THE BEST
LAW
SCHOOLS

ARCO

THE BEST LAW SCHOOLS

▼

Thomas H. Martinson, J.D.

PRENTICE HALL
New York ▼ London ▼ Toronto ▼ Sydney ▼ Tokyo ▼ Singapore

Prentice Hall General Reference
15 Columbus Circle
New York, NY 10023

An Arco Book

Arco, Prentice Hall, and colophons are
registered trademarks of Simon & Schuster, Inc.

Library of Congress Cataloging-in-Publication Data

Martinson, Thomas H.
The best law schools / Thomas H. Martinson.
       p.   cm.
At head of title: Arco.
   ISBN 0-671-84858-5
   1. Law schools—United States. I. Title.
KF273.M37   1993   93-5831
340'.071'173—dc20   CIP

Manufactured in the United States of America

1   2   3   4   5   6   7   8   9   10

CONTENTS

▼

Introduction / 1

I think with reasonable GPA (3.3 - 3.5) and reasonable LSAT. you can get into several of these schools. MW

THE RUNNERS-UP

INTRODUCTION

▼

This is a guidebook to top United States law schools. Like any other guidebook, its purpose is to assist travelers by showing them the way through a strange place and by noting landmarks and other objects of interest that they may find there. In this guidebook, you will find:

- General information about each law school, including a numerical profile, a description of the school and its setting, a sketch of the student body, and a list of noteworthy graduates
- Detailed descriptions of key law school functions, such as admissions, education, and placement
- Commentary on student life, the educational experience, and the search for employment

By virtue of this information, each entry in this book is a guide to a particular law school.

While each entry can be used as a guide to specific places (the individual schools), the book as a whole has another, broader function: overall, its organization makes it a guidebook to the *region* of top law schools. The parallel ordering of the elements of each entry will let you compare and contrast different law schools along different lines. By attending to the many similarities between and among the individual schools, you will understand better the factors that help to define a law school as "top"; and by attending to the many differences between and among them, you will come to realize that each has its own "personality." Using the guide in this way will help you to appreciate better the law school experience and to find a school that seems right for you.

Finally, a guidebook is an aid for travelers. Its description of a place is never intended to substitute for an actual visit. So too, this book is intended to help you learn about the places that you might want to visit and what you might want to see for yourself when you arrive. A guidebook is no substitute for experience.

USING THIS GUIDEBOOK

In order to have confidence in a guidebook, you must know how the information was gathered. You must also be aware that a guide has limitations, and you should know what those limitations are.

The Entries. All numerical data and descriptive statements, including tables, descriptions of the law school, dean's message, outline of admissions practices, summary of placement activities, sketch of the student body, and list of note-worthy graduates, are derived from administration responses to written inquiries, published material, or follow-up telephone inquiries. Where applicable, remarks are attributed to their source, whether they were submitted in writing or made in conversation. Prior to publication, the part of the entry generated by a law school's administration was submitted to the dean of the law school to ensure its accuracy and fairness.[1]

The "commentary" portions of each entry attempt to capture prevailing *student opinion* regarding environment (setting, physical plant, morale), education (philosophy, teaching styles, faculty accessibility), and placement by summarizing student reports. The information that forms the basis of the commentary was gathered through telephone interviews with students at the various schools. The commentary is editorial in nature and solely my responsibility. As such, commentary was not submitted to law schools for a final review. In fact, in many cases the commentary suggests that students view their law school in a different light from that of the administration—or at least that they perceive certain functions of the law school differently from the administration.

As noted, the commentary is based on received reports; in this respect, this guidebook differs from others that users might encounter. If, for example, it is asserted in the commentary that students at a certain law school are "well pleased with the library's expansive reading room," the assertion should not be understood to say that I or some member of the research staff would describe the reading room as expansive, nor that anyone visited the law school to verify that the reading room is, in fact, expansive. Rather, the commentary is asserting that it is a generally shared opinion of students at that school that the reading room is expansive, and further, that they are pleased with it.

Also, because there is no single and unique law school experience, free of all ambivalence, the commentary should not be taken as the final word on conditions at any of the law schools treated in this directory. Still, a conscientious effort was made to create a sketch of each institution that is accurate, if not complete in every detail. All students interviewed were assured at the outset that their remarks were not for attribution and that identities (where provided or otherwise known) would be concealed; care was taken to secure interviews from students with a variety of viewpoints and to obtain from them contacts who might have different views; students were asked to think reflectively about their answers by finding explanations for phenomena or by illustrating generaliza-

---

[1]An exception is the "Student/Faculty" ratio in the profile table for each law school. Different law schools calculate this ratio in different ways, so in the interest of fairness, all entries for this directory were recalculated using simply the total number of J.D. candidates in the student body and the total number of teachers who are listed in the bulletin as "Professor of Law," "Assistant Professor of Law," or "Associate Professor of Law."

tions. By and large, the students interviewed were remarkably candid, broad-minded, and reflective.

In light of these points, you should consider it to be the primary function of the commentary to raise questions rather than to answer them. It can introduce you to the kinds of issues that concern today's law students, but that should be the beginning of your inquiry rather than the end. Once alerted to some of the factors that define student life at a law school and differentiate one law school from another, you will be better able to profit from visits to those schools in which you have the greatest interest.

The Ranking System. The plan of this directory was always to treat in detail a limited number of law schools, so it was necessary to have some method by which to identify the schools to be included. A strategy that naturally came to mind was to defer to some authoritative ranking of law schools prepared by a professional organization or an academic body. No such ranking was found. In fact, the preeminent professional organization for lawyers, the American Bar Association (ABA), explicitly disavows any attempt to rank law schools:

> No rating of law schools beyond the simple statement of their accreditation status is attempted or advocated by the official organizations in legal education. Qualities that make one kind of school good for one student may not be as important to another. The American Bar Association and its Section of Legal Education and Admissions to the Bar have issued disclaimers of any law school rating system.[2]

On the academic side is the Law School Admission Council (LSAC), a non-profit association of American and Canadian law schools. LSAC implicitly defers to the ABA as the proper authority for any official ranking and does not offer a ranking system of its own.[3]

Since no official ranking of law schools was available, it became necessary to create a ranking system from scratch. But wouldn't the attempt to create a ranking be doomed to failure since, as the ABA points out, different people might look for different qualities in a law school? Not at all! One might as well conclude that the new car rankings published by automotive magazines are worthless on the ground that different drivers look for different qualities in an automobile. Most people who consult comparative ratings of any product or ser-

---

[2] The American Bar Association, Statement 20, *Policies of the Council of the Section of Legal Education and Admission to the Bar and of the Accreditation Committee* (Indianapolis, IN: 1987), p. 18.

[3] Law School Admissions Services, Inc., *The Official Guide to U.S. Law Schools, 1992–1993* (Newtown, PA: 1992), p. 19.

vice don't expect the rankings to be tailored to their unique circumstances, and they rely on such rankings even if not prepared by an industry association nor given the imprimatur of a regulatory body. People who ask for a comparison of law schools, even when they ask about "best" law schools, are not usually expecting the names of law schools judged "best" by some absolute standard, nor the names of law schools "best" suited to their individual circumstances. Instead, what most people ask of a ranking system is that it be *serviceable,* to wit, that it be factually reliable and employ reasonable standards.

The task, then, of selecting schools for this guidebook became to create a serviceable ranking system. The first element of such a ranking system—factual reliability—was guaranteed by the source of the data: the law schools themselves. The task then became to establish ranking criteria that would be useful to most people consulting the guidebook. Over 15 years of experience counseling law school applicants have taught me that when people ask, "What are the top schools?", they generally expect an answer that ranks schools according to three criteria: admissions selectivity, educational effectiveness, and placement power. The next job, then, was to identify measures for each criterion.

For selectivity, median Law School Admissions Test (LSAT) score and median grade point average (GPA) of the students at a law school are easily available measures. After all, if those measures can be used by admissions officers to identify "top" law school applicants, then it seems fair to use them also to help identify "top" law schools. Another measure of a law school's selectivity is the ratio of acceptances to applications. The lower the ratio of acceptances to applications, the more difficult it is to gain admission.

Measuring educational effectiveness is more problematic. Indeed, it is sometimes argued, though usually facetiously, that the claim that so-called top schools provide a more effective education than other law schools is an example of the *post hoc ergo propter hoc* fallacy: a top school attracts very talented applicants who would go on to become successful professionals no matter where they went to school; those talented people study at that school for three years; after graduation, those talented people become successful professionals, and the law school claims credit for their success. Setting that suggestion aside, one way of measuring a school's academic "reputation" is by the success its graduates have obtaining judicial clerkships.

A judicial clerkship is a one- or two-year assistantship to a judge and is an experience highly regarded by members of the legal profession. Since it is a judge who extends the job offer in the case of a clerkship, the offer is an implicit recognition by a leading legal authority that the person offered the clerkship has received a top-notch legal education. The ranking system uses the percent of students who accept clerkships with the U.S. Supreme Court, a U.S. Court of Appeals, a U.S. District Court, or a state's highest court.

Finally, a school's placement power can be measured fairly directly by the percentage of students in a graduating class who have jobs at graduation. And, of course, median starting salary is also a measure of a law school's placement success.

For purposes of this directory, then, "top" law schools are identified by their relative standings on three criteria:

Selectivity
      As measured by   median LSAT score
                          median GPA
                          acceptances-to-applications ratio

Educational Effectiveness
      As measured by   percent of graduates accepting certain clerkships

Placement Power
      As measured by   percentage placed at graduation
                          median starting salary

For each of the six specific measures, schools were awarded points based on standing in the list, with the top-ranked school on the list receiving the maximum number of points (a number equal to the number of schools in the list), the second-ranked school receiving one point less than the top-ranked school, and so on. (In cases of ties, points were distributed among the schools tied.) For Selectivity and Placement, scores are simply averages of the scores for each of the specific measures for that criterion. Educational Effectiveness is simply the clerkship ranking. The overall ranking is just the average of scores of each of the three criteria. A more detailed discussion of the calculations is provided in the Appendix.

Some might object that the system is too simple, even crude. Perhaps, but to others it will no doubt seem highly intuitive and very accessible. And as long as you understand the following limitations of the system, it is serviceable.

One, the ranking system is intended to provide an answer, though not the only possible answer, to the question about *top* law schools. As the LSAC rightly advises in its literature, there are many factors that help to make up a law school's reputation that do not lend themselves to quantification.[4] Indeed, most of the space in each entry of this guidebook is devoted to nonquantifiable factors, such as physical setting, faculty style, and student life. The ranking system, while logically necessary to the design of the project, is a relatively minor part of the final product.

Two, you should not place too much emphasis on small differences in rankings. It is not at all clear, for example, that the ranking system does very much to distinguish the first-ranked school from, say, the fifth. Instead of viewing the rankings as evidence of a uniform continuum, you should probably think of the system as identifying "tiers" or "clusters" of schools (e.g., break the list into quartiles).

Three, and this point is particularly important, do not make too much of the fact that a school included in the initial survey for this directory does not appear

---

[4] *The Official Guide to U.S. Law Schools, 1992–93.*

on the list of 25 top schools. The length of the list was dictated in large part by production concerns, and the distinction between appearing on the list of 25 and not appearing on that list has more to do with the way books are printed than with the relative merits of the schools in question.

Changing Conditions. A publication such as this requires months to research and months more to be taken from manuscript to bound volumes. This time lag is inherent in the nature of things. Conditions at law schools, however, can change dramatically in a much shorter time. For example, between the time that law schools submitted their data for this guidebook and the time that this manuscript was ready for submission, the job market for recent law school graduates took a pronounced downward turn. During the interview phase of the research for this guidebook, student comments attested to widespread concern about placement opportunities. Students reported that they were receiving fewer offers than their counterparts from previous years and noted a decline in the number of firms participating in on-campus recruitment programs.

Conclusive proof of the downturn and quantification was provided by a placement officer at one of the schools included in this guidebook, who was concerned that users of this edition be alerted to the trend. At the law school in question, the percentage of students placed at graduation declined by almost five points from 1990 to 1992. Of course, the majority of graduates from the top schools still find jobs, but users of this guidebook are advised to make inquiries of their own.

If so widespread a change as the one just cited, affecting law schools in general, can occur in so short a time, then how much more quickly can change occur at a particular law school? A change in deans, for example, could conceivably alter, for better or worse, the opinion of the student body about the administration. The completion of a new wing on the library or even just the announcement of a long-term building plan could drastically change student perceptions of the law school's physical plant. A single dramatic incident might set into motion events that color the perceptions of many students of their entire law school experience. In creating the commentary, great effort has been made to minimize the influence of these random factors and to distill from the volatile mixture of observations a stable commentary. Nonetheless, you are hereby reminded of the obvious: things change!

APPLYING TO A TOP SCHOOL

The law school application process is both lengthy and expensive. From the time you begin your initial investigations to the time you actually learn whether you have been accepted can take more than a year, and during that time you will invest many hours reading about law schools, preparing applications, and studying for the LSAT. And by the time you have paid for all the administrative costs, such as phone calls and postage, for all the application fees, and perhaps for some LSAT preparation, you will have spent several hundred dollars—at minimum. As you begin this process, there are several things you should know.

Targeting Top Law Schools. One of the features of this guidebook that will no doubt be attractive to many users is the table of admissions data included for each law school. You should not expect, however, that these tables with their medians and totals will enable you to quantify precisely your chance for admission at any law school. In particular, you should exercise caution in drawing any conclusion based on reports of median LSAT score or median GPA. For any given category, just about half the population is above the median and half below. Thus, at every law school, many applicants with LSAT scores and GPAs above the medians of the school's entering class were not accepted; and, conversely, many applicants with LSAT scores and GPAs below the medians were admitted.

The fact that the data in the tables will not enable you to predict whether or not you will be accepted at a particular school is not a reason for disappointment. Rather, it should be viewed as a benefit of the admissions processes of law schools: decisions are not made on the basis of some simple mathematical formula but take into account instead a variety of factors. As you read the information provided by admissions officers at the law schools and review the "Student Sampler" feature of the entries, you may be pleasantly surprised to learn just how flexible and how accommodating of individuality the decision-making process at a top law school can be. Admissions officers at each school emphasized that in addition to the LSAT score and GPA, an applicant's personal history, significant accomplishments, unusual experiences, employment record, and professional aspirations are important.

On the other hand, while the admissions offices of top law schools are not factories that grind out acceptances and rejections based entirely on LSAT scores and GPAs, you should not imagine that numbers are irrelevant. In spite of the disclaimers by law school admissions officers that the process is not mechanical, and despite their assurances that "many factors" other than scores and grades are taken into account, it is nonetheless a fact that your GPA and your LSAT score will be important. Indeed, even a small difference in the LSAT score and the GPA can be the difference that makes a difference. But to say that a small difference in an LSAT score or a GPA can make a difference in the disposition of an application is not to contradict the claims of law school admissions officers nor to make an indictment of the admissions process. Rather, it is merely to point out an inherent feature of a selection process that relies on numbers in a meaningful way: if the score is at all important, then at some point on the scale, a difference in the score must be the difference that makes a difference in the decision.

If LSAT scores and GPAs are not the entire story but not irrelevant either, where does this leave someone trying to decide whether or not to apply to a top law school? Obviously, the answer to this question depends in part on the person's LSAT score and GPA. Most people with numbers substantially above the medians published by top schools can apply to those schools with the reasonable expectation of being accepted by some—though probably not all. Indeed, every admissions officer who contributed to this guidebook could probably tell you stories of applicants with "super" numbers who were turned down for one reason or another. Those with numbers at or near the published medians have good reason to believe that they are competitive for a seat at a top law school, but the outcome of the application process will depend greatly on the unquantifiable factors in their backgrounds. Finally, those with numbers substantially below the published medians should not necessarily pass on the opportunity to apply to top schools. Again, every admissions officer could tell stories of applicants who were granted admission in spite of numbers that seemed to be unacceptably low. In general, however, the further below the medians an applicant's numbers fall, the lower the chances of admission and the more impressive the unquantifiable factors must be.

Perhaps the best advice for those thinking of applying to top schools is to caution against targeting only top schools. The schools included in this directory are so competitive that no one is guaranteed acceptance at a particular school. To maximize your chances of acceptance at a top school while guarding against the disappointment of having no offers at all, apply to a range of schools. For those with numbers substantially above the published medians, the strategy requires applications to one or two "safety" schools where admission seems almost certain. For those with numbers at or near the published medians, this strategy suggests targeting a mix of schools, some at the very top, some in the middle, and again, one or two safety schools. For those with numbers that make admission to a top law school problematic, the strategy is applied by targeting one or two top schools as long-shot schools and submitting applications to other schools where the chances for admission are greater.

The average number of schools targeted by applicants is 4.5.[5] Applicants who are competitive for top schools and who have a strong desire to attend a top school should consider applying to more than four or five schools because of the severity of the competition at those schools. To be sure, increasing the number of targeted schools will increase the cost of the application process; but as the placement tables in this guidebook show, the incremental increase in the cost of application may be more than covered by the difference in the size of the first paycheck after graduation.

Finally, if you are considering top law schools, then you should do a *realistic* assessment of the unquantifiable factors that will be found in your application. While admissions officers are hungry for students with something extra to offer, you must realize that more than just a few people applying to the top law schools have that extra dimension. If you take a moment to consult the "Student Sampler" feature of each entry, you will find that law schools are able to boast

---

[5] *The Official Guide to U.S. Law Schools, 1992–93*, p. 15.

of many students with unique experiences. In order, then, to best estimate your chances of success at top schools, you must keep in mind that you will be a member of an applicant pool that is drawn from across the country and from foreign countries as well and that includes many people with impressive unquantifiable credentials. As part of your "realistic assessment," you should read the next section on unquantifiable factors so that you will understand the role such factors play in the admissions process.

Crafting a Top Application.   Admissions officers stress repeatedly that unquantifiable as well as numerical factors are considered in making admissions decisions. Indeed, many elements of the application—questions about personal accomplishments and experiences, the personal statement, the letters of recommendation—are designed to elicit information about such factors. The effectiveness of your application will depend in large measure on whether you respond to the application prompts with answers that provide information an admissions officer will find relevant to the inquiry.

Although admissions officers emphasize that applicants are viewed as individuals and not just LSAT scores and GPAs, you should not imagine that the admissions process at a top law school is a free-for-all in which outcomes are unpredictable and in which every applicant has an equal chance. To the contrary, though the unique qualities of different applicants are important, the *significance* of those unique qualities is determined by the general criteria used in the admissions process: those general criteria are shaped by both policy and institutional goals and do not change from applicant to applicant. In fact, the general concerns that make unique factors relevant to the admissions process are the same ones that make the LSAT score and the GPA so important.

What are the general goals that structure the admissions process? Based on the comments submitted by the various admissions officers, we may conclude that they are to select an entering class (1) of well-qualified candidates, (2) who will apply themselves to their studies, (3) who bring with them a variety of experiences, and (4) who are more or less representative of our society at large. If you reflect for a moment on the function of an admissions office, you will see why each of these four goals is important and you will understand better what admissions officers are looking for.

First, the admissions process is obviously designed to select only those applicants who have the ability to complete successfully the program of study. Second, the process is designed to select only those who have seriously committed themselves to three years of fairly arduous work. Third, since a top law school receives many more well-qualified applicants than can be accepted, the admissions office is able to consider the unusual contributions that applicants might make as students. Fourth, given that law is powerful social force, law school admissions officers recognize that they have a moral responsibility to try to ensure that the make-up of the bar more or less reflects the make-up of our society.

What factors in an applicant's background would indicate that the applicant possesses the first two characteristics? Many different experiences might suggest that a candidate has the academic ability, analytical skills, language mastery, and personal qualities that are needed for studying law, and admissions officers are alert for any indicia of ability. There is, however, one experience that virtually all law school applicants have in common, namely, three to four years of undergraduate study; and previous academic performance would seem to be as good a predictor as any of future academic performance. That is the reason that the admissions process compares applicants in terms of their undergraduate GPAs.

Of course, a GPA is just a number, but colleges and universities vary in their requirements and grading standards. Consequently, the same number means different things for applicants who come from different undergraduate institutions. One way of correcting for the deficiency of the GPA as a measure of ability would be to require all applicants to take a test—the same test. The entire applicant pool could then be ranked on the basis of a single, uniform measure. That, of course, is the theory that underlies the use of LSAT scores: the exam is intended to provide "a standard measure of acquired verbal reading and reasoning skills that law schools can use in assessing applicants."[6] These observations on the GPA and the LSAT score help to explain the great importance that those numbers have in the law school admissions process, but they also cast some light on what additional factors might be relevant.

In addition to the flaw mentioned in the preceding paragraph, the GPA has another limitation: a grade point *average* does not give a very detailed picture of an applicant's past performance. For this reason, admissions officers often interpret the GPA in light of a transcript. By looking at the details provided in a transcript, an admissions officer may be able to spot a trend or an anomaly in the applicant's grades. An applicant whose upperclass marks are considerably better than earlier grades might be expected to continue to improve in law school, so an admissions officer might discount a somewhat low GPA and give more emphasis to the later, higher grades. Or again, an admissions officer might be inclined to forgive a single sub-par semester, particularly if the applicant offers a reason to believe that it was, in fact, an anomaly.

In examining the applicant's transcript, an admissions officer would also be trying to ascertain whether the coursework had prepared the applicant for the rigors of law school study. An applicant's GPA might be given an informal upward adjustment if the transcript shows a number of very challenging courses; conversely, it might be given a nudge downward if the course load was not very taxing. Additionally, an admissions officer would like to know something about any personal circumstances that might have helped to shape the GPA. For example, students who work part-time during the academic year probably have a more difficult time maintaining their averages than do students who do not need to work. The GPA for an applicant who worked and studied at the same time

---

[6] *The Official Guide to U.S. Law Schools, 1992–93*, p. 7.

10

might get a small upward push. By the same reasoning, any other hurdles that an applicant had to overcome in order to get a particular GPA would be relevant.

Many applicants continued their studies beyond college, and their academic performance on the graduate level also bears on the issue of ability. Of course, graduate school GPAs cannot play the same role in the admissions process that undergraduate GPAs do. Not all applicants have one, and among those who do, the significance of the number varies widely. Still, a good performance in graduate school is evidence of academic ability; and while the weight of that evidence can't be quantified, it is still something that admissions officers consider.

Another factor that cannot be assigned a numerical value is extracurricular and other, similar experiences. Clearly, such experiences are relevant to the law school admissions process, but it is very important to keep in mind that they have value in this context only insofar as they provide evidence that an applicant has one or more of the characteristics mentioned above. For example, the fact that an applicant was a member of a debating club or participated in a political forum may suggest to an admissions officer that the applicant has learned skills that would be valuable to a law student. The fact that an applicant contributed time to an athletic team or a volunteer organization suggests seriousness of purpose. Again, an applicant who has lived in a different country or is an accomplished musician has something unique to contribute to the learning and living experience at a law school.

Yet another unquantifiable factor that may be relevant to the admissions process is an applicant's work experience. Even part-time work experience is important to the extent that it requires some ability or demonstrates something about the applicant's maturity, but part-time work experience while in college may be relatively less important to an admissions officer than the other unquantifiable factors discussed above. For a certain group of applicants, however, work experience may be as important as, if not more important than, the undergraduate experience.

If you consult the "average age" entry in the profile tables for the law schools in this guidebook, you will learn that the average age of entering students at these schools is around 23 or 24. Obviously, many applicants to these schools have been away from school for one or even many years, so most will have significant work experience. Although it is not possible to assign a numerical value to the quality of an applicant's work experience, that experience is nonetheless an important factor in the admissions process. And the longer an applicant has been away from school, the more important this work experience is likely to be in the mind of an admissions officer.

Nor is it necessary that work experience be in a law-related field to be important. Rather, the conditions that make other unquantifiable factors relevant to the law school admissions process also operate to determine the significance of work experience. To the extent that an applicant's professional responsibilities demonstrate ability, maturity, or an unusual perspective, the work experience will be relevant.

One more unquantifiable factor deserves special mention: ethnic status. Ethnic/minority status[7] is important because certain ethnic or minority groups have traditionally been underrepresented in the legal profession, and admissions officers are acutely aware of the need to redress any such imbalances. Ethnic or minority status is also important because applicants from different ethnic or minority groups have experiences that may not be shared by other students and so have something special to contribute to the learning and living experience at a law school. It is interesting to note that some of the law schools included in this directory specifically require an additional personal statement from applicants who wish to be considered as members of ethnic or minority groups, and in those statements, applicants must describe their linguistic or cultural heritage and comment on its significance.

The unquantifiable factors discussed above are not the only ones that are relevant to the law school admissions process. In the final analysis, virtually any accomplishment or experience could be of interest to an admissions officer. As you respond to the questions on the application form and prepare your personal statement, you must always keep in mind that it is not the *fact* of the accomplishment or the experience that is important, but its *significance* as judged by the goals of the admissions process.

Preparing for the LSAT. Of all the factors that are important in the admissions process at top schools, the LSAT is the only one over which you can exercise any short-term control. In order to maximize your score, you must be fully prepared to take the LSAT.

The two main approaches to LSAT study are live coaching courses and self-study materials, and these options differ greatly in terms of cost. Test preparation materials can be purchased in most bookstores or through Law School Admissions Services (LSAS) and usually cost less than $20. Commercial courses, which are not available in all areas, typically cost $500 to $700. Some cost less; others cost even more.

Is there a very great difference between test preparation books and live courses in terms of content? Perhaps, perhaps not. Books and courses vary considerably in approach and content. Some books and some courses use the "drill and review" approach: work practice problems and review the answer. Other books and courses provide comprehensive and systematic programs of instruction backed up by reinforcement exercises. Before buying, you need to do some comparison shopping.

Finally, the two options differ greatly in terms of style. In the one case, you read for yourself directly the content of the lesson; in the other case, you sit in a classroom and listen to the teacher deliver the content of the lesson. Are there

---

[7] You will find that the law schools treated in this directory describe such characteristics using different terms, and there is a debate as to the appropriate designation.

any reasons to prefer the second method? Perhaps. Some people who enroll in coaching courses mention favorably the discipline that the course schedule imposes on their study. And it cannot be denied that an effective teacher who is able to answer questions is a great asset. But whether these advantages are worth the cost of the coaching program is an individual matter.

Designing a personal test prep program must strike a balance among the competing considerations mentioned above, but it is a difficult task unless one knows how much and what sort of preparation one needs. And those are questions that may not be answerable unless the program is already underway. One approach that many people find effective is to make a small initial investment: purchase a test preparation manual at a bookstore and a previously released LSAT from Law School Admissions Services (LSAS). Study the manual and then use the previously released LSAT to determine exactly where you stand. If you are not satisfied that you are achieving your maximum score in this way, then you can consider enrolling in a commercial test preparation course. But don't commit to a large expenditure unless you first determine that it is necessary to do so.

THE TOP LAW SCHOOL EXPERIENCE

Judging from responses to questions about their expectations and experiences, many law students arrive at law school with what might be called "Paper Chase Anxiety." As the phrase suggests, "Paper Chase Anxiety" may be brought on by exposure to the film *The Paper Chase*.[8] Whatever the source of the beliefs, many students acknowledged that they entered law school with one or more preconceptions about what was in store for them, only to find that these notions were considerably oversimplified, overstated, or even just plain wrong.

Classmates and Competition. Many people worry that the environment at a top school is inherently one of unhealthy and cutthroat competition. They anticipate that the first year in particular will be a mad scramble for grades and class ranking, and they may expect the worst of their classmates. That this view is both erroneous and widely held by entering students is proven by the comments made by second- and third-year students about their first-year experiences. When asked whether their classmates "work and play well with others," second-

---

[8] For those not familiar with the film, *The Paper Chase* depicts the experiences of a handful of first-year students at Harvard Law School—their worries about grades, their friendships and fights, and their struggles with a cantankerous and mean-spirited professor by the name of Kingsfield. The images conveyed by the film are evidently fairly powerful, for many student responses to inquiries about first-year student life at a top law school began with "It's not really like the movies."

and third-year students typically answered "Oh, we don't have any of the problems at our school that you hear of at other schools, such as missing pages or stolen books." On the face of it, the response seems plausible enough and a very nice thing to say in praise of one's school, but students at every law school included in this guidebook said the same thing!

Thus, one after the other, students distinguished their law schools from "other law schools" by pointing out that they had not encountered missing pages or stolen books. The result of the inquiry was puzzling: although it seemed to be common knowledge that some law schools are characterized by cutthroat competition, the names of those schools never emerged. No one ever commented, "Here at this law school students are really unscrupulous and will steal your class notes or hide important reference books." It seemed, then, that either students were not entirely truthful in describing their experiences, perhaps in an effort to avoid tarnishing a law school's image, or the impression among students that such incidents regularly occur at other, unnamed schools is simply incorrect. Given that most students interviewed seemed to speak reflectively and candidly about other aspects of their law school experiences, it appears unlikely that the paradox can be explained by a cover-up. The more likely explanation is that the first-year experience at top law schools is no longer like the movies—if it ever was.

This is not to say, however, that there were literally no reports of missing pages or stolen notes, for a handful of students did say that they had first-hand knowledge of such incidents. So too, there doubtless are other students or younger members of the legal profession who were not interviewed for this guidebook and who might tell similar stories. Even so, this anecdotal evidence does not validate the "Paper Chase" view of law students as ruthless competitors. In fact, when students told such stories, they were usually quick to add that the problem was an "isolated incident" that caused surprise and indignation among students. Surprise and indignation, however, are appropriate reactions only because the incidents described stood in stark relief to the sense of fair play that otherwise prevails at the law school.

If the good news is that the desire to perform well does not automatically cause students at top law schools to act toward one another with depraved indifference, then the bad news is that, like the characters in the film, most students interviewed admitted to feeling some performance anxiety during the first year. In addition to worries about grades and employment prospects, many students experience what might be called "personal performance anxiety." As one student put it, "You have a group of people who are accustomed to ranking at or near the top of the class; but, after the first set of exams, half of them are going to be in the bottom of the class."

The Socratic Method.   Many people considering law school apparently also have a mistaken conception of the Socratic method. The phrase, of course, refers to the ancient Greek philosopher Socrates, or at least to the Socrates character of Plato's *Dialogues*. The aspect of those philosophical investigations that is most familiar is the question-and-answer format, in which Socrates prompts participants with interrogatory suggestions to examine or to reexamine their answers to questions such as "What is justice?" Thus, the Socratic method, in which participants are challenged to state and to defend their own positions, is distinguished from a direct and authoritative exposition of some already developed thesis by a lecturer.[9] It is in this respect that many law school classes can be said to proceed according to the Socratic method: the professor prompts students to think through positions on their own rather than give them prepackaged, authoritative answers to questions.

While the phrase "Socratic method" is often bandied about in a way that suggests that the question-and-answer format is the defining characteristic of law school classes, the use of the Socratic method rather than lectures is dictated, at least in part, by reliance on the "case method"—a teaching method generally credited to Professor C. C. Langdell, dean of the Harvard Law School in the late nineteenth century.[10] In the case method system of teaching law, students read court decisions and the arguments written by judges to justify those decisions. The casebook is thus the law school analogue of the college textbook, but it is not primarily an authoritative exposition of important legal principles. Rather, the heart of a casebook is a compilation of judicial opinions on a selected subject, such as contracts or criminal law. Professors then use the question-and-answer format of the Socratic method to prompt students to attempt to articulate the important principles of decisions; to test the application of those principles to other situations; and to criticize those principles.

The phrase "Socratic method" is also used inaccurately and pejoratively, even by law students, to refer to the very formal and sometimes brutal use of the question-and-answer method that is depicted in the film version of the novel *The Paper Chase*. Consequently, when asked about the classroom experience, a law student might reply, "No one really uses the Socratic method anymore," or "Professors here use a modified Socratic method and let you know a week in advance when you'll be called on." Clearly these remarks do not mean that the Socratic method, that is, the question-and-answer format of studying a problem, has been abandoned, but rather that teaching styles have changed. After all, even in a class where participation in the question-and-answer format is entirely voluntary, the method is nonetheless Socratic.

***The Paper Chase* Revisited—A Personal Note.** The movie version of *The Paper Chase* was made while I was a student at Harvard Law School. Some of

---

[9] *See* "Socrates" in *The Encyclopedia of Philosophy*, Vol. 7, p. 480.
[10] *See* Bernard L. Diamond, "Psychological Problems of Law Students," in *Looking at Law Schools*, Stephen Gillers, ed. (Penguin Books USA, Inc.: 1990), p. 68.

the filming was actually done at the Law School, and I answered the "cattle call" for extras. Unfortunately, I took up a position on the wrong end of the student lounge and was never even seen by the casting crew. Some of my friends, however, got a day's work and the $25 that went with it.

Only a few of the movie's scenes were filmed at Harvard Law School. The classroom scenes, for example, were filmed at some other university. But if you pay careful attention to the relatively unimportant scenes of students changing classes and the like, you can occasionally catch brief glimpses of real Harvard Law students. In those fleeting moments, the film is a fairly accurate depiction of Harvard Law School. The rest of the film should be taken as what it really is—a work of fiction.

Even though my classmates and I knew that the film was a fictionalized account of the first-year law school experience, and though we knew that there was no Professor Kingsfield at Harvard, we still speculated about which member of the faculty had been the inspiration for the Kingsfield character. Many thought it might have been Clark Byse, who taught Contracts to my first-year section. I had forgotten about the identification of Kingsfield with Byse until an article about Professor Byse came to my attention during my research for this guidebook. The article, which features an interview with Professor Byse, appeared in a recent issue of the University of Wisconsin Law School's *Gargoyle* and was fortuitously included by them as part of their response to my survey questionnaire for this directory:

> Featured Alumni: Clark Byse ('38)
> Byse is one of the alleged models for the character of Professor Kingsfield in the novel *The Paper Chase*. Byse commented, "The movie was shown at Harvard Law School and afterwards a poll was conducted to determine whether Kingsfield was patterned after any present member of the faculty. I won hands down. One of the students was reported to have said, 'It's Byse all right, but Byse isn't sadistic. Besides, Byse is a better actor.'"

Whether the student was correct to identify Byse as the inspiration for the Kingsfield character is moot, but the student's other two points are well taken. First, Byse was not sadistic. I have seen *The Paper Chase,* and I have been subjected to Professor Byse's use of the Socratic method. *The Paper Chase* is an interesting film, but Professor Kingsfield is not Professor Byse. Professor Byse's use of the Socratic method, while rigorous, never seemed to me to be intended to denigrate anyone, nor did Professor Byse ever, to my recollection, badger students who might not be prepared on a particular day.

In fact, I recall that one day a classmate whose chair was next to mine but on the aisle was absent, so I took the aisle seat in order to have more leg room. About midway through the class, Professor Byse looked up from the seating chart on the top of the lectern, pointed in my general direction, and asked, "Mr.

Martinson, what about that?" I had not prepared the day's assignment because I did not expect to be called upon, but I had overestimated the safety of being one out of 130 or so students.

In any event, there was silence as Professor Byse waited for an answer, and while I debated whether it would be worse to admit that I was not prepared or to run the risk of saying something truly inane. Suddenly, inspiration struck: I pointed to my own empty seat and said as casually as I could, "Professor Byse, apparently Mr. Martinson isn't here today." The seating chart on the lectern, of course, had my photograph in the position of my seat, but Professor Byse simply turned in the other direction and called on a different student.

Professor Byse was also much more entertaining than the Kingsfield character. He was very lively in his classroom demeanor and used his wonderful sense of humor to brighten the classroom atmosphere. I recall that one day a classmate had brought his brother to Contracts class so that he might see Professor Byse in action. My classmate was sitting in his regular seat in the center of one of the front rows, his brother next to him. At some point during the class, Byse pointed to my classmate and called on him by name for an analysis of some case. My classmate, who had probably been busy the previous evening entertaining his brother from out of town, had not prepared the assignment for the day and said "I'm sorry, Professor Byse, but I haven't read that case."

At that point, without consulting the seating chart in front of him, Professor Byse simply moved on to the next closest person—the brother—and asked "What is your opinion of the case?" Startled practically out of his wits, the poor visitor gesticulated wildly in the direction of his brother and in a panic blurted out, "I haven't read the case! I'm his brother!" Professor Byse, in turn, grasped the lectern with both hands, leaned over it so far that his heels came off the floor, and thundered in mock anger, "Well, is there anyone in your family who has read this case?!!!"

Now Professor Emeritus at Harvard, Byse is currently a Visiting Professor of Law at Boston University. As part of my research for this guidebook, I reviewed other law school guides and paid particular attention to their coverage of the schools included herein. In its discussion of Harvard Law School, one guide made a point of saying that only two or three professors at Harvard now use the Socratic method, as though readers would understand by that comment that students considering Harvard Law School can breathe easier knowing that Kingsfield no longer dominates the classroom there. What exquisite irony it is, therefore, to find in that same guidebook, in the entry for Boston University, the statement: "[F]aculty stars include Clark Bice [sic] . . ."

THE TOP TWENTY-FIVE LAW SCHOOLS

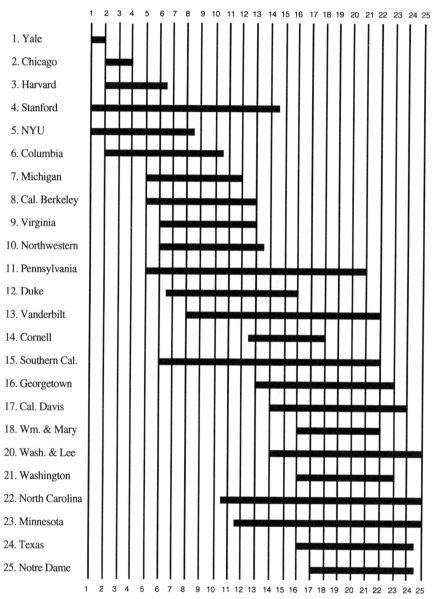

The table presents the law schools as they are ranked using three criteria: selectivity (as measured by median LSAT score, median GPA, and percent of applicants accepted), reputation (as measured by the percent of graduates who obtain clerkships with the U.S. Supreme Court, a U.S. Court of Appeals, a U.S. District Court, or a state's highest court), and placement success (as measured by the percent of students who have jobs at graduation and median starting salary). The end points of the bars mark the highest and lowest scores given each school, and the bars indicate the range of scores. (The lower the number, the better the score.)

19

THE TOP 25

UNIVERSITY OF CALIFORNIA, BERKELEY

SCHOOL OF LAW (BOALT HALL)
BERKELEY, CA 94720
(510) 642-1741

ADMISSIONS

Applied: 5,665

Accepted: 796

Enrolled: 267

Median LSAT: 97th percentile

Median GPA: 3.7

STUDENT BODY

Total: 900

Women: 47%

Minorities: 31%

Average Age: 24 (Over 30: 15%)

ACADEMIC RESOURCES

Library Volumes: 600,000+

Computer Services: WESTLAW, LEXIS, word processors

Student/Faculty Ratio: 20:1

FINANCES (ACADEMIC YEAR)

Tuition:	
Resident:	$ 3,688
Nonresident	$11,387
Housing and Food:	$ 6,840
Books, Personal:	$ 2,180
Total:	
Resident:	$12,708
Nonresident	$20,407

ENVIRONMENT The University of California at Berkeley has a student body of 31,000, 9,000 of whom are graduate students, and is known for its intellectual, social, and political atmosphere. San Francisco is less than half an hour away by car or by BART, the subway system; and the Bay Area offers a variety of recreational and cultural activities. Off-campus, within walking distance of the law school, are shopping areas and numerous coffee houses and restaurants, many serving specialty cuisines.

Until 1951, the law school occupied the original Boalt Hall of Law, built as a memorial to Judge John H. Boalt—hence, the popular name for the law school, "Boalt Hall." The university campus is situated at the base of wooded hills which, with large lawns and groves throughout the campus, help to create a parklike atmosphere.

The law school faculty strives to be available to students at the personal as well as at the professional level, and students consistently maintain a spirit of friendliness and cooperation. Thus, students and faculty at Boalt Hall take their work very seriously but try to create an atmosphere in which they do not take themselves too seriously.

Commentary. Students confirm what the administration says about the Bay Area: it does offer something for everyone. Some students mentioned cultural activities such as opera and ballet; others cited outdoor recreation such as hiking and bicycling; others noted the city's professional sports teams; still others described restaurants such as those found in Chinatown; and many praised the Bay Area's climate. The area around the Berkeley campus, however, received mixed reviews. In particular, student comments focused on a stretch of Telegraph Avenue just a few blocks from the law school. It was said that the area is frequented by many homeless people, that it is a magnet for older adolescents who hang out, that the streets in the area are dirty, that windows to shops are often broken, and that the area has on occasion been the scene of crowd violence. For these and perhaps other reasons, most students concluded that area is not very safe and that conditions deteriorate as one moves farther from campus.

One female student said, for example, that she would not come into that area of Berkeley after dark. Another female student said that she would visit the law school at night but added that after ten o'clock she would avail herself of the campus "walk system" and arrange for an escort to the BART station. One student opined, perhaps facetiously, that even campus security might be unwilling to make the trip to the BART station late at night. To put these comments into perspective, it should be noted that the quality of the neighborhood in which the law school is located seems to be one of the less important factors in students' evaluations of their school. Students indicated that they do, in fact, patronize the coffee shops near the law school during the day, but many law students do not reside in the area immediately around the law school, preferring instead to settle in other parts of Berkeley or in San Francisco or Oakland. Additionally, because the law school itself, which stands on one corner of the campus, is fairly isolated from its surroundings, it is possible to study law at Berkeley without becoming involved with the surrounding community.

Students also agreed that the Berkeley campus, with its trees and surrounding hills, is beautiful, but students were markedly less enthusiastic about the law school's physical plant. Reviews included: "nothing to write home about," "a bit of a downer," "fairly old," and "cramped." Students added, however, that the law school is in the process of renovating some classrooms.

24

As for morale, students said that the law school is remarkably free of competitive pressures, though they allowed that each class has a certain number of students who are very competitive. When asked to account for the lack of competition, some students theorized that Boalt has a reputation for a very supportive atmosphere and attracts students who want to live in such an environment. Other students said that the law school's faculty tries to foster a sense of community and cooperation rather than competition. Other students theorized that the grading system, under which over half of the grades awarded to a class are simply "P" for pass, tends to remove any incentive to compete against one's classmates. In fact, one student went so far as to suggest that the distribution of grades is really random, in which case there would be literally no incentive to try to distinguish oneself from classmates. This last remark was almost surely hyperbole and intended merely to dramatize the fact that the grading system doesn't encourage competition, but the grading system was seriously described as "screwy" and "ridiculous." A corollary of this "grading system" thesis maintains that the law school offers so many different activities that it is possible for virtually everyone to earn a "participation gold star" that helps to fill out the resume and that for this reason grades tend to be less important than at other schools. Finally, it was suggested that because the student body tends to be a bit older than those of other law schools (over 15% of Berkeley students are over 30), the added maturity helps students to keep a balanced perspective on law school life.

To a certain extent, students at the law school seem to be heirs to the tradition of Berkeley political activism. Students described their classmates as moderate to liberal but added that there is ample room at Berkeley for conservatives as well and noted that the law school has a fairly large contingent of Federalists, members of the conservative law society. Further, students remarked that their classmates seemed to be particularly interested in various political issues and that the law school has many activist organizations. Yet, in spite of the fact that students hold strong political views and are committed to various activist programs, they said that their classmates get along well with one another. By way of illustrating this collegiality, a student noted that earlier in the day a particularly heated discussion on legal ethics had erupted in a class with the battle line drawn between right and left. At the end of class, however, all parties to the debate simply packed their books and went out for coffee together. In fact, when asked about the single greatest advantage of studying at Berkeley, students most often said simply "the student body," meaning the diversity, talent, and energy of their classmates.

ACADEMICS According to former Dean of the Law School Jesse H. Choper, the educational program at Boalt is constantly undergoing reexamination and evolution as the law school responds to the ever-present challenge of balancing competing yet mutually reinforcing claims of theoretical and practical learning. Students must be taught not just to understand legal doctrine but to comprehend the forces that shape it. To be sure, Mr. Choper emphasizes, students must be given experience in the basic working skills of the lawyer, who must be able to grow and function for half a century in constantly changing legal systems, but they must also be prepared for the policy-making roles that lawyers are inevitably called upon to fill in a complex world.

One way of meeting this challenge, Mr. Choper notes, is to adjust the content of the curriculum, and the more than 120 curriculum offerings at Boalt include courses and seminars designed to respond to emerging areas of legal problems. A second approach, Mr. Choper continues, focuses not so much on new areas of study as on new methods of study, specifically, increased independent study, clinical education, and other specialized skills training. Clinical opportunities at Boalt range from units of credit for individually arranged experience to a more structured program that permits students to obtain a semester's credit through full-time supervised legal work. Finally, Mr. Choper adds, students can take advantage of the law school's interdisciplinary offerings that range from specialized courses to joint degree programs.

Commentary.   The introduction to this guidebook emphasizes that conditions at a law school can change quickly, and Berkeley is a case in point. Between the time that the initial survey questionnaire for this book was completed by the law school's administration and the start of the student interview phase of the research, Jesse H. Choper was replaced by Herma Hill Kay as Dean of the Law School. This shift in deans seems to have changed student attitudes about the law school experience at Berkeley in some important ways.

CURRICULUM

First-Year Courses: Orientation, Civil Procedure (yearlong), Contracts (yearlong), Constitutional Law (spring), Criminal Law (fall), Legal Research and Writing (fall), Moot Court (spring), Property (spring), The Legal Profession (spring), Torts (fall)

Interesting Electives: Bible and Talmud Law; Bilingualism and the Law; Business Law and Ethics; Comparative Environmental Law; Computer Software Protection; Chinese Investment Law; Disability Rights; Entertainment Law; Environment and Culture: Protection of Our Heritage; Genes, Embryos and Shifting Maps of Persons and Parenthood; Health Care and Market Policy; Indigenous Americans and U.S. Law; Ocean Resources and Law of the Sea; Street Law; Work and Gender

Several students reported that during Dean Choper's term, relationships between the administration and students were strained and thought that the dean was especially hostile to legitimate student concerns over the lack of ideological diversity on the faculty. A few other students, while allowing that the tension was evident, suggested that the tension was more easily explained by the fact that Dean Choper's policies were simply out of favor with the predominantly liberal student body. Now, even though students still disagree over the merits of Dean Choper's administration, Dean Hill Kay seems to enjoy some measure of confidence among the students: one student praised the new dean's "hands on" approach; another said that the new dean is "listening to students"; and another called the new dean "very supportive." Some students, however, are only cautiously optimistic about Dean Hill Kay's ability to effect meaningful change. As one student noted regarding the diversity issue, tenured faculty positions become available only infrequently, so the new dean will necessarily operate within institutional constraints. Others, however, mentioned projects that can be implemented in the short run and noted that the new dean seems to support the expansion of the clinical programs that many students advocate. On balance, students at Boalt seem to be upbeat about the prospects for the immediate future at the law school.

As the preceding paragraphs suggest, while students describe their classmates as predominantly liberal, they describe the faculty as predominantly conservative, and the question of ethnic and ideological diversity among teachers is important to many students. But to put this debate into perspective, students pointed out that while it can become heated, it is not divisive of the student body.

As for the teaching styles of professors, students said that they "go out of their way to make the first-year experience okay." Some professors are more formal in their use of the Socratic method than others, but no one seemed to be especially traumatized by that aspect of the law school experience. Students noted that many professors used some type of order for calling on students so that it is possible to know when to be prepared, that it is acceptable to "pass" if unprepared, and that some professors try to rely primarily on voluntary participation.

Regarding the accessibility of the faculty, some students said that professors are very accessible, while others said that accessibility depends on the professor. At minimum, professors have office hours and are available then. Beyond that, students mentioned devices such as the assignment of faculty advisors that encourage student contact with the faculty. And beyond that, some students said that the faculty are very interested in students as individuals and participate in "icebreakers." Some students mentioned professors who invited students to their homes or who participated in student activities such as softball games. In light of these different experiences, the report of one student, who said "students here don't really care about accessibility," suggests that faculty are about as accessible as students want them to be, neither more nor less, and that accessibility is just not an issue.

ADMISSIONS | According to Edward G. Tom, Director of Admissions and Financial Aid, applicants are selected on the basis of potential for law study and potential for achievement in and contribution to the field of law. In a typical year, Mr. Tom expects to receive more than 5,500 applications for fewer than 300 places. Mr. Tom states that the LSAT score and undergraduate GPA are the two major criteria used to evaluate academic ability. The LSDAS (Law School Data Assembly Service) combines these two numbers, according to weights provided by the law school, into a single value called the Index and prints the Index on the LSDAS score report. The formula for calculating the Index was not made available, but the law school suggests using the median LSAT score and median GPA of applicants accepted (shown below) as a guideline of chances for admissions. Every file, once complete, is evaluated by a member of the admissions staff on the basis of the admissions criteria. A limited number of applicants who clearly rank highest are admitted immediately. Similarly, others whose numerical indicators are low, and whose files do not show a "plus" indicating some special quality, are denied. The remainder are then given more extended consideration by the Committee on Admissions, which is composed of faculty and students. (Student members participate in the review and evaluation of an application only if the applicant specifically authorizes their participation.)

LSAT scores are evaluated in light of an applicant's familiarity with the test. Multiple LSAT scores are averaged. GPAs are evaluated in the context of possible grade inflation, age of grades, grade trends or discrepancies among the applicant's grades, academic caliber of college attended, exceptionally high grades, difficulty of course work, and time commitments while attending college. No single "pre-law" major is required, recommended, or favored.

The Personal Statement. A personal statement is required and is, according to Mr. Tom, the applicant's opportunity to submit information that would help the reader of the file to evaluate the application. A resume or chronological list of activities may accompany the personal statement.

Recommendations. Letters of recommendation are not required, but Mr. Tom says that the admission committee finds them useful—and most applicants submit them. The law school recommends two or three letters from professors familiar with the applicant's academic performance and who are able to assess the applicant's potential for the study of law. For applicants who have been away from academia for some time, letters from work colleagues are often valuable. Applicants are given the option of waiving access to letters, but in the evaluation of the letters, no weight is given to whether the waiver has been signed.

ADMISSIONS DATA

	Class of 1993	Class of 1994
Applied	5,936	6,527
Median LSAT	86.1 percentile	86.1 percentile
Median GPA	3.31	3.33
Accepted	807	741
Median LSAT	95.9 percentile	97.5 percentile
Median GPA	3.6	3.7
Enrolled	312	214
Median LSAT	95.9 percentile	97.5 percentile
Median GPA	3.67	3.70

Interviews. Mr. Tom states that because of the large number of applicants, interviews are not used as an aspect of determining admission. Candidates are welcome, however, to visit the law school on an informal basis and may stop by the Admissions Office with questions about the school or the admissions process.

Minority Applications. According to Mr. Tom, the law school seeks a racially and culturally diverse student body. In making admissions decisions, it gives positive weight to membership in cultural, ethnic, or racial groups that have not had a fair opportunity to develop potential for academic achievement and that would contribute to the diversity of the entering class. In recent years, these groups primarily have been African-Americans, Chicanos, Latinos, American Indians, Chinese, Koreans, Southeast Asians, and Pacific Islanders.

Residency. The law school, Mr. Tom notes, is a public institution supported by the State of California. Under a policy adopted by the law school, approximately 75 percent of the entering class must be residents of California. Since half of the applicants in any year are residents of other states and only 25 percent of the places in the class may be allotted to them, competition for these places may be somewhat more intense.

Application Tips.   Mr. Tom suggests the following as appropriate topics for the personal statement:

- Academic honors, awards or other recognitions *not* based solely on GPA
- Personal data such as cultural, ethnic, or racial background
- Physical and learning disabilities and any effect they might have on applicant's credentials
- Extracurricular, community, or other achievements
- Work experience, including nature and amount of outside employment while in college and after college
- Description of graduate studies
- Analysis of one's history of standardized testing (comparing LSAT scores with those on other tests)
- College grading and course selection and grade trends
- Any additional information that would be relevant

Mr. Tom also suggested that students still in a position to structure their curricula might do the following: develop skills in communication (both verbal and written), and take courses in which written work is vigorously edited; develop analytical and problem-solving skills; obtain breadth in humanities and social sciences in order to understand the social context within which legal problems arise; and acquire a general understanding of economics, because legal problems are related to the economic functioning of society.

Applicants may wish to present documentation of prior poor performance on standardized tests.

P LACEMENT | According to the Office of Career Services, Boalt has no difficulty attracting employers, and about 350 visit the campus in a typical year. The law school does an annual mailing to all who have conducted on-campus interviews in the past and to those who express an interest in interviewing for the fall and spring programs. Students are given in-house handouts containing general information on interviewing techniques and on dealing with employment offers. In addition, the placement office holds workshops and mock interviews.

Commentary.   Student comments about the placement office at Boalt are similar to those made by students about placement offices at some other law schools. Students generally find the efforts of the placement office acceptable but are not enthusiastic about its operations, and instead attribute the place-

PLACEMENT DATA

	Class of 1991	Class of 1990
Placed at Graduation	94.3%	96.6%
Placed within 90 Days	94.3[1]	96.6[1]
U.S. Supreme Court Clerks	N/A	1
U.S. Appellate Court Clerks	15	15[2]
U.S. District Court Clerks	18	18[2]
State Appellate Court Clerks	1[3]	2[3]
Other Judicial Clerks	1	N/A
Median Starting Salary	$65,000	$65,000

[1]Similariity of numbers may be attributable to fact that students who are committed to public interest work often have to wait for bar results, and results are not announced in California until five months after graduation.
[2]Estimated.
[3]California State Court of Appeals does not generally offer clerkships but hires staff attorneys instead. Positions reported were for states other than California.

ment office's good record to the quality of the school's graduates rather than the functioning of the placement office. Further, students reported that the focus of the placement office's efforts seems to be finding students jobs at large firms, while students interested in areas such as public interest law or government service are expected to make efforts on their own. A couple of students theorized that the change in deans might result in changes in placement office policies but added that it is too soon to tell, and further, that competition for scarce resources at the law school may make expansion of nontraditional opportunities a low priority.

A STUDENT SAMPLER Current Boalt students did their undergraduate work at over 100 different universities, about half coming from schools outside California, with the greatest numbers from Harvard, Yale, and Michigan outside the state and Berkeley, Stanford, and UCLA within. Of the most recent entering class, 24% have at least a master's degree, nine have Ph.D.s, and three have M.D.s. The class includes a ballerina, a cartoonist, an economist, a journalist, a molecular biologist, and a physicist.

NOTEWORTHY GRADUATES

Melvin Belli, prominent trial attorney; Hon. Cathy Silak, recently the first woman appointed to the Idaho Supreme Court; Dale Minami, a partner in the San Francisco firm of Minami, Lew, Tamaki and Lee, who represented Fred Korematsu against the United States government in the case that triggered reparations legislation for Japanese-Americans wrongfully interred during World War II; Earl Warren, the late Chief Justice of the United States Supreme Court

UNIVERSITY OF CALIFORNIA, DAVIS

SCHOOL OF LAW—KING HALL
DAVIS, CALIFORNIA 95616
(916) 752-6477

ADMISSIONS

Applied: 4,006

Accepted: 675

Enrolled: 158

Median LSAT: 92nd percentile

Median GPA: 3.41

STUDENT BODY

Total: 481

Women: 47%

Minorities: 27%

Average Age: 25

ACADEMIC RESOURCES

Library Volumes: 295,000

Computer Services: LEXIS, WESTLAW

Student/Faculty Ratio: 20:1

FINANCES (ACADEMIC YEAR)

Tuition:	
Resident:	$ 3,057.50
Nonresident	$10,756.50
Housing	$ 3,446
Food:	$ 1,556
Books and Supplies:	$ 782
Personal:	$ 1,974
Transportation:	$ 751
Total:	
Resident:	$11,566.50
Nonresident	$19,265.50

ENVIRONMENT Davis is a small, progressive college town of some 51,000 people, located in the fertile Sacramento Valley, 20 minutes by car or rapid transit bus from Sacramento, California's capital. The San Francisco Bay area is little more than an hour away. The streets and parks of Davis are laced with bicycle paths, and most law students live within biking distance of the school. The town is devoted to orderly growth, and University students are responsible participants in town government. The air is clean, the community atmosphere friendly, and the climate temperate.

The Davis campus, with a total enrollment of 23,000, consists of 3,600 acres located in prime farm lands. A multi-million-dollar sports and recreation complex houses the University's extensive intramural sports program and provides individual recreational opportunities. Additionally, Davis is equidistant from the Sierra Nevada mountains and the Pacific Ocean, so it is ideally suited for access to outdoor recreational activities. The ski areas of the Lake Tahoe region are close enough for relaxed one-day ski trips. Less than two hours away are good beaches to the west and the rugged wilderness area of Lassen National Park to the north. Davis also offers a wide variety of cultural events, including a professional resident theater; professional art galleries; and programs of concerts, lectures, and films. Also close at hand are the urban facilities of Sacramento, which include a symphony orchestra, several theater groups, and a number of excellent art collections.

The law building is named after the late Martin Luther King, Jr., in recognition of his efforts to achieve social and political justice for the poor and disadvantaged by orderly means. The building was designed especially to meet the school's needs and includes a model courtroom for moot court and mock trials, a well-furnished student lounge, comfortable study carrels, and offices for student organizations. Another section of the building contains seminar and meeting rooms, offices, and a student snack area. The building is constructed around a sunny central courtyard with trees, flowers, and places to relax and talk.

Commentary. Students confirmed that one of the defining characteristics of Davis is its "small-town feeling." For those accustomed to the activity of a large city such as Los Angeles, the serenity of Davis may be tedious, but most students cited living conditions in the law school's host city as a definite advantage of studying at King Hall and described Davis as "very livable," "safe, clean, and quiet," and "politically progressive and socially correct." The lifestyle of the city's residents, which was described as "very earthy," "friendly," and "laid back," apparently also becomes the lifestyle of many law students who mentioned participating in "potluck dinners" or "sipping mocha" at one of the little coffee houses in the downtown area. For those with an appetite for greater excitement, Sacramento is just 11 miles away—an arrangement considered highly satisfactory by those students who prize the small-town feeling of Davis and are pleased that the City has "no ghettos, slums, or other bad areas, just nice, residential neighborhoods."

The Central Valley region is primarily agricultural, and the University, which is surrounded by rice fields, has strong agricultural and animal husbandry programs. One of the advantages of living in such a region is the "farmers' markets" that offer fresh produce, and one of the disadvantages is the odor that emanates from the Ag School's pig farm when the wind is blowing in the wrong direction.

Thus far, Davis may sound very much like many other smaller college towns, but student reports indicate that the city is characterized also by a collective social conscience that makes it highly unusual if not truly unique. This additional dimension is epitomized by the logo on the city government's stationery: a bicycle. Bicycling is the mode of transportation of choice in Davis, a city that is noted as a champion of alternative energy sources. As one student put it, "Davis is a bicycle town." The City's flat landscape is conducive to pedaling, and the mild climate makes the outdoor activity comfortable almost year-round. The City's road system was designed with bicycles in mind, and virtually every road has a bicycle lane. Cyclists are required to register their bikes with the town, and at last count, 50,000 had been registered—10,000 more than the number of residents in Davis. The town even has its own "bicycle police" who wear official uniforms that include cycling shorts and who write summonses to cyclists who speed or who fail to stop at intersections. Davis also has a clean air act that bans smoking in restaurants, city offices, and other public buildings, and even outdoor public events. In fact, the law is so broad that it is illegal to smoke on a sidewalk unless one is moving.

Law students did not express very profound feelings about their physical plant. It was described as a "well-maintained brick structure with timeless institutional looks." One positive aspect of studying at Davis, and one that was mentioned several times, is the law school's policy of assigning to each student a library study carrel. Actually, first-year students generally have to share a carrel with another student, but space assignments take account of class schedules so that one carrel-mate is likely to be in class while the other is studying. Then, in the second and third years, it is possible to have exclusive use of a carrel.

Given student descriptions of the lifestyle in Davis, it would be extraordinarily surprising to learn that the law school is a hotbed of vicious competition; and, in fact, students described the atmosphere at the law school as "nurturing" and "supportive." As one student said, the feeling at Davis is that the three years are a "learning experience rather than a job competition." This is not to say, however, that Davis students are not interested in doing well. Rather, it is to say that they understand that "people learn more effectively by working together."

Finally, it should be noted that there is one aspect of the law school, as an institution, that is not admired by many students. Although UC Davis is located in a city known for its progressive social and political climate and though the law school building is named for a great civil rights leader, the faculty was described by students as "mostly Caucasian and predominantly male." The lack of diversity is a sore spot for many students, and one that was aggravated by a recent hiring decision: on the short list for a tenure-track position were eight candidates—seven women and one man—and the job went to the man. When asked what institutional forces operated to shape this decision and others that have resulted in the loss of women teachers, students cited the "old-boy network" and added that closing the gender gap on the faculty is going to be particularly difficult given the budgetary cuts that are affecting all public universities in California.

ACADEMICS | According to Acting Dean of the Law School Edward Rabin, the program at the School of Law of the University of California at Davis (King Hall) is constructed to create a cohesive community of professors, students, and staff. The law school building was originally designed for 500 students, and the dean states that the law school has firmly resisted any temptation to expand beyond that number. Consequently, the law school of UC Davis is the smallest school in California that is fully accredited by the American Bar Association. The dean says that because of the law school's small size, and because Davis is a typical small college town, students and faculty get to know each other both in and outside of class, and many strong and lasting friendships are formed at the law school.

The dean continues the discussion of the law school's academic philosophy by explaining that the law school strives to maintain a friendly and supportive atmosphere in which students can concentrate on the important task of mastering the law, rather than overcoming a hostile environment. The dean contrasts the first-year curriculum, in which every student is assigned a second- or third-year student as a tutor, to the "sink or swim" method of instruction that characterizes other law schools. Additionally, every first-year student takes at least one course in a small section of about 35 students, and these small sections are almost always taught by a regular faculty member. Consequently, each first-year student gets to know at least one faculty member, someone who, the dean says, often becomes the student's "unofficial advisor."

Expanding on the "tutor" program, the dean notes that tutors are chosen both for their academic ability and for their ability to be accessible and helpful to first-year students. While the tutors' activities vary somewhat, the program imposes three general requirements. First, a tutor must attend all classes of his or her course to know what is being covered in class and to be accessible to the students before and after class. Second, a tutor must be available for individual consultation with students who have academic or personal questions. Third, tutors schedule review sessions to supplement the formal classes conducted by professors.

Dean Rabin concludes by stating that the law school offers a demanding and rigorous legal education by outstanding teachers who, in many cases, are nationally or internationally recognized scholars. The law school believes, however, that the best learning occurs in a supportive and caring environment and makes such an environment a high priority.

Commentary. Students by and large endorsed Dean Rabin's description of the educational philosophy of the law school and mentioned favorably the "tutor

CURRICULUM

First-Year Courses: Introduction to Law (one week), Contracts (first and second semesters), Civil Procedure (first), Constitutional Law (second), Criminal Law (first), Property (second), Torts (first and second), Legal Research (first), Legal Writing (second)

Interesting Electives: American Indian Law; Employment Discrimination; Energy Law; Foreign Relations; Gender-Based Discrimination; International Human Rights; Jewish Law (Seminar); Law, Medicine, and Ethics; Legal Imagination; Mass Media Law; Mexican-American Legal Relations; Public Sector Labor Law; Securities Regulation; Toxics Law; Wildlife Protection

program." Each class (e.g., contracts, torts, property) is assigned a second- or third-year student who monitors the progress of the course, holds review sessions, and is available to answer questions on course content and who also handles collateral topics such as a professor's peculiar likes and dislikes as well. Students contrasted the effectiveness of the program at Davis, where virtually no one fails, with law schools such as nearby McGeorge, where the attrition rate is nearly 33 percent.

When asked whether anything distinguishes the curriculum at Davis, students pointed out that the small size of the law school constrains the number and variety of courses that can be offered. Recently, students expressed an interest in having a course on sports law, but the subject had never before been offered and the law school did not have a faculty member qualified and willing to teach the course. Students took the initiative and found two attorneys in Los Angeles who come to Davis each week to teach the course. In general, students said that they take a lot of responsibility for their education.

Students also cited a second feature of the Davis curriculum: its bar courses. These are courses that teach concepts that one must have mastered in order to pass the California bar examination and be admitted to the practice of law in that state. In fact, it is a source of some considerable pride among Davis students that the law school has the highest pass rate for the California bar exam—about 90 percent. Thus, students explained, Davis has a reputation for producing "quality attorneys who don't have to be trained by their employers" and not "theoreticians who aren't really much good to anyone but another law professor."

As for teaching styles, students reported that professors use a variety of techniques in first-year classes. They range from a Socratic method that includes the element of surprise to a "kinder and gentler" question-and-answer method that requires student participation, but in a systematic manner. And students said that professors are usually in their offices when not teaching and that doors are left open so that students can come to them with questions. One student explained also that it is reassuring to see professors on days off dressed in casual attire because it "makes them real people," but reports suggest that student-faculty interaction is largely limited to the academic setting and does not enter the social sphere except on those occasions that are designed specifically to bring faculty and students together.

ADMISSIONS | According to Sharon Pinkney, Director of Admissions, all applications are read by the Director of Admissions who then makes a recommendation on each to the admissions committee, a group of four faculty members and two third-year students. The director uses an "admissions index" to assist in the initial sorting of files, but the index is used as a guideline only and does not determine the director's final recommendation. Rather, Ms. Pinkney stresses, all applications are read in their entirety, and no decisions are made solely on the basis of numbers.

The reading of the files begins in early January, and the first decisions are made public in mid- to late January. For the purpose of evaluating the files, committee members work in panels of three. Regarding the director's recommendation, Ms. Pinkney states that approximately 500 applicants are recommended for admission, less than one-third to the committee for further consideration, and the remainder for denial. Files recommended for admissions and denial must be made available to the committee for 48 hours in which they can agree or disagree with the recommendation of the director. Files referred to the committee are sent in equal batches to each panel. They must then make a unanimous decision to admit, deny, or waitlist.

The Personal Statement. All applicants are required to provide a personal statement as part of the completed application for admission. Ms. Pinkney stresses that because personal interviews are not a part of the law school's admissions process, the personal statement is the *only* opportunity to advocate on one's own behalf. Ms. Pinkney says that the personal statement can take any form the applicant chooses and that it is also the appropriate forum to explain any discrepancies in an undergraduate GPA or LSAT score.

Recommendations. Two recommendations are required to complete the application file. The admissions committee prefers that they come from professors under whom the applicant has studied. Letters from employers, Ms. Pinkney says, are acceptable but often do not provide information relative to academic preparation for law study. In general, according to Ms. Pinkney, the committee is interested in learning about an applicant's writing, analytical, and reasoning skills and overall academic preparation.

ADMISSIONS DATA

	Class of 1993	Class of 1994
Applied	3,242	4,006
Median LSAT	74th percentile	79.6 percentile
Median GPA	3.21	3.24
Accepted	661	675
Median LSAT	92.3 percentile	94.5 percentile
Median GPA	3.49	3.51
Enrolled	170	156
Median LSAT	92.3 percentile	92.3 percentile
Median GPA	3.44	3.41

Interviews. Ms. Pinkney says that interviews are not part of the admissions process but adds that prospective applicants may make an appointment to meet with staff to ask questions about the process. Further, group information sessions are scheduled in November, December, and January.

Minority Applications. Ms. Pinkney says that ethnic/racial identity is considered a positive factor in the admissions process and adds that if a candidate wishes to have the factor considered, information to support that request must be included in the personal statement.

Application Tips. When asked whether the law school has a minimum LSAT score or GPA below which an application does not have a "realistic" chance for acceptance, Ms. Pinkney responds that offers of admissions are rarely extended to applicants with *both* a GPA below 3.0 *and* an LSAT score below the 45th percentile. Ms. Pinkney also points out that the law school's application materials include a "numerical profile grid" that breaks down the applications received by the law school in the previous year according to LSAT score and GPA and reports the number that were accepted. Although the "numerical profile grid" can be used to get a general idea of the chances an applicant might have, Ms. Pinkney also points out that the admission committee takes into consideration a lot of factors which may have had an effect on the "numbers." Thus, an application with an LSAT score below the 45th percentile but a very high GPA or one with a GPA below 3.0 but a very high LSAT score could still receive serious consideration.

Regarding the mechanics of the application, Ms. Pinkney encourages candidates to apply early in the application season, noting that 65% of all applications are received by the admissions office in January, a volume that creates a "tremendous paper backlog." As for the personal statement, for most people, Ms. Pinkney notes, two to three double-spaced, typewritten pages is the appropriate length. Finally, Ms. Pinkney suggests that those candidates who plan to make ethnic/racial identity a factor in their applications may want to contact a student organization at the law school for assistance. Members of some student organizations such as Asian Law Students, La Raza Law Students, Black Law Students, Native American Law Students, Filipino Law Students, and the Women's Caucus participate in this effort.

PLACEMENT According to its Director, Jane Thomson, the Career Services Office (CSO) at UC Davis makes extensive efforts to recruit prospective employers. Twice each year, letters are sent to a mailing list of several thousand law firms, government agencies, and public interest organizations inviting them to recruit on campus or by mail. Alumni are contacted individually and through publications and mass mailings and are urged to contact the law school regarding openings for students and graduates. Job development outreach to small firms and specialized practitioners is conducted through local, minority, and specialty bar organizations. The office collaborates on an annual regional public interest job fair and assists in promoting regional minority job fairs. Ms. Thomson notes that the CSO at UC Davis initiated a minority summer clerking program in Sacramento. In addition to the on-campus interviewing programs, the CSO maintains listings for part-time, summer, and post-JD opportunities and produces a bi-weekly job bulletin for graduates.

Ms. Thomson says that the office also offers a variety of services and resources to help students to identify legal career options and to develop the requisite strategies and skills to obtain the jobs they seek. These services and resources include lectures, panel presentations, and workshops by attorneys from diverse practice areas; a resource library with guidebooks, directories, pamphlets, and other materials to assist in the career building process; career service publications such as manuals, handouts, and a weekly newsletter tailored specifically to the concerns and interest of the King Hall student population; and individual consultations with the director on issues ranging from polishing a resume or cover letter to negotiating with potential employers to rethinking career goals altogether.

Commentary. It is perhaps a good thing that Davis has the reputation for turning out graduates who are already equipped to practice law because descriptions

PLACEMENT DATA

	Class of 1991	Class of 1990
Placed at Graduation	72%	75%
Placed within 90 Days	N/A[1]	N/A[1]
U.S. Supreme Court Clerks	0	0
U.S. Appellate Court Clerks	1	3
U.S. District Court Clerks	5	12
State Appellate Court Clerks	5	8
Other Judicial Clerks	N/A	N/A

[1] Percent placed within six months was 88% for the Class of 1991, 89% for the Class of 1990.

of the Career Services Office suggest that the placement activities of the law school are not particularly effective. As one student said, "People either love or hate the director, and there is a lot more hate going on right now than love." Students were even critical of the on-campus interviewing program, one of the main placement activities. They felt that McGeorge students have better access to jobs in Sacramento and Berkeley students to jobs in San Francisco, and that Los Angeles firms just make token appearances. These are serious criticisms, since about 27% of Davis graduates wind up working in the Bay Area, 20% in Sacramento, and 22% in Los Angeles. On the other hand, most Davis students get jobs; but reports suggest that employment is often the result of serious individual effort rather than a free ticket from the placement office.

A STUDENT SAMPLER The student body includes a number of former interns and staff members to state and federal legislators as well as several former newspaper reporters, one of whom covered Congress. Also included are former aerospace, marine, and chemical engineers; secondary school teachers; a minister; a physician from Indonesia; an environmental regulatory analyst; military officers; public relations specialists; and a university museum curator. One student counseled disturbed and delinquent children in group homes and operated a respite home for the poor. Two students were professional actors before entering law school; another pursued the career of an opera singer in Germany; one worked as a business and legal affairs executive for a feature film production company; one was a producer of public radio; and another worked as a researcher for the British Broadcasting Company.

NOTEWORTHY GRADUATES

Simone Campbell, member of the Order of the Sisters of Social Service and founder of the Community Law Center in Oakland; Elihu Harris, Mayor, City of Oakland; Gus Lee, author of the best-selling novel *China Boy*; Representative George Miller; Hon. Jane Restani, U.S. Court of International Trade; Art Torres, State Senator, California Legislature; Keith Zajic, Vice President of Music and Business Affairs, Warner Bros.

UNIVERSITY OF CHICAGO

LAW SCHOOL
1111 EAST 60TH STREET
CHICAGO, ILLINOIS 60637
(312) 702-9484

ADMISSIONS

Applied: 3,500

Accepted: N/A

Enrolled: 177

Median LSAT: 98th percentile

Median GPA: 3.75[1]

STUDENT BODY

Total: 546

Women: 38%

Minorities: 15%

Average Age: 25/26

ACADEMIC RESOURCES

Library Volumes: 550,000

Computer Services: LEXIS, WEST-LAW, Nexus, computer lab with 20 PCs and MACs

Student/Faculty Ratio: 16:1

FINANCES (ACADEMIC YEAR)

Tuition:	$16,980
Housing, Food, and Personal:	$10,081
Books and Supplies:	$ 800
Health Services Fee:	$ 210[2]
Total	$28,080

---

[1]Median of those accepted, not those who matriculated.

[2]All students pay a $210 annual fee for the use of the university's Student Health Service. University policy requires also that each student be covered by adequate health and hospitalization insurance. Students must pay a quarterly premium for this supplemental insurance or supply evidence of comparable protection from an individual or family health policy.

E NVIRONMENT The University of Chicago is located on the South Side of Chicago. While many of those who live in Hyde Park are associated with the University, about three-fourths work downtown or in other parts of the city and live in Hyde Park by choice. The University of Chicago Law School is located on the south campus and is separated from the main campus by the Midway Plaisance, which served as the midway for the 1983 World's Columbian Exposition and is now an open recreational field.

The law school is relatively small and places a special value on ease of access to the faculty, so the law school building was designed to facilitate student-faculty interaction. Offices are arranged around the working floors of the library, and the custom is for students to drop in on faculty members at any time without going through secretaries or other staff.

Commentary. The university distributes a pamphlet entitled "Hyde Park and Chicago: A View from the University of Chicago," which contains beautiful color photographs and glowing descriptions. Many who are familiar with the area allow that the university's literature may overstate the case a little, but they do agree that the area has considerable charm and point out that Chicago offers the amenities one expects to find in a large city.

Hyde Park does have its detractors, and one of their concerns is security or, more precisely, personal safety. One student, who moved his family out of the area, insisted that personal safety is a general concern among female law students. He noted that students who plan to work late at the library move their cars closer to the campus in late afternoon. Yet a female student dismissed that idea by saying that Hyde Park is "statistically one of the safest areas of Chicago"— and safer, she feels, than the areas around Columbia or Yale. As for reparking cars, she explained that people do like to park as close to the library as possible but that parking around the library is restricted until 3:30 P.M. Only then do those choice spaces become available to law students. So whom is one to believe? Some sensible advice came from Mr. Rudolph Nimmocks, Director of the University of Chicago Police and a longtime resident of Hyde park: "This is a city, and you have to use common sense. If people are concerned, they should come and visit the area."

In general, students and recent graduates seem to be pretty well satisfied with the law school's physical plant—though one student expressed a preference for the Neo-Gothic architecture of the main campus over the modern law school building. And virtually all confirmed that the design of the law school does provide easy access to the faculty. In fact, access can sometimes be too easy, according to students who have had the misfortune of coming face to face in the library stacks with a professor whose class they have just cut.

As might be expected, the small size of the law school also has implications for the quality of student life. Although perceptions regarding "performance pressure" vary individually, most students wanted to make it very clear that the atmosphere is not one of cutthroat competition. When asked about student life, many students used words such as "cooperation" and "congenial." Specifically, students said that classmates are generally willing to share study outlines and notes from missed classes. One recent graduate, who confessed to being a not-so-dedicated law student who finished near the bottom of the class, was a member of a study group composed primarily of members of the *Law Review*.

Chicago also has a reputation as a conservative law school, but some students were quick to dismiss this notion as a non-issue. First, they disputed the characterization of the school as a bastion of conservativism. Regarding the faculty, they pointed to "nonconservatives" such as Dean Stone, who served on the Board of Directors of the ACLU (Illinois Division). Nor are students necessarily more conservative than those at other schools. Of the recent entering class, approximately a third are affiliated with the Law School Democrats Club. Ultimately, said one student, the impression of conservatism may be due to the fact that the conservative elements are just more organized than others.

Second and more important, students reported that political orientation is a non-issue because thoughtful disagreement is welcome. Faculty members of radically different viewpoints are collegial, and students with opposing politics respect one another. It was suggested that this civility is a conservative force that retards change, and some recent graduates do think that in the past the law school has shortchanged students going into public interest law; but even they acknowledged that the law school may have "turned the corner" on this issue. Or again, some students opined that the law school does not yet have enough women or minority faculty but also acknowledged that the school seems committed to change on this score. Finally, some students applauded the sincerity of the law school's efforts to recruit minority students but expressed some disappointment at the lack of more rapid progress.

ACADEMICS According to Dean of the Law School Geoffrey R. Stone, Chicago has always been home to great legal scholars, but it is equally a teaching institution. Like most other law schools, Chicago aims fundamentally at training generalists by teaching broad and basic concepts of law, by imparting an understanding of the legal process, and by refining analytical skills. What the Dean believes distinguishes Chicago from other law schools is its special interest in the relationships between law and other social studies and in the interaction of law with its social and human context.

Commentary. When asked about any special emphasis at the law school, students reported that many courses, though not all, include analysis of the relative economic efficiencies of various laws. One recent graduate estimated that the number of courses in which this approach is emphasized is about one-third to one-half of the offerings, but he added that some topics simply do not lend

CURRICULUM

First-Year Courses: Contracts, Torts, Property, Criminal Law, Civil Procedure, Elements of Law (Autumn Quarter), one elective (Spring Quarter), Legal Writing Program

Interesting Electives: AIDS: Legal and Public Issues; Ancient Greek Law; Current Issues in Racism and Law; Economic Liberties; Employment Discrimination; Epistemology of Law; Feminist Theory; History of Canon Law; Intellectual Origins of the U.S. Constitution; Law Concerning American Indians; Mining Law; Protectionism in U.S. Trade Policy; Section 1983 Civil Rights Litigation; Structuring Venture Capital and Entrepreneurial Transactions; Thomas Hobbes

themselves to economic analysis and that some professors are less inclined than others to use this approach. Still, the emphasis is important enough that one student said that economic analysis becomes "a way of life."

Teachers use the Socratic method, and students appreciate the value of the question-and-answer format as a teaching tool. They reported that it is not used in a mean-spirited or denigrating manner. One student remarked that teachers are available for questions at the end of class and address any seemingly widespread confusion that surfaces at such meetings at the start of the next class.

Finally, the Chicago faculty has a deserved reputation for its scholarly output, but students were adamant that the faculty's research activity does not compromise the educational mission of the law school. And they offered evidence to support that claim. Recently, one new professor took the time to learn the name and face of every student in the course from law school records *before* the first class. Even on the first day, the professor was able to call on and to answer students by name. Or, a visiting professor at the law school remarked to students that the faculty at Chicago seems to spend more time on preparation for class than faculty at many other schools. Or again, a student was having difficulty with the "Coase Theorem," named for its author Ronald Coase, who was awarded the 1991 Nobel Prize in Economics. Since Professor Coase happens to be a member of the law school faculty, the student visited his office and was able to ask questions of the Nobel Prize winner himself.

ADMISSIONS | According to Dean of Students Richard I. Badger, the law school has a four-member admissions committee. Every file is read by at least one member of the committee; some files are read by several members of the committee. The committee does not use an index or a mathematical formula, and each application is examined from an overall perspective. Although there are no cutoffs, chances of admission decline as GPA and LSAT scores decline, as recent statistics show:

GPA	Percent of Applicants Admitted
3.7 and Above	31%
3.5 to 3.7	19%
3.3 to 3.5	8%
3.1 to 3.3	5%
Below 3.1	3%

LSAT Score	Percent of Applicants Admitted
98th Percentile and Above	37%
95th to 97th Percentile	29%
91st to 94th Percentile	12%
85th to 90th Percentile	5%
Below 85th Percentile	2%

The committee does take into account the quality of an applicant's undergraduate school, as judged by the performance of other graduates who have attended the law school and by the performance of all students of that institution who have taken the LSAT in recent years. The committee also looks at the mix of courses shown on the college transcript to determine whether an applicant has had the opportunity to develop analytical skills and the ability to communicate with precision. The further an applicant is removed from college, the less weight is given to the undergraduate academic record. Multiple LSAT scores are usually averaged, though a substantially higher subsequent score may be used alone if there is reason to discount an earlier score.

The Personal Statement. Chicago does not require an essay or writing sample, but applicants are encouraged to submit one. It is permissible to use a copy of a personal statement used in other applications, and the substance of the essay is as important as its demonstration of an ability to write well.

Recommendations. Chicago asks for two letters and strongly encourages the submission of three. Why? According to Dean Bader, it is often difficult for the admissions committee to evaluate an individual's academic record, and it is especially so when the committee is not familiar with the applicant's school,

ADMISSIONS DATA

	Class of 1993	Class of 1994
Applied	3,600	3,500
Median LSAT	N/A	N/A
Median GPA	N/A	N/A
Accepted	N/A	N/A
Median LSAT	98th percentile	98th percentile
Median GPA	3.73	3.75
Enrolled	194	177
Median LSAT	N/A	N/A
Median GPA	N/A	N/A

program of study, or the individual courses taken. For this reason, the dean explains, the best letters are those that come from faculty members who are in a position to comment on a candidate's intellectual strengths and weaknesses. Extra weight is given to a letter from a professor, advisor, or department head who can compare the candidate with other students at the same institution and comment informatively about the candidate's overall academic record, rather than on the candidate's performance in just one or two courses. There is no objection to submitting more than three letters provided that the additional letters are likely to help the committee evaluate an applicant's qualifications. The admissions committee realizes that applicants who have been out of school for some time are likely to have to rely on employers or colleagues for recommendations.

Interviews. Chicago is one of the few law schools that does use evaluative interviews as part of the admissions process, though most applicants will receive a final admission decision without being invited to an interview. Applicants who are invited for evaluative interviews are those whose applications were neither finally accepted nor finally denied but which were placed in a deferred decision category. Applicants in the deferred decision category are invited to submit supplemental information and are encouraged to come to the law school for an evaluative interview. Each year, about 700 applicants are placed in the deferred decision category; about 400 come for interviews.

Minority Applications.   Dean Badger stated that "special efforts are made to recruit minority applicants and to admit minority candidates."

Application Tips.   You should be careful when using the data supplied regarding the percentage of students accepted with particular qualifications. For example, though fewer than a third of the applicants with GPAs above 3.7 and a little more than a third of applicants with LSAT scores in the 98th percentile or above were accepted, the percentage of applicants with GPAs above 3.7 *and* LSAT scores in the 98th percentile or above was probably much higher.

Dean Badger also remarked that personal statements having "a narrow focus are generally more effective than those attempting to make a broad integration of the law with one's general career or scholarly goals." You should notice that this observation is consistent with Dean Stone's statement of the law school's educational philosophy: the law school curriculum aims at training generalists. Therefore, unless some considerable personal experience shaped a particular career objective, your statement will probably be better received if you focus on your background rather than trying to map out your legal career. For example, you can describe *the significance* of any academic honors or other accomplishments or provide explanations for what may appear to be any weakness in your academic record.

Another important feature of this particular admissions process is that it solicits three rather than two letters of recommendation. Dean Badger indicated that in a significant number of cases each year the additional letter is "decisive." Although it is always important to obtain strong letters of recommendation, for Chicago you will have to go the extra distance.

PLACEMENT   The placement office does four mailings each year to encourage prospective employers to visit the law school campus, and approximately 400 recruiters visit the law school each year. It conducts interview workshops and mock interviews for students who request or need simulations. Additionally, upon request, the placement office debriefs students on actual interviews immediately after the interviews take place.

Commentary.   Students seem satisfied with the placement opportunities for Chicago students. For example, one student reported success in getting interviews with all 10 targeted law firms. Another noted that summer employment is plentiful. And a recent graduate mentioned having multiple job offers despite being toward the bottom of the class.

Students and graduates attributed this happy situation to two factors. One, because Chicago is a small law school, Chicago graduates are scarce, creating a

PLACEMENT DATA

	Class of 1991	Class of 1990
Placed at Graduation	98%	98%
Placed within 90 days	99%	99%
U.S. Supreme Court Clerks	5	4
U.S. Appellate Court Clerks	28	32
U.S. District Court Clerks	9	6
State Appellate Court Clerks	12	7
Other Judicial Clerks	0	0
Median Starting Salary	$70,000	$70,000

kind of competition for them among employers. Two, grades at the Law School tend to cluster tightly in the middle and class rankings are not published. Thus, it is difficult for employers to distinguish someone in the 60th percentile from someone in the 40th percentile. Consequently, job offers are spread around.

A striking feature of the placement statistics is the extraordinarily high number of judicial clerkships: nearly a third of the most recent graduating class obtained judicial clerkships. Furthermore, those were all positions with federal courts or state appellate courts. And five were with the United States Supreme Court. In fact, based on the records of the U.S. Supreme Court, Dean Stone determined that over the last several years, Chicago's per capita production of Supreme Court clerks was second only to that of Yale.

A STUDENT SAMPLER The students at Chicago come from over 170 undergraduate institutions. A recent survey of the student body showed that the largest number come from Amherst (21), Brown (16), Berkeley (14), Chicago (23), Cornell (11), Dartmouth (9), Duke (12), Georgetown (13), Harvard (33), University of Illinois, Urbana-Champaign (24), Michigan (18), Northwestern (16), Pennsylvania (21), Princeton (21), Stanford (15), and Yale (39).

The student body at the Law School includes: a state policewoman, a publisher of educational books, a management consultant, an IBM marketing representative, a Navy officer, an advertising executive, a professional musician, a professional water polo player, a social worker, a newspaper reporter, a television reporter, a screenwriter, a talent agent, a congressional staff member, an engineer, a college professor, an accountant, an investment banker, a paralegal, a high school teacher, a CIA officer, a research scientist, a financial analyst, a Peace Corps volunteer, a college fundraiser, a government economist, an ESPN account executive, and an opera singer.

Of the students in a recent graduating class, 68 percent accepted positions with law firms, and 25 percent accepted judicial clerkships; the remaining 7 percent went with corporations, the government, or public interest organizations; continued their educations; or accepted employment outside the field of law.

NOTEWORTHY GRADUATES

John Ashcroft, Governor of Missouri; Robert Bork, research associate, American Enterprise Institute; Carol Moseley Braun, U.S. Senator; Ramsey Clark, former Attorney General of the United States; Herma Hill Kay, Dean of the University of California at Berkeley; Edward H. Levi, former Attorney General of the United States; Professor Thomas Morgan, Former president, American Association of Law Schools; Ralph Neas, executive director, Leadership Conference for Civil Rights; Lawrence Rosen, Professor, Princeton Department of Anthropology; Hon. Mary Schroeder, U.S. Court of Appeals for the Ninth Circuit

COLUMBIA UNIVERSITY

SCHOOL OF LAW
435 WEST 116TH STREET
NEW YORK, NEW YORK 10027
(212) 854-2670

ADMISSIONS

Applied: 5,395

Accepted: 930

Enrolled: 341

Median LSAT: 97th percentile

Median GPA: 3.6

STUDENT BODY

Total: 935

Women: 40%

Minorities: 24%

Average Age: N/A

ACADEMIC RESOURCES

Library Volumes: 735,000

Computer Services: LEXIS, WEST-LAW, word processors

Student/Faculty Ratio: 18:1

FINANCES (ACADEMIC YEAR)

Tuition:	$17,310
Food and Housing:	$ 7,110
Other Expenses:	$ 2,500
Total:	$26,920

ENVIRONMENT New York City provides a rich and challenging setting for the study of law. The city is home to much of the nation's—indeed, the world's—legal talent. Leading practitioners and policy makers in many areas of the law regularly visit Columbia to teach a class or to talk with students in informal lectures, panels, or brown-bag lunch discussions.

The Columbia campus is located in the Morningside Heights section of Manhattan, a diverse family neighborhood with special character. Educational institutions and students are the dominant presence in the area; in addition to Columbia, there are Barnard College, Teachers College, Bank Street College of Education, Union Theological Seminary, the Jewish Theological Seminary, and the Manhattan School of Music. One can sample food from at least fifteen different ethnic restaurants. There are seven bookstores, a legendary family-owned chocolate shop, a record store, three supermarkets, and three green-grocers. Riverside Park, a block away from campus, runs along the Hudson River, and jazz and comedy are offered almost every night at the West End Gate, a neighborhood institution. Plus, Columbia has one of the safest campuses among the nation's urban universities, and the crime rate in the area is one of the lowest in New York City.

Commentary. The students who were interviewed at Columbia gave high marks to life in New York City and mentioned activities ranging from cultural offerings such as art museums (for example, the visiting Matisse exhibit at the Museum of Modern Art), to sporting events at Madison Square Garden (professional hockey and basketball), to Broadway and Off-Broadway shows (for which there are reduced student or same-day tickets), to less formal diversions such as an evening at the West End Gate (mentioned above, "where law students really do hang out"), or the Amsterdam Cafe (located a block from the law school and featuring live music and comedy), or at any one of the many bars or dance clubs along Amsterdam or Columbus Avenues in the 70s or 80s (a part of Manhattan's Upper West Side) or in Greenwich Village. As might be expected, some of the students who came from less densely populated areas evidenced some ambivalence about New York City. One student from the South, for example, called the city "both fabulous and terrible." Further conversation with the student revealed, however, that the "terrible" pertained primarily to the routine activities of living such as getting from place to place. Once one becomes accustomed to those "challenges," the student explained, the city is "really great."

Reports taken at other law schools included in this guide indicate that the area surrounding Columbia University has a reputation among students at other schools as unsafe. Indeed, students at one or another urban school sometimes claimed as one of the advantages of the school the fact that it is located in a neighborhood that is "much better than that surrounding Columbia University." Given this opinion that is so widely held about Morningside Heights by those not actually enrolled at Columbia, one might expect to hear even worse comments from those law students most familiar with the neighborhood. In fact, the descriptions of the neighborhood provided by Columbia students were positive rather than negative!

While Columbia law students acknowledged that the area in which the University is located has the *reputation* (at least in some quarters) of being unsafe, they were adamant that the area around the University is in actuality on a par with other parts of New York City. By and large, the students interviewed endorsed the description of the area given by the administration, and one student specifically described it as "neighborhoody." In fact, those who have heard the area described in unfavorable terms may be pleasantly surprised to hear that Columbia law students mentioned as an advantage of the school the convenience of the nearby subway stop!

53

Which of the two views of Morningside Heights just sketched is more accurate? In the first place, Columbia students are describing the area *immediately* around the University. It is there that one finds the restaurants, bars, and shops mentioned by both administration and students. Also in that area, Columbia University owns a number of apartment houses and other buildings that are used for student housing. (In fact, as one student pointed out, Columbia University is the largest landlord in New York City!) Students said, however, that as one moves away from the Columbia University area, the neighborhood becomes less attractive. One student from a smaller city who seemed quite pleased with Columbia said, "I know that there are areas that are obviously dangerous—I have even heard gunshots—so I avoid those areas." Or as another student (who described himself as 6'4" with a black belt in karate) explained, "The University is located at 116th Street. I won't go past 120th Street at night, and I just will not go as far as 125th Street alone." What lies beyond 125th Street? "One of the most poverty-stricken areas in the country." Furthermore, it should be noted that Columbia University does have a campus and that it is possible to live in a dorm very near the law school building. One dorm resident said that the effect is to create a "little world of one's own" right in the middle of the city. Finally, students explained that the subway line that serves the area is a good one and that it is heavily used. Consequently, one is likely to be riding on a train with many other people rather than alone, and so students are comfortable traveling the subway system to and from the law school. Thus, it appears that Columbia University has created a substantial enclave on the fringe of an urban area that many law students regard as frightening.

If the Columbia University area gets an unfair rap from those not really familiar with it, then the law school has for many years had a reputation for being very competitive, even cut-throat, that was, until recently, entirely justified. Students are quick to point out, however, that conditions at the law school have changed for the better. As one student remarked, "Although there is a certain underlying competitiveness that is perhaps inherent in law school, now one gets nothing but support from one's peers." By way of illustrating this new attitude, one student said that someone who misses class can always count on borrowing notes and can be assured that a classmate will take an extra handout if one is distributed. Students also mentioned that the law school has hired a new Dean of Students, one of whose goals is to ensure that the law school remains free of cut-throat competition.

While the law school's New York City location and new spirit of cooperation may be good reasons to study at Columbia, students reported that the law school's physical plant is not entirely satisfactory. Several times, questions about the building elicited snickers rather than spoken responses. One student called the building "stunningly ugly" and suggested that it be "blown up." Specifically, students said the building is short of space ("the building lacks a student lounge") and that classrooms are not particularly inviting ("very few windows and the blinds are never opened" and "climate control tends to be a bit erratic"). On the other hand, students grudgingly admitted that the facilities are functional ("by and large things work") and even had good things to say about the recently renovated library ("modern," "great," and "a brighter space with large windows"). Furthermore, some students said that the law school does have plans to add a student lounge, and there was even a report that an architect has already been hired for the project. Another student, however, commented that a student lounge is an "eternal promise" not likely to be fulfilled by the law school during the present fiscal crunch. Finally, students mentioned very favorably the recent addition of various computer services at the law school. Particularly worthy of note is the new "E-Mail Center." There are two terminals outside the library and two more in the entryway to the law school that students can use to leave messages for and retrieve messages from classmates, faculty, and administration.

ACADEMICS The description provided of the academic philosophy at Columbia uses phrases such as "enable," "think for themselves," and "self-development." Dean of the Law School Lance Liebman explains that the faculty at Columbia "endeavor to educate students who will function successfully in a legal world, the nature of which can only dimly be perceived." Consequently, the curriculum encourages students to develop their own powers to learn, to analyze, to question, to research, to write, and to think, because, the dean says, ultimately "law is in large part self-taught."

The dean goes on to explain how the curriculum is designed to equip students to handle the "diverse and exciting range of career opportunities [that] will challenge tomorrow's graduates." After completing a rigorous training in legal skills in the Foundation Curriculum, second- and third-year students may select their own program from a large number of courses, clinics, and seminars and may choose as they see fit between intensive study in specific fields or broad exposure to many different areas of the law. Law students may also broaden their programs by enrolling in courses given by other schools within the university, and opportunities for independent scholarship abound at the law school. On the other hand, Dean Liebman notes, while there is great freedom of choice, the faculty at Columbia feel that there are some subjects that no one should neglect: constitutional law, corporations, federal income taxation, and some jurisprudential or comparative law offering.

The ultimate goal of this balance in the curriculum, Dean Liebman concludes, is to give students the chance to achieve "self-development in a profession with almost limitless choices to work for the betterment of society, while finding personal and professional fulfillment."

Commentary. When asked what distinguishes the curriculum at Columbia from that of other law schools, students most often mentioned the "foundation curriculum." (The first-year courses plus one additional course taken in the first

CURRICULUM

First-Year Courses: Contracts, Law and Economics, Civil Procedure, Legal Method, Torts, Constitutional Law, Criminal Law, Foundations of the Regulatory State, Perspectives on Legal Thought, Property

Interesting Electives: American Indians and the Law; Biotechnology: Public Policy, Law, and an Emerging Industry; Black Letter Law of White-Collar Crime; Children and the Law; Chinese Attitudes toward International Law; Civil Rights Law and Social Change; Employment Law; Environmental Litigation; Historical Introduction to Common Law Literature; The Presidency: Office and Powers; Racist Speech and Equal Opportunity; The Trial in American Life; Technological Properties; Women in Society and the Law; Urban Development Controls

term of the second year constitute what is called the "foundation curriculum.") Aside from some adjustments in the length and timing of first-year courses, it is the three courses—"Foundations of the Regulatory State," "Law and Economics," and "Perspectives on Legal Thought"—that distinguish the foundation curriculum at Columbia from the first-year course work at many other law schools. The first is designed to introduce students to methods and procedures of governmental regulation, the second to basic economic concepts useful as tools for contemporary legal analysis, and the third to considerations about the values that underpin traditional legal methodology and its modern variants. Students reported that the third course in particular can be very theoretical (one professor included readings from Kant) but seemed generally to have faith in the concept of the foundation curriculum, if not in every detail of its present configuration. As for the upper-level courses, students noted various areas of strength in the curriculum (e.g., intellectual property) and weakness (e.g., the clinical program). One student claimed that the law school has the "premier corporate program in the country" and added regarding any weaknesses that the administration is "willing to revise what is not working very well."

Questions about the first-year classroom experience did not elicit very strong responses. Students said, for example, that professors use a "soft Socratic method" (asking for volunteers, assigning panels, or following some predetermined order) and further that the first-year classroom atmosphere is "comfortable."

Finally, faculty accessibility was described in terms such as "good," "they have office hours," and "they try to be flexible." In general, comments about accessibility suggest that the faculty are available to handle inquiries about academic matters but that "they are not usually in the mood just to philosophize about life." And student reports suggest that aside from a few scheduled events, students and faculty do not generally interact socially.

56

ADMISSIONS | According to Dean of Admissions James Milligan, the process of reading applications begins shortly after Thanksgiving. The admissions committee first reviews the 400 to 500 applications submitted under the law school's Early Decision Program, an option unique to Columbia among law schools. Under this program, candidates whose first choice of law schools is Columbia can receive an early commitment of admission and, if applicable, financial aid. In return, the law school requires from an Early Decision applicant a prior and definite commitment to attend the law school—if accepted. (And to take certain steps to demonstrate that commitment such as withdrawing applications pending at other law schools.) After disposing of the Early Decision applications, the staff takes up the "regular" applicant pool. "Regular" applications are generally reviewed in the order in which they are received.

Dean Milligan explains that the Columbia Law School admissions system does not recognize any applicant as either a "presumptive admit" or a "presumptive deny" based solely on quantifiable indices of LSAT score or GPA. The system does not use any LSAT "cut-off" or "threshold" scores above or below which an applicant is admitted or rejected, and the GPA is interpreted in light of factors such as the rigor of the curriculum, institutional grade inflation patterns, and the selectivity and reputation of the undergraduate institution. The idea, says Dean Milligan, is to go "both behind and beyond the numbers." To accomplish this goal, the committee examines the applicant's personal essay or statement and letters of recommendation as well as the following pertinent information elicited in the application: course selection, special honors and awards, fellowship opportunities, publications, extracurricular involvement, community service, political activity, professional contributions, and other work experience.

Although the committee places primary emphasis on demonstrated qualities and proven skills that are necessary for academic success and intellectual engagement at the law school, Dean Milligan emphasizes that Columbia also values very highly manifest personal strengths that it believes predict professional distinction and public service. Consequently, the committee weighs carefully elements of the application that speak to a candidate's background, interest, and goals and that evidence sound character, judgment, and values.

Dean Milligan explains further that the activity of the admissions staff at Columbia is not limited to reviewing applications. In the fall, before the "reading season" begins, the dean and staff visit 40 or 50 undergraduate campuses. Though these visits are commonly called "recruitment" visits, the dean explains that their true objective is to provide a public service to prospective applicants—not to stimulate application volume. The admissions staff is particularly concerned to reach people who, for whatever reason, might not otherwise consider Columbia Law School as an option. The dean and staff visit historically black colleges such as Morehouse and Spelman, large pubic and land-grant universities such as Wisconsin and Iowa, small private colleges such as Bates and Bowdoin, and the law school's major feeder colleges to offer educational admissions seminars. The dean and staff also attend the six Law School Admission

Forums, held around the country with the objective of coming into contact with candidates who are no longer students.

ADMISSIONS DATA

	Class of 1993	*Class of 1994*
Applied	6,208	5,395
Median LSAT	89.7 percentile	86.5 percentile
Median GPA	3.4	3.4
Accepted	997	930
Median LSAT	97 percentile	97 percentile
Median GPA	3.7	3.7
Enrolled	330	341
Median LSAT	97 percentile	97 percentile
Median GPA	3.6	3.6

The Personal Statement.   Dean Milligan states that the personal statement is "accorded significant decisional weight." It is, the dean stresses, *the* opportunity for a candidate to inform the committee of reasons for choosing to study law; to educate the committee as to how that choice is consonant with personal values and professional goals; to demonstrate intellectual power and academic skills; to describe various life experiences including disadvantages and opportunities; to communicate information about personal, academic, and professional objectives; and to share with the committee a sense of the responsibilities of (as well as the benefits of) membership in the legal profession.

Recommendations.   According to Dean Milligan, recommendations play an important, sometimes determinant, role in the selection process at Columbia. Even though, as one might expect, most of the letters are positive and even exaggerative, the dean says that they are helpful in selecting the most outstanding applicants from a generally outstanding applicant pool.

Interviews.   Regrettably, says Dean Milligan, the large number of applicants from all over the country and the world makes it impossible for personal interviews to be a part of the selection process. It is logistically impossible to grant so many interviews, and such a procedure might give an unfair advantage to applicants living near the law school and to those able to afford a special trip.

Minority Applications.　According to Dean Milligan, Columbia Law School has an Associate Director and Coordinator of Minority Recruitment who is actively engaged in recruiting African-American, Hispanic/Latino, Asian, and Native American applicants and counseling them throughout the application process. In most cases, minority files are read first by the Associate Director and Coordinator of Minority Recruitment (and later, like all other files, by at least two admissions offers).

Application Tips.　Dean Milligan states that candidates for regular admission should submit their applications as soon as possible after September 1 of the year preceding their desired matriculation. The dean adds that applications are not reviewed until *all* required materials have been received, including the LSDAS report.

With regard to the personal statement, Dean Milligan points out that any seasoned admissions officer knows that any applicant may compose an essay laying claim to strong character, sound values, noble ideals, and impressive achievements. The Admissions Office at Columbia, however, places the professed claims of the essay into the context of the rest of the application, indeed into the context of the applicant's life, says Dean Milligan. The admissions committee looks for *demonstrated* evidence to validate any claims that a candidate makes regarding qualifications and studies the application to see how the candidate has *actually chosen* to commit time, energies, and talents.

As for letters of recommendation, the dean says that those most helpful to the committee are those where the author can speak *meaningfully* about the applicant because the author has been in a position to observe the applicant over a period of time, in different settings, and under different conditions, and to comment on the applicant's intellect, character, and personality *in action*. The dean cautions that it is a mistake, a mistake commonly made by applicants, to solicit recommendations from individuals in high places who cannot make such an evaluation. Finally, the dean adds that in addition to the obvious qualities of intelligence and academic skills, the committee wants to learn from recommenders about an applicant's self-discipline, industry, energy, commitment, and ability to learn and work collaboratively with peers.

PLACEMENT　According to Associate Dean of Students Howard F. Maltby, the Law Placement Office invites about 3,000 employers each year to visit the Columbia Law School campus, including every employer known to the Law Placement Office that has historically hired either second- or third-year students from the law school. Even in the somewhat soft market for law school graduates, over 425 employers accept their invitations. Additionally, the Law Placement Office conducts specialized solicitations on behalf of the law school's foreign-trained LLM candidates and for third-year students who ask for help finding positions with employers who do not usually interview on campus.

The Law Placement Office provides students with very extensive written materials, including a 520-page *Employer Directory* that gives detailed information on law firms, corporations, and management consulting firms; a separate 224-page *Public Interest Employer Directory*, published in conjunction with the University of Chicago Law School; and numerous other booklets and memoranda on placement possibilities and procedures. In addition to receiving written materials, students participate in videotaped mock interviews and meet with career advisors. The Associate Dean for Career Services and the Law Placement Office staff also meet with students on a one-on-one basis. Finally, in order to assist students in making effective interview choices, the Law Placement Office provides them with a five-year history of employer activity at the law school, including correlations between hiring decisions and student academic records.

Commentary. The response of the Law Placement Office to the survey questionnaire used to gather information for this guidebook was carefully weighed—

PLACEMENT DATA

	Class of 1991	Class of 1990
Placed at Graduation	95.85%	97.76%
Placed within 90 Days	N/A	N/A
U.S. Supreme Court clerks	1	1
U.S. Appellate Court Clerks	14	12
U.S. District Court Clerks	22	30
State Appellate Court Clerks	4	3
Other Judicial Clerks	N/A	N/A
Median Starting Salary	$74,030	$78,325

literally. Dean Maltby shipped a boxful of materials that are distributed to, or otherwise made available to students at Columbia, including (but not limited to) the directories mentioned above. This is not to say, of course, that other law schools do not have similar materials (and just chose not to send them as part of their responses), but student reports suggest that the effort expended by Dean Maltby to respond to a survey is typical of that made generally to help students find employment—an effort that was described as "tremendous."

Students noted that the placement office had warned them of the declining opportunities for first-time placement and implied that the placement office redoubled its efforts "in the last two years to provide a host of services." Students mentioned added speakers who conducted seminars on various employment alternatives, such as large firms, public interest law, and legal defense work. They also mentioned a "huge board of new job listings from all over the country." And the law school recently added a new Director of Public Interest Career Placement.

Of course, not everyone was completely satisfied with the placement efforts at the law school. One criticism focused on the law school's traditional orientation toward private firms, but that is an orientation that is subject to revision in light of the changes just noted. A second criticism suggested that the placement office might be a little too closely tied to the New York City legal community to the exclusion of firms from other cities. But that may be because Columbia is just very strong in New York City—period—and not that it is relatively weaker in other cities. A third criticism suggested that the law school does not have as much success as it should placing its students in the most competitive clerkship positions, though one student theorized that the law school's peculiar grading system puts Columbia students at a disadvantage in the competition for clerkships (of the five grades—E, VG, G, P, and U—most students receive G, and there is no ranking system).

A Student Sampler
About 65 percent of the typical entering class at Columbia have spent some years after college fulfilling professional and/or family responsibilities. Typically, such older students have engaged in a variety of amateur and professional endeavors. The student body often includes one or more representatives of the following groups: educators, community and labor organizers, nurses, medical doctors, engineers, professional dancers, artists, actors and actresses, musicians, steelworkers, accountants, psychologists, literary critics, historians, linguists, the military, the foreign service, police officers, bankers, film producers, television directors, corporate executives, advocates for the homeless, scientists, nationally ranked athletes, journalists, creative writers, economists, publishers, and museum curators.

NOTEWORTHY GRADUATES

U.S. Presidents Theodore Roosevelt, Franklin Delano Roosevelt; U.S. Supreme Court Justices Charles Evans Hughes, Benjamin Cardozo, Harlan Fiske Stone, William O. Douglas; Paul Robeson, singer and activist; Jack Greenberg, Vilma Martinez, civil rights lawyers

CORNELL UNIVERSITY

CORNELL LAW SCHOOL
MYRON TAYLOR HALL
ITHACA, NY 14853-4901
(607) 255-3626

ADMISSIONS

Applied: 4,426

Accepted: N/A

Enrolled: 190

Median LSAT: 94.5 percentile

Median GPA: 3.55

STUDENT BODY

Total: 570

Women: 40%

Minorities: 21%

Average Age: 24

ACADEMIC RESOURCES

Library Volumes: 507,221

Computer Services: LEXIS, WEST-LAW, access to INTERNET, word processors for students

Student/Faculty Ratio: 18:1

FINANCES (ACADEMIC YEAR)

Tuition:	$17,000
Housing & Food:	$ 6,150
Books and Supplies:	$ 690
Personal Expenses:	$ 3,400
Total:	$27,240

ENVIRONMENT Cornell University is located in Ithaca, a city of 40,000 in the Finger Lakes region of New York. Ithaca recently tied for first place as "The Best Small City in the Northeast," a distinction recognized by *American Demographics* magazine. The area surrounding Ithaca is rural—a region of rolling hills, deep valleys and gorges, and clear lakes. Open countryside, state parks, vineyards, and year-round recreational facilities are convenient to the campus. Ithaca is about one hour by plane and four to five hours by car from New York City.

The cultural and intellectual life of the university community is large and varied. Cornell University, with a student population on the Ithaca campus of about 18,000 provides many opportunities for the enjoyment of art, athletics, cinema, music, and theater, as well as direct participation in those activities.

The law school building, Myron Taylor Hall, is located in the heart of the university's main campus and was recently renovated and expanded. Cornell proudly notes that it resisted the temptation to expand class size in recent years despite the increase in the number of people applying for admission to law school. Consequently, it remains a medium-size school characterized by a "strong feeling of collegiality."

Commentary. When asked about the physical setting of the law school, students echoed the comments found in the law school's literature, giving high marks to the campus, to the city of Ithaca, and to the surrounding area. One enthusiastic student cited a bumper sticker sported by automobiles in the area: "Ithaca is gorge-ous." Another fan of the area remarked, "It is one of the most beautiful places I have ever seen." An older student, who had lived in Ithaca for several years, received a perfect LSAT score but applied only to Cornell Law School in order to remain in the area. The least enthusiastic reviews given the physical setting were "very pretty" and "beautiful." In addition to its aesthetic merits, the Finger Lakes region offers a variety of outdoor activities including hiking, swimming, biking, and boating.

The one "knock" on the University's location is the fairly long upstate New York winter. Several students remarked, however, that the worst part of the winter season is not the cold but the gray winter sky that lasts from November until April. By contrast, several students literally raved about the summer and fall seasons.

Students also noted that because Ithaca is a smaller city, people have relatively few worries about their personal safety. This is not to say that the law school is oblivious to matters of security. After a certain hour, doors are locked and students need keys or identification cards to gain access to school facilities. Still, aside from the residuum of concern that one might have living anywhere, personal safety is a non-issue at Cornell.

Given the idyllic setting of the Cornell Law School, one might expect to hear also of the disadvantages of being located so far from a major city. In fact, students were quick to deny that the relative isolation of the law school is a disadvantage and pointed to the many cultural amenities of the area, including music, theater, and cinema. Specifically, students cited recent concerts by classical artists Yo-Yo Ma, Isaac Stern, and Kathleen Battle, performances by popular groups, presentations by university drama groups, and the offerings of over a half dozen multiplex cinemas.

Students also mentioned restaurants that offer a variety of cuisines including Chinese, Vietnamese, Thai, and Japanese. One student, who had just returned from dinner, was particularly enthusiastic about the Moosewood Restaurant, a vegetarian establishment and source of the *Moosewood Cookbook*. The student, incidentally, is not a vegetarian.

While Cornell law students can take advantage of a variety of cultural activities, one student emphasized that "Ithaca cannot offer the depth and continuity of attractions that are available in a large city." Consequently, special events are just that—special. Though the lack of an intense and constant nightlife might be considered a disadvantage by some, others thought that Ithaca offers a nice balance between serenity for study and entertainment for diversion.

Students also commented favorably on the law school's physical plant. Recalling a first impression, one student said, "As my parents and I drove up to the school with its Gothic-style architecture and ivied walls, I though to myself 'This is exactly what a law school ought to look like.'" The law school building has recently been renovated and enlarged. It is entirely self-contained and includes a dormitory, a cafeteria that is open for breakfast and lunch, a squash court, a locker room, and conference rooms. Students said that the library is well-lighted and a good place to study.

Students provided several examples of the attention given to the physical plant. For the recent renovation, an old quarry was reopened and stone extracted for the exterior of the addition in order to ensure that the new facade would match as closely as possible the old. Another student commented approvingly on the landscaped grounds that are carefully maintained. Finally, one student mentioned, by way of illustrating the care that is taken of the building, a brass railing somewhere in the facility that is "polished literally every day."

As for the atmosphere at the law school, students reported that the small class size does help to foster an atmosphere that is competitive but not unhealthy. As might be expected, each entering class includes a few "gunners," a term used by some Cornell law students to describe classmates who are aiming for top grades, but they are few in number. Students said that most of their classmates study with one another, share outlines, and generally provide each other with assistance. Many students commented that they know virtually all of their classmates by name. The competition that does exist is attributed by students to the grading curve and the job market. About half the law school's first-year students live in Hughs Hall, a part of the law school complex. According to second- and third-year students, those first-years may feel a bit more pressure than their classmates who don't live on campus because of their proximity to the library and to one another.

ACADEMICS According to the dean of the Cornell Law School, Russell K. Osgood, the law school's educational philosophy can be summed up in a single word: humanity. "For over a hundred years," according to Dean Osgood, "Cornell Law School has upheld the principle that law must be studied within the context of its ultimate humanity." That principle, explains the dean, demands the same dedication, enthusiasm, and critical spirit that infuses all liberal study. Thus, the purpose of the law school is to prepare lawyers who will render the highest quality of professional service to their clients, who will further legal progress and reform, and who can fulfill the vital role of the lawyer as a community leader and a protector of ordered liberty. The dean identifies five elements necessary to accomplish that purpose: a talented and dedicated faculty, a diverse and well-structured curriculum, highly qualified students, excellent physical facilities, and a strong relationship with an outstanding university.

Ultimately, in Dean Osgood's view, what makes Cornell Law School unique is not just *what* is taught nor *who* does the teaching. Rather, the important difference is the philosophy that guides the teachers. Cornell's faculty have a preference for, and concentration on, legal scholarship and teaching. So too, Dean Osgood goes on, Cornell wants students who understand that there is more to being a lawyer than sitting through three years of classes, answering questions, and graduating. Cornell wants its graduates to *understand* the law and to be able to think about what that knowledge represents.

CURRICULUM

First-Year Courses: Civil Procedure, Constitutional Law, Contracts, Criminal Justice, Legal Process, Practice Training, Property, Torts

Interesting Electives: Admiralty; African-Americans and the Supreme Court; American Indian Law; Asian Americans, Civil Rights, and the Law; Bioethics and Law; Corporate Deleveraging: Workouts and Bankruptcies; Election Law and the Law of Campaign Finance; Entertainment Law; Environmental Litigation; Feminist Jurisprudence; Gender Discrimination; International Human Rights; Law and Medicine; Modern Japanese Law; Sports Law

Commentary. If "law in the context of humanity" is a guiding principle at the law school, then it shapes the Cornell experience in ways that students are not aware of. When asked about their educational experience, students described the Cornell Law School education as covering fairly standard topics and as proceeding in a fairly traditional manner. Some students stated specifically that they believe that Cornell has a reputation—rightly or wrongly—for training lawyers for large, corporate firms, and many students are pushing to add course offerings that do not fall into the traditional "corporate" category.

In the debate over finding the right mix of courses, some students theorized that the school's size and location make it difficult for Cornell Law School to do some of the projects done at larger schools in urban areas, such as extensive clinical work. The school is, however, fairly liberal in approving credit for projects undertaken away from the law school. It was also pointed out that new courses have been added to the curriculum; for example, one on organized crime that is taught by the head of the Organized Crime Task Force, who flies into Ithaca each week to conduct the seminar. And if the number of openings in clinical programs is somewhat limited, then so too are the number of students seeking those positions because of the size of the law school.

Additionally, while some students voiced concern over the lack of diversity on the faculty, others pointed to recent hiring decisions designed to increase the number of teachers who are not white and male. Those who defend the administration's record argue that the law school's relatively isolated location makes it more difficult to attract qualified minority and women teachers, while those who want speedier action on the diversity issue dismiss that argument as rationalization. Diversity among the student body is also an issue, and the "War Board," a bulletin board in the student lounge, often includes notices expressing opinions on both sides. Still, one of the students, an African-American woman, who discussed the diversity question in some detail, said that the debate is "not divisive" and does not generally create ill will among classmates. Another student, who seems to hold fairly reflective opinions about the law school, said that Cornell does not appear to be radically different from many other law schools in this respect.

Though the debates over diversity and curriculum proceed but do not rage out of control at Cornell, there has been some student dissatisfaction with the administration. Several students said that the administration sometimes communicates the feeling that it is not especially interested in student points of view, and further, that the administration often acts unilaterally on matters of great importance to students. Indeed, these feelings were so strong among some students that they vigorously opposed the recent reappointment of the dean to another term.

As for the classroom experience, students indicated that Cornell professors rely heavily on the Socratic method during the first year, sometimes even abusing the method in the opinion of a few students. Others said, however, that the question-and-answer technique, while rigorous and even intimidating at times, was not demeaning and that in the second and third years it is not particularly widespread. Several students theorized that the faculty either consciously or unconsciously use the first year to "toughen" students and felt that the Socratic method classes were a sort of rite of passage.

Student comments regarding faculty accessibility suggest that those studying at Cornell Law School can have fairly different experiences with their teachers. Some students stated that the faculty is somewhat conventional and that an air of formality works to create a barrier between faculty and students, though they added that professors are available by appointment. This view was qualified by other students who distinguished between older teachers and younger ones. Younger teachers, they reported, are more likely to be accessible on an informal basis. Still other students described the faculty as having an "open door" policy and felt comfortable dropping in on teachers or other professors unannounced. Given these different experiences, it seems that there may be no single overarching principle that governs faculty accessibility at the law school, and rather that the frequency and quality student-faculty contacts are determined by the idiosyncrasies of students and teachers.

ADMISSIONS | According to Dean of Admissions Richard D. Geiger, admission to Cornell Law School is highly selective: about 4,500 people apply for 180 to 190 places. According to Dean Geiger, because of the relatively small size of the student body, Cornell pays particular attention to the parts of the application that provide a look at the applicant as an individual. The law school does not use cut-off indexes to make decisions. The admission office reviews the applicant's entire file to determine whether the applicant has the ability to thrive at the school both personally and intellectually.

ADMISSIONS DATA

	Class of 1993	Class of 1994
Applied	4,650	4,426
Median LSAT	N/A	N/A
Median GPA	N/A	N/A
Accepted	N/A	N/A
Median LSAT	96.1	96.1
Median GPA	3.6	3.6
Enrolled	179	190
Median LSAT	94.5	94.5
Median GPA	3.51	3.55

The Personal Statement. A personal statement is required as part of the application. The general instructions for the application include the following:

"Part of your application is the separate Personal Statement discussing any matter you feel is relevant to our admission decision. The choice of subject is left to you, but our desire is to learn something about you that we may not be able to learn from the other elements of the application. If possible, please type the Personal Statement, and try to limit it to two pages."

According to Dean Geiger, the personal statement is "very important."

Recommendations.   The application includes two faculty recommendations, which the instructions say should be given to faculty members in a position to provide detailed comments about academic ability. For applicants several years removed from college, the instructions suggest giving the forms to an employer or some other person, but they stress that the primary value of the letter is the recommender's judgement about academic ability and potential for success in the legal profession.

The dean emphasizes that recommendations from "friends of the family," local judges, neighbors or celebrities are not particularly useful unless they have something specific to say about the applicant's potential for studying law. Instead, recommendations should come from people familiar with an applicant's work.

As for their importance, the dean explains that letters of recommendation help the admissions committee "put flesh on a transcript or an experience." The ideal letter establishes the identity of the writer, explains how the writer knows the applicant, and then states how the applicant compares—academically and personally—to others whom the writer has known and recommended.

Interviews.   Cornell is one of the few schools that uses evaluative interviews in the admissions process, but interviews are not used on a wholesale basis. Rather, in recent years, the admissions committee has *invited* about 200 applicants per year for interviews. Additionally, applicants who are placed on the summer waiting list may request an interview with the admissions committee.

Minority Applications.   The application form includes a question that asks applicants whether they want to be considered as a minority applicant. If so, they are asked to submit a separate statement describing their cultural, economic, ethnic, or other background. This information is viewed as a positive aspect of an application.

Application Tips.   According to Dean Geiger, the personal statement is "intentionally very open-ended." Its purpose is to help the admissions committee get to know "each applicant a *little* better." The dean adds, "Because of our relatively small size, the statement plays an important role in our process."

Additionally, the dean counsels that applicants should try to "be themselves." "Contrivances and gimmicks," says the dean, "don't work." When asked what type of applicant is typically accepted, the dean responds "those who have set their own agendas in life and have accomplished the goals they have set."

P LACEMENT Cornell uses direct mail to invite over 5,000 legal employers to visit the campus to interview its students or to send information about their hiring needs for student reference in the placement library. In a typical year, between 300 and 350 recruiters will visit the campus. Additionally, the law school administers regional interviewing programs in Boston, New York, Washington, Los Angeles, San Francisco, and Seattle to attract small to medium-size employers who are not able to come to Ithaca to recruit. The placement office also offers special assistance for those interested in public interest law, including a loan repayment assistance program, individual counselling, and a public interest job fair.

The placement office offers a mock interview program and individual counselling for people with special concerns. It also provides students with guidance and practice questions, a collection of interview skills books and audiotapes in the placement library, and videotapes of panels of employers giving advice on interviewing.

PLACEMENT DATA

	Class of 1991	Class of 1990
Placed at Graduation	87%	84%
Placed within 90 Days	93%	91%
U.S. Supreme Court Clerks	0	0
U.S. Appellate Court Clerks	6	8
U.S. District Court Clerks	12	6
State Appellate Court Clerks	4	0
Other Judicial Clerks	1	0
Median Starting Salary	N/A	N/A

Commentary. Student opinions about the placement office were varied and often intense. Some students applauded the efforts of the staff, calling the people "very helpful," "warm and empathetic," or "hardworking." Others, when asked about placement resources, described the office as "abysmal," "poorly managed," or "overwhelmed." There is a reason for this divergence of student opinion.

According to a source familiar with the workings of the placement office, it had grown disorganized and ineffective. A couple of years ago, however, a different dean was given the responsibility for overseeing the placement office and new facilities and staff were added. According to this source, the recent changes have borne fruit and the track record of the placement office as judged by students is improving. In particular, the law school has committed time and money to expanding the public interest resources available to its students.

If the law school's placement office is indeed in a transition phase, it nonetheless seems likely that change will require time and that, in the words of the source, "some criticism will continue." In the first place, the job market will probably make the staff's job difficult. As some students point out, Ithaca is one of the first cities likely to be dropped from a smaller firm's recruitment agenda when hiring is scaled back. Additionally, most students agreed that placement services have traditionally been oriented toward private firms, but now students looking for public interest work are demanding more assistance. It should be noted that students themselves assist classmates interested in public interest work by supporting the Public Interest Law Fund (PILF). Each year, PILF holds an auction, selling off goods and services donated by faculty or area merchants to raise money to subsidize students who take summer jobs in public interest areas.

A STUDENT SAMPLER

In a typical year, the 570 or so students at Cornell Law School will represent most states and about 250 colleges. About 40 percent of the students will be women, and 20 percent or so members of minority groups.

It is possible to get some idea of the diversity of the student body at Cornell by looking at short biographies of four students:

V.C. was born in Jamaica and raised in the South Bronx Projects of New York City. After graduating from Long Island University, V.C. became a successful sales representative for a major pharmaceutical company. After 18 months, V.C. became interested in real estate and took an M.B.A. at Baruch College. By age 26, V.C. had already made enough money in Manhattan real estate to cover much of the cost of a law school education. V.C. wants to be a real estate developer as well as a lawyer and to become a consultant in the newly emerging field of affordable housing.

J.F. is a graduate of the U.S. Naval Academy and had anticipated making the service a career. After four years of flying Navy F1 Tomcats in the Middle East, J.F. decided that the six-month tours of duty were too taxing on his family and decided to substitute law as a career. When asked to compare law school to life aboard a ship, J.F. says that law school is a "piece of cake." J.F. has accepted a clerkship with a U.S. Circuit Court of Appeals judge.

S.K. is a child of immigrants—Polish father (a survivor of the German concentration camps) and her mother a native of Tunisia. The family's adopted country is Belgium. The family spoke French at home, but S.K. was educated in Dutch; and Belgium's proximity to German- and English-speaking countries offered early experience in those languages and cultures as well. The result was not only a facility in five languages (Hebrew is the fifth), but an appreciation of those cultures as well. S.K. plans a career in international trade and financial transactions.

K.G. attended Princeton University and received certificates from the program in American studies and the program in theater and dance. K.G. wrote an award-winning thesis on the political understanding of Herman Melville. K.G. plays keyboards in the law school band, "I'm Not Prepared Today," in regular appearances at night spots in Ithaca. After graduation, K.G. will join a newly formed intellectual property law firm in Chicago and concentrate on copyright and trademark work.

In a typical year about 80 percent of the graduating class will go into private practice; 11 percent will take judicial clerkships; 5 percent will obtain employment with public agencies, government agencies, and legal-service organizations; and 5 percent will pursue other interests such as business, teaching, or further study.

NOTEWORTHY GRADUATES

Barber B. Conable, former Congressman, former President of the World Bank; Debra James, General Counsel, Roosevelt Island Operating Corporation; Douglas Lansdon, founder and executive director of Legal Action for the Homeless; Sol M. Linowitz, Senior Counsel, Coudert Brothers, former U.S. Ambassador, negotiated Panama Canal and Middle East Peace Treaties; Edmund Muskie, partner, Chadbourne & Parke, former U.S. Senator and Secretary of State; Rosemary Pye, Director, National Labor Relations Board; William P. Rogers, senior partner, Rogers & Wells, former U.S. Attorney General and Secretary of State

DUKE UNIVERSITY

SCHOOL OF LAW
DURHAM, NORTH CAROLINA 27706
(919) 489-0556

ADMISSIONS

Applied: 4,345

Accepted: 810

Enrolled: 200

Median LSAT: 96.1 percentile

Median GPA: 3.65

STUDENT BODY

Total: 605

Women: 37%

Minorities: 16%

Average Age: 23

ACADEMIC RESOURCES

Library Volumes: 400,000

Computer Services: LEXIS, WEST-
LAW, word processing

Student/Faculty Ratio: 16:1

FINANCES (ACADEMIC YEAR)

Tuition:	$16,400
Fees:	$ 350
Books and Supplies:	$ 850
Personal Expenses:	$ 8,950
Total:	$26,590

ENVIRONMENT Duke Law School is located on the main university campus just a couple of miles from downtown Durham, once a principal center of the tobacco industry. Today, the city's economy is based more on service industries, and there is also a lively local arts scene; old tobacco warehouses on the edge of the east campus have been converted into shopping and living spaces. The law school building is less handsome than most others at Duke, and in 1986 two committees formed to review the law school commented adversely on the building's modest size and appearance. Since those reports, the law school has undertaken plans for renovation and enlargement, and the first part of that project was completed in 1989. The small size and relative isolation of the school work to produce a sociability among students; and since Duke students disperse widely at graduation, they are rarely in competition for the same first job. Thus, the competitive environment at Duke is more supportive than that of other schools.

Commentary. According to students, the fact that Duke's mailing address says "Durham" is not particularly important. Even though the downtown area can be reached by car in only ten minutes, there is little reason for students to make the trip. Shopping and eating facilities are available near the campus; and when students want a taste of night life, they usually drive to Chapel Hill, fifteen minutes away. To be sure, the law school does take steps to ensure the personal safety of its students. For example, the doors to the library lock at a certain time (though students have 24-hour access to the building), and students escort one another to cars in the parking lot. It is important to understand, however, that concern for personal safety on a campus like Duke's is not the same concern that one might experience in a large urban setting. The safety procedures are designed to protect primarily against the occasional uninvited visitor. In fact, in interviews, the name "Durham" was perhaps most often used not to refer to the downtown area of the city but in conjunction with the name "Bulls," as in "Durham Bulls," a minor league baseball team that can count among its supporters many Duke law students. (Duke law students also boasted—justifiably— of the success of the Blue Devils basketball team and said that they are willing to camp out on line in order to get tickets to the games.)

The administration candidly admits that the law school facility is modest but moves quickly to reassure prospective applicants that the renovation and construction already underway and scheduled for completion in late 1993 will remedy any deficiencies. Interestingly enough, most students do not seem to regard the current physical plant as a serious drawback of the law school. A representative description of the building was "this brick thing," and the worst reviews of the building by students were "adequate—but just barely" and "not exactly fabulous"—hardly very serious indictments of a law school. And everyone agreed that the new facility, once completed, will be a big improvement: "more than sufficient space with a good look," said one student. Thus, the administration's concerns about the law school's present physical plant should perhaps not be given too much weight by those considering Duke; in any event, those who will be students after the new facility is in service can look forward to enjoying a pleasant new working space.

As for morale at the law school, most students said that they know virtually all of their classmates by sight if not by name, but they gave only a qualified endorsement to the administration's claim that the atmosphere at the school is one of cooperation rather than competition. Although the school does not publish a class ranking, several students said that classmates often have an obsessive and even morbid curiosity about the grades of others. Students also observed that the general rule that Duke graduates are not competing against one another for first-time employment does not hold true for Atlanta and Washington, D.C., the major urban centers closest to Duke, and many admit that the fabric of cooperation begins to fray during the interviewing season. Still, a good many students insisted that they compete only against themselves and that competition among students, when it exists, is not detrimental.

ACADEMICS | According to Dean Pamela Gann, herself a graduate of Duke Law School (class of '73), the goal of the law school is to provide "a place where professors and students share an effort to explore, to master, and to illuminate the law." Dean Gann candidly acknowledges that this general statement of Duke's aim probably won't distinguish Duke from other university law schools, most of which could make similar claims. What is distinctive about Duke Law School, according to the dean, is the way it seeks to achieve this goal: through "professionalization."

Dean Gann explains that in recent decades law school faculties have become increasingly "academized," a term used by the dean to describe a widening separation between the study of law as an academic activity and the practice of law as a professional activity. Duke, however, seeks to retain an emphasis on training students for professional work. The faculty includes leading scholars in fields such as business organizations, taxation, real estate finance, intellectual property, civil procedure, criminal procedure, and economic regulation, with fewer scholars of constitutional law or legal theory. Additionally, most professors who have recently been granted tenure have had significant professional experience. Finally, through devices such as an intensive tutorial writing program and a clinical program, the law school attempts to develop professional skills.

CURRICULUM

First-Year Courses: Civil Procedure, Constitutional Law, Contracts, Criminal Law, Property, Torts, Professional Advocacy (one week), Legal Writing and Advocacy, Legal Institutions

Interesting Electives: Athletics and the Legal Process; Black Legal Scholarship; Chinese Legal History; Corporate Restructuring: Acquisitions, Recapitulations, and Workouts; Economic Analysis of the Law; Environmental Law; Feminist Legal Theory; Forensic Psychiatry (Clinical Course); International Transactions with Japan; Intellectual Property I: Law and the Arts; Intellectual Property II: Business Intellectual Property; Law and National Defense; Professional Liability; Regulating Hazardous Waste; Social Science Evidence and Law

---

Commentary. Although the dean mentions "professionalization" as an important element of the law school's philosophy, most students just cannot give any content to that notion. One student remarked, "I couldn't tell you the philosophy of the Duke Law School if you pointed a gun at me." A few students, however, interpreted the term "professionalization" to mean that Duke is primarily, though not exclusively, concerned with training practitioners for placement in large firms; they cited with approval courses such as "Estate and Gift Taxation" and "Trusts and Estates."

The dean's remarks about "professionalization" should not, however, be misconstrued to suggest that Duke's curriculum is designed to teach only "black letter law," for that is not the case. Although the curriculum stresses courses that are of interest to practitioners and is implemented by teachers who have practical experience as lawyers, students reported that courses do offer a distinctly theoretical perspective as well. If Duke Law School has a single guiding principle that shapes the experience of its students, it is perhaps best summarized by a student who remarked, "Here at Duke, we are fed meat and potatoes with a side order of law and economics."

Students reported that only a few professors rely heavily on the Socratic method and that, in any event, even those classes in which the Socratic method is used are "nonconfrontational." For example, one professor, in order to compensate for the trauma that is necessarily experienced by the first student to be called on in the very first class, presented that unfortunate person with a pair of tickets to a Durham Bulls game. Students also said that the faculty are accessible to them both in and out of the office. Some mentioned playing golf or running with teachers; others mentioned lunching with the faculty; and still others recalled a barbecue at a teacher's home.

If Duke's small size is an advantage in terms of congeniality, then it is a disadvantage in terms of course offerings: many students mentioned that when professors are away for sabbatical or visiting term at another law school, certain courses just aren't available. In fact, a review of a recent *Bulletin* shows a number of "Not offered this year" entries. When asked about the policy of listing courses not open to enrollment (a practice by no means unique to Duke), Senior Associate Dean for Academic Affairs Paul Haagen explained that internal procedures governing curriculum at the law school make it necessary for professors to seek reapproval for courses that have been dropped from the *Bulletin*—a process that is administratively cumbersome. For that reason, courses are carried on the roster even though they are not actually open to enrollment. Still, a significant number of students expressed disappointment at being unable to schedule courses they had wanted to take.

Finally, nearly 40 percent of the students at Duke do some sort of *pro bono* work, and there is a feeling in some quarters that the law school ought to grant academic credit for those efforts. The administration has traditionally regarded such work as co-curricular and to be done without compensation in the form of academic credit. In response to student entreaties, the administration is planning to appoint a committee to study the issue, though the outcome is uncertain.

ADMISSIONS | Director of Admissions Elizabeth Gustafson explains that at Duke an admissions committee, composed of four law professors and three students, together with the Associate Dean for Student Affairs and the Director of Admissions, makes all policy decisions regarding the admissions process. She adds, however, that student members of the committee do not read individual files. Instead, applications are reviewed by the Director of Admissions, and the final admissions decision is made by the admissions committee and the associate dean. Review of completed applications begins in December and continues until the class is filled. Decisions are made on a rolling admissions basis with the earliest offers of admission extended in mid-to-late January.

The three most important admissions criteria at Duke are LSAT score, undergraduate GPA, and undergraduate experience. Careful consideration, however, is also given to more subjective factors such as proven capacity for leadership, dedication to community service, excellence in a particular field, motivation, graduate study in another discipline, work experience, extracurricular activities, personal and character information provided in letters of recommendation, and indications that an applicant can bring to Duke unique personal qualities or talents.

ADMISSIONS DATA

	Class of 1993	Class of 1994
Applied	4,254	4,345
Median LSAT	89.7 percentile	89.7 percentile
Median GPA	3.38	3.44
Accepted	601	810
Median LSAT	96.1 percentile	96.1 percentile
Median GPA	3.63	3.70
Enrolled	204	200
Median LSAT	96.1 percentile	96.1 percentile
Median GPA	3.51	3.65

The Personal Statement. Applicants are strongly encouraged to submit a personal statement, and most of those admitted have articulated, thoughtful reasons for pursuing a legal education. The statement provides an applicant the opportunity to demonstrate his or her strengths and to emphasize nonacademic as well as academic achievements, employment experience, community involvement, and other law-related activities. The statement also provides an applicant the means to demonstrate an ability to write effectively.

Recommendations. The admissions committee considers recommendations to be a valuable aid in evaluating applicants, and each applicant is required to submit three academic references. (One of these references must be completed by an appropriate dean at the undergraduate school last attended.) The law school suggests that the other two references be written by professors who know the applicant well and can attest to the applicant's intellectual abilities and potential to succeed in law school. Professors in the applicant's major often provide the best recommendations. If the applicant has been out of school for a number of years and has acquired significant work experience, an additional reference letter from a supervisor with knowledge of the applicant's personal traits and intellectual abilities may be beneficial.

Interviews. Personal interviews on campus generally are not considered in making admissions decision and, therefore, are not required. Interviews may be arranged, however, if there are special circumstances that cannot be described adequately in writing or by telephone.

Minority Applications. Duke has a faculty-initiated affirmative action program for minority admissions. Special care is taken in evaluating applications from members of minority groups who traditionally have not been well represented in the legal profession. No quotas are employed in the admissions process, but the law school makes a conscious effort to achieve diversity in each entering class.

Application Tips. Because Duke uses a rolling review process, candidates should have applications completed and ready for submission early in the application season. The review process begins in December, and the first offers for admissions are made in January. Thus, candidates who submit applications after the middle of January may have compromised their chances for acceptance.

The "articulated, thoughtful reasons for pursuing a legal career" mentioned in the discussion of the personal statement do not necessarily refer to ultimate career goals. Dean Gann makes it clear that the law school does not expect that students will arrive at Duke with well-defined career plans. Indeed, she says that such plans are "premature" and "often ill-conceived." The message beneath the text is that it is not necessary in the personal statement for an applicant to identify a particular first-employment position and that an attempt to do so—in the absence of strong experiential considerations—may seem contrived.

Finally, the fact that Duke's affirmative action program is "faculty-initiated" does not mean that it is necessarily different from those at other law schools, nor that faculty members play some special role in evaluating minority applications that they do not also play in evaluating other applications. According to Dean Haagen, it is just that historically at Duke it was the faculty who provided the initial push for the plan.

PLACEMENT | Each year the Office of Career Planning and Placement invites over 1100 employers to come to the school in the fall to recruit second- and third-year students; over 400 come. The placement office attempts to provide personal service including lunch during the recruiting day, a placement bulletin that includes photographs and brief resumes of the upperclass students, and written confirmation of interview dates.

The placement office offers workshops and individual assistance to all students on creating a resume, cover letters, interviewing strategies, and career planning. It also provides opportunities for students to have practice interviews that are videotaped and which can then be critiqued if a student so requests.

PLACEMENT DATA

	Class of 1991	*Class of 1990*
Placed at Gruaduation	91%	92%
Placed within 90 Days	95%	96%
U.S. Supreme Court Clerks	0	0
U.S. Appellate Court Clerks	16	13
U.S. District Court Clerks	8	7
State Appellate Court Clerks	9	1
Other Judicial Clerks	2	1
Median Starting Salary	$58,753	$60,172

Commentary. While Duke law students seem generally very well pleased with their school, there is—unfortunately—no denying that the placement office has incurred the wrath of many. Even those who are reluctant to say something negative about the school damn the placement office with faint praise such as "They are really nice people" and "They are trying very hard."

Of course, some of the dissatisfaction with the placement office must be attributed to the current state of the economy and job market for lawyers. And some negative comments about the procedures used by the placement office, for example, the lottery system for allocating interview slots, can be heard at other schools as well. Still, it cannot be denied that many Duke law students are not happy with the placement office, and there are just too many specific reports to write off this dissatisfaction to the state of the economy or to student anxiety.

One student complained of being dropped from the placement office's records because the staff was not sufficiently familiar with new record-keeping software. Another student described the office's resource library as "two or three shelves of junk." For another student, the most recent edition of a publication listing particular job opportunities was years out of date. And several students remarked that the advice given by the staff consists of unhelpful homilies such as "Be creative!" and "Iron your clothes!"

To be sure, by and large, Duke graduates find jobs, and the placement record above speaks for itself. Yet the criticism voiced by students strongly suggests that the school's placement record should be credited to the excellence of the school and its graduates and not to the efforts of the placement office.

A STUDENT SAMPLER

A recent entering class at Duke included students from 37 states and 93 undergraduate institutions. For that class, the law school drew heavily from the South (34 percent) and the Northeast (44 percent), with 11 percent of its students coming from the West and 10 percent from the Midwest. The class also included two students from countries other than the United States. The average age was 23, and 13 percent of the class was 25 years or older.

As for interesting personalities, Dean Haagen stated that Duke has "its fair share" of doctors, musicians, actors, people who have served in the military, people who have worked on Capital Hill, and people from other countries. On the spur of the moment, the dean was able to mention specifically a professional baseball player, an assistant coach in the NBA, a high-ranking advisor to a major Presidential candidate (whose admission was deferred pending the outcome of the election), and the winner of the 1991 Miss America contest.

As a recent graduating class illustrates, most Duke students go to private firms (79 percent). The rest accept clerkships (12 percent) or find positions in business (3 percent), government (1 percent), public interest/service (0.7 percent), or academia (0.7 percent). As for geographical distribution, 35 percent accepted placements in the Northeast, 27 percent in the Southeast, 11 percent in the Midwest, and 25 percent in the West.

NOTEWORTHY GRADUATES

John Adams, Executive Director of the Natural Resources Defense Council; Barbara Arnwine, Executive Director of the Lawyers Committee for Civil Rights under the Law; Daniel Blue, Speaker of the North Carolina House of Representatives (the first African-American since Reconstruction to be Speaker of any legislature in the South); James Buck, Vice-President of the New York Stock Exchange; Paul Hardin III, Chancellor of the University of North Carolina at Chapel Hill; Hon. James Moore, Justice, Supreme Court of South Carolina; Jay Moyer, Executive Vice President of the National Football League; Richard M. Nixon, former President of the United States; Hon. Gerald Tjoflat, Chief Judge, U.S. Court of Appeals, 11th Circuit

FORDHAM UNIVERSITY

SCHOOL OF LAW
LINCOLN CENTER
140 WEST 62ND STREET
NEW YORK, NY 10023
(212) 636-6810

ADMISSIONS

	Full-Time	Part-Time
Applied:	4,176	907
Accepted:	846	212
Enrolled:	334	124
Median LSAT:	41	40
Median GPA:	3.32	3.22

STUDENT BODY

Total:	1,018	372

Women: 43%

Minorities: 16%

Average Age: 27

ACADEMIC RESOURCES

Library Volumes: 430,000

Computer Services: LEXIS, WEST-LAW, word processors

Student/Faculty Ratio: 23:1

FINANCES (ACADEMIC YEAR)

Tuition and Fees:	
Full-Time	$15,100
Part-Time	$11,325
Housing and Food:	$ 8,650
Books and Personal Expenses:	$ 3,850
Total:	
Full-Time	$27,850
Part-Time	$24,075

ENVIRONMENT Fordham University is a private institution, located in New York City, with an enrollment of 13,000 students. It has three campuses and offers more than 70 academic programs in its 10 schools. The university was established under Catholic auspices and has benefited from the services of hundreds of members of the Society of Jesus, a religious order of men who devote much of their energy to higher education.

The School of Law is located in the heart of New York City, next door to Lincoln Center for the Performing Arts, which includes the New York State

82

Theater, featuring the New York City Ballet and the New York City Opera; Avery Fisher Hall, home of the New York Philharmonic; and the Metropolitan Opera House. Fordham is also literally minutes away from most major attractions in New York City, including the Metropolitan Museum of Art and the Museum of Modern Art as well as Broadway and Off-Broadway theaters. In addition, the law school is only one block from Columbus Circle, a major subway stop, which puts students within a few minutes of Greenwich Village, SoHo, and the world's leading legal and financial centers. New York's Central Park lies two blocks to the east and offers a zoo, concert stages, cafes, playing fields, and paths for walking, jogging, biking, and horseback riding.

The Lincoln Center campus enrolls 6,000 in graduate schools of law, business, education, and social services, and in an undergraduate school, the College at Lincoln Center. A twenty-story apartment residence on the campus houses almost 900 students.

Fordham is a member of the Patriot League, whose members include West Point, Bucknell, Colgate, Holy Cross, Lafayette, Lehigh, and Annapolis. Fordham law students may use the Vincent T. Lombardi Athletic Facility located at the university's Rose Hill campus, located in the Bronx. The facility features exercise rooms; a swimming pool and diving area; weight rooms; saunas; volleyball, basketball, squash, and tennis courts; and a 220-yard track. The university operates a frequently-scheduled commuter van transportation service between the Lincoln Center campus, where the law school is located, and the Rose Hill campus.

Commentary. Students consider the law school's Lincoln Center location a definite advantage of studying law at Fordham. As one student put it, "Whereas Columbia is very far north in Manhattan and NYU somewhat to the south, here you are right in the middle of everything!" Continuing the description of the area, the student went on to explain that there are at least nine movie theaters within three blocks of the law school and that Columbus and Amsterdam Avenues, two main streets, have "hundreds of restaurants." As for the high culture offerings of the Lincoln Center complex, comments suggest that Fordham law students are probably neither more nor less interested in such events than their counterparts farther to the north or south, and no student reported having chosen Fordham simply for its proximity to the Metropolitan Opera House. During a particularly animated interview with three students, one student joked, "I went to the ballet—once!" Another student, however, in a more serious vein, noted that the proximity of the law school to Lincoln Center makes it very easy for law students to attend performances. Consequently, whereas law students at other schools would have to plan an evening at the opera or ballet well in advance of the performance and so might pass up an opportunity, Fordham students are already in the area and can buy tickets on impulse the day of a performance.

Students also explained that the law school has traditionally not provided housing for students but noted that a new dormitory is scheduled to open sometime in 1993. Many students live in apartments on the Upper West Side of Manhattan, the neighborhood just to the north of Lincoln Center. Housing on the Upper West Side is convenient to the law school—no more than 20 to 25 blocks or just a mile or two and a short walk or subway ride from the law school—but the area is a high-rent district and apartments do not come cheap. Other students—especially those with families or permanent residences already established in the metropolitan area—elect to live in other neighborhoods in Manhattan, in other boroughs of the city, or even in New Jersey, where rents are more manageable, though the commute is anywhere from 30 minutes to an hour. Most students denied that Fordham is a "commuter school" and speculated that the opening of the new dorm can only strengthen the sense of community at the law school.

If Fordham students are not more likely to see the inside of the Metropolitan Opera House than their counterparts at Columbia or NYU, they nonetheless gave the "outside" of those buildings high marks and mentioned relaxing or studying by the fountain in the center of the plaza at Lincoln Center. They also mentioned doing the same in nearby Central Park. One student preparing for the bar exam during the spring thought that two hours in the park each day was mandatory for a healthy state of mind. As for athletic activities, student reports suggest that few law students are likely to make the "Ram Van" trip to the Bronx just to use the athletic facilities at the Rose Hill campus. Instead, students are more likely to join one or another health club in the midtown area or to go jogging or cycling in Central Park. Students also mentioned ice skating at Wollman Rink and playing softball in the "meadow," also in Central Park.

For those unfamiliar with New York City who might be concerned about the law school's proximity to Central Park, students pointed out that Central Park is very large and that while one might avoid the inner regions of the park at night and some of the more remote areas altogether, the areas near the law school are heavily travelled and therefore safe. As for the Lincoln Center area, it was described as "definitely safe" and "as safe as you can be in New York City." Students mentioned also that the law school had recently tightened security at its building in response to a series of minor thefts of personal articles. Of course, Fordham Law School and Lincoln Center are in a major city, and it is necessary to exercise some common sense. As one student perhaps put it best, though the neighborhood is safe, "the foolish can always find trouble."

The physical plant at the law school does not seem to be particularly important to students, perhaps because it is satisfactory in most respects and because the law school's advantageous location is so important to students. Some students did mention in positive terms a new addition to the library and its atrium filled with greenery, while others noted in a negative vein that the library has no bathrooms. Reports also mentioned that various parts of the law school are scheduled for refurbishing. Finally, several students praised very highly the law school's new computer facility. Reflecting on this program of expansion and renovation (the new dormitory, the addition to the library, refurbishing of office and classroom space), one student theorized that the administration is simply improving its physical plant to bring it into line with the quality of other aspects of the law school—a top building for a top law school.

If Fordham students do not have very strong opinions about the law school's physical plant, they do have definite ideas about their classmates. When asked to characterize the atmosphere at the law school, the first word used by virtually every student interviewed was "friendly"—not "congenial," not "supportive," not "cooperative"—just "friendly." In fact, more than one student referred to Fordham as "the friendly law school." When pressed to explain how a law school, an institution likely to engender competition, could produce such a friendly atmosphere, students noted that Fordham has a reputation for such an atmosphere and attracts such students, and further, that from the very first day the administration stresses the value of such an attitude. All of the emphasis on amity might suggest to skeptics that the atmosphere is the product of a public relations campaign by the administration, but one student, a self-confessed skeptic who acknowledged having had such misgivings prior to arriving at the law school, just insisted "No, it really is a friendly place!"

Given student descriptions of the atmosphere at the law school, it was not surprising to hear students emphasize that Fordham students work and play well with each other. Reports indicate that students form study groups and share notes and other work products. As one student phrased it, "This is a work-hard, play-hard school," meaning that while people are interested in doing well, they do not plan to do so at the expense of their friends.

ACADEMICS

According to Dean of the Law School John D. Feerick, the Fordham School of Law is a community of lawyer-scholars. Of the 49 full-time professors, 10 hold Ph.D.'s as well as J.D. degrees. This full-time faculty is augmented by 102 men and women who are "outstanding members of the bench and bar." Hence, says Dean Feerick, the law school is characterized by a diversity of legal scholarship and jurisprudence which has as its goal the creation of well-rounded lawyers.

Dean Feerick explains that the first-year course of study focuses on the traditional core academic subjects but adds that they are supplemented by an extensive writing program. In the second and third years, students are free to take a variety of courses covering various areas of practice, such as civil litigation, criminal law, business and financial regulatory law, intellectual property, tax law, and international law. The dean adds that there are numerous legal theory courses, courses in which simulation techniques are used, an active clinical program in which students are trained to function as attorneys, and a comprehensive system of seminars and independent study programs. Finally, the dean notes that the School of Law is aware of its obligation to the bar and the public, and requires of its students a course in Legal Ethics and Professional Responsibility.

By way of summary, Dean Feerick says that "the philosophy of the Fordham University School of Law is to educate well-rounded students who understand the process of the law, and to develop in these students a sense of service and professional responsibility." To that end, the law school has developed an extensive volunteer public service program.

CURRICULUM

First-Year Courses: Civil Procedure, Contracts, Constitutional Law, Criminal Justice, Legal Process (one week), Legal Writing, Property, Torts

Interesting Electives: Admiralty and International Maritime Law, Advanced Trademarks and Unfair Competition, Civil Rights Seminar, Collective Bargaining, Computer Law, Employment Discrimination, Far Eastern Contract and Commercial Law, Feminist Jurisprudence, Health Care Law, Mass Media Law, Municipal Law and Finance, Protection of the Global Environment, Real Estate Financing, Space Law, Women and the Law

---

Commentary. Several students at Fordham reported that the law school offers a fairly traditional curriculum—in the words of one student, "a good solid legal education." Another student who shared this opinion said, "Fordham makes really good lawyers, not philosophers." Students also mentioned the law school's clinical programs, which make available a variety of options that range from interning with a judge or prosecutor to representing criminal defendants. For example, one third-year student who was participating in a litigation clinic had made two solo courtroom appearances. Other students pointed out that the law school is placing greater emphasis on public interest law. As evidence of this new commitment, they pointed to the most recent annual "PILF" (Public Interest Law Fund) auction, which raised $56,000, money that will be used to supplement the salaries of students who take lower-paying summer jobs in the public interest sector. Finally, several students also mentioned that the law school requires three credit hours of study in professional responsibility.

While some students expressly thought the curriculum at Fordham was the standard law school bill of fare, assorted comments from others implied that it might be in the initial phase of a transition to a more diversified mix of courses. One student, for example, noted a recent influx of "new blood," meaning younger professors with different perspectives, and added that some students had recently formed a Critical Legal Studies Group. Another interviewee noted that the law school is now beginning to stress the hiring of "high-caliber, academic-type faculty members." And still another expressed the hope that the law school would hire faculty to teach courses such as American Indian Law. This is not to say, of course, that Fordham does not currently have a broad curriculum nor that it lacks noted scholars, for the students just mentioned did not believe that they were reporting shortcomings of the law school. Rather, the remarks might be best understood by comparing them to one student's observation about the new dormitory: "It's not that we really need a dormitory, but it will help the law school attract top law students from all around the country."

As for the first-year classroom experience, students noted that teaching effectiveness varies from professor to professor and that one expects and gets "the good and the bad." Regarding teaching style, one student quipped that "the Socratic method is known and hated at the law school" but added that "everyone gets used to it." Again, styles reportedly vary individually, with younger professors being more relaxed in their use of the question-and-answer format. In the final analysis, as one interviewee phrased it, "All the professors were human beings, and no student was really terrorized."

Finally, as for accessibility, professors generally have posted office hours, but they are available at other times as well. One student interviewed had just run into a professor in a hallway and was able to get an answer to a question —not about a problem discussed in class but about a personal legal matter. Another said that if a teacher's door were open, most students would have no qualms about knocking and entering. On the other hand, others stated that professors were not likely to be seen in the student lounge and that students were not likely to be seen in the professors' dining room. And a few students reported that some professors, again younger ones, make a special effort to engage students outside of the confines of the law school building by arranging for small groups to go to lunch.

ADMISSIONS | Director of Admissions Kevin Downey described the admissions process at Fordham Law School. Applications are accepted between August 1 and March 1 for admission into the class matriculating the following September and are reviewed on a rolling basis. Each application is read in its entirety by at least two members of the admissions committee, and some applications are read by three, four, five, or even all members of the committee. Mr. Downey emphasizes that there are no "cut-off" scores. On the one hand, strong academic records and high LSAT scores do not alone assure admission; and on the other hand, a less than optimum performance in

87

ADMISSIONS DATA

	Class of 1993		Class of 1994	
	Full-Time	Part-Time	Full-Time	Part-Time
Applied	4,395	922	4,176	907
Median LSAT	N/A	N/A	N/A	N/A
Median GPA	N/A	N/A	N/A	N/A
Accepted	916	254	846	212
Median LSAT	N/A	N/A	N/A	N/A
Median GPA	N/A	N/A	N/A	N/A
Enrolled	294	149	334	124
Median LSAT	89.7 percentile	79.6 percentile	89.7 percentile	86.5 percentile
Median GPA	3.30	3.15	3.32	3.2

either area does not mean an automatic rejection. Factors considered for admission include academic achievement as demonstrated by undergraduate and graduate records; aptitude as revealed by LSAT scores; leadership potential as revealed by extracurricular, athletic, public service, or work activities; and, in the interest of student body diversity, a candidate's background.

The Personal Statement.   According to Mr. Downey, the personal statement is very important to the admissions process, as it allows the admissions committee to assess in greater detail an applicant's abilities. From the applicant's perspective, the personal statement provides "an opportunity to illuminate factors outside of the scope of the other questions included in the application."

Recommendations.   Letters of recommendation are not required but may be submitted, up to a maximum of three. Mr. Downey notes that a "candid and specific recommendation from someone well-acquainted with the applicant" can be very helpful.

Interviews.   The Admissions Committee does not grant interviews.

Minority Applications. Mr. Downey says that the law school encourages minority applications and notes that Fordham continues to place a high priority on enrolling a racially, economically, and geographically diverse student body.

Application Tips. If a personal statement recounts a significant experience, Mr. Downey says that the account must "ring true." The most successful applications, Mr. Downey explains, are those which make the reader experience what the applicant has. Above all, that requires good writing. "Significant accomplishments" which are least impressive are those which bore the reader. For example, it is not a good idea, Mr. Downey notes, simply to recount the daily routine of a law office from the perspective of a legal assistant or a paralegal. The lawyers on the admissions committee are already familiar with that routine. On the other hand, if the experience gained as a legal assistant or a paralegal is *significant* because it leads to a career choice, then it should be discussed and interpreted in that light.

PLACEMENT According to Kathleen Brady, Assistant Dean and Director of the Career Planning and Placement Office, the placement office does a mass mail campaign twice each year, targeting NALE members nationwide as well as smaller, regional employers. Additionally, the staff does follow-up calls to alumni and other personal contacts and cultivates

PLACEMENT DATA

	Class of 1991	Class of 1990
Placed at Graduation	72%	89%
Placed within 90 days	92%	94%
U.S. Supreme Court Clerks	0	0
U.S. Appellate Court Clerks	8	8
U.S. District Court Clerks	12	12
State Appellate Court Clerks	2	2
Other Judicial Clerks	4	2
Median Starting Salary	$64,402	$64,880

relations with local bar associations. Finally, Ms. Brady notes that the professional staff attends all alumni functions and that the Director travels nationwide with the Assistant Dean of Alumni Affairs establishing alumni networks for students and graduates. Over 250 employers visit the law school each year, generating over 700 interviews.

Ms. Brady explains further that part of the mission of the Career Planning Center is "to empower and support the Fordham Law Community in planning and accomplishing their work and life goals." To that end, the center provides individual career counseling and a wide variety of seminars, including eight on interviewing skills and four on resume preparation. Some of the seminar names are "The Career Smorgasbord," "Marketing Yourself," "Women in the Profession—a Look at the Next Five Years," "The Truth About Finding a Job," "Public Service Careers Orientation," and "The Human Side of Practicing Law." The center also provides an overnight Resume/Cover Letter critique service, a videotaped mock interview program, and a wide variety of publications to assist students in the job search.

Commentary. Students generally gave the placement office good marks for "effort." They mentioned that, in addition to its extensive recruitment program, the placement office tries to keep students informed of job openings by leaving messages at the voice mail center for student organizations and by publishing announcements in law school publications. Students added that the placement office also has tried some unusual strategies such as sponsoring alumni/career dinners. Indeed, several students mentioned as a real strength of the placement office at Fordham its contacts with its graduates in practice. On the other hand, the praise for the "efforts" of the placement office at Fordham seemed also to reflect the depressed condition of the job market and included comments such as "They are pretty good," "They do as much as they can," and "I doubt that they could do more than they do." On balance, then, it seems as though Fordham students are satisfied with the operations of the placement office if not with the economy.

A STUDENT SAMPLER The Fordham Law School enrolls students from over 140 colleges, from 37 states and 22 foreign countries. Approximately 12 percent of Fordham law students hold advanced degrees, including four M.D.'s. Students have a variety of different cultural backgrounds; 5.4% of the student body is African-American, 5.9% Asian, and 4.8% Latino. Three students are Native Americans, and 46% of the students are women. The student body includes former professional tennis and football players, a Peace Corps volunteer who worked in Kenya, a former Marine Corps lieutenant, several professional musicians, schoolteachers, social workers, engineers, police officers, and journalists.

NOTEWORTHY GRADUATES

Richard J. Bennett, former President and Chairman, Shering-Plough Corp.;
Geraldine Ferraro, first woman candidate for Vice President of the United
States; Elizabeth McCann, Broadway Producer (*Nicholas Nickleby, The Gin
Game, The Elephant Man*, and *Amadeus*, among others); Joseph McLaugh-
lin, former law school dean and member of the U.S. Court of Appeals,
Second Circuit; Archibald Murray, Executive Director, Legal Aid Society
of New York, and first African-American president of the New York State
Bar Association; Cesar Perales, Deputy Mayor of New York City and former
head of the Puerto Rican Legal Defense and Education Fund

GEORGETOWN UNIVERSITY

LAW CENTER
600 NEW JERSEY AVENUE, N.W.
WASHINGTON, D.C. 20001
(202) 662-9010

ADMISSIONS

Applied: 9,400

Accepted: 2,030

Enrolled: 625

Median LSAT: 94.5 percentile

Median GPA: 3.51

STUDENT BODY

Total Enrollment: 1,875

Women: 50%

Minorities: 24%

Average Age: 24

ACADEMIC RESOURCES

Library Volumes: 500,000

Computer Services: LEXIS, WEST-LAW, word processors

Student/Faculty Ratio: 23:1

FINANCES (ACADEMIC YEAR)

Tuition:	$16,650
Other (rent, food, books, transportation and personal expenses):	$11,200
Total:	$27,850

ENVIRONMENT The Georgetown University Law Center's main building, McDonough Hall, is located 35 blocks from the main campus and stands in the shadow of the U.S. Capitol. Adjoining the main building on the north side is the five-floor Edward Bennet Williams Law Library, opened in 1989. On the south side, Gewirz Student Center will provide apartments for 300 students as well as facilities and services for the entire law school community. All Law Center facilities are within walking distance of Judiciary Square, the Supreme Court, and the Library of Congress, in addition to the United States Capitol.

Commentary. Student reports indicate that the experience of studying law at Georgetown is shaped in several important ways by the law school's physical proximity to powerful governmental institutions. As the law school's literature makes clear, the Law Center is not part of the main university campus; and, on first hearing, some people may be disappointed to learn that the law school is not situated in fashionable Georgetown. Most law students, though by no means all, seemed fairly well satisfied with the school's location in downtown D.C. They mentioned as advantages of the law school's location its proximity to the U.S. Capitol, the Supreme Court Building, and the Library of Congress. Many spoke of seeking part-time positions on the Hill, of volunteering time for government agencies, or of watching oral arguments before the Supreme Court. In general, students seem to share a certain "Washingtonian" attitude of being on the "inside."

Also, most students seem to enjoy the D.C. area, though a few from larger cities find Washington a little small. Many students mentioned favorably the variety of restaurants in the city, performances at the Kennedy Center, and the wealth of museums. Actually, some students who mentioned Washington's cultural amenities confessed that they do not avail themselves of those amenities on a regular basis but noted that "just knowing that they are there is a big plus for the city." So even if a typical afternoon would not find several Georgetown law students in the Smithsonian, most said that it was a comfortable feeling knowing that the museums were nonetheless available. And if students don't visit the monuments and memorials on a regular basis, it is again an advantage of going to school in Washington to be able to show off the sights to visiting family members and friends.

Several students cautioned that Washington, D.C. is a city with serious urban problems but did not want to make too much of that fact and wanted to make sure that prospective students were not deterred from enrolling at Georgetown on that account. Law students find living accommodations in acceptable areas of the city or in northern Virginia.

Students described the Law Center's physical plant as satisfactory and even pleasing and were very enthusiastic about the library. A favorite adjective used to describe that facility was "light"—referring to its windows and the natural light that illuminates its spaces. Additionally, a new dormitory building is in the final stages of construction, and several students opined that its completion would go far toward changing Georgetown's reputation as a "commuter school." Still, students acknowledged that the Law Center itself is not at present particularly conducive to socializing, but they added that law students do meet for fun and discussion off campus—at various pubs such as the *Irish Times*, or at one another's homes.

Students also noted that the Law Center is *near* an area that is regarded as not particularly secure. In particular, several students cited the Law Center's proximity to a shelter for the homeless as indicative of the character of the area near the school. Most students agreed, however, that the buildings of the Law

Center are themselves secure and that it is possible to move in and out of the area safely by exercising reasonable precautions. Because of the location, parking near the Law Center is not plentiful. One student noted that those who arrive after 8:00 or 8:10 A.M. are likely to have to park in a lot at a cost of somewhere between three and six dollars for the day. Public transportation is a good alternative, according to many students who gave the Metro high marks.

Students were fairly unanimous that the opening of the new Gewirz Student Center will have a great impact on the Law Center, but they offered different opinions about the possible outcomes. Some students speculated that the new facility would provide a new focus for student life in general, with spaces for students to meet and to socialize. Others opined that the students who will live in the new facility are likely to feel isolated, inasmuch as the Law Center is not located very close to any eating establishments or shopping facilities.

As for the atmosphere at the Law Center, students said that it is not one of cutthroat competition. In the words of one student, "People here are pretty down-to-earth; an extraordinarily bright crowd, but few hyperintellectuals." Not only did students want to make it clear that "razoring of pages from books" is virtually unheard of at Georgetown, many also stressed that in spite of the large size of the classes there is a "surprisingly supportive" atmosphere at the school. For example, one first-year section included a student who, due to visual impairment, was unable to read from casebooks and other sources. Classmates took turns reading aloud for that student. Or again, during the year, another student lost a parent. Sectionmates all signed a card to express their sympathy, and over three dozen attended a memorial service.

Students from both sides of the political spectrum agreed that the student body at the Law Center has a distinctly liberal political outlook. One student, for example, claimed to have been the only Republican in a course with an enrollment of over 35 students. Still, the conservative students did not seem to regard the political make-up of the student body as a serious disadvantage of studying at Georgetown, but they did warn that they found it necessary to be on their toes. And despite the liberal color of the outlook at the Law Center, most students still wind up at large firms—even those who might otherwise incline toward public interest law often bow to the pressure of debt incurred in obtaining the J.D.

As might be expected, students in the evening division tend to be a little older and perhaps more mature. One student who had transferred from the evening to the day division thought that classroom discussion in the evening division tended to be more interesting than that in the day division because many evening students work by day in a profession such as government or medicine and have something specific to contribute. On the other hand, the student explained that it is extremely difficult to work full-time and go to school at night: "It requires a lot of sacrifices; and, consequently, evening students don't cut classes."

ACADEMICS According to Dean Judith Areen, the Georgetown University Law Center seeks to prepare its graduates to excel in a range of legal careers from private practice to teaching and public service of all kinds. Moreover, says the dean, the Law Center is dedicated to the principle that law is but the means, justice is the end.

To be sure, the dean states, the Law Center seeks to equip its students with the tools of the lawyer's trade by providing a thorough, sound, and practical exposure to law and the lawyering process, but the Law Center's goal is also education in the widest sense of that term. Thus, the curriculum at the Law Center goes beyond a mastery of "black-letter law" to address the philosophical, political, social, and ethical dimensions of the law. To that end, the Law Center aims at awakening an abiding curiosity about the nature and purpose of law and at instilling in its students a sense of responsibility for the law's development and direction.

Finally, Dean Areen notes that the Law Center is committed to the belief that an educational community best serves its goals when it brings within it diversity of experience, heritage, belief, and orientation. To that end, the Law Center assembles from around the nation, and indeed from around the world, students from a multitude of racial, ethnic, and religious backgrounds and with a remarkable array of goals and values. The result, says the Dean, is a vital, exciting

CURRICULUM

First-Year ("A" Curriculum): Civil Procedure, Constitutional Law I: The Federal System, Contracts, Criminal Justice, Legal Research and Writing, Property, Torts

First-Year ("B" Curriculum): Bargain, Liability and Exchange; Democracy and Coercion; Government Processes; Integration; Legal Justice; Legal Research and Writing; Process; Property in Time

Interesting Electives: Arms Control and National Security Seminar, Congressional Law and Procedure Seminar, Entertainment Law Seminar, Feminist Legal Theory Seminar, Food and Drug Law, International Human Rights, Law and the Aging Seminar, Legislative Investigations Seminar, Local Government Law, Mediation Seminar, Personal Privacy in an Information Age, Regulation of Medical Technology Seminar, Sexual Orientation and the Law, Space Law Seminar, Sports Industry Legal Issues Seminar

intellectual community in which learning occurs on many levels, both inside and outside the classroom.

Commentary. The Georgetown Law Center does not seem to be governed by any particular theoretical point of view. Students reported that they are exposed to a variety of perspectives, including Critical Legal Studies, law and economics, law and history, black-letter law, and practical experience. And these remarks are consistent with the dean's statement. On this view, the law school is not about exotic theories but about law as a profession in all of its manifestations, including large firms, public interest work, and government service. One student described the curriculum as "very meat-and-potatoes."

Teaching styles vary from professor to professor, and students reported that a couple of professors still rely on an older form of the Socratic method, calling on students by name and asking a series of questions. Other professors proceed alphabetically or by seating order. Although several students said that the first-year experience can be "unpleasant," it did not seem to have left any lasting scars, nor seem any worse at Georgetown than at other law schools. In fact, many students made a point of emphasizing that professors at the Law Center are genuinely concerned teachers.

Students at Georgetown reported that the faculty are fairly accessible and mentioned that they are available on an informal basis after class and during their office hours. It was also reported that faculty give out their home telephone numbers and make themselves more accessible during exam time.

One of the most rewarding aspects of studying at Georgetown seems to be the exposure to people who either are or recently were actually involved in "making law"—attorneys, regulators, and judges. Students pointed out that the Law Center is able to attract as adjunct professors people who are actively engaged in the practice of law. Students gave high marks to a recently retired judge who taught a course on the rules of evidence. Another student mentioned taking a course in intellectual property with a former attorney in the office of the General Counsel to the U.S. Copyright Office. Finally, yet another student mentioned taking a course with retired Supreme Court Justice Brennan, who met the seminar on an informal basis during the luncheon hour, with students bringing their own brown bag lunches.

Although students seem to find the Law Center's curriculum exciting, it does have its disadvantages. The attorney or judge who teaches a class at the Law Center necessarily has other responsibilities and may not be as easily accessible as a full-time faculty member. Or again, the most special offerings, like the seminar with Justice Brennan, may be difficult to get into. In fact, even routine offerings may be allocated by lottery; and one student regretted having gotten only one out of four requested courses, having to settle for back-up selections in the other positions. Still, even those who had been disadvantaged by the lottery method of allocating class assignments seemed to accept that risk as the cost of having access to the exciting mix of courses and faculty offered by the Law Center.

ADMISSIONS According to Dean of Admissions Andrew P. Cornblatt, the Law Center's Committee on Admissions uses a rolling admissions process, and completed applications are reviewed beginning in late November. Dean Cornblatt emphasized that the Committee does not use numerical cutoffs and does read all applications and consider all credentials. Both objective data and personal information are used to evaluate candidates for admission. Objective data include the candidate's undergraduate (and, in some cases, graduate) record and LSAT score; personal information includes extracurricular activities, recommendations by school officials, professors, or employers, work experience, and biographical data. Unquantifiable information is most often used to distinguish between applicants with similarly strong credentials.

ADMISSIONS DATA

	Class of 1993	Class of 1994
Applied	9,500	9,400
Median LSAT	N/A	N/A
Median GPA	N/A	N/A
Accepted	2,065	2,030
Median LSAT	94.5 percentile	94.5 percentile
Median GPA	3.54	3.55
Enrolled	625	625
Median LSAT	94.5 percentile	94.5 percentile
Median GPA	3.5	3.51

The Personal Statement. The personal statement, according to Dean Cornblatt, is an applicant's opportunity to have his/her voice heard in the admissions process and is one of the most important nonobjective elements of the application. The dean noted also that the personal statement is evaluated on the basis of quality of writing and studied to find information that is not otherwise found in an application. It should be focused and to the point—two pages, suggested the dean.

Recommendations. Dean Cornblatt stated that letters of recommendation are important in the admissions process for two reasons. First, they allow the admissions committee an opportunity to hear from someone who knows the applicant and can comment on the applicant's academic or job-related abilities and potential. Beyond this evaluative value, explained the dean, these letters also help to supply the admissions committee with information about the applicant that might not otherwise be available, i.e., difficulty of courses, extracurricular involvement, or other personal information. In addition to such information, the "ideal" letter, in Dean Cornblatt's view, would include an *honest* evaluation of the applicant and how he or she compares with other students or workers.

Interviews. The Law Center does not have evaluative interviews, but Dean Cornblatt added that appointments can be made to visit the school to meet with an admissions officer for informational purposes.

Minority Applications. The Law Center has a longstanding commitment to diversity for two reasons. First, exposure to diverse perspectives enriches a student's legal education. Second, the Law Center is cognizant of the history of discrimination and disadvantage experienced by racial and ethnic minorities.

Application Tips. Although the admissions committee does not use numerical cut-offs and does read all applications, Dean Cornblatt acknowledged that applicants with a GPA below 2.8 and an LSAT score below the forty-seventh percentile are accepted only when the personal information is "compelling." It is also important to note that the admissions committee is looking for candidates who have *both* strong objective and personal qualifications. This indicates that nonobjective qualifications are necessary but not in and of themselves sufficient for acceptance. In other words, an interesting personal history is not a substitute for good numbers, as measured by the median LSAT score and GPA of the applicants who were accepted.

As for the content of the application, several times the dean used the word "honest." This strongly suggests that personal statements that seem contrived or letters of recommendation that are overstated are likely to have a pronounced negative impact on the committee. The dean also stresses that the personal statement should be unified and to the point. So, if it is necessary to provide an explanation for any seeming weakness in the application (such as a poor LSAT score compared with a good GPA, a poor GPA compared with a good

LSAT score, a single bad semester, or a bad LSAT score compared with a good LSAT score), the additional information should be presented in a separate addendum to the regular application.

As for the mechanics of the application, since the committee takes a "no nonsense" approach to the admissions process, gimmicks such as tapes, poems, or songs are not only unlikely to be effective, they are likely to be harmful. Additionally, the application should be completed neatly and according to instructions, e.g., if a resume is to be included it should not be offered in lieu of answers to specific questions on the application form.

PLACEMENT According to Marilyn Tucker, Director of the Career Services Center, about 600 recruiters visit the Law Center's campus each year. Ms. Tucker notes that the placement office also schedules regional interview programs in several cities throughout the country for employers who are unable to visit the campus in Washington, D.C. To assist students in the job search, the Office of Career Services distributes several handouts on interviewing techniques and maintains a resource library on prospective employers. Individual counseling is available, and, Ms. Tucker notes, students may request mock interviews that are videotaped and then critiqued.

Commentary. As might be expected at a school the size of Georgetown, different students have different experiences with the placement office. In general,

PLACEMENT DATA

	Class of 1991	Class of 1990
Placed at Graduation	86%	90%
Placed within 90 days	91%	96%
U.S. Supreme Court Clerks	2	0
U.S. Appellate Court Clerks	6	14
U.S. District Court Clerks	14	12
State Appellate Court Clerks	10	13
Other Judicial Clerks	18	11
Median Starting Salary	$62,705	$62,000

students seemed particularly well pleased with the placement office's efforts on the East Coast. One referred to the route from the Law Center to large private firms in Washington and New York as a "greased slide." Others thought, however, that the placement office does not put enough emphasis on alternatives to the greased slide.

Many students were critical of the system used by the placement office to allocate interview slots during the recruiting season. Students are permitted to sign up for only a limited number of interviews—a couple of dozen. When student demand for a particular employer exceeds the number of available appointments with that employer, interviews are allocated by lottery. Though the system was designed to ensure the equitable distribution of interviews, it has had some bizarre consequences. It was reported, for example, that one student in the top 10 percent of the class got only one of the two dozen interviews requested. Students also felt that the system encourages some people to ask for interviews for positions for which they are not truly competitive, though the placement office tries to discourage that.

A STUDENT SAMPLER The typical entering class at Georgetown is divided about equally between men and women; almost 25 percent of the students are members of minority groups. The class includes people from nearly every state and from several foreign countries. Almost 250 academic institutions are represented.

In addition to many former professors, teachers, journalists, physicians, foreign service officers, police officers, and members of the armed forces, the student body has recently included an assistant producer of "60 Minutes," a senior analyst in the White House situation room, a cellist in the Granada (Spain) Symphony, a starting defensive back for the Washington Redskins, a platoon commander in the Marines, an executive assistant to the Queen of Jordan, and a *Time* magazine White House correspondent. Those with public service experience include former Peace Corps volunteers and adult literacy tutors, the director of the North Carolina Rural Communities Assistance Project, a volunteer for a community development program in Paraguay, the vice-president of a shipping company in charge of the Food for Peace Program to the Sudan, and an AID official working in Pakistan with Afghan refugees.

Upon graduation, about three-fourths of the students go directly into private practice, with 10 percent taking judicial clerkships. Of the rest, 7 percent take government positions, 3 percent positions in business, 2 percent public interest jobs, 1 percent military appointments, and 3 percent nonlegal positions. Nearly three-fourths of Georgetown graduates remain in the Northeast, with 11 percent going to the West, 6 percent to the Southeast, 7 percent to the Midwest, 2 percent to the Southwest, and the rest to countries other than the United States.

NOTEWORTHY GRADUATES

Julian Cooke, Chief Judge, U.S. District Court (Eastern District of Michigan); James Denny, Vice Chairman of Sears, Roebuck and Company; Jim Jones, President of the American Stock Exchange; Sandy Litvak, Executive Vice President of Walt Disney Corporation; Judge Mary Lupo, who presided at the trial of William Kennedy Smith; U.S. Senator George Mitchell, Ken Pye, President of Southern Methodist University; Eugene Sullivan, Chief Justice of the U.S. Court of Military Appeals

H ARVARD U NIVERSITY

HARVARD LAW SCHOOL
POUND 303
CAMBRIDGE, MA 02138
(617) 549-3109

ADMISSIONS

Applied: 7,415

Accepted: 837

Enrolled: 542

Median LSAT: N/A

Median GPA: N/A

STUDENT BODY

Total: 1,620

Women: 42%

Minorities: 28%

Average Age: 23 (6% over 30)

ACADEMIC RESOURCES

Library Volumes: 1,450,000

Computer Services: LEXIS, WEST-
LAW, word processors

Student/Faculty Ratio: 26:1

FINANCES (ACADEMIC YEAR)

Tuition:	$16,725
Housing & Food:	$ 7,643
Medical Fees:	
Health Fee:	$ 584
Blue Cross/	
Blue Shield:	$ 600
Books and Supplies:	$ 798
Personal Expenses:	$ 2,360
Total:	$29,210

E NVIRONMENT | Harvard University is located in Cambridge, Massachusetts, across the Charles River from Boston. The law school has a student body of eighteen hundred, including graduate students, and is housed in sixteen buildings, including seven dormitories, a dining commons, and an International Legal Studies building. Harvard Law School is an exciting, dynamic place with a talented and diverse student body and a distinguished faculty. Students can meet and interact with people from almost anywhere in the world. In addition to a challenging curriculum, there are numerous extracurricular activities.

Commentary. The student body at Harvard Law School is large and very diverse; and, as might be expected, questions about Boston elicit a variety of reactions. A common way of describing the city is by reference to New York City. One student called Boston a "kinder and gentler New York." Another student, a native New Yorker, said that though Boston is "cleaner and more civilized" than New York City, it is also "duller and closes down earlier." Some students mentioned favorably opportunities for theater, music, and museums, while others thought Boston "too crowded." There was no disagreement, however, about the climate, for no one remarked positively on the long and sometimes severe New England winters.

Likewise, questions about Harvard Square evoked a variety of responses. Everyone agreed that Harvard Square has bookstores, restaurants, and shops and that it is frequented by many people, some of them unusual in dress or behavior; but evaluations of the area ranged from the positive such as "Bohemian," "hip," and "like Greenwich Village," to the negative such as "weird," "bizarre," and "the Times Square of Boston." In the final analysis, however, students agreed that the law school is sufficiently removed from Harvard Square that the goings-on there do not affect daily life at the law school. Students also indicated that in spite of the law school's urban location, concern for their personal safety in and immediately around the law school is minimal though not entirely lacking.

Just as the student body includes people of diverse backgrounds, so too the buildings that make up the law school's physical plant are varied in architecture and age. A couple of buildings received high marks from students: Hastings Hall for its dormitory rooms with wood panelling and fireplaces, and Austin Hall, an older classroom building, for its unusual architecture. Generally, however, students seemed to be disappointed in the physical plant, noting that the architectural grouping is at best "eclectic" and at worst "haphazard" and specifically calling various buildings "old and run-down," "worn and a little leaky," or "old and beat-up."

Students were virtually unanimous in their condemnation of the Gropius Complex, a group of concrete block buildings designed by Walter Gropius and built in the 1950s. The dormitories were described as "atrocious beehives" with "tiny" rooms, serious criticism since many first-year students end up living in one of them; and Harkness Commons, the dining facility, was labeled an "architectural nightmare." Architectural nightmare or not, Harkness Commons and connected structures are the only public buildings in the United States designed by Gropius that are still standing, and they have attracted the interest of various historical societies and are protected as landmarks. Thus, the law school is very limited in what it can do to the buildings.

Hemenway Gymnasium too received some serious criticism. Though technically not a part of the law school, it is situated between Hastings Hall and Gannett Hall, which houses the Law Review. Its basketball court is old and the floor not maintained, and activities such as pick-up games and volleyball compete for limited space. Additionally, the gym has only "four run-down exercise bikes and an antique rowing machine." Finally, the weight room equipment was described by one student, who thought it dangerous, as "a tort in progress."

The law school is constructing a new facility, scheduled for completion in December 1993, on Holmes Field that will provide new faculty offices and additional classroom space; but a single new building is not likely to address the wide range of complaints the students have about the physical plant.

As for the atmosphere at the law school, students fairly consistently denounced as inaccurate books and films depicting Harvard law students scrambling over one another for grades in order to secure top jobs. Several students mentioned cooperative ventures like study groups and shared outlines, and one student pointed out that the law school is so large that it is impossible to identify personally those students with whom one might be in direct competition. On the other hand, one person noted that students are prone to seek out classmates whom they regard as likely to make important contributions to a study group, and another mentioned an incident in which two students were expelled by classmates from an outline group for lack of productivity. Still, most students seemed to believe that the atmosphere at the law school is not one of cutthroat competition.

This is not to say, however, that there is no pressure to do well, for there is—at least in the first year. But the worry about grades is only partly explained by the sense of urgency about employment prospects. One student, who stands near the top of the class, theorized that the pressure to do well is what one might call performance anxiety. Students who come to the Harvard Law School generally have extraordinary records of success, and this history of success is an essential part of their conceptions of themselves. It is in the nature of things, however, that at the end of the first year half of the students will form the bottom half of the class. And that prospect, for many, is frightening, so they worry as they work. After first-year grades have become a reality and not a dream or a nightmare, the pressure subsides. The mood was summarized by one third-year student as "Pay your fee, and get your B."

If the good news is that the Harvard Law School experience is not defined by ruthless competition for grades, then the bad news is that many students are nonetheless unhappy. Their dissatisfaction ranges from ennui ("There is no cohesion among students or faculty") to outright hostility toward the institution ("If you are smart enough to get into Harvard Law School, then you are smart enough not to come here!").

Several factors seem to work together to create this atmosphere. First, students reported that the administration is not particularly sensitive to the desires of students. Indeed, some students went further and said that the administration gives the impression that it wishes to have a law school without students altogether.

Second, the law school is large (over 500 students in each class), so it is difficult, students reported, to feel a sense of community with one's classmates. Even students who enjoy some sense of camaraderie with classmates reported that it is necessary to take the initiative and to seek out opportunities and other students. The result is a Balkanization of the student body—many groups with specific interests, such as a journal, but no general sense of community. And, students added, this is a situation that does not seem to concern the administration.

A third factor mentioned by students as contributing to the malaise is, paradoxically, the highly energized political atmosphere at the law school. Students reported that debate often degenerates into name-calling: some students will accuse classmates of racism or sexism; they in turn will be accused of overreacting; and both groups will then be described by other students as "acting out." Regarding this phenomenon, one student joked that a frequently-used rhetorical strategy is to take offense at a classmate's remark, to use the slight to claim the moral high ground, and from that presumed advantage to declare victory on the substantive underlying issue.

A fourth factor cited by students is the dissension among the faculty. They think that the disagreements there are reflected in the student body. It was even suggested that certain faculty actions somehow authorize or validate a parallel in discourse and actions among students—even as the students struggle to escape from that influence.

Of course, not every student is caught up in one of the many political debates. A large number of students, probably the majority, regard themselves as neutral observers; but even they acknowledge that the sometimes acrimonious disagreements are a defining characteristic of the Harvard Law School experience.

ACADEMICS According to Dean Robert Clark, the goal of Harvard Law School is to develop a student's ability to analyze the web of facts at the core of a problem and then to solve that problem using legal methods. To that end, the faculty seek to impart the enduring principles of law, legal philosophy, and the historical development of institutions, rather than to emphasize the mastery of legal detail and memorization of terminology. It is the belief of the dean that a firm understanding of judicial principles and reasoning better equips students to deal with new legal problems as the law changes and evolves.

The dean goes on to explain that while Harvard stresses the importance of understanding the principles of law and legal philosophy, the law school also teaches the basic skills that are the tools of the law. Students at Harvard are required to do legal research, write briefs, and deliver oral arguments, and extracurricular activities provide students with opportunities to practice these skills outside of the classroom. In addition, while acting under faculty supervision, students can handle criminal cases in district court; draft lawsuits in environmental cases; study regulatory agencies; and work with other students and professionals in sociology and psychiatry on actual cases in family law, welfare, and mental health.

The dean also notes that the law school does not stress any single area of law. The curriculum includes courses in civil liberties as well as corporate finance, environmental law as well as accounting, and the legal implications of sex discrimination as well as international trade. The dean also emphasizes that there is no standard teaching method at Harvard; class formats vary widely, and different courses and professors employ different techniques. Lectures and seminars are common, but other courses use strategies such as simulated negotiations, computer-assisted legal research, or reviews of videotaped counselling sessions. The dean also acknowledges that the case method is widely used and that lectures are not merely a one-way flow of information. Rather, students will frequently be called upon individually to state the facts of a case or otherwise contribute comments and analysis.

CURRICULUM

First-Year Courses: Torts, Contracts, Property, Criminal Law, Civil Procedure, Introduction to Lawyering, Moot Court, plus one elective

Interesting Electives: AIDS and the Law; Alternative Parenting; Banking Regulation; Church and State; Comparative Law: The Islamic Legal System; Consumer Protection; Feminism and Gender Discrimination; International Finance; Law and Literature; Foreign Relations and National Security Law; Nonprofit, Cooperative, and Mutual Organizations; Political Violence and Terrorism; Race, Racism, and American Law; Sexual Orientation and the Law; Thinking About Thinking; Transnational Corporations and Third World Development

Commentary. Given the charged atmosphere at the law school, one might expect the educational experience here to be informed by the different theoretical perspectives of the teachers, and students reported that they are exposed to a variety of theoretical tools, from traditional economic analysis to the more radical Critical Legal Studies approach. For most students, however, the difference in approaches doesn't seem to make much difference. Regarding Critical Legal Studies, one student observed that "people have pretty much lost faith in the usefulness of noting that law has indeterminate meanings." Consequently, traditional analysis reasserts itself, and the vocabulary of law and economics predominates.

Students reported that the Socratic questioning that one often identifies with the Harvard Law School has been considerably modified. Most professors try to rely on voluntary class participation, and some name panels of students to be prepared on particular days. A handful of professors, notably those with ties to an earlier era at the law school, continue to call upon students randomly and by name, but even their students do not appear to have been traumatized by their classroom experiences.

Students said the faculty at Harvard are accessible, but their remarks indicate that accessibility is subject to both formal and informal constraints. While professors are willing to remain after class to answer questions, they are otherwise accessible only during office hours. And several students said that during those times many students may be competing for limited opportunities to meet with professors. Consequently, it is sometimes necessary to make an appointment. Furthermore, students observed that there is a general deference accorded the faculty—a recognition among students that the faculty are engaged in important scholarly research or other activities and should not be disturbed for frivolous reasons. Finally, students noted that professors are seldom found in the places frequented by students. As one student put it: "I have no idea where they are when they are not in class." This is not to say, however, that students at the law school thought this to be a great disadvantage of studying at Harvard, for none said so. It seems, however, that despite student affirmations of the faculty's accessibility, to a certain extent psychological barriers operate to insulate faculty from their students.

ADMISSIONS According to Joyce Curll, Assistant Dean for Admissions and Financial Aid, the large volume of applications makes the admissions process at Harvard "very selective." Dean Curll stresses, however, that quantitative factors, while important, are not determinative. The admissions committee, consisting of administrators and faculty, does not use a computational method for making decisions, nor any other mechanical shortcuts. Thus, at no point on any objective scale of qualifications are the chances for admission to Harvard 0 or 100 percent. Instead, three types of factors are considered: academic skills, LSAT scores, and personal qualifications.

College grades are adjusted in two ways. First, a candidate's GPA is weighted according to a comparison of the performance at Harvard Law School of students from the candidate's college or group of colleges with that of a control group; and second, it is interpreted in light of unquantifiable criteria including diversity, depth, and difficulty of the course work and performance patterns. In considering personal accomplishments, the committee evaluates all available information, including extracurricular and community activities, work experience, personal background, letters of recommendation, and any demonstrated societal, economic, or educational disadvantage a candidate has had to overcome.

Applications are considered roughly in the order in which they are completed, beginning in early December, and are given one of four statuses: admit, deny, waitlist, or hold. Applications placed in the "hold" category are reconsidered in April or May when the admissions committee has more complete information about the entire applicant pool.

The Personal Statement. As Dean Curll emphasizes, the admissions process is designed to take account of a variety of factors and to ensure diversity of

ADMISSIONS DATA

	Class of 1993	Class of 1994
Applied	8,516	7,415
Median LSAT	N/A	N/A
Median GPA	N/A	N/A
Accepted	834	837
Median LSAT	N/A	N/A
Median GPA	N/A	N/A
Enrolled	542	542
Median LSAT	N/A	N/A
Median GPA	N/A	N/A

interest, background, and experience among members of each entering class. The personal statement is important in this regard because it helps the members of the admissions committee get a sense of the applicant "as a person." The instructions do not specify any content for the personal statement; but, according to Dean Curll, simple, straightforward, well-thought-out, and well-written statements are best.

Recommendations. Harvard requires two recommendations, and Dean Curll says that they should come from people who have had an opportunity to evaluate the candidate carefully and individually over a sufficient period of time to make a reasonable evaluation. At least one letter should deal with academic and scholarly abilities. Candidates who have been out of school for a number of years may find it necessary to substitute a letter from an employer or someone with whom they have worked closely.

Interviews. Dean Curll states that evaluative interviews are not used as part of the selection process for three reasons. First, it is the experience of the admissions committee that most applicants present qualifications that leave no doubt about their ability to do the academic work at the law school. Thus, such interviews are not needed. Second, it is simply not possible for the committee to schedule appointments for any substantial portion of qualified applicants, so their use is not feasible. Finally, it is the belief of the committee that it is not possible to make a meaningful comparison of personal qualities on the basis of a brief interview.

Minority Applications. According to Dean Curll, all applications receive the same full and fair consideration by the committee. The committee looks for diversity in the student body, in background, experience, and interests. It takes into account personal accomplishments in academics, work, and community experience in the context of any demonstrated societal, economic, or educational disadvantages overcome by the candidate.

Application Tips. As the "N/As" in the table above indicate, Harvard no longer makes available information about the quantitative characteristics of its applicant pool or student body. The most recent information available is for the class of 1993. The applicant pool for that class had an average LSAT score in the 89.7 percentile and an average GPA of 3.5. Of the 1,500 candidates for 1990 admission with LSAT scores above the 96th percentile and GPAs above 3.5, slightly more than one-third were offered admission. Finally, more than half of the applicants accepted for the 1990 entering class had an LSAT score above the 96th percentile and a GPA of 3.70 or better.[1] When asked why Harvard no longer makes available detailed admissions data, an admissions office spokesperson said that the selection process at Harvard takes into account too many factors and is too complex to be represented fully or fairly by a GPA/LSAT profile chart.

When asked to describe the kind of "significant accomplishments" that the admissions committee regards with favor, Dean Curll mentioned advanced degrees such as an M.D. or a Ph.D.; fellowships such as a Rhodes, Marshall, or Truman; activities such as Leadership America or the Peace Corps; and any other projects which require a candidate to demonstrate initiative or leadership skills.

PLACEMENT Each year the Office of Career Services and Office of Public Interest Advising send mailings to almost 5,000 legal employers asking them to visit the law school or to list openings. About 1,400 interviewers from approximately 600 firms visit the campus in a typical

---

[1] *The Official Guide to U.S. Law Schools, 1991–92* (Law School Admissions Services, Inc.: 1991), p. 176. The data on the applicant pool is said to describe the 1988–89 pool, but that is apparently an error. A comparison of the language with that of the previous edition of the *Official Guide* suggests that the reference to "1988–89" should have been updated to read "1989–90." The rest of the language clearly refers to the class that entered in 1990.

year. The Offices of Career Services, Student Life Counseling, and Public Interest Advising run seminars on resume writing, interviewing strategies, and interviewing skills. Practicing attorneys are brought in to share their experiences and to offer advice to students; and counselors meet with students individually or in small groups to provide guidance, advice, and support.

PLACEMENT DATA

	Class of 1991	Class of 1990
Placed at Graduation	98%	98%
Placed within 90 Days	99%	99%
U.S. Supreme Court Clerks	12	10
U.S. Appellate Court Clerks	61	45
U.S. District Court Clerks	66	63
State Court Clerks	16	17
Other Judicial Clerks	1	1
Median Starting Salary	$67,815	$66,601

Commentary. Students seemed generally well-satisfied with the placement efforts made on their behalf. Indeed, if students at Harvard have a complaint about the Office of Career Services, it is that it is too efficient and "funnels" students in the direction of private firms. The law school also has an Office of Public Interest Advising, but its resources do not compare with those of the Office of Career Services. Still, students gave those in charge of finding alternative placements high marks for "guerrilla" strategies that include brown-bag lunches and support groups.

A STUDENT SAMPLER Members of a recent entering class at Harvard included representatives from 43 states, the United Kingdom, Costa Rica, Iran, Japan, Korea, Sri Lanka, Argentina, the Philippines, and Canada. One hundred forty-seven colleges and universities were represented. The top 10 "feeder schools" were Harvard College with 78 admitted, Yale with 43, Princeton 31, Dartmouth 22, Stanford 18, Berkeley 18, Brown 15, Michigan 13, Cornell 13, and UCLA 13.

The median age of the class at the time of entering the law school was 24, with 35 people (seven percent) over 30. Sixty percent of the students had been out of school for a year or more.

Some of the more notable prior occupations of the entering students included: one of the first female Army battery commanders, a veteran sentinel at the Tomb of the Unknown Soldier, a television reporter, a television producer, a number of martial arts experts, a Japanese vice consul from New York, three former Jesuits, an emergency relief worker in the Sudan, a member of the CIA, a Soviet emigre, a New York City firefighter, a Navy air traffic controller, a professional actress, a professional ballet dancer, a well-digger in India, three medical doctors, two Peace Corps volunteers, a migrant farm worker, a veterinarian, a rock-and-roll musician, a state champion gymnast, and a military police officer.

NOTEWORTHY GRADUATES

Supreme Court Justices William Joseph Brennan, Jr., Harry Andrew Blackmun, Antonin Gregory Scalia, Anthony Kennedy, and David H. Souter; Senator Brock Adams of Washington State; Senator John H. Chafee of Rhode Island; Representative Patricia Schroeder of Colorado; Ralph Nader, Director, Center for Responsive Law; Nadine Strossen, President, American Civil Liberties Union

UNIVERSITY OF MICHIGAN

LAW SCHOOL
HUTCHINS HALL
ANN ARBOR, MICHIGAN 48109
(313) 764-0537

ADMISSIONS

Applied: 6,666

Accepted: 945

Enrolled: 632

Median LSAT: 96.1 percentile

Median GPA: 3.63

STUDENT BODY

Total: 1,080

Women: 48%

Minorities: 25%

Average Age: N/A

ACADEMIC RESOURCES

Library Volumes: 710,000

Computer Services: LEXIS, WEST-LAW, word processors

Student/Faculty Ratio: 18.5:1

FINANCES (ACADEMIC YEAR)

Tuition and Fees:
Resident:	$ 9,125
Nonresident:	$17,099

Housing and Food:
Resident:	$ 9,880
Nonresident:	$ 9,880

Total:
Resident:	$19,005
Nonresident:	$26,979

ENVIRONMENT Ann Arbor, a city with a population of more than 100,000, is situated in southeastern Michigan and is easily accessible to Detroit, Chicago, and Toronto. Physically, the city is known for its beautiful tree-lined streets, contemporary and traditional architecture, and extensive park system. It is surrounded by rivers, lakes, farmland, and forests. Additionally, Ann Arbor is culturally diverse and supports literally dozens of theaters, film cooperatives, dramatic and musical performance groups, public and private galleries, and museums. The city's cultural diversity is also reflected in the variety of eating establishments that offer cuisines from around the world.

The law school occupies the W.W. Cook Law Quadrangle, situated on a 10-acre tract immediately south of the central university campus. Three main shopping and restaurant districts—South University, State/Liberty, and Main Street—are all within walking distance. The buildings of the Quadrangle, which are in late Gothic or Jacobean style, were designed to achieve the maximum of convenience, adaptation to purpose, and beauty. The university has three intramural sports complexes with courts for paddleball, racquetball, handball, squash, and basketball, and facilities for indoor and outdoor track and field, gymnastics, weight-lifting, boxing, and judo. There are additional facilities for tennis, skating, and hockey, and team field sports such as baseball. The university also offers two golf courses and four swimming pools.

Commentary.   Students agreed that Ann Arbor is an "inviting," "agreeable," and "interesting" place to live. According to reports, housing is plentiful, and most students live within walking distance of the school. The University of Michigan is large and offers a variety of activities. Some students mentioned the availability of excellent athletic facilities and a thriving intramural sports program; and many students become fans of the college's successful athletic teams. One student said that home football games find many law students seated in the same area of the stadium because of the way tickets are allocated.

Students said that the university's Hill Auditorium is noted for its fine acoustics and that the seating arrangement of the nearby "Power Center" puts most in the audience very close to the stage. In recent memory students have had the opportunity to hear Itzhak Perlman, Wynton Marsalis, Kathleen Battle, and YoYo Ma and to see a production of Tosca by the New York City Opera's touring company. Ann Arbor also has numerous bars that present jazz groups, "cutting edge" bands, or simply a congenial atmosphere for chatting with others over beer or coffee. A couple of students from larger cities added by way of footnote, however, that the bars are by law required to close by 2:00 A.M. and frequently close earlier if not busy. For those who require a larger city, Detroit is only an hour away—though most students said "No one goes there, because it is unsafe and there's nothing to do." Chicago is five hours away, and students sometimes go there for a weekend.

Students also reported that Ann Arbor has many restaurants offering a variety of cuisines, including Thai, Chinese, Vietnamese, Indian, Mexican, Cajun, and Italian. One self-proclaimed epicure, when challenged to name a cuisine not represented in Ann Arbor, could not think of one. Another student, a graduate of Michigan who had lived in Ann Arbor for almost six years, had just returned from eating for the first time at a small Italian restaurant in downtown Ann Arbor.

In addition, students reported that Ann Arbor is a very safe city and that people enjoy walking to various destinations, even if they are a bit cautious late at night. For example, one female student said that she feels comfortable walking around the law school campus even as late as 2:00 A.M., though she added that she would not do so wearing a stereo headset.

The Law Quadrangle, with its Gothic-style buildings, also received favorable reviews from students. The library and classroom buildings are connected, and the main law school dormitory is nearby. Students explained that the law school facility is nearly self-contained and closed off from the rest of the campus and from undergraduates. Students were particularly enthusiastic about the library, noting that it is fairly new, well-illuminated by natural light, and spacious.

Students reported that classmates interact well with one another. Although first-year classes typically have 90 to 100 people, students are assigned to first-year sections of 30. All students in a small section are assigned to the same large classes as well as one smaller class. Thus, the small section becomes the nucleus for friendships. Students also said that classmates share notes. One student reported, for example, doing only one outline but, through the largesse of classmates, having outlines for every single subject. Another rarely bought a textbook, relying instead on used books provided by classmates. No one recalled any incident in which a student attempted to gain an unfair advantage over classmates by stealing or otherwise misusing study resources.

As might be expected, however, students said that they observed an increase in competition with the decline in the job market. And generally, the atmosphere of cooperation becomes somewhat strained during exam periods. In addition, the law school has a mandatory grading curve which students believe depresses marks at the law school and tends to hurt Michigan students in the job search.

Students who enroll in the law school's "Summer Starter" program may have a slightly different experience from that of the typical first-year student. One hundred "Summer Starter" students begin their studies in June and graduate one semester earlier than their classmates (in December). Some "Summer Starter" students suggested that their first semester was somewhat less stressful than that of the typical fall starter and offered two theories to explain the phenomenon: the group is smaller and professors may be more relaxed during the summer months. In any event, by the time the rest of the class arrives, the "Summer Starters" are seasoned veterans.

ACADEMICS | According to Lee Bollinger, Dean of the Law School, the general educational philosophy of the law school is simple: Bring together a faculty of the brightest minds and best teachers with students who are extraordinarily gifted and diverse, and let them teach each other. With respect to its faculty and students, the dean maintains that Michigan Law School is second to none.

As for methods of education, Dean Bollinger explains that the law school seeks to link the professional training it provides firmly to the opportunity for reflection and thought about fundamental public questions, such as the nature of law itself and the character of constitutional democracy, as well as the examination of how the law can address issues of real social urgency—from crime and the environment to child abuse and the effects of racism and sexism in our culture. The idea of Michigan is that the proper education for a lawyer is not only the acquisition of a set of professional techniques but a true education that will help the student make the most of his or her capacity for a full life in the law.

Dean Bollinger also emphasizes that Michigan is a national leader in interdisciplinary legal studies. According to the dean, Michigan's strength in this area is apparent both in the way traditional courses are taught and in the wide array of specialized courses taught by faculty who are lawyers with advanced degrees in other disciplines and joint appointments in other departments in the University. As examples, the dean notes that a law professor who is also a distinguished sociologist teaches "Sociology of Law" and "Law and the Social Sciences," and a practicing psychologist examines "The Lawyer as Negotiator." The dean goes on to add that Michigan's strength in the interdisciplinary approach to legal study does not mean, however, that the law school neglects traditional study and research, and points out that several of the nation's leading treatises on topics such as Evidence, Securities Regulation, and Criminal Procedure are the work of Michigan faculty.

CURRICULUM

First-Year Courses: Civil Procedure, Contracts, Criminal Law, Introduction to Constitutional Law, Property, Torts, Writing and Advocacy Program, and one elective[1]

Interesting Electives: The American Urban Underclass; Asian Legal Systems; Bloodfeuds; Cultural Treasures: Government Preservation and Patronage; Employment Discrimination; The First Amendment; Greek Law and Rhetoric; Health Law; Indian Law; Land Finance Law; Mass Media; Race, Racism, and American Law; Religious Law; Sports Law; Sex Equality

---

[1]One group of randomly chosen first-year students is assigned to the "new section," which has a somewhat different curriculum. One of the required first-year courses is shortened by a semester and the second semester elective eliminated to make room for two courses unique to the "new section"—Legal Process and Public Law.

Commentary. When asked about the law school's academic philosophy, most students suggested that the curriculum is probably similar to that of many other top law schools and is not distinguished by any particular philosophical princi-

115

ple. When prompted by Dean Bollinger's reference to interdisciplinary studies, students did add, however, that professors with advanced degrees in areas other than law do bring an additional perspective to the law school classroom. One student mentioned as an example an evidence professor who is also a psychologist. Another student mentioned a professor who has a degree in political science and another a degree in business administration. And yet another student mentioned taking a course in political theory with a professor who also holds an advanced degree in philosophy.

According to students, professors use a variety of teaching styles, including the Socratic method. A couple of professors reportedly rely exclusively upon the question-and-answer format—even in second- and third-year classes. Still, one student said that most classes have an atmosphere "in which students are really not afraid to make a mistake." For that student, only one professor called on first-year students at random. Other professors assigned dates in advance for students to be prepared to answer questions. Another student agreed that it is not an unpardonable sin to beg off a question when unprepared but added that the professor would likely come back with a question in a couple of days and then it would be important to be prepared.

While students reported that faculty members are in general reasonably accessible, most agreed that "accessibility" does not usually mean dropping in on a professor for no good reason at all. Professors have office hours and are likely to give students their home telephone numbers. Beyond that, accessibility varies from teacher to teacher. Students mentioned one teacher, who regularly plays basketball with students, as having "extended office hours" and being very accessible. Another professor was said to be "very private" and so relatively less accessible. Yet another professor was described as so busy that one student tried more than 10 times—unsuccessfully—to find a mutually agreeable time for a meeting. Still, even those students who did not feel the need for contact with the faculty said they felt that they could have had access to teachers had they chosen to seek it.

There are a few scheduled occasions on which students and professors socialize, such as a semester's end luncheon; and students can chat informally with professors over coffee or juice in the student lounge. Again, however, this sort of interaction varies from professor to professor. While some professors prefer to socialize within the more formal setting of a scheduled luncheon, one professor invited for Thanksgiving dinner any students who were not returning home for the holiday break; 10 students accepted.

ADMISSIONS According to Dennis Shields, Assistant Dean and Director of Admissions at Michigan Law School, admissions decisions are made by the admissions office according to standards established by the faculty. Applications are accepted between September 1 and February 15 of each admissions season; but candidates are strongly advised to apply early in the season because the office begins to make decisions on the strongest of the completed applications in December.

In reaching decisions, the admissions office relies heavily on LSAT scores, on undergraduate course work and performance, and on studies of the past performance of similar students at Michigan. All applications are read in their entirety, but the admissions office does use a weighted average of LSAT score and grades, an index, as a rough sorting device to help to establish the order in which the files are to be read. The index, however, is never used as a cut-off, and all of the information elicited by the application is factored into the admissions decision. The admissions office uses the average of multiple LSAT scores, although the results of all tests are reported and are considered in evaluating an application.

The admissions office gives serious consideration to an applicant's potential to make a notable contribution to the law school by way of a particular strength in one or more of the many attainments and characteristics examined in the application process (e.g., an unusual intellectual achievement, employment experience, nonacademic performance, or personal background). Additionally, according to Dean Shields, selections among applicants are guided by the purpose of making the law school a better and livelier place in which to learn and improving its service to the profession and the public. Finally, as Michigan is a public institution, 40% of the places are reserved for residents of the state.

ADMISSIONS DATA

	Class of 1993	Class of 1994
Applied	6,645	6,666
Median LSAT	86.5 percentile	86.5 percentile
Median GPA	3.38	3.40
Accepted	1,083	945
Median LSAT	97.4 percentile	97.4 percentile
Median GPA	3.67	3.70
Enrolled	358	362
Median LSAT	96.1 percentile	96.1 percentile
Median GPA	3.57	3.63

The Personal Statement. Michigan requires a personal statement and invites candidates to submit one or even two other statements. First, candidates must supplement their applications with personal statements. Dean Shields suggests that candidates may wish to elaborate on significant professional and personal experiences, academic and intellectual interests, personal background, talents, evidence of leadership or motivation, or any other matter that might help the admissions office evaluate the candidate's probability of success as a student or potential contribution to the education of others at the law school.

Candidates are also invited to submit an essay of approximately 250 words that provides evidence of the quality of the candidate's education and intellect and that reveals something about the way the candidate thinks. Suggested topics for this second statement include some intellectual or social problem faced by the candidate or a book that was particularly important to the candidate.

Finally, applicants may provide, if they wish, an essay that elaborates on those features of their background and experience which suggest that they might make special contributions to the diversity that the law school wishes to foster. In this essay, it is appropriate to discuss aspects of the applicant's background, upbringing, or life experiences which gives a perspective on the world or the law that is unlikely to be shared by most law students or to discuss any similar set of individuating circumstances.

Recommendations. Michigan requires at least one letter of recommendation, and applicants may choose to arrange for additional letters of support. Dean Shields recommends that three be submitted but adds that beyond that number, more is not necessarily better. At least one letter should be from a college instructor, but the law school recognizes that candidates who have been out of school for a significant period of time may choose to submit a recommendation from an employer.

Interviews. Interviews with the staff of the admissions office are not a routine part of the admissions process, and they do not affect the likelihood of acceptance. To the extent that time and staff resources permit, the admissions office attempts to schedule individual or small group meetings with candidates for informational purposes. Applicants with questions about the law school are welcome to contact the admissions office, and those who wish are encouraged to visit the campus.

Minority Applications. Dean Shields states that Michigan has a strong commitment to racial and ethnic diversity, with special reference to the inclusion of students from groups such as African-Americans, Hispanics, and Native

Americans, groups who have historically been discriminated against and who, without this commitment, might not be represented in the student body in meaningful numbers. The law school believes that these students are particularly likely to have experiences and perspectives of special importance to their classmates and to the mission of the law school.

Application Tips. According to Dean Shields, it is important to complete applications in a timely fashion. Candidates who delay completing their applications (later than February 15) may well be at a considerable disadvantage.

When asked to give content to the phrase "significant accomplishment," Dean Shields noted that over half of the typical entering class at Michigan is a year or more away from undergraduate study. Their experiences during that time range from stints in the Peace Corps to work in investment banking. Many candidates have already earned advanced degrees in fields which they wish to link with the law—often with a view to an academic career, a path that the law school encourages. Additionally, a commitment to public interest law—as evidenced by work experience as well as statements—makes a candidate more attractive.

Dean Shields also said that the successful candidate is typically someone who has demonstrated an ability to write well by submitting "attractive" personal statements. Regarding the content of the personal statement, Deans Shields noted that it is not so much what a candidate has accomplished as what that accomplishment means to the candidate and how it is described. "An internship in the White House," Dean Shields points out, "is only as important a credential as the candidate is capable of representing it to be."

With regard to recommendations, Dean Shields said that the importance of recommendations in the decision-making process varies. If a candidate has a superb record and an outstanding LSAT score, recommenders will only add to the "chorus of praise." If a candidate's LSAT score is weak and the academic record shaky, then not even the most laudatory recommendations will overcome those disadvantages. In the typical case, however, recommendations provide additional insight into the candidate's intellectual interests and promise.

PLACEMENT | According to Nancy Krieger, Director of the Placement Office, Michigan has long had a very large on-campus interviewing program because its student body is highly regarded by the Bar. Nonetheless, the placement office nurtures this program by offering the best possible service to employers who interview on campus. In a typical year, approximately 900 potential employers from all parts of the country actually visit the campus. The placement office also receives requests and information from a substantial number of employers who are not able to visit. Typically, the latter group comprises small private firms, government agencies, and public interest employers. The placement office also encourages small firms, government agencies, and public interest employers to visit the campus by scheduling special interviewing days for them and organizing programming for them. In addition to the contacts generated by the placement office, students have available to them the resource materials and data bases of the placement office library.

As part of its effort to help students find positions, the placement office invites students to attend panel discussions, participate in mock interviews, and attend informational meetings with alumni and staff. Individual counseling is also readily available from the staff of the placement office.

PLACEMENT DATA

	Class of 1991	Class of 1990
Placed at Graduation	92%	93%
Placed within 90 Days	96%	98%
U.S. Supreme Court Clerks	1	2
U.S. Appellate Court Clerks	26	11
U.S. District Court Clerks	25	33
State Appellate Court Clerks	11	7
Other Judicial Clerks	4	1
Median Starting Salary	$65,000	$60,000

Commentary. Students at Michigan seem to be pretty well satisfied with the law school's placement efforts. Students said that the staff does a good job of gathering materials, scheduling recruiter interviews, and helping students to contact potential employers. Some students, however, theorized that the placement office faces several difficulties not really under its control. One theory maintains that students at Michigan are at a disadvantage because the law school does not have a ready-to-hand domestic job market like the ones that are available to students in New York, Chicago, or Los Angeles. Another, though less widely argued, theory holds that East Coast firms interview Michigan students almost as an afterthought. A refinement of this second theory suggests that the large size of the class puts Michigan students somewhat at a disadvantage because employers from both coasts are looking to hire only one or two Michigan graduates in any given year. And advocates of this second theory also hypothesize that smaller firms from both coasts that regularly recruit in large cities simply cannot afford to make the trip to Ann Arbor. Third, several students suggested that the law school has traditionally been oriented toward private firms and said that not enough emphasis is given to public interest work. Even so, those who made these observations about the job search at Michigan in no way blamed the placement office. Instead, they attributed the difficulties to geographical or financial factors outside the control of the placement office staff. In any event, the excellent placement record of the law school speaks for itself.

A STUDENT SAMPLER In a typical class at Michigan, students will come from at least 40 different states and 10 or so foreign countries. Women make up approximately 48 percent of the student body, Michigan residents 40 percent, and students of color 25 percent. Over 50 different undergraduate majors may be represented. Recent Michigan students came from a wide range of backgrounds and had a variety of accomplishments prior to entering law school, e.g.:

S.B., a *Law Review* editor, was captain of the varsity swim team at Harvard, and swam the English Channel in what was then the 17th best time;

B.H., one of eight children of a family of migrant farm workers, first came to the state of Michigan as a child to work on the fruit harvest;

D.K. wrote a book, *Off the Track*, documenting the decline of the inter-city passenger train from peak years of the luxury limiteds to the present;

S.M., as a recently divorced mother of two preschool children, took a course in motorcycle mechanics and landed a purchasing position with a motorcycle parts store before moving to the Ford Motor Company's computer operations division;

D.N., a graduate of the Eastern School of Music, composed scores for documentary films, the Detroit Institute of Arts, and PBS.

NOTEWORTHY GRADUATES

George R. Ariyoshi, former Governor of Hawaii; Mary Frances Berry, history and law educator, recipient of the Roy Wilkins Civil Rights award, NAACP, 1983, the Rosa Parks award, SCLC, 1986, and the Woman of the Year award, *Ms.* magazine, 1986; Clarence Darrow, defended John T. Scopes, 1925 (Technically, Darrow is not a "noteworthy graduate," for he was never awarded a degree. At that time, it was not uncommon for students to leave school for the practice of law before completing their studies, and Michigan claims Darrow as one of its own.); Representative Richard Gephardt, House Majority Leader; Hon. Amalya L. Kearse, Circuit Judge, Second Circuit; Frederic David Krupp, Executive Director of the Environmental Defense Fund; Branch Wesley Rickey, President and General Manager of the Brooklyn Dodgers, 1942 to 1950 (signed Jackie Robinson to the Dodgers' Montreal farm team and brought him to the majors in 1947); Eli J. Segal, Clinton campaign, Chief of Staff; Lucy Sankey Russell, Attorney, Office of General Counsel, Food and Drug Division of the U.S. Department of Health and Human Services

UNIVERSITY OF MINNESOTA

LAW SCHOOL
229 19TH AVENUE SOUTH
MINNEAPOLIS, MN 55455
(612) 625-5005

ADMISSIONS

Applied: 2,423

Accepted: 657

Enrolled: 270

Median LSAT: 89.7 percentile

Median GPA: 3.56

STUDENT BODY

Total: 780

Women: 45%

Minorities: 16%

Average Age: 25

ACADEMIC RESOURCES

Library Volumes: 750,000

Computer Services: WESTLAW, LEXIS, computer lab

Student/Faculty Ratio: 24:1

FINANCES (ACADEMIC YEAR)

Tuition:	
Resident:	$ 6,970
Nonresident:	$13,726
Living Expenses:	
Resident:	$ 7,410
Nonresident:	$ 7,410
Total:	
Resident:	$14,380
Nonresident:	$21,136

ENVIRONMENT The Twin Cities of Minneapolis and St. Paul are a progressive, distinctive, and very livable metropolitan area of two million people. Both are thriving commercial centers, boasting new skyscrapers and retail-office complexes as well as restored historic structures and riverfront redevelopments. Law students have easy access to many federal, state, regional, and local government agencies and courts—including the U.S. District Court for Minnesota and the U.S. Court of Appeals for the Eighth Circuit, which regularly sits in St. Paul. The Twin Cities legal community engages in a sophisticated practice of law, serving many national and international clients as well as local concerns and offering a wide range of clerkship and career opportunities.

The Twin Cities have long been noted for their progressive political climate and spirit of civic cooperation. On a cultural note, Minnesotans are proud of the Minnesota Orchestra, the St. Paul Chamber Orchestra, the Guthrie Theater, the Minneapolis Institute of Art, and the Walker Art Center, all of which are premier institutions in their respective fields. A host of other orchestras, theater groups, museums, dance companies, musicians, and festivals offer a wide spectrum of cultural opportunities. Major-league sports fans can see Vikings football, Twins baseball, Timberwolves NBA basketball, and horse racing at Canterbury Downs. In addition, there is a wide range of Golden Gopher teams at various Big 10 events. Outdoor enthusiasts can explore the 150 parks and 200 lakes nearby.

The University of Minnesota is one of the largest public institutions of higher learning in the United States. Its Twin Cities campus is located on two close campuses, separated by the Mississippi River. The law school is located on the West Bank of the Minneapolis campus in a building dedicated in 1978.

Commentary. Students at the University of Minnesota Law School described the Twin Cities in very positive phrases such as "a vibrant community," "pretty cosmopolitan," and—more than once, echoing the administration's description—as "very livable." When asked to identify those features of the area that endow it with its "livability," students responded with a variety of specific points; it is this collection of specifics—the presence of certain positive features and the absence of negative ones—that makes the Twin Cities attractive. As for the positive features of the cities, students mentioned the variety of diversions, the strength of the legal community, and the civility of the inhabitants. For entertainment, there are bars and clubs that offer music (a "very intense music scene") or social games such as billiards and darts; there are sporting events, both college and professional (with "reasonably priced tickets"); and there are outdoor activities such as water sports and camping (Minnesota—"the land of 10,000 lakes"). The Twin Cities also offer a variety of opportunities for both permanent and full-time employment as well as for clinical education. Several students who were interviewed were participating in the law school's Civil or Misdemeanor Prosecution/Defense Clinics or were working for a government agency such as the Attorney General's office. Finally, students emphasized that Minnesota is characterized by a "friendliness" or "civility" that they say is lacking in other cities. As examples of this last feature, students offered: "Motorists will let you onto the freeway"; "People hold doors for one another"; and "Students smile and say hello to each other in the hallways."

On the other side of the coin, students also noted that Minneapolis and St. Paul are not afflicted by the ills that afflict other urban areas—or at least not to the same extent. Traffic, for example, was reported to be less annoying than that in other cities. One student who lives several miles from the law school noted that the morning commute was an easy five to 10 minutes by freeway. Others mentioned that parking near the law school is very easy to find. And virtually all agreed that despite the fact that the law school is situated very near to downtown Minneapolis and is therefore an urban environment, concern for personal safety is not a major issue for law students—though this last point should be qualified slightly because, as one student noted, it is always "dangerous to do something foolhardy." In the final analysis, this balance of characteristics that constitutes the "livability" of the Twin Cities was perhaps best described by the student who said that the Twin Cities offer a "nice combination of big and small."

The one "knock" on the Twin Cities seems to be Minnesota's cold winters. Regarding this aspect of the climate, students observed that "the winters are notorious," that "winter is very cold," and that "it is colder than sin for a long period of time around here."

While the law school's host city received high marks for its "livability," the law school's physical plant did not. Regarding the exterior of the building, students said "it doesn't have much character" and "it is not beautiful"; and of the architectural style, one student said, "It might best be called 'adventures in concrete.'" A more serious criticism of the structure, and one that was voiced by several students, focused on the fact that most classrooms are in the lower stories and are partially or totally below ground. The problem created by the lack of natural lighting was compounded when the administration, as a cost-cutting measure, installed fluorescent fixtures in those areas. The result, said one student, is a "really dismal atmosphere" in parts of the building. On the positive side, however, students said that the library is easy to use and that its collection is so large—with multiple copies of reporters and reference books—that one hardly ever has difficulty finding needed volumes. Further, several students mentioned as an advantage of the law school its location on the west bank of the river, where it is fairly isolated from the undergraduate part of the university, so that the law school building is pretty much used only by law students. Finally, students are given keys to the doors of various law school facilities, such as the library, so that they can come and go as they please—even on weekends and late at night—a policy that is also good evidence that the Twin Cities truly are "livable."

The atmosphere at the law school was described by students as "really cooperative," "never threatening," and "supportive." Some interviewees qualified these descriptions by noting that there will always be a few students who are more competitive than their classmates but added that the competition that does exist is not "cut-throat" and does not manifest itself in ways that contravene the norms of civility at the law school. Social life at the law school is to a great extent structured by the organization of the first-year class into five sections of approximately 50 students each. These sections meet independently or in combination with other sections, and it is within the small group sections that initial and lasting friendships are likely to form.

125

Finally, some students also commented on the "progressive" attitude of Minnesotans that is mentioned by the administration in its description of the region, noting that the state really is fairly liberal. One student recalled that the state had even jokingly been called by a conservative colleague "The Peoples' Republic of Minnesota." Another student, trying to give content to the "progressive" label, described the predominant attitude of people in the region as a product of a "Lutheran ethic" that manifests itself in an unconscious tension between "social progressivism and moral prudishness"—as evidenced by the state's fairly liberal social legislation and its rather conservative "blue laws" governing the sale of alcohol. In the final analysis, while it may be somewhat difficult to put into words, it does seem, then, that there is an upper Midwestern quality that characterizes life in the Twin Cities and that contributes to their "livability."

ACADEMICS | According to Dean of the Law School Robert A. Stein, the educational mission of the University of Minnesota Law School is to prepare men and women for their roles as lawyers and professionals. The dean explains that the law school carries out this task by providing an intellectually stimulating environment that sharpens the minds of some of the best law students in the country and by offering a variety of educational opportunities, including clinical programs, moot court competitions, law journal writing, international exchange programs, and computer-assisted instruction. By way of illustrating the law school's academic philosophy, Dean Stein points to the pioneering role that Minnesota has played in the development of new applications for tutorial and clinical instruction and notes that the law school continues to expand opportunities for students to study international and comparative law with internationally renowned scholars both at home and abroad. Furthermore, the dean adds that the majority of the law school's faculty are entering their most productive years of scholarship and teaching.

Dean Stein notes also that Minnesota takes "very seriously" its responsibility to prepare students for significant contributions to the public interest. This ethic of service, the dean continues, is tied closely to the school's upper Midwestern origins and the area's history of public and private cooperation. The region's tradition of progressive community life has also attracted to the law school faculty and students with the talent and motivation to improve society in many areas.

By way of conclusion, Dean Stein states, "The University of Minnesota offers a high-quality legal education that prepares its graduates for the diverse and changing demands that they will face throughout their careers." That it succeeds in its missions, the Dean observes, is evidenced by the many accomplishments of the law school's faculty, students, and alumni in scholarship, private practice, business leadership, and government service.

CURRICULUM

First-Year Courses: Constitutional Law, Contracts, Criminal Law, Legal Research and Writing, Legislation, Civil Procedure, Property, Torts

Interesting Electives: Agricultural Law; American Indian Law; Biomedical Ethics; Civil Liberties; Computer Applications in Law; Domestic Abuse; Environmental Law; Intellectual Property Moot Court; Law and Medicine; Media Law; Patents; Pension Law; Psychology, Psychiatry, and the Law; Public International Organizations; U.S. Foreign Trade Law

Commentary. Students at Minnesota did not think that the law school's curriculum is unique and described it as "fairly straightforward," "fairly practical," and "fairly nontheoretical." An advantage of the curriculum, students noted, is the variety of clinical programs that are made possible by the law school's urban location. Students noted that each year several participants actually get to try cases before a jury—under faculty supervision, of course. The one criticism of the curriculum focused on the legal writing program, which was said even by one student-instructor to fail to prepare students adequately for writing assignments in actual professional positions.

First-year classes are said to be, by and large, conducted in a Socratic style that is "non-intimidating" and "humane" (for example, by calling on students in reverse alphabetical order), and most professors are primarily interested in helping students to answer questions. There are, however, one or two exceptions to this rule, including one professor described by a student as using "the old lightning bolt" technique of cross-examination; but, on balance, the use of the Socratic method during the first year did not seem to be a particularly important issue among students.

Finally, faculty accessibility was rated "as somewhere in the middle" between a literal open-door policy and a restrictive "office hours only" policy. Teachers remain after class to answer questions and can be found at other times in their offices. Students said that it is understood, however, that the professors at the law school are busy working on research and lectures and "usually don't have time to chat about the weather." There are also a few events each year that bring students and faculty together outside of the academic setting, such as the annual softball game, but reports indicate that faculty and students generally move in different social circles.

ADMISSIONS | According to Edward A. Kawczynski, Director of Admission, when an application to the law school is complete, it is reviewed in its entirety and placed in one of three categories: accepted, denied, or deferred. This initial screening, Mr. Kawczynski explains, is based on an initial review of the file, along with the LSAT score and cumulative undergraduate grade point average, using a formula devised from a study of past admissions. The applicant is immediately notified of the first screening action. Approximately half of the entering class is selected on the basis of the statistical prediction of their success in law study.

The remaining half of the class, Mr. Kawczynski explains, is selected from the "deferred" group of applicants. All "deferred" applications are reviewed by the admissions committee, which comprises student and faculty representatives. In addition to considering LSAT scores and transcripts, the committee pays particular attention to extracurricular and community activities, scholastic honors, recommendations, work experience, personal statements, and other factors that reflect character and academic promise.

ADMISSIONS DATA

	Class of 1993	Class of 1994
Applied	2,245	2,423
Median LSAT	N/A	N/A
Median GPA	N/A	N/A
Accepted	702	657
Median LSAT	N/A	N/A
Median GPA	N/A	N/A
Enrolled	276	270
Median LSAT	89.7 percentile	89.7 percentile
Median GPA	3.54	3.56

The Personal Statement.   According to Mr. Kawczynski, the personal statement plays "a very important role" in the admissions process. The law school considers the personal statement as a "sort of cover letter that introduces candidates to the admissions committee." Mr. Kawczynski notes that the law school is interested in persons not only with strong academic backgrounds, but also a wide range of skills and experiences that will contribute to the quality of the class as a whole and to the learning process of its members.

Recommendations.   Two letters of recommendation are required. If possible, Mr. Kawczynski says, these should be from persons in an academic setting or, if a student has been out of college for more than two years, from persons in a nonacademic setting.

Interviews. Interviews are not held for evaluative purposes, but Mr. Kawczynski adds that students are encouraged to visit the school and to meet with the Director of Admissions.

Minority Applications. Mr. Kawczynski states that the faculty affirms its support of an affirmative action program in admissions to the law school. The purpose of this program is to attract and to admit law students from minority and other diverse backgrounds. The precise numbers of minority and other diversity applicants to be admitted, Mr. Kawczynski explains, depends on the comparative credentials of all applications; no racial or ethnic quotas are fixed that exclude any applicants from consideration for any place in an entering class. Those students who believe that they will contribute to the diversity of the class should include a separate statement describing aspects of their ethnic, cultural, and linguistic heritage that they deem relevant, noting any related academic or extracurricular activities.

Residency. Although the law school is part of the University of Minnesota system, residents from other states have constituted roughly 35% of each incoming class in recent years. The number of nonresident applicants increases each year, and, Mr. Kawczynski says, nonresidents are encouraged to submit applications.

Application Tips. In addition to providing the admissions data entered above, Mr. Kawczynski says that the law school encourages students to contact the Office of Admissions to check their credentials against the admissions profile with recently admitted classes. As for the decision-making process, Mr. Kawczynski notes that the admissions committee is interested in knowing about any facts or circumstances that may warrant special consideration. These additional facts or circumstances can be discussed in the personal statement. Students who have been out of college for more than five years should provide additional letters of recommendation covering that period to aid the admissions committee in evaluating their applications. The "ideal" letter of recommendation is one that compares and contrasts the candidate with other individuals. Further, Mr. Kawczynski notes that it is not possible to describe applications that are "typically successful or typically unsuccessful," adding that "students are best equipped to list and define their own significant accomplishments." "Ultimately," says Mr. Kawczynski, "we want students to tell us what is important to them." Finally, it should be noted that the state of Minnesota has tuition reciprocity agreements with Manitoba, North Dakota, South Dakota, and Wisconsin.

PLACEMENT According to its director, Susan Gainen, the Office of Career Planning and Placement sends written invitations to all members of the National Association of Legal Employers to participate in the law school's fall On-Campus Interviewing (OCI) program. Invitations are also sent to corporations, government agencies, and public interest organizations, as well as Minnesota law firms and solo practitioners. The office schedules recruiter interviews, collects students' resumes, and distributes schedules and resumes to recruiters at least one week prior to the interview date. In December, the office sends information on its spring OCI program to those employers who have requested it. Approximately 200 employers interview second- and third-year students on campus in a typical year. Throughout the year, the office solicits job opportunities for current students and for graduates, and posts job opportunities in the career resource office. When available, the office publishes openings in the Alumni Placement Bulletin.

Ms. Gainen explains also that the Office of Career Planning and Placement provides informational sessions and seminars on topics such as "Tips for Successful On-Campus Interviewing" and offers students mock interview sessions. The office also makes available several handouts such as "Legal and Illegal Interviewing" and encourages students to make individual counselling appointments.

PLACEMENT DATA

	Class of 1991	Class of 1990
Placed at Graduation	70%	72%
Placed after 90 Days[1]	N/A	N/A
U.S. Supreme Court Clerks	1	0
U.S. Appellate Court Clerks	7	6
U.S. District Court Clerks	4	9
State Appellate Court Clerks	17	22
Other Judicial Clerks	5	11
Median Starting Salary	$50,862	$45,598

[1] At 6 months, 96% and 96%, respectively.

Commentary. In the introduction to this guidebook, it was noted that conditions at a law school can change dramatically from one year to the next and that student perceptions are often shaped by the personality of one or another key players at the school. The placement office at Minnesota is a case in point. In recent history, it has had three different directors and was described by one student as "the weakest link in the chain" of the services provided by the law school. Now, however, an interim director has been replaced with a new permanent director, Sue Gainen, who was described by students as a "windstorm" and a "ball of fire." One report said that it is even rumored among students that Ms. Gainen once sold used cars for a living and that this experience accounts for a new "coming at you" approach that now characterizes the placement office. On the other hand, optimism about the new director is tempered by the realization that the job market for lawyers is weak.

The new director's job may also be made more difficult by the fact that Minnesota is a midwestern state university, a fact that some students believe helps to explain why its students are not as strongly recruited by East and West Coast firms as they might otherwise be, given the law school's national reputation. Still another student said, however, that there is room for improvement even within the geographical constraint just mentioned. During a visit to the University of Wisconsin Law School, another Midwestern institution with a substantial national reputation, the student specifically compared listings for Chicago positions on the placement office's bulletin board there with those at Minnesota and concluded that Wisconsin is doing a better job of attracting recruiters from that city. Some students also expressed a desire that the placement office at Minnesota do more for those who are interested in government work and public interest law. Finally, some students commented favorably on the law school's close ties to the Minnesota bar, noting that firms in the Twin Cities and elsewhere in the state are filled with graduates of the law school, an advantage for those seeking positions in the region.

A STUDENT SAMPLER Typically, over 25% of the entering class at Minnesota are members of Phi Beta Kappa or some other academic honor society. The majority claim the Midwest as home, but students represent more than 200 undergraduate schools located in 40 states and 5 countries. Students come from positions such as business leaders and engineers, politicians and nurses, student advocates and teachers, and from many other backgrounds. A recent entering class included a volunteer for AIDS patients' estate planning, a former Miss Minnesota, an Olympic speed skater, a former NHL hockey player, and a sumo wrestler.

NOTEWORTHY GRADUATES

James J. Blanchard, Governor of the State of Michigan; Hon. William C. Canby, Jr., U.S. Court of Appeals, Ninth Circuit; A.W. Clausen, President of the World Bank and CEO, BankAmerica; Hon. Sandra Gardebring, Minnesota Supreme Court; Hon. George E. MacKinnon, U.S. Court of Appeal, D.C. Circuit; Walter Mondale, former Vice President of the United States

---

NEW YORK UNIVERSITY

▼

SCHOOL OF LAW
40 WASHINGTON SQUARE SOUTH, ROOM 419
NEW YORK, NY 10012
(212) 998-6060

ADMISSIONS

Applied: 7,241

Accepted: 1,172

Enrolled: 400

Median LSAT: N/A

Median GPA: N/A

STUDENT BODY

Total: 1,200

Women: 47%

Minorities: 18%

Average Age: 25

ACADEMIC RESOURCES

Library Volumes: 825,000

Computer Services: WESTLAW, LEXIS, word processors

Student/Faculty Ratio: 19:1

FINANCES (ACADEMIC YEAR)

Tuition:	$17,910
Food and Housing:	$ 8,710
Fees:	$ 595
Books & Course Materials:	$ 675
Total:	$30,600

ENVIRONMENT The main campus of New York University is located on Washington Square in Greenwich Village. The School of Law comprises 10 buildings (five academic buildings and five residential buildings). The main building is Vanderbilt Hall, which contains classrooms, seminar rooms, lounges, faculty and administrative offices, the auditorium, and the library. Fuchsberg Hall is devoted to clinical education and contains courtrooms, seminar rooms (designed for videotaping and viewing), and faculty offices. The law school's principal residential facilities are two nearby apartment-style residence halls that house more than 1,000 people, including J.D. and graduate law students and their spouses. The law school has been able to house virtually all students who have requested housing for the last several years, including those admitted from the wait list.

New York City provides a rich professional backdrop for a law school. The opportunities the city offers for involvement in public affairs and in private professional activities are useful in teaching and scholarship. The School of Law is a 20-minute walk from one of the great legal and financial centers of the world. NYU students have unequaled access to the courts and to the offices of major public interest and public sector organizations, as well as to the business and financial communities and the law firms that represent them.

Of all the neighborhoods in New York City, Greenwich Village is perhaps the most enigmatic. For artists, writers, performers, and many law students, it is truly the center of the world. Bounded by the Hudson River, Broadway, Houston Street, and Fourteenth Street, the Village is a town-within-a-city. While the use of the word "town" suggests a level of cultural and social homogeneity, the Village is the opposite. It is radical and reactionary, elegant and ordinary, frenetic and calm. The number of excellent restaurants, clubs, theaters, shops, and other diversions is staggering. Visitors and residents—including NYU law students—can amuse themselves for hours by doing nothing more than wandering through the Village.

Commentary.   When asked about living in New York City, students pointed out that the city consists of many neighborhoods and that these neighborhoods exhibit widely varying characteristics. The law school is located in Greenwich Village; while many law students do live in the neighborhood, either in law school housing or in privately owned buildings, a substantial number of students reside in other Manhattan neighborhoods, in Brooklyn, or even in New Jersey.

The Greenwich Village neighborhood was described by students as "vibrant," "exciting," "offering everything," and "an experience in itself." Students said that the Village offers a wide variety of eating and entertainment establishments and echoed remarks contained in the law school's literature about the diverse group of characters whom one is likely to see on the streets. Students usually added that Greenwich Village is still a part of New York City and emphasized the importance of developing a reliable sense of "street smarts." The area immediately around the law school was described as "well lit," "crowded," and "relatively safe," though one student recalled that a University security guard had once been held up. Still, those familiar with the Washington Square area called it "one of the safest neighborhoods" in New York City; and New Yorkers studying law at NYU described the area in which the law school is located as "considerably safer" than that surrounding the Columbia Law School.

Students also explained that the NYU campus is not clearly demarcated by physical boundaries. University buildings are located around and near Washington Square Park; but the park is public, not university, property, and university buildings stand next to privately owned buildings. The lack of a well-defined and self-contained university campus has both advantages and disadvantages. One student, whose undergraduate years were spent at a college with a nationally ranked football team, joked that school spirit at the law school certainly does not derive from the "NYU Violets." Another student noted seriously, "You don't have the feeling of being in an ivory tower; instead, you are close to the people in the neighborhood."

Even though the NYU Law School is not characterized by Gothic architecture and a well-defined "quad," students gave the law school's physical plant good marks. The recently renovated library received excellent evaluations. It was described as "stunning," "phenomenal," "outstanding," and "aesthetically pleasing." Students praised the wide variety of study spaces available, from open reading rooms with reference books, to lounge areas for informal discussion, to cloistered recesses for intense study. One student quipped that the law library's security staff has difficulty keeping other NYU students out of the library because it is such a nice place to study.

Classrooms were rated as "more than satisfactory but not great." A few students commented on the lack of precise climate control; and one student, after some reflection, finally concluded that the old wooden chairs in some classrooms are not particularly comfortable but added that they do give the law school a certain "prestigious old law school feeling." These shortcomings, however, did not seem particularly important to students in the overall scheme of things, and students also noted that the law school has an ongoing renovation program.

Of the law school dormitories, students said that the newer one, located immediately behind the main law school building, has somewhat cramped accommodations and that both dormitories are expensive when compared with other housing alternatives. On the other hand, students said that the dormitories offer advantages of convenience and ease of renting.

Though allowing that there might be a few exceptions, students at the law school described themselves and their classmates as "hardworking but not cutthroat" and the atmosphere at the law school as "collegial." People were said to be good about sharing notes with classmates—so good, said one student, that it is possible to end up with more notes than one can use. Many of the journals keep copies of particularly good course outlines prepared by previous students, and those outlines are available to all—even those not working for the journal. Students also theorized that the "very tight grading system," under which few people get grades below B- or above B+, also tends to relieve some of the pressure that one might otherwise expect to experience at a top law school. As one student put it, "Grades are generally neither a source of great friction nor great pleasure."

Several students described the student body as predominantly liberal but added that the occasional outbreak of political strife does not serve to define the NYU Law School experience. A couple of conservative students suggested, however, that the predominantly liberal outlook of students tends to "smother dissension under a blanket of liberalism." But even those students who identified themselves as moderates or conservatives by way of distinguishing themselves from their classmates did not feel that they had been abused by their class-mates—even though they thought their classmates in error on certain issues.

Several students also said that the administration is responsive to student views on issues such as faculty hiring. One student, on the losing side of a pol-icy debate when the administration refused to take a certain action, nonetheless supported the position articulated by classmates that the administration is inter-ested in student views. Others specifically said that the dean of the law school, John Sexton, makes a considerable effort to be accessible to students. For exam-ple, each weekend the dean and some faculty members play basketball, and stu-dents are invited to participate in the game.

ACADEMICS | According to John Sexton, Dean of the Law School, the philosophy of New York University Law School can be captured in one word: engagement. As a major research and teaching institution, the law school seeks to foster a climate in which faculty members become engaged with each other in discussion about research and teaching; in which stu-dents become engaged with each other in discussion of the great legal issues of the day; and in which the faculty and students become engaged with each other around those topics. The law school strives to become ever more fully a com-munity of diverse backgrounds and diverse viewpoints, in which individuals test their intellectual positions in a civil, but intense and rigorous, discourse.

As for the curriculum, Dean Sexton states that while the law school enjoys a national reputation for its scholarship and teaching in traditional fields, two innovations serve to distinguish it from other law schools: the clinical programs

---

CURRICULUM

First-Year Courses: Contracts, Criminal Law, Civil Procedure, Property, Torts, Lawyering

Interesting Electives: Artists, Authors, and the Law; Civil Rights at the Crossroads; Close Corporations; Commodities Futures Regulation; Con-stitutional Law of the United Nations; Employment Discrimination Law; Juvenile Rights Clinic; Law and Science; Law in the People's Republic of China; Philanthropy, Nonprofits, and the Law; Post-Convictions Proceedings; Race and the Law—U.S. and South Africa; Regulating Toxic Hazards; Statistics for Lawyers

---

and the interdisciplinary studies. First, noting that clinical education is a key element in the future of legal study, Dean Sexton points out that NYU has been a pioneer in this area. Because of this tradition, the dean says that NYU can now lay claim to the most advanced and successful clinical program in the United States. It begins in the first year with a course on Lawyering; in the second year it enriches traditional academic subjects with simulation of real-world circumstances; and in the final year it incorporates field-work clinics. Second, Dean Sexton states that NYU Law School is home to some of the finest interdisciplinary scholarship and teaching in the nation and cites several examples, including its Law and Philosophy Program, Criminal Justice Colloquium, and Colloquium on Lawyering Theory. Finally, the dean adds that the NYU Law School, with several "world-class" faculty members, is also a vital center for the study of international law.

Commentary. Dean Sexton's remarks about the law school's clinical programs struck responsive chords in many, though not all, students. Students spoke highly of the required first-year Lawyering course. During the first semester, the emphasis is on traditional research and writing skills; but during the second semester, students are presented with a series of simulations, e.g., a settlement negotiation or a client interview. The importance of clinical-type work during the second and third years is a more individual matter since participation in clinical programs in those years is a matter of voluntary course selection; but students mentioned a variety of offerings for those who are interested in such training. The clinical offerings, however, tend to have titles such as "Family Defense Clinic" and "Urban Law Clinic." Students whose primary interest is in traditional corporate law topics such as securities regulation or taxation may find that the clinical programs do not necessarily enrich their educational experiences. And for people who are very interested in clinical subjects, the "knock" on the law school's clinical programs is that excessive student demand for some of the clinics means that admission to those programs is not automatic. On the other hand, one student pointed out that *pro bono* work is always available through the law school. So it is usually possible for students to find noncredit, volunteer positions working on a project of particular interest and on a schedule that is convenient. And, according to some students, the law school's practical dimension makes graduates who have availed themselves of these opportunities particularly attractive to employers.

Students also remarked on the availability of a variety of learning opportunities outside of the classroom that are more theoretical in nature than the clinical programs. Specifically mentioned were various speaker programs, roundtable discussions, and debates.

According to students, teaching styles, particularly during the first year, vary from professor to professor. One professor with years of experience was said to employ a "very Socratic approach," calling on students at random. Even so, it was reported that interrogations were limited to five minutes or so and that it was no great embarrassment to ask to be passed over on a particular day. At the other extreme is a professor whose efforts to stimulate voluntary class participation were so relaxed that the professor was said, somewhat derisively by one student, to emulate Phil Donahue.

Most students described professors as "accessible," but that term is used differently by different students at the law school and is applied differently to different professors. To one student, "accessible" means that it is "easy to schedule an appointment" with a professor. To another student, the term means being able to drop in on for an informal chat with one or two especially friendly teachers but not on others. One student specifically noted that the doors to faculty offices are usually closed and that students do not routinely have incidental contact with teachers in the hallways or eating areas. In terms of accessibility, one of the school's strong points, the use of practicing attorneys as professors in certain fields, is also a disadvantage: because they have full-time practices, they do not have the time to be available to students.

ADMISSIONS | According to Nan McNamara, Assistant Dean for Admissions, a Committee on Admissions has the responsibility for implementing the faculty's admissions policies and for making admissions decisions. Committee members include faculty, the Assistant Dean for Admissions, and third-year students. According to Dean McNamara, NYU uses no index, no cutoff, and no formula to make decisions or even to sort applications. Instead, the committee thoroughly reviews all materials in the applications.

As part of the review of an applicant's undergraduate transcript, the committee pays careful attention to factors such as trends in grades, class rank, ratio of pass/fail to graded courses, the diversity and depth of course work, and the length of time since graduation. The committee also evaluates work experience and extracurricular or community activity for evidence of advancement, leadership, and capacity for assuming responsibility.

According to Dean McNamara, the committee does not use a rolling admissions process, at least not in the strict sense of that phrase. The law school tries to let applicants know the disposition of the application as soon as possible, but decisions are not hurried and offers for admissions are not made on a first-come–first-served basis. If an application is made in timely fashion, it will receive full consideration, and there is no quantifiable disadvantage to filing later in the application season than earlier.

The Personal Statement. The Committee on Admissions recognizes that the application form has certain limitations and cannot convey a complete picture of an applicant. On the other hand, the committee cannot grant interviews. Thus, the personal statement is the vehicle that candidates should use to describe

ADMISSIONS DATA

	Class of 1993	Class of 1994
Applied	7,105	7,241
Median LSAT	N/A	N/A
Median GPA	N/A	N/A
Accepted	1,176	1,172
Median LSAT	N/A	N/A
Median GPA	N/A	N/A
Enrolled	396	400
Median LSAT	N/A	N/A
Median GPA	N/A	N/A

important or unusual aspects of their backgrounds that are not otherwise apparent from the rest of the application. The "Instructions for Applicants" do not specify any content for the personal statement, and the length of the statement is also left to the applicant's discretion and may be as short or as long as necessary.

Recommendations. NYU requires one letter of recommendation for candidates for admission to the law school, but candidates may submit additional letters if they choose—and many do. According to Dean McNamara, recommendations should come from faculty members, or, if the candidate graduated some time ago, from employers who know the candidate's work well.

Interviews. When asked what role evaluative interviews play in the admissions process at NYU, Dean McNamara responded simply, "None."

Minority Applications. Dean McNamara states that factors other than undergraduate grades and LSAT scores are particularly significant for applicants who are members of minority groups, who are older, or who have experienced educational disadvantage. In its effort to enroll a student body from a broad spectrum of society, the committee specifically invites members of groups underrepresented in the legal profession to submit a separate statement describing special circumstances in their background that are relevant to the application.

Application Tips.   NYU does not release the median LSAT score or GPA of its classes, but Dean McNamara supplied the following information about the law school's applicant group for the 1991–1992 academic year:

LSAT Score	Percent of Applicants Admitted
Above 95th percentile	46.6%
91st to 95th percentile	23.4%
81st to 90th percentile	13.2%
Below 81st percentile	3.6%

GPA	Percent of Applicants Admitted
Above 3.74	47.9%
3.50 to 3.74	35.2%
3.25 to 3.49	9.5%
Below 3.25	2.4%

Of course, these data say nothing about the raw numerical chances of a candidate with a certain *combination* of LSAT score and GPA. For more detailed information, Dean McNamara encourages prospective applicants to consult NYU's entry in the *Official Guide to U.S. Law Schools*. Still, the numbers do show that while the LSAT score and GPA are important, they are by no means dispositive of applications at NYU, and other factors are very important.

As for those other factors, Dean McNamara said of the personal statement that it is very important. The dean suggested that applicants may wish to complete or clarify responses to items on the application forms, to bring to the committee's attention additional information, or to discuss reasons for applying to NYU. And regarding recommendations, Dean McNamara said that a recommendation is of "particular value" when the writer provides substantive information about an applicant's abilities, activities, and personal qualities.

P LACEMENT The Office of Career Counseling and Placement has 12 full-time staff members aided by 10 part-time college students. Each year, the staff sends invitations to visit the NYU campus to 7,000 law firms, 3,500 government agencies and public interest organizations, and 2,000 corporations. For the academic year 1990–1991, 770 employers sent 1,231 interviewers. The office also coordinates off-campus recruitment programs in Washington, D.C., Los Angeles, San Francisco, and Seattle as well as a "Resume Only" program for employers who cannot visit the campus.

PLACEMENT DATA

	Class of 1991	Class of 1990
Placed at Graduation	96%	97%
Placed within 90 days	98%	98%
U.S. Supreme Court Clerks	1	0
U.S. Appellate Court Clerks	6	14
U.S. District Court Clerks	32	43
State Appellate Court Clerks	5	4
Other Judicial Clerks	7	3
Median Starting Salary	$77,287[1]	$76,677[1]

[1]Graduates going into private practice, approximately 75% of class.

During the year, the office holds 35 career panels, each with six speakers, and 25 job search workshops. Videotapes of the panels as well as other research material are available to students in the office. Other placement strategies include videotaping and critiquing mock interviews.

Commentary. By and large, students at the NYU Law School seem to be extremely well pleased with the workings of the placement office. Phrases used to describe the placement office included "strong," "tireless," and "very knowledgeable." In the words of one enthusiastic student, "On a scale of one to 10, the placement office gets at least an 11," while another, slightly less enthusiastic student rated the placement office only "10.5 on a scale of 10." One student said categorically, "Everybody *loves* the placement office." This last statement may not be literally true, but it is the case that the reputation of the placement office extends beyond the confines of the NYU Law School. A student at another top law school included in this directory, at which the placement office received mixed reviews, stated that the placement office there planned to study the procedures of the placement office at NYU as part of a plan to improve its own operations.

When asked to identify the specific strengths of the placement office, students often commented on the depth and breadth of the research done by the staff. One student told of visiting the placement office as a first-year student and asking for a list of partners in firms of specific cities who had graduated from a particular college and whose practice had a special emphasis. Given these parameters, the placement office data base provided the student with a highly specific list that eventually yielded a summer placement. Another student described the information available on judicial clerkships and stated that the data base includes information on just about every judge in the country. Others referred to the placement office's efforts to help find positions for students looking for placements in public interest areas; and whereas students at some other top law schools described the public interest efforts of their placement offices as weak, NYU students said specifically their placement office has a lot of material on public interest positions and counselors who specifically work on that type of placement.

Students also judged the placement office favorably for its organization and attention to detail. One student described the placement office's "early interview week" as a "monumental accomplishment" and credited this device with helping students to secure positions they might not otherwise have obtained. Several students mentioned that the placement office frequently sends to students through the campus mail informational bulletins and notices about the availability of specific positions.

Finally, students also praised the placement office staff for the energy that it expends on behalf of students. For example, a student said that Dean Sexton had given a talk on procedures for obtaining a judicial clerkship one Friday afternoon. At the end of the talk, the dean encouraged students to visit the placement office. At 5:45 on a Friday afternoon, the placement office was still open. This kind of effort, said one student, is strong evidence that the placement office "really wants to see students get hired." Finally, one student offered a comparison of the NYU placement office with perhaps a half dozen others at various top law schools. Shortly after receiving acceptances, the student, who had prior professional experience and particular career objectives, telephoned the placement office of each institution that had extended an offer of admission to inquire about their resources. All but one rebuffed the student. The placement office at NYU, however, spent 90 minutes on the telephone assisting a person who had not yet formally accepted NYU's offer of admission.

A STUDENT SAMPLER

The student body at NYU Law School includes students from all fifty states and several foreign countries and more than 200 colleges and universities. The undergraduate institutions most represented at the law school are NYU with 71 students, Pennsylvania with 50, Cornell with 46, Columbia with 42, Yale with 41, Michigan with 39, Brown with 35, Harvard with 35, Princeton with 31, and Georgetown with 24.

As a rule, more than 60 percent of entering students are at least one year out of college; and in recent history, about 18 percent have been out of college for at least five years. About 10 percent have completed other graduate or professional degrees, and those with work experience include business executives, entrepreneurs, medical doctors, creative and performing artists, police officers, scientists, construction workers, journalists, athletes, military officers, health care administrators, and social workers.

NOTEWORTHY GRADUATES

Peter Guber, CEO of SONY—Columbia Pictures and producer of *The Color Purple*, *Flashdance*, *Rain Man*, and *Batman*; Robert M. Hayes, founder and former Counsel of the Coalition for the Homeless; Hon. Judith Kaye, Chief Judge, New York State Court of Appeals; Ed Koch, former Mayor of New York City; Hon. Pauline Newman, U.S. Court of Appeals for the Federal Circuit; Jose Marie Ruda, President, World Court; Paul Tagliabue, Commissioner of the National Football League

UNIVERSITY OF NORTH CAROLINA, CHAPEL HILL

▼

SCHOOL OF LAW
CB #3380, VAN HECKE-WETTACH HALL
CHAPEL HILL, NC 27599
(919) 962-8108

ADMISSIONS

Applied: 3,290

Accepted: 570

Enrolled: 235

Median LSAT: 89.7 percentile

Median GPA: 3.51

STUDENT BODY

Total: 690

Women: 44%

Minorities: 13%

Average Age: N/A

ACADEMIC RESOURCES

Library Volumes: 346,999

Computer Services: LEXIS, WEST-LAW, word processors

Student/Faculty Ratio: 22:1

FINANCES (ACADEMIC YEAR)

Tuition:
Resident:	$ 1,150
Nonresident	$ 7,013

Living Expenses:
Resident:	$ 6,375
Nonresident:	$ 6,375

Books:
Resident:	$ 500
Nonresident:	$ 500

Total:
Resident:	$ 8,025
Nonresident:	$13,888

ENVIRONMENT Although it still calls itself a town, and some of its residents prefer to think of it as a village, Chapel Hill is a bustling community of 38,000 people with a progressive atmosphere in central North Carolina. Its four distinct seasons are a bonus that has inspired some to refer to it as "The Southern Part of Heaven." Its winters are short and mild, with temperatures averaging 40 degrees. Winters will bring at least one snowfall, but shorts and t-shirts are the fashion from late spring to early autumn.

Because of its proximity to the state capital of Raleigh and other educational institutions, Chapel Hill offers a stimulating menu of intellectual and cultural events, from art to music to drama. And sports fans can revel in Atlantic Coast Conference basketball. In recent years, Chapel Hill has been enriched by the growth of Research Triangle Park, 12 miles to the east of town. This state-sponsored research center has attracted to the area a distinct population of scientists, engineers, and other professionals who add to the diversity of the area.

When students arrive in Chapel Hill, they discover a campus conducive to learning and living. The beauty of the 687-acre central campus is seductive—regularly converting visitor to resident, skeptic to believer. Ancient oaks and eclectic architecture are laced together by miles of brick walkways and rock walls, all within an easy stroll of a charming downtown area. Author Richard Moll, in his guide to the best U.S. colleges and universities, called Chapel Hill "the perfect college town."

The law school entered a new era when it moved into a new facility, Van Hecke-Wettach Hall, in 1968. Van Hecke-Wettach Hall, located on the eastern boundary of campus, features dramatic contemporary architecture designed to accommodate the needs of modern legal education. Named for two former deans, Maurice T. Van Hecke and Robert Wettach, the structure consists of two buildings joined by a courtyard and connecting bridges.

Commentary.   The students interviewed pretty much endorsed the administration's description of the surroundings of the law school in all respects—save one, discussed below. Several students, for example, mentioned spontaneously the "beautiful weather" of central North Carolina, with its four distinct seasons but mild winters. And, in general, the summary descriptions of Chapel Hill paralleled very closely those provided by the administration and included "classic college town," "proverbial college town," and "archetypal college town." The term "college town," as it is used here, should not, however, be misunderstood to signify just an atmosphere of "drunken debauchery"—though, as one student noted, a "fair share" of that goes on in Chapel Hill. Rather, while the term "college town" obviously denotes a place with a large student population and businesses that cater to a student clientele, it also connotes, as the administration's literature suggests, a "progressive atmosphere" that is characterized by the free exchange of ideas. And as for ACC basketball, one student, when asked about activities for law students, responded with a question: "Do you like basketball?" College basketball at UNC, the student said, becomes "addictive."

Of course, one of the characteristics of this college town is that it offers a variety of student-type activities and amenities. According to reports, Chapel Hill offers many restaurants, including ones serving ethnic cuisines such as Mexican, Thai, Indian, Chinese, and Italian, as well as those serving less specific "continental" fare. Some notion of the variety of eating establishments was suggested by the reaction of the interviewee who, when asked whether or not there is a Chinese restaurant in the area, simply asked in return, "Do you want to pick it up or have it delivered?" The prices for meals range from cheap ("a good, homey diner") to expensive ("where your parents can take you out when they are visiting"). There are "tons" of movies and "lots" of bars and clubs (18 within walking distance of the law school). Theater possibilities include university productions (which may also feature Equity actors), regional theater, and touring companies (recently *The Secret Garden*). Chapel Hill is also home to clubs such as Cat's Cradle, which features original rock bands. Finally, students added that what one cannot find to do in Chapel Hill can almost surely be found in either Durham (which is only 25 minutes away and is where some law students live because housing is less expensive) or in Raleigh (which is only 45 minutes away). In fact, the term "Triangle" refers to the configuration of these three cities as well as to the research facility mentioned by the administration. And all of this is available in a setting that does not include the "hassles" of a large city.

If students generally endorsed the administration's description of Chapel Hill, they rejected its description of the law school's physical plant as featuring "dramatic contemporary architecture," offering instead descriptions such as "not remarkable," "heinous," and "an architectural nightmare." One student said, "On first seeing it, I thought to myself, 'That is the ugliest building I have ever seen.'" On the other hand, students agreed that the greater University campus (with its Georgian architecture) is beautiful and that the wooded setting of the law school is attractive (even if the building is not). And, students allowed that even though the building has other drawbacks, it is nonetheless "functional." There is no student lounge in the building proper (though the "Snack Shack" located in a "trailer" only a couple of hundred yards away has lounge and picnic areas), and the library reading room was described as "uninviting" (though the library was said to have excellent computer facilities). On balance, however, students thought the shortcomings of the physical plant "no reason not to come to UNC." And others noted that the law school plans a fairly substantial renovation and expansion in the next couple of years.

Questions about the atmosphere at the law school elicited responses that ranged from "students here are very relaxed" to "the tension here is almost palpable," but the extreme divergence of opinion is less jarring when these remarks are placed into context. The first interviewee added that a certain amount of competition is probably "inherent in the structure of a law school" and could not identify any particular reason why the UNC law school should be less competitive than others (other than to suggest that students choose the law school with that expectation). The second student confessed to being, by choice, a very "low stress person" but pointed out that the grading curve for the first year is "very severe" and cited an example of a study group formed early during the first year that exacted mutual promises from its members to keep its findings a closely guarded secret. Thus, it seems that the truth is probably somewhere in the middle. Students generally do share outlines and other study resources, but some students are more competitive than others. In the final analysis, the atmosphere at the law school was perhaps best described by the student who said it is "moderately competitive" and who also referred to classmates as "typical law students out there trying to do their best."

During the first year, students are assigned to "small sections" and meet for one course only with their small section (and the other courses in larger groups). The small sections are assigned upperclass advisors who count as one of their responsibilities the scheduling of some social activities. One older, married student said of the system that it helps to introduce students to one another and to engender a sense of camaraderie, but, the student added, "I didn't really 'bond' with my classmates."

ACADEMICS | According to Dean of the Law School Judith W. Wegner, the University of North Carolina School of Law strives to be one of the nation's great public law schools. It is committed, the dean says, to educating a talented and diverse student body, drawn from across the state of North Carolina and the nation. The dean says that as a public institution, the School of Law is especially proud of its commitment to provide legal education at affordable rates to a wide range of individuals, including minority students, women, older students, and those from all economic backgrounds.

The dean explains that the law school's curriculum is designed to prepare students for a wide range of future careers, including private practice in large or small firms, public service, or nontraditional capacities. The curriculum provides students with strong coverage in traditional core areas, a choice of diverse electives in changing areas of the law, and an opportunity to sample interdisciplinary viewpoints. Most students, the dean says, enroll in at least one small section course of 25 to 35 students in each semester of their law school careers. And, the dean adds, the law school also offers opportunities for students to develop skills in research and writing through required courses in each of the three years of law school, and in practical skills through its strong program in trial advocacy and civil or criminal clinics.

Finally, the dean notes that the law school draws upon the University's important strengths and offers joint degree programs in business administration, city and regional planning, public administration, public policy, and public health. The law school has long taken pride in its commitment to excellent teaching, innovative faculty scholarship, and public service by both faculty and students. It also nurtures, the dean says, student interest in varied extracurricular activities and sponsors diverse informal programs designed to enhance its core educational program.

Commentary. Students said that though the coursework at the UNC Law School may be "fairly conventional," "straightforward and traditional" with only a few "cutting edge" courses, it provides a "good, broad-based legal education."

CURRICULUM

First-Year Courses: Civil Procedure I and II, Contracts I and II, Property I and II, Torts I and II, Criminal Law, Introduction to Legal Writing and Bibliography, Legal Research and Writing

Interesting Electives: Bioethics and Law; Children and the Legal System; Constitutional History; Ethical Issues in Trusts and Estates; Environmental Law; Gender-Based Discrimination; Health, Law, and Public Policy; Intellectual Property; International Law; Land Use Control; Law and Literature; Legal History; Ocean and Coastal Law; Race and Poverty: Some Constitutional Dimensions; Scientific Theory and Method for Lawyers

There is a second-year writing requirement that requires in-depth research on a topic and that brings students into direct contact with a professor. Admission to the law school's clinical programs is not automatic, but there is a long list of volunteer activities in which to participate such as the Carolina Aids Wills Project (students prepare living wills, wills, and powers of attorney), Women in Law (which has the Domestic Violence Project), the Prisoners' Rights Project, and the Environmental Law Project, as well as non-lawyering activities such as cooking at a homeless shelter or tutoring at-risk children.

The classroom teaching styles of the first-year professors are said to vary from teacher to teacher. Some call on students at random; others proceed in some sort of order so that it is possible to know when it is absolutely essential to be prepared. Some teachers are "rather hard" in their use of the Socratic method, while others were said to be more relaxed. In any event, students agreed that in spite of the fact that answering questions in front of 150 very bright classmates is an experience that is inherently stressful, the professors did not go out of their way to make it more so than necessary. Representative descriptions of the first-year experience were "Profs ask tough questions, but they are not abusive" and "They might grind you—not to humiliate you but to make you think."

Reports indicate that the faculty are fairly accessible to students, though, as might be expected, accessibility depends upon both student and teacher. Professors remain after class to answer questions; and if they are in their offices, then it is appropriate to knock (whether the door is open or not) and ask whether the professor has time for a consultation. One student said, "But I have never called on a professor who did not have time to talk." Beyond that sort of contact, there are some opportunities for students and faculty to socialize. Small section professors (first year) may invite students for a dinner at their homes, or an upperclass seminar may occasionally meet at a professor's house. In general, however, students did not mention a lot of social interaction with professors.

147

ADMISSIONS | According to J. Elizabeth Furr, Assistant Dean for Admissions and Student Affairs, admission to the School of Law is a competitive process, and those applicants with the strongest records are given priority. Dean Furr explains that a "substantial majority" of admissions decisions are made on the basis of combining LSAT scores with undergraduate grade point average, and those applicants who rank among the highest or lowest using this standard are offered or denied admission primarily on this basis. Still, Dean Furr says, there is no minimum LSAT score or GPA below which applicants are automatically denied and adds that letters of recommendation are reviewed for all applicants. Further, in order to ensure the educational benefits of a meaningful diversity of background and other enriching qualities in the class, candidates may be considered by the admissions committee on the basis of various other factors including: extracurricular activities, unique work or service experience, leadership potential, maturity, demonstrated compassion, a history of overcoming disadvantage (including physical disability), ability to communicate with the poor, exceptional personal talents, race or ethnic origin, trends or development in academic program, writing skill, demonstrated analytical skills, strength of undergraduate program, and graduate school grades.

The Personal Statement.   Dean Furr states that the personal statement is carefully evaluated for evidence of writing skill, motivation for the study of law, and for any enriching qualities that an applicant would bring to a law school class.

ADMISSIONS DATA

	Class of 1993	*Class of 1994*
Applied	3,419	3,290
Median LSAT	N/A	N/A
Median GPA	N/A	N/A
Accepted	549	570
Median LSAT	N/A	N/A
Median GPA	N/A	N/A
Enrolled	223	235
Median LSAT	89.7 percentile	89.7 percentile
Median GPA	3.39	3.51

Recommendations. Dean Furr says that two letters of recommendation are required and should be completed by professors or employers who know the applicant personally and who have knowledge of the applicant's academic performance or other achievements.

Interviews. When asked what role evaluative interviews play in the admissions process at North Carolina, Dean Furr says simply, "None."

Minority Applications. Although there are no special or separate procedures for handling minority applications, Dean Furr states that the law school has an "aggressive" affirmative action program.

Residency. Approximately 75 percent of entering students are legal residents of the state of North Carolina.

Application Tips. Dean Furr says that the most helpful letters of recommendation are ones that focus on academic or analytical abilities of the applicant. She adds that an "in-depth, candid" evaluation is more useful than "broad, generalized statements."

PLACEMENT According to the Director of Career Development and Services (CDS), Amanda V. Harding, CDS mails over 2,000 invitations each year to employers nationwide in both the private and public sector. In a typical year, about 275 to 300 recruiters visit the campus. Plus, the placement office receives about 1,200 mail solicitations each year. Additionally, the faculty and administration speak with alumni and other potential employers at conferences to encourage them to hire UNC students. CDS also offers interview skills workshops, mock interviews with upper-level students and alumni/ae, individual counseling sessions, and extensive library resources including books and videotapes on interviewing, resumes, and cover letters.

Commentary. Recruitment, career counseling, and other employment services at UNC are lodged in the Career Development and Services Office—CDS for short. According to students, the director of CDS insists upon the name of the office because it is descriptive of CDS's proper function and emphatically denies that CDS is a "placement agency." As one student explained, the avowed function of the office is not "to place" students in positions of employment but "to help" them find a job. This is a distinction that is a source of dissatisfaction

PLACEMENT DATA

	Class of 1991	Class of 1990
Placed at Graduation	70%	75%
Placed within 90 Days	79%	83%
U.S. Supreme Court Clerks	0	0
U.S. Appellate Court Clerks	2	0
U.S. District Court Clerks	6	4
State Appellate Court Clerks	6	9
Other Judicial Clerks	6	1
Median Starting Salary	$45,000	$42,000

among some students, particularly those who expect that a top law school should be able to "place" them in positions of employment. In the final analysis, however, the distinction insisted upon by the director may represent a certain frankness about the ability of a "placement office" at a law school that, while highly ranked, does not draw recruiters from all parts of the nation. Students reported that UNC students are vigorously recruited by North Carolina firms but said that recruiters from large firms outside of the state come primarily from Atlanta, Washington, D.C., and New York. And the firms from the three large cities are likely to be interested primarily in the top quarter of the class. Indeed, fully one-half of the law school's graduates typically take jobs in North Carolina with another quarter going to Delaware, D.C., Florida, Georgia, Maryland, South Carolina, or West Virginia. Given that distribution, it is probably just not reasonable to expect that the on-campus recruitment program will be the answer to the job search for every student. Consequently, CDS emphasizes alternative strategies, and the results are evident in the "Placement Data" table above.

A STUDENT SAMPLER

A recent entering class included representatives from 21 states and the District of Columbia and from 75 colleges and universities. The ages of the entering class ranged from 20 to 40. Some of those with interesting pre-law school accomplishments were a musician who had recorded two albums, a concert violinist with the North Carolina Symphony, a soccer coach and participant at the World Maccabi Games, an English teacher in Kenya, a national debate champion, a former hand surgeon (65 years old), and a former college professor in biochemistry.

NOTEWORTHY GRADUATES

Julius Chambers, Director and Legal Counsel for the NAACP Legal Defense and Education Fund; C. Boyden Gray, former Counsel to the President of the United States; Hon. K. Edward Greene, Judge, North Carolina Court of Appeals; A. Richard Golub, entertainment attorney (clients have included Donald Trump, Christie Brinkley, Yasmin Kahn, and Cornelia Guest) who has written and recorded the rap number "He Is My Lawyer"; James B. Hunt, former Governor of North Carolina; Reef D. Ivey, II, director and co-owner of Nutri/System, Inc.; William F. Maready, attorney who successfully represented the family of one of the victims of *The Challenger* space shuttle disaster; Terry Sanford, United States Senator and former Governor of North Carolina

NORTHWESTERN UNIVERSITY

SCHOOL OF LAW
357 EAST CHICAGO AVENUE
CHICAGO, ILLINOIS 60611
(312) 503-8465

ADMISSIONS

Applied: 4,654

Accepted: 728

Enrolled: 201

Median LSAT: N/A

Median GPA: N/A

STUDENT BODY

Total: 600

Women: 40%

Minorities: 21%

Average Age: 24

ACADEMIC RESOURCES

Library Volumes: 550,000

Computer Services: WESTLAW, LEXIS, CCH access, word processors

Student/Faculty Ratio: 15:1

FINANCES (ACADEMIC YEAR)

Tuition:	$16,386
Food and Lodging:	$ 6,102
Books & Supplies:	$ 870
Personal Expenses:	$ 2,697
Total:	$26,055

ENVIRONMENT The School of Law is located on the 20-acre Chicago campus of Northwestern University, between Lake Shore Drive to the east and the stretch of Michigan Avenue known as "the Magnificent Mile" to the west. With a population approaching 3 million, Chicago is a center for the arts, education, finance and trade, law, commerce, and government. The city offers a blend of distinguished architecture and public art, vibrant neighborhoods, ethnic restaurants, stimulating theater, memorable jazz, great and less-than-great professional sports, and a political scene of interest second to none.

Many law students live in the university's Lake Shore Center, one block north of the law school, or in Abbott Hall, across the street to the south. Both facilities are on the lake front and provide convenient living quarters in one of the city's most desirable residential districts at a price within student budgets. Other students choose to live off-campus, in the residential districts within walking distance of the law school or a short bus ride away.

The three School of Law buildings are a blend of academic Gothic and contemporary architecture. A glass-enclosed atrium connects the three buildings and is used as a student commons and gathering place for members of the law school community.

It is the law school's hope that each entering Northwestern student—intelligent, individualistic, and venturesome—will become a member of a small, closely knit community bound together by a common pursuit and by the rich tradition of the law school. The law school strives to foster a healthy spirit of competition which is complemented by the comradeship and mutual respect characteristic of the legal profession.

Commentary. Students at the Northwestern School of Law seem to be genuinely pleased with their surroundings, and if law students perhaps do not have the wherewithal to shop regularly at the high-priced stores of the "Magnificant Mile," then the law school's proximity to that shopping district puts it in "one of the nicest areas of Chicago." Students reported that the law school is accessible by automobile and by public transportation from/to the various parts of the city, but it was also said to be sufficiently far removed from the downtown area that the campus itself is quiet. One student, who compared several law schools before choosing Northwestern, described the law school as a "small community in a larger urban setting." Pursuing this idea, another student said that a review of data on reported crimes shows that the incidence of crime is fairly low in the area, and another touted the law school's lake-shore location by contrasting it with the "war zone down in Hyde Park."

The law school's physical plant also received high marks from students. The law school shares a relatively new building with the American Bar Association and has an older building that, according to students, has considerable charm. The library, which looks out over Lake Michigan, was specifically mentioned by many students as being a particularly enjoyable aspect of studying at Northwestern. In fact, one student noted that the library is so attractive that students from other schools come to the law school to study. Recently, according to the student, the library staff found it necessary to limit access to the building by outsiders to certain areas so that Northwestern law students would not be inconvenienced.

Most students, though not all, described the atmosphere at the law school in terms such as "friendly," "congenial," and "cooperative." They noted specifically that students share outlines with classmates and pass them down from year to year. Students also form study groups, and one is not likely to be denied access to study material on the grounds that one's own contribution to the group effort was below par. To be sure, it was acknowledged that the class is likely to include a few "gunners," those people aiming for the very best grades; but as one student put it, the School of Law is "quietly competitive," meaning that competition is primarily with oneself. Another student described Northwestern as a "kinder, gentler law school."

On the other hand, students complained that the grading system at the law school, under which averages can be calculated with decimal-point precision, tends to overemphasize small differences in grade point averages. Several students described the system as "ridiculous" and suggested that it leads prospective employers to place too much weight on relatively insignificant differences in grade point averages. Some employers, for example, do not give serious consideration to students with averages below a certain number. It is curious, then, that students would remain so cooperative in the face of so austere a grading system. When asked to resolve this seeming paradox, one student theorized that the grading system somehow galvanizes students so that "instincts of cooperation overwhelm instincts for personal survival." Still, the grading system may help to explain the occasional report of the student or students who seemed to transgress the bounds of what the administration calls a "healthy spirit of competition."

Some students maintained that Northwestern students are fairly sociable. One student mentioned as an example the "Bar Review," a procedure by which Northwestern law students socialize with one another by designating a different bar each week as a Thursday evening meeting place. Another insisted that students at Northwestern are a more sociable group than their counterparts at the University of Chicago Law School. On the other hand, another, perhaps more reflective student theorized that students at Northwestern are neither more nor less sociable than students at other law schools, noting that one's social interests depend in important ways on one's living arrangements (off- versus on-campus) and family status and on one's extracurricular interests. Ultimately, it seems as though the School of Law is perhaps not defined by a single, transcendent sense of *the* law school community. Rather, students coalesce into groups according to their interest in and their participation in various student activities and organizations. To quote one law student, "People are looking for their niche."

ACADEMICS According to Dean Robert Bennett, Northwestern University School of Law seeks to provide the best legal education available at any law school in the country—without exception. It does this with the aim of training people for the practice of law, in the best tradition of the legal profession, as well as for positions of leadership in government, business, and the academic world.

How does a law school provide its students with the best legal education available? The single most important criterion of excellence, according to the dean, is the faculty. To claim excellence, the dean explains, a law faculty must be composed of respected scholars with a broad range of professional experience, interdisciplinary perspectives, and research interests. It must also embrace the teaching of the law as its primary responsibility. Northwestern University School of Law faculty members have published widely and are committed to teaching. Their knowledge and experience afford students the opportunity to examine the law in its broadest context.

Faculty at Northwestern employ a variety of instructional tools including seminars, clinics, and instruction in legal writing. In the first year, however, the case method of instruction is widely used. Under the case system, students prepare thoroughly before class using a casebook, a collection of actual court decisions. In class, Socratic dialogue between students and teacher tests students' understanding of the cases, the considerations that controlled the decisions, the implication for similar cases, and the relation to other decisions. While professors may depart from the interrogative role to provide legal background or give direction to the discussion, the essence of the case method is the collective probing and searching that develops and tempers students' own powers of reason.

CURRICULUM

First-Year Courses: Civil Procedure I, Contracts I, Criminal Law, Legal Writing, Property, Torts I, with an elective such as American Legal History, Application of Economics to Legal Institutions, International Law, Law and Economics, Law and Social Change, Law and the Social Order, or Legislation

Interesting Electives: AIDS and the Law, Civil Rights, Computers and the Law, Employment Discrimination, Post-Critical Perspectives on English Legal History, Entertainment Law, Federal Hazardous Waste Regulation, Feminist Legal Theory, Theory of Free Expression, Gender-Based Discrimination, Health Care Law, Intellectual Property, Japanese Law, Taxation of Foreign Income, White-Collar Criminal Prosecution and Defense

---

Commentary. Students described the curriculum at Northwestern as being fairly traditional. The theoretical component of a class is likely to center on public policy analysis of the consequences of a law or a judicial decision; and despite the presence of a couple of more radical thinkers on the faculty, students accept that the faculty is fairly conservative. As one student remarked approvingly,

"Northwestern just isn't about Critical Legal Studies." Those not interested in alternatives to law and economics suggested that a few of their classmates "grumble" about the mix of views on the faculty but expressed their own satisfaction with their teachers. On the other hand, students who voiced concern about the lack of ideological diversity among teachers observed that the faculty includes no representatives of the Critical Legal Studies movement and only one or two people who approach law from the perspective of feminist legal theory. This difference of opinion does not, however, seem to polarize the law school, and students reported that there is a free exchange of ideas and articles on the issue. The majority of students seem to be satisfied with the mix of viewpoints on the faculty, and the minority who argue for greater ideological diversity have taken some steps of their own, such as forming a student group devoted to Critical Legal Studies.

As for teaching styles, students reported that some faculty members use the Socratic method in a somewhat formal manner and that others do not. Some professors, for example, call on students in alphabetical order so that it is possible to know "when one's number—or rather letter—is up." In any event, the experience of most seemed to be that the use of the question-and-answer method was not at all "brutal." Students also expressed enthusiasm for the law school's clinical programs, which use "big firm" lawyers to supervise the work of students.

Students called the faculty "friendly" and "enormously accessible," but those terms, of course, mean different things to different people. One student explained that it is possible just to drop in on a professor without an appointment, though one must expect that it might be necessary to return at a more convenient time if the professor is busy. Another student especially emphasized that an advantage of the law school is that one does not have to be a "protege" to get the attention of a teacher. Students also mentioned opportunities for students to work with professors on individual research projects. Nonetheless, students said that contact with professors was likely to be limited to the academic setting and that students and professors were not likely to be found socializing outside of school.

ADMISSIONS | According to Susan Curnick, Assistant Dean for Admission and Financial Aid, the admissions process at Northwestern is conducted on a "rolling basis," beginning October 1 for the following academic year. Candidates who complete their applications by the February 1 filing deadline will receive a decision by April 15. Applications are reviewed by members of an admission committee consisting of six faculty members and the Assistant Dean for Admission and Financial Aid. Most applications are circulated among three or four committee members, and decisions are based on a consensus vote.

Assistant Dean Curnick acknowledges that the GPA and the LSAT are important factors in the admissions process at Northwestern but stresses that no predetermined weight is assigned to the quantitative measures. The assistant dean states categorically that "no mathematical formula is used to sort or to arrange applications into a hierarchy" and that "there are no minimum cut-offs for either the GPA or the LSAT." Rather, the committee seeks to "individualize" the admissions process: in evaluating a candidate's GPA, the committee takes account of course selection and grade trends; or again, if a candidate has taken the LSAT more than once, the committee considers all scores and the circumstances of each testing experience. Ultimately, says the assistant dean, admission decisions are based on a combination of factors including GPA, LSAT score, the personal statement, letters of recommendation, and any and all other information provided by the candidate.

ADMISSIONS DATA

	Class of 1993	Class of 1994
Applied	4,934	4,654
Median LSAT	N/A	N/A
Median GPA	N/A	N/A
Accepted	686	728
Median LSAT	N/A	N/A
Median GPA	N/A	N/A
Enrolled	201	201
Median LSAT	N/A	N/A
Median GPA	N/A	N/A

The Personal Statement. The personal statement, explains Assistant Dean Curnick, is an opportunity for each candidate to introduce himself or herself to the members of the admissions committee and to distinguish himself or herself from approximately 4,600 other candidates. The committee wants to learn about each candidate's personal and professional goals and how that candidate evaluates his or her personal experiences and obstacles overcome. A "well-written" personal statement can greatly assist the committee in getting to know the individual beyond the simple quantitative measures of the LSAT score and the GPA.

Recommendations. According to the assistant dean, a letter of recommendation should provide the admissions committee with an appraisal of a candidate's character, maturity, motivation, and scholarly ability. An "ideal" letter would come from an individual who can offer sound judgments about the prospective student's qualifications for the study of law. Effective letters typically come from a present or former instructor or, in the case of candidates who have been away from their graduate or undergraduate institution for some time, from employers—provided that a faculty recommendation is not available.

Interviews. The Office of Admission and Financial Aid does not conduct evaluative interviews as part of the admission decision process. The law school does, however, encourage applicants to visit the Office of Admission and Financial Aid to gather additional information about the school and the admissions process. If contacted beforehand, the staff can also arrange a tour of the law school.

Application Tips. The Admissions Office does not make available the median GPA or LSAT score of its student body. It has in some years, however, published graphs that summarize its admissions decisions in *The Official Guide to U.S. Law Schools.* From these graphs, it is possible to make an educated guess about the median GPA and LSAT score of the typical entering class at Northwestern. For the class of 1994 the median GPA was probably about 3.6 and the median LSAT about 44 (96.1 percentile).[1]

When asked about the characteristics of applications that are typically accepted or typically rejected, Assistant Dean Curnick again returned to the theme of regarding each candidate as an individual and stated, "With 16 years of law school admission experience, I have logged in excess of 60,000 application reviews and have seen it all; I continue, however, to be struck by the individuality presented by each and every application."

---

[1]In *The Official Guide to U.S. Law Schools* for 1991–1992, the graph for the applicant group for the 1990–1991 academic year at Northwestern divides applicants according to an Index, an artificial number that is calculated by a formula that uses GPAs and LSAT scores on the then-current 10-to-48 scale. For each range, the graph depicts the total number of applications received by the School of Law and the number that were accepted. The formula used for the applicant group for 1990–1991 was:

$$\text{Index} = (\text{GPA} \times 20) + (\text{LSAT} \times 1.25) - 52.5$$

The Admissions Office accepted 686 applications in that year, so using the graph, it is possible to conclude that the median index accepted was approximately 76.

By making the simplifying assumption that students at the median had LSAT scores and GPAs that were of equal weight in the formula, it is possible to calculate the approximate median LSAT score and GPA of those students. By subtracting 8 points from LSAT scores on the 10-to-48 scale and dividing that result by 10, one converts an LSAT

The assistant dean also noted that some candidates apparently think that their prospects for admission are automatically enhanced if they solicit a recommendation from a well-known public figure such as a judge—simply because that person is prominent, without regard to whether the recommender is really familiar with the candidate's abilities. That assumption, according to the assistant dean, is erroneous, for a recommendation from a person, famous or not, who has only a passing knowledge of the candidate is of limited value.

PLACEMENT | According to its director, Jeanne Kraft, the Career Counseling and Placement Office each year invites approximately 6,000 employers to participate in the Fall On-Campus Interview Program and a smaller number of employers to participate in the Winter/Spring Program. Anywhere from 350 to 450 employers come in a typical year. The Career Counseling and Placement Office also participates in a number of job fairs and consortia.

---

score to the same 0-to-4 scale that is usually used for GPAs. For example, an LSAT score of 48 would equal:

$$(48-8) \div 10 = 4.0$$

Thus, a perfect LSAT score would have the same value as the perfect GPA. In general then:

$$(LSAT-8) \div 10 = GPA \text{ equivalent}$$

Using this last equation in conjunction with the formula used by the Admissions Office to calculate an applicant's Index, it is possible to calculate the LSAT score and GPA of a student whose equally weighted measures generated the median value of 76. Using our GPA equivalent in place of GPA:

$$76 = [(LSAT-8) \div 10] \times 20] + (LSAT \times 1.25) - 52.5$$
$$76 = [(LSAT-8) \times 2] + 1.25LSAT - 52.5$$
$$76 = 2LSAT - 16 + 1.25LSAT - 52.5$$
$$144.5 = 3.25LSAT$$
$$LSAT = 44.5$$

Substituting this value for the LSAT score into the formula for calculating the Index to find the GPA:

$$76 = (GPA \times 20) + (44.5 \times 1.25) - 52.5$$
$$76 = 20GPA + 55.625 - 52.5$$
$$76 = 20GPA + 3.125$$
$$72.875 = 20GPA$$
$$GPA = 3.64$$

Thus, the medians for those accepted must have been approximately 3.64 for the GPA and 44.5 for the LSAT. By comparing these data for the candidates accepted by Northwestern to similar data published by comparable schools, it seems reasonable to conclude that the medians for those who finally enrolled in the class of 1994 were about 3.6 and 44 (or 96.1 percentile).

PLACEMENT DATA

	Class of 1991	Class of 1990
Placed at Graduation	90%	98%
Placed within 90 Days	91%	98%
U.S. Supreme Court Clerks	0	1
U.S. Appellate Court Clerks	7	16
U.S. District Court Clerks	12	11
State Appellate Court Clerks	4	2
Other Judicial Clerks	1	2
Median Starting Salary	$67,000	N/A[1]

[1]The average starting salary, including clerkships, for the class of 1990 was $59,918 and for the class of 1991 was $58,644. Given the similarity of those two numbers, one might infer that the median starting salary for the class of 1990 was not substantially different from that for the class of 1991.

In addition to producing handbooks on various topics, the Career Counseling and Placement Office offers individual counseling on the job placement process. The office also offers interviewing skills workshops with videotaped mock interviews and seminars featuring attorneys who speak on a variety of placement and professional issues. And the office also maintains thousands of individual employer files and an extensive resource library of books, directories, manuals, periodicals, and video and audio tapes.

Commentary.   Student comments regarding the placement office at Northwestern were not atypical of those heard generally about the law schools treated in this guidebook. For example, with respect to placement opportunities at large firms, students reported that the placement office "gets the job done," while some students expressed reservations about the placement office's record on alternative career paths such as government employment or public interest work. Students added, however, that the placement office seems to be responsive to this criticism and is working to strengthen its efforts in those areas. If there is something more to be said about the placement office at Northwestern, it is probably implicit in the many remarks that noted that "the information is there if you take advantage of it." In other words, the placement office coordinates the interviewing programs and maintains its resource materials, but it does not spoonfeed the law school's students. As one student, who thought the placement office could be a bit more aggressive, put it, "The placement office just does not operate as an employment agency."

A STUDENT SAMPLER | Typically, more than 40 percent of the 200 people in the first-year class are women and 20 percent are members of minority groups. Recently, the 600 students enrolled in the School of Law held undergraduate and graduate degrees in a variety of disciplines from more than 150 colleges and universities in the United States and from seven foreign institutions.

Members of recent incoming classes have included the holder of a patent for utilization of a digital counting technique to generate the true variable set point of an optimal start programmer; the music director for Interlochen International Music Camp; a staff reporter for the *New York Times*; a college professor; a diplomatic translator; and East Indian dancer; a professional clown; a bassoonist with the Chicago Symphony Orchestra; an advisor to the Minister of Urban Affairs and Housing of Bolivia; a surgeon; a football player with the Dallas Cowboys; the "Most Creative Forklift Operator" at the CBW Company in 1983; campaign workers for Gary Hart, Bob Dole, George Bush, and Michael Dukakis; football players from USC and Ohio State; experts in the martial arts; people proficient in one or more foreign languages; composers, novelists, film makers, and sculptors.

NOTEWORTHY GRADUATES

Ada Kepley, class of 1870, writer, teacher, preacher, WCTU Official, and first woman to receive a law degree in the U.S.; William Jennings Bryan, class of 1883, U.S. Secretary of State, 1913–1915, Presidential candidate 1886, 1900, 1908; Adlai E. Stevenson, class of 1926, Governor of Illinois, 1949–1950, Presidential candidate, 1952, 1956; U.S. Ambassador to the United Nations, 1961–1965; Arthur Goldberg, class of 1930, Secretary of Labor, 1961–1962, Associate Justice, U.S. Supreme Court, 1962–1965, U.S. Ambassador to the United Nations, 1965–1968; John Paul Stevens, class of 1947, Associate Justice, U.S. Supreme Court, 1975–; Dawn Clark Netsch, class of 1952, Illinois State Senator, 1972–1990, Illinois State Comptroller, 1990–, first woman to win a statewide constitutional executive office in Illinois; Harold Washington, class of 1952, Mayor of Chicago, 1983–1987

UNIVERSITY OF NOTRE DAME

NOTRE DAME LAW SCHOOL
P.O. BOX 959
NOTRE DAME, INDIANA 46556
(219) 631-6626

ADMISSIONS

Applied: 3,600

Accepted: N/A

Enrolled: 175

Median LSAT: 90th percentile

Median GPA: 3.45

STUDENT BODY

Total: 552

Women: 40%

Minorities: 17%

Average Age: 25

ACADEMIC RESOURCES

Library Volumes: 330,000

Computer Services: LEXIS, WEST-LAW, word processors

Student/Faculty Ratio: 20:1

FINANCES (ACADEMIC YEAR)

Tuition:	$15,230
Fees:	$ 27
Total:	$15,257

ENVIRONMENT | Notre Dame Law School is located at the entrance to the campus of the University of Notre Dame, a Holy Cross institution founded in 1842 by the Rev. Edward F. Sorin, CSC, a French priest of the Congregation of Holy Cross. The law school is a handsome building with the traditional Tudor/Gothic exterior. The original building was recently refurbished and a major addition was completed in 1987.

Many students live on campus in a newly constructed graduate residence. Off-campus housing is readily available at reasonable cost. Only a few of the available off-campus living accommodations are within walking distance of the school. In most cases, some form of transportation is a necessity; but students who have cars are cooperative, and bus service is available between the University and downtown South Bend. Unfurnished two-bedroom, all-electric apartments close to campus are available to married students in University Village. (Preference is given to those with children.)

Every opportunity is afforded to students to engage in healthful exercise. The indoor program is centered in the Rockne Memorial and the Edmund P. Joyce Athletic and Convocation Center and is devoted to the physical welfare of students and faculty of the University. The facilities include two swimming pools; courts for handball, racquetball, and squash; rooms for boxing and wrestling; a large gymnasium for basketball, indoor tennis, badminton, and other games; general apparatus rooms; and rooms for corrective work. Facilities for outdoor play include an 18-hole golf course, tennis courts, and large playing fields.

Commentary. The mailing address for the law school reads Notre Dame, Indiana; but the law school's host city is for all practical purposes South Bend, and the town of Notre Dame exists as a separate entity only by virtue of the fact that it has a separate post office. South Bend is not a particular favorite of most Notre Dame law students. One student said that South Bend receives a "fair amount of bad-mouthing" from law students. Indeed, the student suggested that the greatest advantage of South Bend is its proximity to Chicago—only 1.5 or 2 hours away, depending on to whom one is speaking. Another student reported that the weather might be considered by some to be an advantage to South Bend because "it is very conducive to studying"; that is, the weather that comes down from the Great Lakes is cold and either rainy or snowy for much of the year, so there is no good reason to go outdoors. One student, about to graduate, perhaps best summarized the prevailing attitude among law students by saying, "A lot of people in my class are looking forward to leaving South Bend."

Reports indicate that South Bend has a symphony, a small museum, and a few decent restaurants—but not much more in the way of cultural amenities. Student social life centers around the university, both the college and the law school. For those who enjoy fall football weekends and college basketball, the Notre Dame teams will obviously have much to offer; but for those who are not "rah, rah Irish fans," the "party element" of such events may be lacking. The university also puts on a "huge" basketball tournament each year, and law students participate. Students also have a "good time" in town, for example, on Wednesday nights when groups will meet at one or another favorite bar or pub. In sum, life in South Bend seems to be just what one might expect in a "mid-sized, midwestern college town."

The university campus was described as "just beautiful." The law school's physical plant has been renovated, but care was taken to preserve the architectural integrity of the building by integrating the renovations into its Tudor/Gothic style. The library was described as "comfortable," and one student explained that one of its advantages is that it offers many different study environments ranging from those floors below ground (said to be "dark and dingy" and eerily quiet) for those who prefer to study like moles, to a main reading room, to a second-floor balcony with windows overlooking the "quad." One complaint heard about the facility was the lack of a full-service student cafeteria in the law school building itself. There is a "Snack Hole," a name which one student suggested is particularly appropriate.

If South Bend did not receive rave reviews from students, then students do seem genuinely pleased with the atmosphere of the law school and said that the administration does a good job of maintaining a sense of an "integrated community." This sense of community manifests itself in a spirit of sharing and cooperation—though as one student remarked, every law school will have a few people who are "petty." For example, one teaching assistant maintains course outlines in a library carrel and invites anyone to copy them. The only restriction on this invitation is "to please put them back." Beyond a general sense of cooperation, the sense of an integrated community manifests itself in strong friendships. One student on the way to a pre-graduation banquet said, "There will be a lot of teary eyes at dinner tonight."

Finally, it should be noted that Notre Dame is a Catholic school. On Sunday evenings, for example, Mass is celebrated in the law school's student lounge. This connection with the Church, it was said, is "very important" to many students, though some non-Catholics may feel "left out" of this aspect of student life.

ACADEMICS According to Dean of the Law School David T. Link, Notre Dame Law School draws its inspiration from two ancient traditions. First, in the tradition of English and American common law, and a peculiarly American contribution to that tradition, it is a university law school. As a university law school it seeks to train intellectuals, not simply technicians. Second, the dean explains, it is a Catholic law school in the tradition of St. Thomas More, who was able to say that he was "the King's good servant, but God's first." The law school supports a Catholic intellectual and liturgical life and thus endeavors to foster its Catholic identity as more than mere background. However, the dean notes, people of all faith traditions, and of no faith tradition, are welcome and valued for the contributions they make to the discourse that is necessary to the intellectual inquiry.

Dean Link continues by explaining that the required program of study is aimed at providing students with the corollary to a liberal education. Coursework in a wide variety of areas of the law is required of each student, so that Notre Dame graduates are conversant with the fundamental principles which are the bases for law and with the various ways that the law mediates the relationship of individual persons to the state and to other persons.

Finally, the dean says that the Notre Dame program aims to educate men and women to become lawyers of extraordinary professional competence who possess a partisanship for justice, an ability to respond to human need, and compassion for their clients and colleagues. Therefore, the dean concludes, the program emphasizes not only skill but service, not only professional ethics but also social and moral ethics.

It should also be noted that Notre Dame is the only law school in the United States that offers study abroad for credit on both a summer school and a year-round basis. The year-abroad London Program has been in continuous operation since 1968. All courses and instruction are in strict conformity to the standards of the Association of American Law Schools and the American Bar Association. Each year, about 30 second-year students who have successfully completed all their first-year courses elect to study in England in course and seminar work under American and English teachers. Students may work as interns in the offices of British barristers or solicitors, or local American law firms, although no compensation and no courtroom participation are possible under British rules. Tuition is the same on the London campus as at the Notre Dame Law School. Classes normally begin in late September and end in June to coincide with the British academic calendar.

CURRICULUM

First-Year Courses: Torts I and II, Contracts I and II, Procedure I and II, Criminal Law, Criminal Procedure, Legal Research I and II (Moot Court), Introduction to Law and Ethics, Legal Writing, Property I

Interesting Electives: Admiralty Law, Agricultural Law, Energy Law, European Legal Institutions, Federal Civil Rights Statutes, Housing Law, Immigration Law, Law and Literature, Law and Religion, Military Law, Minerals Law, Public Lands Law, Regulation of Internal Union Affairs, Street Law, Topics in American Legal History, Water Law

---

In addition, since 1970 Notre Dame has operated a separate summer program for credit in London for its own students and students from other American law schools. The course offerings cover international, comparative, and American subjects.

Commentary. As noted in the commentary on "Environment," students endorsed the description provided by the dean of the connection between the law school and the Catholic Church. Additionally, it was reported, students are encouraged to think about ethical issues, and not just those that arise from the rules governing the behavior of lawyers, but the larger ones that surround the important legal problems of the day. Yet another influence of the Church can be found in the course listing: the law school tends to be a conservative institution. For example, there is no course in feminist jurisprudence, not as a consequence of benign neglect of that method of analysis, but because many of the faculty and administration are "hostile toward it."

The first-year experience at Notre Dame was said to be "usually, very hard, and very stressful." Professors may call on students at random and can be fairly "tough" in their use of the question-and-answer format. As one student said, "Many first-year professors just do not accept 'pass' very well." The second semester is particularly tough, with five courses (and finals) plus the moot court requirement. On the other hand, upperclass teaching assistants do what they can to help first-years through the experience by encouraging them to see each other as friends and not as adversaries and by encouraging group efforts such as cooperative research and writing.

Finally, students described the faculty as "very accessible." One student even said, "I wonder if it is a law school requirement that they be here all the time." A measure of the accessibility of teachers is that they make available to students their home telephone numbers. It was also said that teachers participate in the community life at the law school by attending Mass or participating in events such as the dean's Picnic.

ADMISSIONS

According to Anne C. Hamilton, Coordinator of Admissions, Registration, and Records, one of the most important considerations of the administration and faculty of the Notre Dame Law School is the selection of its students. The goal is to accept for the legal profession the best qualified students who are representative of all segments of American society. To achieve this goal, the dean has appointed an admissions committee to assist in the selection process. The committee is made up of members of the faculty with extensive experience as law school teachers and as practicing attorneys.

The admissions committee begins considering completed applications in December. Decisions are made on a "rolling basis," roughly in the order in which files become complete. If a candidate has multiple LSAT scores, the admissions committee looks at all of them but gives somewhat more weight to the average of all.

Ms. Hamilton explains that the admissions committee members and the dean make their decisions based on the "whole person" concept. To be sure, she acknowledges, academic ability, as reflected in LSAT and grade point averages, is important. The law school recognizes, however, that the real meaning of a GPA will vary with the quality of the institution attended, rigor of courses selected, and degree of grade inflation. The committee considers a broad array of elements in addition to the essential factors of LSAT and GPA, with a view toward assembling a diverse class while at the same time arriving at a fair appraisal of the individual applicant.

The "other elements" that are also taken into account, Ms. Hamilton explains, include the maturing effect on an individual of time spent away from formal education, a rising trend in academic performance versus solid but unexceptional work, financial pressure requiring employment during the undergraduate years, significant personal achievement in extracurricular work at college, postcollege work experiences or military duty, and unusual prior training which promises a significant contribution to the law school community.

Finally, Ms. Hamilton notes that the law school officials who are involved in the admissions process are mindful of the school's objective to produce lawyers who are both competent and compassionate. The admissions decisions are made more difficult because there are many highly qualified candidates; admissions decisions are inevitably the result of selecting a relatively small class from a large number of qualified applicants.

ADMISSIONS DATA

	Class of 1993	Class of 1994
Applied	3,147	3,600
Median LSAT	N/A	N/A
Median GPA	N/A	N/A
Accepted	N/A	N/A
Median LSAT	N/A	N/A
Median GPA	N/A	N/A
Enrolled	195	182
Median LSAT	90th percentile	90th percentile
Median GPA	3.4	3.45

The Personal Statement. Ms. Hamilton calls the personal statement a "significant part" of the admission decision. Candidates may want to use the opportunity to provide additional information about strengths, weaknesses, education, social and economic background, achievements, and goals—and why they feel that Notre Dame Law School will be in harmony with their profiles of themselves.

Recommendations. Two letters of recommendation are required. Ms. Hamilton says that letters of recommendation are important in providing information on academic and scholarly abilities. They should come from those who have known the applicant over a sufficient period of time to comment substantively. At least one of the letters, and preferably both, should address academic and scholarly abilities. The admissions committee recognizes that for those who have been out of school for a number of years, this may be a difficult task. In such cases, letters from employers or others with whom a candidate has worked closely can substitute.

Interviews. Prospective students are encouraged to visit the law school and to sit in on a class, but, Ms. Hamilton says, formal interviews are not a part of the admissions process.

Minority Applications. Ms. Hamilton reiterates that the goal of the Notre Dame Law School is to accept the students best qualified for the legal profession and that they be representative of all segments of American society. The committee fully reviews the files of ethnic minority students with a view toward assembling a diverse class and giving a fair review to each applicant. The legal profession, she notes, needs well-qualified members to serve the needs of all people.

Application Tips. Because Notre Dame uses a "rolling" admissions process, the fact that an application is completed early in the admission process may "improve" the chances of an applicant. Ms. Hamilton also encourages candidates to include recommendations (in *sealed* envelopes) with the application submission to ensure that the application is at that time complete in all respects save for the LSDAS report. Ms. Hamilton also says that the personal statement is examined for its writing as well as for its content.

PLACEMENT | According to Nancy A. Kommers, Placement Director, the placement office mails invitations to over 1,000 legal employers to attend the six-week on-campus recruiting program held each fall. In a typical year, more than 175 will attend. Additionally, the placement office posts notices of job openings and requests for resumes from several hundred other firms, corporations, government agencies, judges, and public interest agencies. A very important source of placement help at the law school, Ms. Kommers notes, is the Notre Dame Law Association—almost 5,000 alumni located all over the country. More than a hundred members of this network have volunteered their services as placement coordinators who act as resource people in their particular locales.

Ms. Kommers says that each year the placement office gives all students a revised placement manual and offers individualized assistance on resume prepa-

PLACEMENT DATA

	Class of 1991	Class of 1990
Placed at Graduation	82%	81%
Placed within 90 Days	N/A[1]	N/A[1]
U.S. Supreme Court Clerks	0	0
U.S. Appellate Court Clerks	5	2
U.S. District Court Clerks	2	6
State Appellate Court Clerks	3	1
Other Judicial Clerks	3	3
Median Starting Salary	$50,671	$53,177

[1]Placed at six months: 90% and 91% for 1991 and 1990, respectively.

ration. In addition, the placement office puts on seminars on a variety of topics including interviewing skills and different types of law practice. The office also videotapes practice interviews for students when requested to do so.

Commentary. Regarding the placement office at the law school, the students had both good news and bad news. First, the bad news: "It is a weak spot," and "A lot of people are dissatisfied with it." To be sure, students allowed that some of the dissatisfaction may reflect the current state of the job market, but even factoring out that influence, the prevailing sentiment seems to be that the placement office is not doing its job, and negative feelings focused in particular on its director. Now the good news: the present director is retiring soon, and Dean Link, who recently returned from a leave of absence, has made the improvement of the placement office a priority. Although students expect a transition period, they are nonetheless looking forward to the change "with anticipation."

A STUDENT SAMPLER The student body comes from every state in the Union—and a few students come from foreign countries. It is typical that at least 100 undergraduate schools are represented in each entering class of 170 students. About 60% of the students are men, 40% women, and 15 to 20% minorities. Notre Dame is a full-time day

169

school—there are very few commuting students. A recent graduating class took the bar exam in 37 states! Students include a German scholar, a Marine who served in Desert Storm, a former probation officer, and an MBA with a degree in engineering.

NOTEWORTHY GRADUATES

Anthony J. Early, President and CEO Long Island Lighting Company; Hon. John J. Kilkenny, U.S. Court of Appeals for the Ninth Circuit; Patricia O'Hara, VP Student Affairs, Professor of Law, Notre Dame; John Francis Sandner, Chairman of the Board, Chicago Mercantile Exchange; Hon. Ann Claire Williams, U.S. District Court, Northern District of Illinois

UNIVERSITY OF PENNSYLVANIA

LAW SCHOOL
3400 CHESTNUT STREET
PHILADELPHIA, PA 19104-6204
(215) 898-7400

ADMISSIONS (CLASS OF '94)

Applied: 4,492

Accepted: 934

Enrolled: 236

Median LSAT: 94.5 precentile

Median GPA: 3.62

STUDENT BODY

Total: 690

Women: 44%

Minorities: 27%

Average Age: 24

ACADEMIC RESOURCES

Library Volumes: 520,000

Computer Services: WESTLAW, LEXIS, word processors

Student/Faculty Ratio: 20:1

FINANCES (ACADEMIC YEAR)

Tuition:	$17,250
Fees:	$ 1,114
Books:	$ 690
Personal Expenses:	$10,036
Total:	$29,090

ENVIRONMENT The law school is part of the University of Pennsylvania, which has a total enrollment of 20,000 students—10,000 undergraduates and 10,000 graduate students. The university is located just west of downtown Philadelphia in an older residential community known as University City, and the downtown area is easily accessible by public transportation. University City, home also to Drexel University, the University City Science Center, and a number of teaching hospitals, is a heterogeneous community of interacting cultures and both period and modern architecture. Lewis Hall, the law school building, was completed in 1900, but it was thoroughly

171

renovated and enlarged during the 1960s. Work on a new library building is scheduled for completion in 1993. The small size of the law school's classes facilitates contact between students and professors.

Commentary. The fact that the law school is part of a major university means different things to different people. For some, it means the opportunity to take a joint degree or at least to cross-register for courses in a school such as Wharton. For others, the university is a source of entertainment or the arts. Most students remarked, however, that the day-to-day lives of law students at Penn proceed pretty much in isolation from the rest of the university.

Many students choose to live in the areas immediately surrounding the university, from which they walk or bicycle to school. The city of Philadelphia received a number of favorable comments for the availability of entertainment, spectator sports, and restaurants. Indeed, more than one student specifically said that Philadelphia is a very underrated city. As might be expected, students at the law school modify their behavior to take account of the urban environment, e.g., after dark they take the university-operated shuttle bus rather than the subway and don't walk around alone late at night. As a part of its orientation program, the law school advises entering first-year students on how to live safely in an urban area, and one student remarked that the campus police seem to be more effective than the city's force.

Beyond the generally heightened sense of awareness that goes with city living, some students pointed with concern to the neighborhood west of the university, calling it one of the "poorer" areas of Philadelphia. But the university itself creates a buffer zone between the law school and the edge of campus, regardless of one's opinion of what lies beyond. Additionally, first-year students work at the student-initiated and student-run Guild Food Stamp Clinic, and second- and third-year students commonly fulfill the law school's public service requirement by working in West Philadelphia. Some students, for example, teach high school students "street law" topics such as consumer rights and Constitutional limitations on police procedures.

As always, it is important not to make too much of such fears. One student from a self-described "privileged background" confessed to having arrived at the law school with grave concerns for personal safety. After fulfilling the *pro bono* requirement by working in West Philadelphia, this student described the experience as "extremely valuable." Ironically, then, what for this person had seemed to be a serious disadvantage of studying at Penn actually became one of its most significant advantages.

Questions about the physical plant do not occasion much controversy, though students acknowledged that quarters are a bit cramped and look forward to the opening of the new library facility in 1993. Paradoxically, however, some of the anticipated benefit of the expansion of the physical plant may be lost because the law school has been forced to increase the size of future entering classes to 270 in order to generate revenues to help pay for the construction project. Still, most students were excited about the new "state-of-the-art" library and wanted prospective students to be reassured that the law school is being greatly improved. They pointed out that the increase in students will be relatively minor and further speculated that the final result may actually be smaller first-year classes if the administration chooses to create three sections of 90 students.

Penn has a reputation for being a law school without the intense competition for grades found at other schools. Students at the law school who said that this was a factor in their decision to go to Penn confirmed that the reputation is deserved. Students theorized that the lack of intense competition can be traced to the confluence of several forces. First, since the school does have this reputation, it tends to attract students for whom a more cooperative environment is an advantage; and these people, as students, tend to interact cooperatively rather than competitively. Second, the law school is not as large as some others, and students do get to know most of their classmates. Finally, the law school grading system reduces the incentive to compete intensely for marks: approximately 20 percent of the class receive "excellent," 40 percent receive "good," and 40 percent receive "qualified." Most students get a mix of those grades over the years, and so wind up in the middle.

In general, students reported that people are willing to share notes and other information; and in particular, that second- and third-year students are very generous in giving outlines and information to first-year students. This in turn engenders a sense of obligation in those students, who will want to help their juniors in their turn, and so creates a system by which assistance is passed from one class to the next. Some of these outlines are "legendary" and have been around for seven or eight years. Although it is difficult to find a single word or phrase that summarizes the attitude at Penn, one student, who came to the law school with some worries about "Ivy League snobs," said that the students at Penn are "remarkable people who have done remarkable things but are pretty normal."

ACADEMICS | According to Dean Colin Diver, the University of Pennsylvania Law School stresses that "Education in the law is not confined to technical training, however sophisticated, and that the complete lawyer must be far more than a craftsman, however proficient." Elaborating on this idea, the dean emphasizes that a complete lawyer must be a "person of broad sympathies, social awareness, and intellectual interest" and must be cognizant of the "relationship between the law and other disciplines, such as philosophy, economics, and the political and behavioral sciences." A lawyer, in the dean's view, must be a reformer as well as a practitioner, alert for imperfections in the law and eager for its improvement. Consequently, the University of Pennsylvania Law School encourages its students to see legal issues in their broadest social and intellectual perspectives.

CURRICULUM

First-Year Courses: Civil Procedure (fall), Constitutional Law (spring), Contracts (fall), Criminal Law (fall), Labor Law (spring), Legal Writing (yearlong), Property (spring), Torts (fall), plus one spring elective from courses such as American Legal History, Economic Analysis of Law, Education Law and Policy, Equality and Inequality and the Role of Law and Lawyers, or Legal Reasoning.

Interesting Electives: Appellate Advocacy, Computers and the Law, Criminal Defense Clinic, The Debtor–Creditor Game, The First Amendment, Health Care Law and Policy, Intellectual Property, International Transfer of Technology, Introduction to Environmental Law, Introduction to Jewish Law, Mediation, Public Health Law in the Time of AIDS, Public Interest Lawyering, Representation of People with Disabilities, Small Business Clinic

The case method, featuring intensive analysis of appellate decisions, is widely used at Penn, especially in the first year. Yet even in the first year, and increasingly thereafter, some professors prefer to orient classroom discussion around problem situations, while still others make extensive use of materials drawn from related nonlegal disciplines. The school's high expectations for the varied careers of its graduates are reflected from the beginning of the three-year program rather than being reserved for a few electives in the upper years. In the first year the program includes traditional private law courses as well as courses whose primary focus is public law.

The first-year curriculum includes the five courses traditionally offered by most law schools, courses that focus primarily on concepts of private law such as ownership, contract, and liability for injury; but the law school has chosen to supplement those offerings with courses in constitutional law, economics of law, American legal history, and legal philosophy. Beyond the obvious effect of exposing first-year students to a wider range of legal concepts, this enriched curriculum has two distinct advantages. One, it exposes students to fundamental public law concepts such as due process, equal protection, and freedom of conscience. Two, it familiarizes students with basic lawmaking institutions other than the courts (to wit, legislatures and administrative agencies), and encourages study of the competence, limitations, and interrelation of all law-making institutions.

Commentary. If the University of Pennsylvania Law School has a guiding principle that shapes the experience of its students, it operates at a level below student consciousness. The dean's remarks regarding "Educational Philosophy" simply do not strike a responsive chord in the law school's students. Some professors assign additional readings in philosophy or economics; others do not. So the teaching has a theoretical element, but is not distinctly theoretical.

Two features of Penn's curriculum are noteworthy. First, as Dean Colin points out, the first-year curriculum offers some courses that are usually not available until the second year. Students had different opinions, however, about the value of the feature. Speaking from their third-year perspective, some students thought they had benefited from taking a course such as Labor Law in their first year; others thought that the timing probably did not make a great deal of difference in their education. Second, the law school requires a total of 70 hours of *pro bono* work of its students during their second and third years. Students take this responsibility seriously and speak favorably of the wide variety of options for fulfilling this obligation. As noted above, some choose to teach high school students in West Philadelphia; others donate their time to the *pro bono* projects of large firms in the city; still others do volunteer work for government agencies. The general feeling about the public service requirement is that while it obviously takes time away from other activities, it is not onerous and can even be interesting and enlightening.

Students said that first-year professors rely heavily on the Socratic method. Most people, however, seem to accept that this teaching method has advantages and don't take very strong exception to the styles of their professors. One student explained that some teachers call on students in rotation while others choose from the class at random. This particular student reported that one first-year professor, when away from the lectern and seating chart, had an annoying tendency to call on the same three or four people—annoying, because this student was one of them. Still, the student, who had more reason than most to object to the teaching method, simply chalked up the experience to the misfortune of having been assigned "the absolute worst seat in the house."

Most students regard the faculty as accessible and have specific experiences to back up that claim. One student, disappointed at a grade on an exam, visited the professor's office. The professor took the examination booklet and two days later returned it to the student with a full-page analysis of the weaknesses of the student's responses. Other students mentioned that faculty participate in social activities such as a Halloween party (in which those teachers who attended came in costume) and the annual "Law Revue." Another student mentioned that one first-year professor made it a point to be at a nearby coffee shop every Friday afternoon for students' questions.

If there is a generally held negative opinion about the academics of this law school, it focuses on the small number of minority teachers on the faculty: few black professors and no full-time Hispanic or Asian teachers. It is important to understand, however, that this is a "concern" of students and not an "issue" and does not seem to have divided the school.

ADMISSIONS | According to Assistant Dean of Admissions Glen Glenn, the law school has evolved a multifaceted admission process which is implemented by a faculty committee on admissions with the dean of admissions and staff. The assistant dean explains that "multifaceted" refers to the variety of factors that are taken into consideration when evaluating applications, including an applicant's personal statement, letters of recommendation, community service, prior employment, and extracurricular activities as well as LSAT score and GPA. Thus, the admissions process is designed to insure that each applicant is evaluated in terms of his or her academic promise and potential contribution to the intellectual life of the law school community. There is no minimum LSAT score or minimum GPA below which an applicant is automatically rejected, but an applicant can get a general feel for his or her chances of acceptance by comparing his or her LSAT score and GPA against the mean LSAT score and GPA for the law school's most recent entering class.

ADMISSIONS DATA

	Class of 1993	Class of 1994
Applied	4,879	4,492
Median LSAT	N/A	N/A
Median GPA	N/A	N/A
Accepted	1,013	934
Median LSAT	N/A	N/A
Median GPA	N/A	N/A
Enrolled	225	236
Median LSAT	94.5 percentile	94.5 percentile
Median GPA	3.60	3.62

The Personal Statement. The personal statement is an essential part of the application file, and in borderline cases it can be of immense importance. The personal statement is used to provide the personal information needed to flesh out an applicant's file.

Recommendations. Letters of recommendation are an "integral part" of decision-making at Penn, and two letters of recommendation are required. An "ideal" letter of recommendation comes from someone who can attest to an applicant's potential to be a successful law student. Thus, recommendations from faculty members familiar with the applicant's analytical skills, reasoning ability, and writing talent are particularly valuable. When it is not possible to obtain recommendations from faculty members, an applicant's employer may prove a suitable substitute.

Personal Interviews. Personal interviews are not used by Penn as a criterion of admission and are, therefore, not required. Nevertheless, a person considering a legal education may find a visit to the law school helpful, and such visits may be arranged through the office of admissions.

Minority Applications. The University of Pennsylvania Law School has a commitment to increase the diversity of the student body by having a strong minority presence in the law school. Consistent with this commitment, minority status is another element considered in the law school admissions process. The files of minority applicants, like the files of the so-called majority applicants, are read by an admissions professional and may be presented to the faculty committee.

Application Tips. When asked to specify what sort of "significant" accomplishments are typical of applicants who are accepted by Penn, Dean Glenn mentioned the following: president of the debate club, editor of the school paper, member of Phi Beta Kappa (or other honors society), leadership role in student government, public service activities such as Big Brother/Big Sister or volunteering with the homeless, extensive involvement in collegiate sports, or successful work experience. It is important to note that the dean used words such as "president," "editor," "extensive," and "successful." It is not enough just to have a long list of activities; the admissions committee is looking for evidence of serious commitment and serious involvement. Most unsuccessful applicants, the dean reported, present a background of limited extracurricular activities.

PLACEMENT The Career Planning and Placement Office of the law school sends invitations to all employers who have had any contact with the law school in the last three years. If an employer does not respond positively, the office contacts the employer by telephone to encourage a campus visit. If a significant number of students are interested in a particular geographic area where Penn graduates haven't typically found employment in the past, the office targets employers in that area, informing them that Penn students would like to work there and providing information about the law school.

The office does a great deal of one-on-one interview training using practice interviews and videotape, and lawyers from the community who are involved in

PLACEMENT DATA

	Class of 1991	Class of 1990
Placed at Graduation	97.4%	97.4%
Placed within 90 Days	N/A	N/A
U.S. Supreme Court Clerkships	—	—
U.S. Appellate Court Clerkships	3[1]	8
U.S. District Court Clerkships	21	21
State Court Clerkships	5	3
Other Judicial Clerks	5	1
Median Starting Salary	$65,000	$64,600

[1]Perhaps an aberration, as class of 1992 had 8.

hiring come in to speak to students about interviewing. The staff also offers advice on specific problems such as handling weak grades, call-back interviews, and interviews for clerkships or public service jobs.

Commentary.   Students seem generally well satisfied with the efforts of the Career Planning and Placement Office, particularly as regards placement at large law firms. In fact, 70 to 80 percent of a typical graduating class ends up in private practice, compared with only 2 to 4 percent in business and industry and only 1 to 3 percent in public interest law. Several students expressed the hope that more could be done to find positions for students in areas other than private law firms and specifically mentioned corporations, clerkships, and public interest activities. These students recognized, however, that there are some inherent limitations on what a placement office can do or should be expected to try.

A STUDENT SAMPLER   A recent entering class at Penn included students from 25 states and five foreign countries and from 93 undergraduate institutions. Twenty-five percent were members of minority groups (26 blacks, 14 Hispanics, 17 Asian-Americans, and one Native American), and 43 percent were women. Forty-six percent did not come directly from undergraduate school, and 8 percent held academic degrees beyond the bachelor's degree. Of the entire student body that year, 26 students came from California, 35 from Connecticut, 11 from the District of Columbia, 40 from Florida, 25 from Illinois, 24 from Maryland, 39 from Massachusetts, 98 from New Jersey, 187 from New York, and 157 from Pennsylvania.

Interesting personalities at the law school usually include people with professional experience in medicine, music, teaching, architecture, police work, business, accounting, social work, nursing, government, journalism, finance, and international relations. Many Penn students have served as political interns to officeholders on local, state, and national levels. Still others have served in the military—including some who were on active duty in Desert Storm—while yet others are peace activists.

The majority of Penn graduates go into private practice (typically 70 to 80 percent), with a substantial number (13 to 18 percent) accepting judicial clerkships. Most of the rest take positions in business and industry (3 to 6 percent), in government (2 to 4 percent), or in a public interest area (1 to 3 percent).

NOTEWORTHY GRADUATES

Sudharm Bhadrakom, Chief Justice, Supreme Court of Thailand; Charles A. Heimbold, Jr., President, Bristol-Meyers Squibb Co.; Phyllis Kravitch, Circuit Judge, U.S. Court of Appeals for the 11th Circuit; Gerald M. Levin, Co-Chairman, Time-Warner, Inc.; Gail Lione, General Counsel, *U.S. News and World Report*; A. Raymond Randolph, Jr., Circuit Judge, U.S. Court of Appeals for the District of Columbia Circuit; Robert N. C. Nix, Jr., Chief Justice, Supreme Court of Pennsylvania; Dolores K. Sloviter, Chief Judge, U.S. Court of Appeals, Third Circuit.

179

UNIVERSITY OF SOUTHERN CALIFORNIA

THE LAW CENTER
UNIVERSITY PARK
LOS ANGELES, CA 90089
(213) 740-7331

ADMISSIONS

Applied: 4,010

Accepted: 754

Enrolled: 184

Median LSAT: 94.5 percentile

Median GPA: 3.4

STUDENT BODY

Total: 570

Women: 40%

Minorities: 25%

Average Age: N/A

ACADEMIC RESOURCES

Library Volumes: 330,000

Computer Services: LEXIS, WEST-LAW, word processors

Student/Faculty Ratio: 19:1

FINANCES (ACADEMIC YEAR)

Tuition:	$17,430
Housing and Food:	$ 7,200
Books, Personal:	$ 4,470
Total:	$29,100

ENVIRONMENT Los Angeles, the second largest city in the United States, spreads out across 70 square miles and is bounded on the north by the snowy peaks of the San Gabriel range and by the Pacific Ocean to the south and west. Much of the architecture and many of the place names, such as Palos Verdes, Encino, and San Fernando, bear witness to the city's Spanish heritage. Los Angeles is a vital center of industry, commerce, international trade, business, and the arts. The city is, of course, well known for the entertainment industry, but it also occupies a leadership position in technology and precision manufacturing. Moreover, Los Angeles has grown into an international business center and is now the United States' major gateway to the Pacific Rim. The National Planning Association has predicted that in the period from 1985 to 2010, Los Angeles will experience the greatest growth in job opportunities of any city in the nation. Finally, the city offers a great variety of cultural and entertainment attractions, and many of the city's theaters, museums, and galleries are in the downtown area and are easily accessible from USC. Notable among these are the Los Angeles Music Center, with its trio of theaters rising from a plaza animated by fountains, mirror pools, and sculpture, and the Museum of Contemporary Art (MOCA) with its distinctive postmodern architecture and sunlit gallery spaces.

USC, with a total enrollment exceeding 30,000, is located in an urban setting—about three miles south of the Los Angeles Civic Center—and is easily accessible by freeway from all outlying areas. The University Park campus is a 150-acre park with green spaces, landscaping, fountains, and sculpture, and is closed to automobile traffic. Adjacent to the campus is University Village, a contemporary shopping center with restaurants, banks, specialty stores, and a market; to the south is Exposition Park with its complex of museums.

The USC Law Center occupies the five-level, 150,000-square-foot Elvon and Mable Musick Building, which has recently been remodeled and expanded. USC is a *small* school and seeks to be a true academic community in which faculty and students are engaged in a common quest for education and new understanding.

Commentary. Most students interviewed gave the City of Los Angeles a favorable review and mentioned generally that the city offers a variety of cultural and other activities. Representative comments were "There is a lot to do here," "L.A. has a lot going for it," and "It offers endless choices." Most interviewees never named specific cultural institutions, clubs, or restaurants to illustrate these claims, but perhaps that is because the possibilities seem endless. Additionally, almost everyone interviewed mentioned Southern California's famed climate with its mild temperatures and sunny days; some students, for the most part those not from Los Angeles, made note of L.A.'s smog. Those who were in a position to make the judgment were quick to point out that Los Angeles is unique among American cities. As one student phrased it, "Los Angeles is not a city for people who like to walk." It was explained that the metropolitan area is actually many "sub-cities" with names such as Century City, Santa Monica, and Pasadena, all connected by freeways. A car, therefore, is a virtual necessity, and people who live in Los Angeles do a lot of driving.

While Los Angeles was generally described in favorable terms, that part of the city immediately around the University of Southern California campus was described specifically in unflattering phrases such as "not the nicest part of the city," "a bad part of town," "unsafe," and even "a ghetto," "dangerous," and "a high crime area." The campus is very near—about 20 blocks from—the center

181

of the recent disturbances in Los Angeles, though the campus was not directly involved in the violence. Few law students live in the area, and commuters reportedly make it a point "to get in and out of the area as quickly as possible."

Before one prematurely strikes USC from a list of law schools to be considered, however, it is important to remember that the descriptions included in the preceding paragraph were all given by people currently enrolled at the USC Law Center! And, as one student noted, the law center's students were not drafted by USC nor assigned there by lottery; they *chose* to study law at USC. The seeming paradox can be resolved—and the negative remarks placed into context and given their proper weight—by adding further detail to the description of the campus. Students explained that the USC campus is a clearly defined enclave with security personnel at entrances to the campus. Further, there is a heightened sense on campus of the need to exercise caution. One manifestation of that heightened sense is the university-operated shuttle that ferries students to their cars after dark and is reportedly used even by male students. By exercising such precautions, students are able to study comfortably at the law center—even late at night during exam periods. Thus, on balance, while no one seemed to be particularly pleased with the location of the law center, not one student interviewed suggested that someone ought to choose another law school over USC simply because of its location.

As for the University's campus, students allowed that it is indeed beautiful. (One student even observed somewhat derisively, "The University obviously spends a lot of money to plant flowers.") Students also mentioned the Lyons Center, described by one student as "a great athletic facility." As for the law center specifically, its building was rated as "very good," "excellent," and "pretty workable." The single building is fairly self-contained and its facilities and amenities were described in favorable terms. Certainly the worst complaints pertained to its concrete exterior (one student called the building a "fortress") and to some problems of climate control inside the classrooms (a couple of students mentioned "freezing temperatures"), but these are comments that really don't touch the essence of the Law Center as an institution. And students mentioned with approval a recent expansion and remodeling of the building.

The class size at the law center is indeed small, and students evidently get to know their classmates—at least in the academic setting. Students also indicated that the atmosphere at the law center is not one of intense competition and further, that outlines and similar resources are freely shared. If there is a single way of describing the atmosphere at the law center, it is perhaps found in the words of a student who described classmates as "fair players—the kind of people you wouldn't mind playing poker with." It was also reported that this sense of civility infuses debates over issues such as diversity that at other law schools may be divisive.

While the small size of the student body clearly influences the quality of life at the law center, reports also suggest that the school's location is a factor at least equally important. In the first place, while the "commuter" mentality does

182

not prevent students from making friends, it is an impediment to the development of a general sense of a law school community. As one student put it, "There is no overarching sense of 'we all.'" Rather, friendships form around common interests or according to age or marital status. And when someone organizes a Thursday night "Bar Review," in which students converge on a designated pub, only those who reside in the part of L.A. in which the pub is located are likely to attend.

ACADEMICS | Dean Scott H. Bice begins the discussion of the academic philosophy of the USC Law Center by noting that all leading American law schools share common attributes: highly regarded faculty, talented and motivated students, solid curricula, sufficient financial resources, and proven placement records. These are attributes, says the dean, to which the law center, as one of the nation's leading law schools, can lay claim; but, Dean Bice continues, USC is distinguished from other law schools by three characteristics: its size, its location, and the orientation of its curriculum and instructional program.

First, the dean states that USC is a small law school and seeks aggressively to capture the positive benefits of its size. Second, he notes that for those who are drawn to the diversity, cultural life, and employment opportunities that a major city can provide, Los Angeles is among the very best in the world. Third, the dean points to the Law Center's interdisciplinary approach to legal education.

Elaborating on this third idea, Dean Bice points out that the law center has a high percentage of faculty who have experience in both law and other disciplines, such as philosophy, economics, religion, and psychology. Beyond the personal backgrounds of the individual faculty members, the dean explains that the orientation of the curriculum results from the faculty's conviction that legal education must explore the social context in which laws are formed and applied, that is, from a conviction that one cannot fully understand law unless one studies the philosophical, technological, economic, political, historical, and psychological forces that shape legal decision-makers and their actions. For example, the dean continues, the first-year course in torts brings materials from welfare economics and moral philosophy to bear on issues of compensation for personal injury, and the course in first-year criminal law uses materials from psychology and the philosophy of science to illuminate discussions of criminal responsibility.

Finally, the dean adds that good academic institutions are dynamic and adapt their programs and activities to meet important trends. The dean notes that, in response to the increasing need for continued training in rapidly changing or emerging areas of law, the law center sponsors an extensive program of continuing education for lawyers and that, in recognition of the increasing internationalization of business, it has established formal faculty exchanges with law schools in other countries.

CURRICULUM

First-Year Courses: Constitutional Law; Contracts; Criminal Law; Law, Language, and Ethics; Introduction to Lawyering Skills; Legal Research; Civil Procedure; Property; Torts

Interesting Electives: Bioethics; The Child in the Legal System; Environmental Law and Policy; Immigration Law; Insurance; International Law; Land Use Controls; Law and Aging; Law and Medicine; Legal Aspects of Motion Picture Production; Patent Law; Psychoanalysis, Psychiatry, and Law; Regulation of Broadcasting; U.S.-Japan Business Transactions; Women and the Law

Commentary. As noted in the previous commentary, student remarks echoed those of Dean Bice regarding the small class size at the law center and, in both positive and negative terms, the school's location as well. The third element of the dean's description, to wit, the orientation of the curriculum, did not strike a responsive chord in the student body. The fact that faculty members hold degrees other than the J.D. or that the law center has established a faculty exchange program did not seem to be particularly important to students. Even when pressed, students found it difficult to point to any aspect of the curriculum that might distinguish USC from other law schools. As one student said, "There is nothing particularly unique about the curriculum; it just has a nice balance between topics such as civil rights and constitutional law and more pragmatic courses such as those on real estate and finance."

One component of the education at the law center that does seem to be very important to students is the policy of encouraging internships and externships. Indeed, so many positions are available that everyone has an opportunity to participate, even those who draw very unfavorable numbers in the assignment lottery, according to a student who had "the very worst number in the entire school" and yet found a very exciting internship that included several court appearances. The program offers a variety of opportunities, including positions with judges, district attorneys, and public defenders. Reports also mentioned the availability of considerable *pro bono* work and further noted that the County Bar awards a "Certificate of Merit" to students who do such work. Finally, students also mentioned that the law center has a strong Public Interest Law Foundation. Each year, "PILF" holds a fund-raising auction to which professors contribute. Recent items donated by professors included dinner for four at the professor's home and a promise "to wash the dirtiest car" anyone could find. The money raised by the auction goes to supplement the summer incomes of students who take relatively lower-paying jobs in the public interest sector.

Students indicated that first-year classes incorporate to a greater or lesser extent the Socratic method and that teachers have individual styles. A couple of professors, it was said, call randomly on students for summaries and analyses, but others do so systematically, e.g., according to the seating arrangement. And the rigor of the question-and-answer format too is a matter of individual style. Students said that one or two professors emulate the "Kingsfield" character in the movie *The Paper Chase* but explained that most do not. As one interviewee put it, "When a student founders, a professor is more likely to throw a lifeline than an anchor."

Finally, reports indicated that students at the law center are fairly satisfied with the accessibility of the faculty. They noted that most teachers remain after class, perhaps even as long as half an hour, in order to answer questions. Additionally, students feel comfortable dropping in on most professors without regard to posted office hours and without an appointment. As one might expect, there is some variation in accessibility. At the extremes, one professor was said to be "endlessly available," while another, it was reported, specifically announces at the beginning of the semester that access is severely restricted. Overall, one student rated faculty accessibility at the law center "a six or a seven on a scale of 10."

ADMISSIONS | According to Director of Admissions Diana Thompson, USC is a small school, and admission is, therefore, selective. In recent years, Ms. Thompson notes, the law center has received over 4,000 applications for the 185 to 195 places in the entering class.

As for the mechanics of the decision-making process, Ms. Thompson explains that applications are read by the Director of Admissions, the Associate Dean, and members of the Admissions and Financial Aid Committees. The committee reads all files thoroughly and considers each application on an individual basis. Multiple LSAT scores are automatically averaged. If, however, an applicant believes the performance on any particular LSAT was impaired by unusual circumstances (illness, interruptions, disturbances, etc.), the applicant should call this fact to the committee's attention. In the case of illness, a verifying letter from a physician is required. The law center does not use a rolling admissions process.

Describing the criteria used in the decision-making process, Ms. Thompson states that the admission committee's primary concern is with the applicant's potential as a student of law and that applicants with strong academic records and high test scores have the best chance of gaining admission. In reviewing applicant files, the committee focuses on the student's college grades, academic major, selection of courses, and significant scholarly achievements. The admissions committee also looks for qualities that will enhance the diversity of the student body and enrich the law center's educational environment. An applicant is regarded as having such potential if he or she has characteristics that would not ordinarily be well represented in the law center student body. Such characteristics

185

include geographic background, race, ethnic group, sexual orientation, special educational experience, extracurricular achievement (including community service), work experience, physical characteristics (disability or prowess), economic disadvantage, age, and career goals. Applicants who wish to have these characteristics considered should provide detailed written information about their background and experience.

ADMISSIONS DATA

	Class of 1993	Class of 1994
Applied	3,184	4,010
Median LSAT	N/A	N/A
Median GPA	N/A	N/A
Accepted	673	754
Median LSAT	94.5 percentile	94.5 percentile
Median GPA	3.5	3.4
Enrolled	215	184
Median LSAT	94.5 percentile	94.5 percentile
Median GPA	3.4	3.4

The Personal Statement.   A personal statement is required. Applicants may discuss their academic history, events which led to the decision to study law, significant experiences, or the ways in which the applicant could contribute to the diversity of the law center student body. Ms. Thompson calls the personal statement a "significant part" of any application and adds that it may be "particularly important if an applicant's numerical predictors are right at the averages." In such case, Ms. Thompson explains, the personal statement may help to set the applicant apart from hundreds of other applicants with similar predictors.

Recommendations.   Ms. Thompson points out that each applicant must provide at least one letter of recommendation, preferably academic in nature. If an academic recommendation is not available, an employer's recommendation which focuses on academic skills (reading, writing, analytical ability) may be substituted.

Interviews. Evaluative interviews are not granted as part of the application process.

Minority Applications. Ms. Thompson notes that it is a primary goal of the admissions committee to recruit and enroll as diverse a class as possible while maintaining the highest academic standards possible. Thirty-one percent of the most recent entering class are minority students. Ms. Thompson states that the diversity of the law center's student body is the result of many years of aggressive affirmative action effort.

Application Tips. According to Ms. Thompson, no single program of study is favored by the admissions committee, but she adds that courses that help to develop writing skills and analytic ability and courses that require active participation in classroom dialogue and intensely researched written projects are particularly valuable. Regarding recommendations, Ms. Thompson explains that while recommendations that are not academic may be helpful, academic recommendations carry the greatest weight because they supply more specific information and insight into the applicant's academic ability. Finally, readers should note that the statement of USC's policy with regard to the diversity of its student body includes the characteristic "sexual orientation." A representative of the Gay and Lesbian Law Union at the law center said that USC was one of the first law schools (if not the first) to include sexual orientation as a characteristic of a diverse student body.

PLACEMENT | According to Lori Nelson, Director of the Career Services Offices, each year several hundred recruiters from private firms, government agencies, and corporations come to the law center campus to interview students for employment. Hundreds of additional employers solicit applications from law center students through the Career Services Office. The Career Services Office does major mailings to employers twice a year. The Director of Career Services makes several trips annually to regions of the country in which students have expressed an interest in finding employment. Additionally, the director meets with representatives of federal agencies in Washington, D.C., and attends major career fairs such as the National Association for Public Interest Law. The Career Services Office offers individual counseling to students and presents numerous career-related programs throughout the year.

The Law Center is committed to encouraging students to consider public interest employment. The school maintains a loan repayment assistance program for graduates who follow public interest careers, and it also has a popular student-

PLACEMENT DATA

	Class of 1991	Class of 1990
Placed at Graduation	88%	98%
Placed within 90 Days	88%	98%
U.S. Supreme Court Clerks	0	0
U.S. Appellate Court Clerks	0	0
U.S. District Court Clerks	13	11
State Supreme Court Clerks	2	0
Other Judicial Clerks	2	0
Median Starting Salary	$65,750	$66,934

initiated Public Interest Law Foundation that provides funding for summer employment in public interest offices throughout the country to USC law students and makes available a post-graduate Fellowship to assist recent Law Center graduates beginning careers in public interest law.

Commentary. Reports from the law center suggest that students there think that "the placement office is doing just about everything a placement office can do" to help them find positions. For those whose search efforts had met with success, that description was a favorable review of the placement office; for those still looking for a position, that description was an expression of dissatisfaction—not so much with the placement office as with the state of the job market. In fact, students, when they were asked about the operation of the law center's placement office, often focused on its director, specifically mentioning Lori Nelson by name; and the descriptions were uniformly positive and included remarks such as "very accessible," "friendly," and "attentive to individual needs."

A STUDENT SAMPLER The student body at the law center includes people who have had successful careers in business, public service, journalism, publishing, and real estate. Others have played professional sports, worked in government, served in the armed forces, raised families of their own, or pursued careers in the entertainment industry.

188

NOTEWORTHY GRADUATES

Hon. Candace Cooper, President, California Judges Association; Mr. Larry Flax, co-owner and President, "California Pizza Kitchen"; Ms. Katherine Krause, former Executive Director, Los Angeles Legal Aid; Hon. Malcolm Lucas, Chief Justice, Supreme Court of California; Ms. Aulana Peters, former Commissioner of the Securities and Exchange Commission; Mr. Frank Rothman, former CEO and President, MGM/UA; Mr. Abraham Somer, attorney to Rolling Stones and Rod Stewart; Joseph Wapner, Judge, "The People's Court"

STANFORD UNIVERSITY

STANFORD LAW SCHOOL
CROWN QUADRANGLE
STANFORD, CALIFORNIA 94305
(415) 723-2465

ADMISSIONS

Applied: 6,006

Accepted: 471

Enrolled: 180

Median LSAT: 96.1 percentile

Median GPA: 3.64

STUDENT BODY

Total: 539

Women: 43%

Minorities: 47%

Average Age: 24.8

ACADEMIC RESOURCES

Library Volumes: 337,000

Computer Services: LEXIS, WEST-LAW, word processors

Student/Faculty Ratio: 12.5:1

FINANCES (ACADEMIC YEAR)

Tuition:	$14,894
Housing and Food:	$ 6,200
Books:	$ 870
Miscellaneous:	$ 1,720
Total:	$23,684

ENVIRONMENT Stanford University, a private institution located adjacent to Palo Alto (abon ut 35 miles south of San Francisco), has a student body of approximately 13,000, about half of whom are graduate students. The 8,400-acre campus, situated at the foot of the Santa Cruz mountains, provides an outdoor environment. The climate is moderate, undergoing full seasonal changes, but within a temperature range that is seldom below freezing or above 80 degrees.

Palo Alto and its environs are rich in cultural and recreational opportunities, many of which are accessible by foot, bicycle, motor scooter, or campus bus ser-

190

vice. Southern Pacific commuter trains also provide service to San Francisco from two railroad stations near campus; the trip takes about 50 minutes. A car, however, is a considerable convenience for shopping and for longer trips.

The law school is housed at the center of the university campus in Crown Quadrangle, a modern complex built in 1975 specifically for legal education. The size of the entering class is limited to approximately 175 students in order to preserve a personal educational environment and ensure opportunities for individualized instruction.

Commentary. By all reports, the geographical location and setting of Stanford University are significant factors in the decisions of many students to study at the law school. Some students mentioned the school's proximity to San Francisco with its night-life and professional sports teams. Others cited the availability of outdoor recreational activities such as hiking, camping, and mountain biking. Still others reeled off lists of facilities available at the university: golf course, riding stable, swimming pools, tennis courts, gymnasiums. Some law students follow the university's football and basketball teams, and there is a group of avid fans of the women's volleyball team. As one student said, "It's like going off to summer camp for three years."

This is not to say, of course, that Stanford students do not work hard. The student quoted in the preceding paragraph was referring to the *physical* setting of the school. The proper balance between study and recreation was perhaps best summarized by another student who quipped, "It's not so bad studying torts, if you can do it while sitting outside in the sun."

Students said that all of life's necessities and even luxuries are readily available. Palo Alto, though reported to be a bit "pricey," still offers a variety of restaurants, including beer and burger pubs as well as formal dining. The Stanford Shopping Center, adjacent to the campus, has a Neiman Marcus and a Gap as well as a Macy's. And while it may be true that a car is a convenience, students who live on campus, as many first-year students do, said that it is also possible to do quite well with a bicycle or just by walking. Those who live off-campus, however, seemed to regard a car as a necessity.

The physical plant consists of two buildings connected by a "Law Lounge," a gallery with a snack bar that is frequented by faculty as well as students; and while questions about the location and setting of the university generate enthusiastic responses, questions about the law school facility do not elicit strong reactions. Typical comments are "fairly modern," "standard classrooms," "not particularly lovely," "comfortable," and "library carrels always available." Indeed, students seemed sometimes to be almost puzzled by questions about the physical plant, as though they could not quite grasp why anyone would bother to ask. That fact itself suggests that the facility, if "not particularly lovely," does everything expected of it without calling attention to itself—like a pair of comfortable shoes.

If students at Stanford don't have very strong opinions about the physical plant, most do have strong, very positive feelings about their classmates. Students described one another as "very cooperative," "friendly," and "helpful." It was reported, for example, that students freely share outlines with one another with little regard for the weight of an individual's contribution to the joint project. It was also said that even during the heat of the recruiting season, students compare notes about their interviews and that there is no feeling that it is necessary "to beat someone else out of a job." Additionally, during the orientation period for first-year students, faculty members attempt to instill a "cooperative mentality."

On the other hand, some students, while not willing to contradict these specific statements, worried that the unfavorable job market is putting a strain on the fabric of cooperation and that some of their classmates are becoming overly concerned about grades. They reported, for example, that in the past year one or two outlines have been "lost" and that there is a growing debate over the law school's grading policies. Even so, the concern was not so much that Stanford has become a pressure cooker as that its cooperative atmosphere is threatened. And every student seemed to want to keep the law school free of destructive competition.

ACADEMICS | According to Dean of the Law School Paul Brest, Stanford is distinguished by four characteristics. First, the law school offers an unusual variety of curricular choices, study programs, and degree options, a variety that allows students to shape their legal educations to their own intellectual interests and career plans. While students do receive a broad liberal education in the law, they may also pursue advanced work to acquire the sophistication necessary for a well-trained lawyer or policy maker in a particular field.

Second, Stanford emphasizes less the static law of any particular time and more the dynamics of the law and legal process; less the learning of legal rules and more the inquiry into why particular rules exist and how they might be improved; less the accumulation of a body of existing knowledge and more the development of a framework for analysis; less answers to particular problems and more the development of modes of problem solving.

Third, Stanford strives to prepare lawyers who will add significant value to society—who will enter the profession with the attitudes and skills of facilitators and problem-solvers rather than problem-makers.

Fourth, the dean adds that a lawyer's specialized knowledge and power entails special obligations to clients, adversaries, and society at large. Thus, pervading the Stanford curriculum is a systematic undertaking to introduce students to the actualities and aspirations of the legal profession and requiring them to address important problems of legal ethics. Stanford has pioneered in the development of the so-called "pervasive" method, in which issues of legal ethics and

---

CURRICULUM

First-Year Courses: Introduction to Courts and Cases (orientation), Civil Procedure (fall), Constitutional Law (spring), Contracts (fall), Criminal Law (fall), Property (spring), Torts (fall), Research and Legal Writing (yearlong), plus at least two electives from a prescribed list, e.g., Economics, Finance Theory, History of American Law, and Jurisprudence

Interesting Electives: Art and the Law, Artificial Intelligence and Legal Reasoning, Child Abuse and Neglect, Conflict Resolution in School Cultures, Corporate Governance and Social Responsibility, Eastern European Labor Relations, Health Law and Policy, Law and High Technology, Law in the Pacific Community, National Security Law, Politics of Procedure, Protection of Personality, Sexual Identity and the Law, Tobacco in American Society, Venture Capital and Start-Up Companies, Water Law

---

professionalism are taught contextually through integration into standard substantive courses.

Commentary.　Students confirmed that the four features described by Dean Brest do help to shape the learning experience at Stanford. Classes include a definite theoretical component, perhaps too much theory for the tastes of some students, but then other students commented favorably on clinical programs taught by practitioners. Students also pointed out that it is possible to pursue "concentrations" in areas such as law and business, law and social change, and law and the environment, though a "track" is not required. Additionally, students reported that ethical issues are likely to crop up in any class, thus providing the contextual study of ethics mentioned by the dean. Finally, students also acknowledged that there is considerable emphasis on strategies of negotiation and mediation, again, perhaps too much emphasis according to some students.

As for teaching styles, students made a point of saying that the "old Socratic method is dead at Stanford." To be sure, professors still pose questions and expect student answers, but participation in the classroom discussion is largely voluntary and, students reported, usually forthcoming. To take some of the dread out of the method, some professors appoint "panels" of students who then must be prepared on certain days to participate in classroom discussion. Still, the atmosphere is sufficiently relaxed that one group of students presented a professor with a hammer and a pair of tongs in ironic appreciation of the professor's metaphor for working through legal problems. Or to take another example, in seminar classes, which last three hours, some professors designate panels of students to provide refreshments on particular days so that students can enjoy a "milk and cookies" break.

Some students described the law school as having a decidedly liberal political orientation with, however, a strong conservative contingent. Conservative students stated that they sometimes feel that faculty members do not give their views the same consideration that is given to the views of liberal students. The complaint is not that professors argue strongly against conservative interpretations of the issues; rather that professors tend to dismiss conservative views as wrong-headed and not really worthy of study. Other students say it is not the faculty who shut off the discussion but other students: a conservative idea is likely to be greeted with a host of liberal hands all eager to offer a rebuttal. Those who hold such views did not want to discourage people with conservative ideas from applying to Stanford, but one student sighed and said "You just have to be willing to be in the minority."

Students reported that professors are very accessible and mentioned that the faculty have adopted an "open door" policy, a phrase that is a literal description: office doors are left open except during conferences and the like. Additionally, psychological barriers to accessibility seem to be minimal. One student explained that Stanford students are likely to be on a first-name basis with professors with whom they have taken courses but would probably address other members of the faculty as "Professor So-and-So." Even so, the student recalled making a spontaneous call on a professor who was a total stranger. While walking in the corridor, the student noticed some sports paraphernalia on the professor's wall, specifically, some booster items for the Boston Celtics. Being a Celtics fan, the student went into the office and enjoyed a 90-minute conversation with the professor on various sports topics.

Students also explained that Stanford provides faculty and students with money for get-togethers that bring faculty and students together in a social setting. Students gave Halloween and pool parties as examples. Furthermore, students said that the faculty can also be found in the "Law Lounge." One incident was reported of a student who, having finished a somewhat critical discourse on a certain professor's handling of a particular topic, turned around to find that professor standing there—hot coffee in hand. The professor, however, was amused rather than angry and so drank the coffee.

ADMISSIONS | According to Faye Deal, Director of Admissions and Financial Aid, Stanford uses a "rolling" admissions process, so applications are reviewed and determinations are made over the course of the application season. Some applications, however, are "held" until the admissions committee has had the opportunity to review the entire applicant pool; in April and May these applications are given a second review and the class if filled. Applications must be postmarked after September 15 and before March 1, but the committee does not begin consideration of applications until January.

ADMISSIONS DATA

	Class of 1993	Class of 1994
Applied	5,719	6,006
Median LSAT	N/A	N/A
Median GPA	N/A	N/A
Accepted	456	471
Median LSAT	98.3 percentile	98.3 percentile
Median GPA	3.75	3.75
Enrolled	170	180
Median LSAT	96.1 percentile	96.1 percentile
Median GPA	3.75	3.64

Admission to Stanford is based primarily upon superior academic achievement and potential to contribute to the development of the law, but the committee does not make decisions based solely on numerical quotients. Instead, the committee considers a variety of factors such as advanced degrees or advanced studies, significant work experience, publications, extracurricular and community activities, and cultural or political projects.

The Personal Statement. According to Ms. Deal, the personal statement is "very important." It should be about two pages in length and should describe important or unusual aspects of the applicant not otherwise apparent in the application. Of particular interest is information about or clarification of a candidate's academic achievements or personal background. Applicants are encouraged to describe how factors including advanced studies, significant work experience, publications, extracurricular or community activities, and cultural or political projects would relate to their law school studies or their careers.

Recommendations. A letter of recommendation should, if possible, come from an instructor who has personal knowledge of the candidate's work, preferably someone who has known the candidate through a seminar, small class, or tutorial program. Applicants who have been out of school for a significant period may substitute a letter from an employer or business associate. Additional letters of recommendation, although not required, are welcome; but they are helpful only if written by persons in a position to make a critical and informed appraisal of the candidate's qualifications.

Interviews. The admissions committee does not grant interviews as part of the admissions process. Applicants can, however, arrange a visit to the school and can meet with students or members of the admissions committee to obtain answers to questions about the law school and its admissions process.

Minority Applications. According to Ms. Deal, the law school seeks a student body "diverse in backgrounds and experience." While the goal of diversity is by no means limited to race and ethnicity, the law school does give special consideration to applications from American Indians, Alaska Natives, blacks/African-Americans, Mexican-Americans/Chicanos, and Puerto Ricans. Candidates who claim minority or ethnic status must, either in their personal statements or other supporting documents, describe their ethnic, cultural, and linguistic heritage; campus and off-campus activities related to this heritage; and the ways in which this heritage is likely to contribute to the law school or to the legal profession.

Application Tips. The description of the personal statement above uses the language "law school studies or . . . careers," but Ms. Deal made it clear that it is definitely not necessary to project a specific career path in the statement. She agreed that for many candidates it is simply not possible to articulate particular career goals, though a few applicants—those with specialized training—might have very specific job objectives. Instead, Ms. Deal explained, the form for the personal statement is basically a "blank sheet" and that candidates are not restricted to writing about professional plans. As Ms. Deal put it: "Anything goes!" In the past successful candidates have talked about trips abroad, unusual characters, family background, and many other things. Further, candidates often submit additional supporting documentation, such as a senior thesis or a piece of creative writing. One applicant, an architect, highlighted that extra qualification by submitting a set of original building plans.

The admissions office also supplied additional data to help readers determine their chances of acceptance at Stanford.

PLACEMENT The Office of Career Services (OCS) reported that it has a database of approximately 1,300 employers throughout the nation and that each year about 300 recruiters visit the Stanford campus. The majority of the recruiters represent private law firms; the rest come from gov-

CLASS OF 1994

LSAT Score	Applied	Accepted
96th to 99th percentile	1,927	302
91st to 95th percentile	954	56
81st to 90th percentile	1,172	69
61st to 80th percentile	997	30
Below 61st percentile	880	5

GPA	Applied	Accepted
3.75 to 4.00	1,198	232
3.50 to 3.74	1,806	129
3.25 to 3.49	1,336	72
Below 3.25	1,590	29

ernment and public agencies and from business and industry. Additionally, OCS offers to students a range of services including advice on resumes, practice interviews, and panel discussions on practice specialities.

Commentary. With the Office of Career Services "batting a thousand," one would expect to hear only favorable comments about their efforts. And students do, in fact, praise the director, Gloria Pyszka, as "very experienced" and as someone who takes a personal interest in students. According to students, OCS works to stay current with developments in the employment market and to advise students about them. In fact, a couple of students thought that OCS "overreacted" to the recent downturn in the job market for lawyers and unnecessarily alarmed students about their prospects. Whether that is accurate or not remains to be seen. And, in any event, to say of a placement office that it is perhaps overzealous in doing its job is hardly a serious indictment.

Some students did say that OCS seemed to have stronger contacts with employers in the West than in the East. One student mentioned specifically that only five employers from Atlanta visited the school. Students theorized, however, that this situation probably has less to do with the competence of the placement office than with the law school's geographical location and small size.

197

PLACEMENT DATA

	Class of 1991	Class of 1990
Placed at Graduation	100%	100%
Placed within 90 Days	100%	100%
U.S. Supreme Court Clerks	N/A	2
U.S. Appellate Court Clerks	19	18
U.S. District Court Clerks	10	18
State Appellate Court Clerks	3	6
Other Judicial Clerks	0	1
Median Starting Salary	$65,000	$58,000

A STUDENT SAMPLER

In spite of the law school's small size, Stanford has students from over 40 states, the District of Columbia, Guam, Puerto Rico, and a dozen or so countries other than the United States. Similarly, students at the law school earned bachelor's or advanced degrees from about 180 different institutions. The best represented schools are Brown (12), Berkeley (37), UCLA (20), Chicago (9), Columbia (12), Cornell (9), Harvard (56), Michigan (9), Penn (14), Princeton (20), USC (10), Stanford (48), Texas (9), and Yale (40). Of the 180 students who entered in the fall of 1991, 23 are Asian-American, 22 are African-American, 22 Chicano, 8 Native American, and 8 Puerto Rican. The average age of the students in the class, at the time they began their studies, was 24.8, and nearly 25 of them were 30 or over.

As the average age suggests, many students have prior work experience: in accounting, marketing, consulting, or law firms, or as journalists or television producers or directors. Several students have either worked in or contributed substantial amounts of time to social concerns, e.g., environmental issues, rights of battered women, abortion rights, and the problem of child abuse. A number of students have engineering backgrounds and have worked in space communications. The student body also includes people who were professors, including ones who taught art history, philosophy, and theology. About 35 students in each class have advanced degrees, and the student body includes several Rhodes and Fulbright Scholars as well as a couple of lawyers from other countries.

Most recent graduates of the law school chose first-time employment in law firms (52 percent), with a substantial number taking judicial clerkships (28 percent). Another 10 percent took public interest, government, or non-law positions, or pursued a course of further education. One percent went into business. And the remaining 9 percent did not enter into employment immediately after graduation because of travel or other plans.

NOTEWORTHY GRADUATES

William Rehnquist, Chief Justice, United States Supreme Court; Sandra Day O'Connor, Associate Justice, United States Supreme Court; Ni Zhengyu, International Court of Justice; Robert H. Ames, Hopi Tribal Court; Warren Christopher, Secretary of State; Phillip S. Berry, President, Sierra Club; David M. Margolick, journalist, *New York Times*; Susan J. Wolfe, recipient 1990 Edgar Award, Best First Novel

UNIVERSITY OF TEXAS, AUSTIN

SCHOOL OF LAW
727 EAST 26TH STREET
AUSTIN, TX 78705
(512) 471-3207

ADMISSIONS

Applied: 4,364

Accepted: 927

Enrolled: 508

Median LSAT: 92.3 percentile

Median GPA: 3.55

STUDENT BODY

Total: 1,539

Women: 42%

Minorities: 20%

Average Age: 26.5

ACADEMIC RESOURCES

Library Volumes: 824,000

Computer Services: LEXIS, WEST-LAW, access to 50 personal computers

Student/Faculty Ratio: 25:1

FINANCES (ACADEMIC YEAR)

Tuition and Fees:
Resident	$ 4,440
Nonresident	$ 8,620

ENVIRONMENT Austin offers many sources of diversion and entertainment, often free or inexpensive, and a pleasant climate in which to take advantage of them. Some of the major cultural programs held in Austin are sponsored by the University. These include Cultural Entertainment Committee events, Solo Artists' Series, UT drama productions, and art gallery exhibits. Campus film programs include three to five choices each weekend and at least one film every night. Outside the University community there are theater productions by six theatrical groups; symphony concerts; jazz programs; the best of rock, folk, bluegrass, and progressive country and western music; nightclubs; movie theaters; and many other types of entertainment. Austin is also located in the center of a vast system of lakes that are available for sailing, boating, waterskiing, fishing, and swimming; and the rivers surrounding Austin are considered fine waterways for canoeing, sculling, and kayaking. These waterways are all close enough for an afternoon jaunt. In addition, the city has several parks that include hike-and-bike trails, Barton Springs pool and other natural spring-fed pools for swimming, and large open areas for other recreational activities.

The law school is located in the northeast corner of the University of Texas campus, near the Lyndon Baines Johnson Presidential Library and the Fine Arts complex. The law school complex includes seven large amphitheater-type classrooms, a number of smaller classrooms and seminar rooms, an auditorium that seats 200 people, and office space for faculty, staff, and student organizations. A cafeteria and several lounges are available for students' use. Each year, various federal or state court trials are held in the law school's courtroom, and the United States Court of Appeals for the Fifth Circuit often hears appellate cases in the courtroom.

Commentary. Students thought the Austin location of the school a definite advantage to studying law at the University of Texas and described the city as "workable," "most livable," and "one of the greatest cities in the world." When asked to give content to these descriptions, students offered many observations. One student described Austin as "a nice size." Another noted that the city is "big enough" but that it is still possible to drive across town in twenty minutes. And another explained that the city has been careful about environmental standards, keeping out heavy industry likely to cause serious pollution. That student also described the area as "laid back" and noted that one of the growth industries, computers, is attracting a lot of people from California. Finally, students pointed out that while the University of Texas is an important presence in the city, Austin is certainly much more than a "college town."

Students also endorsed the administration's description of the variety of activities available in Austin. Almost every interviewee, when asked about entertainment possibilities, immediately mentioned the large number of clubs and bars that feature live bands; and they were quick to point out that the music played in them falls into many different categories including country, blues, jazz, fusion, funk, rock, rap, and reggae. Indeed, students explained that Austin is an important center for live music and that performers regard Austin as a good place "to get a start."

Students spoke favorably of the region's climate as well. The late spring and early fall seasons were said to be ideal for the water sports mentioned by the administration (including just plain old "tubing" on nearby rapids) as well as for other outdoor activities such as frisbee or softball in the park or a game of pick-up baseball somewhere on the campus. The winters are mild, or at least so chortled one student who claimed to be wearing shorts while the Blizzard of 1993 buried the eastern portion of the country with snow. In fact, the one "knock" on the climate seems to be the intense heat of July and August that can "make things pretty miserable"; but, it was pointed out, those are months during which many law students are likely to be working in summer positions in other cities—perhaps ones with milder summers.

There were a few slightly negative remarks about Austin, but even so, they seemed always to be nicely balanced by other positive observations. On the one hand, the city does not have its own opera or ballet company; but, on the other hand, various touring companies make Austin a regular performance stop. The city may not have the variety of exotic restaurants found in larger cities, but it does have restaurants serving good food of various regional cuisines such as Mexican, barbecue, and country fare. It may not have professional sports, but it does have Texas Longhorns athletics. The city may not be as large as San Antonio, Dallas, or Houston, but those cities are only one to three hours away—and law students at the University of Texas don't worry all that much about riding the city bus home from school at midnight.

Finally, in addition to its amenities and diversions, Austin is also the state capital, so there is a large government presence as well with attendant opportunities for law students. In addition to the usual array of clinics, the law school offers a Texas Supreme Court Internship for academic credit; and students often find part-time employment with other judges, with the Attorney General's office, or as legislative aides.

The students who were interviewed pretty much had only good things to say about the law school's physical plant. It was said to be "fairly modern," "well designed," and (with the exception of a few smaller classrooms that are used infrequently) "spacious." Students mentioned that the library has comfortable places to relax, and that it is very large with many places to study. One student, who was familiar with the facilities of a couple of law schools located in large cities, was particularly enthusiastic about the spaciousness of the library and proclaimed, "Everything truly is bigger here in Texas." In fact, the library was likened more than once to a "museum."

As it turns out, the use of the term "museum" by law students to describe the library was not just metaphorical. The Tarlton Law Library houses elements of the Hyder Collection. Mr. Michael Horn, its curator, explained that the collection includes some 4,000 historical or artistic museum-quality items, ranging from the very small to the very large, on semi-permanent loan from Elton M. Hyder, Jr., who assembled them specifically for the law school's library and other buildings. The collection includes law-related art: oil portraits or portrait prints of prominent historical figures such as judges or legislators and other legal scenes such as trials, as well as decorative art and furnishings, all of which are distributed throughout the law school. The purpose of placing these items, both thematic and not, both functional and decorative, in the library is to give the institutional setting the warmer feeling of a private library—a feeling more conducive to study. (Who could have imagined that a law school library would need a curator?)

Finally, students described the atmosphere at the law school as being "competitive for grades" while denying that the competition is "dirty." (One student had *heard* of an incident regarding a "misplaced" reference book, but that was a second-hand report and would not in any event demonstrate a pattern of widespread "dirty" competition.) Students also explained that whether someone joins into a cooperative study venture is largely a matter of personal style: many do; others keep to themselves. In general, it might be said that the large size of the law school makes it possible for students to have fairly different law school experiences and that no one course of behavior is "expected" or "prescribed."

The organization of social life at the law school is also a function of the large size of the student body. In the first year, students are divided into five sections of about 100 students each. Each section is then assigned five "Teaching Quizmasters." A "TQ" is a third-year law student who teaches two first-year, one-hour courses in Legal Research and Writing and Brief Writing and Oral Advocacy to a group of 25 or so students from the same small section. But TQs also serve another important function. In addition to acting as course instructors, TQs serve as counselors to their students and are charged with organizing athletic and other social activities. The advantage of the small groups with their TQs is that they make the academic and social challenges of the first year "more manageable." Not only do students meet their section mates more easily, but the section then becomes the base from which to meet other classmates as the sections are intermingled for various classes. In the second and third years, the "small section" social framework gives way to one governed by organizational interests, as friendships tend to develop around common interests in the various journals and other activities at the law school.

ACADEMICS The University of Texas Law School was founded in 1883 and is one of the oldest law schools in the nation. Although it is a state university with a student body largely made up of Texas residents (80 percent by law), Texas is a national school in the sense that the training received and the courses offered provide the necessary legal education for practice in any part of the United States. It offers a wide variety of courses, seminars, and co-curricular educational programs.

The inquiry in each of the law school's courses is twofold and ranges from specific technical questions of little apparent public interest to general ones of great contemporary social concern. First, in each course one aim is to qualify the student as a craftsman and advocate, properly equipped with the knowledge, insight, and skills needed for professional services to clients in advising, negotiating, planning, and assisting them in accomplishing their myriad goals, as well as in representing them in litigation. A second aim is to qualify the student as a responsible and enlightened member of a profession that, throughout the history of the United States, has been prominent in the resolution of social, economic, and political problems and that has been profoundly concerned with the public welfare, both locally and nationally. Hence, in every law school course, the constant need for new resolutions of conflicts between individuals, or between the individual and society, is a focus of attention.

CURRICULUM

First-Year Courses: (Fall) Property, Torts, Contracts, Civil Procedure, Criminal Law, Legal Research and Writing; (Spring) Property, Torts, Contracts (continued), Constitutional Law I, Brief Writing and Oral Advocacy

Interesting Electives: American Legal History; Computers and the Law; Consumer Law; Employment Discrimination, Entertainment Law; Environmental Law; Feminist Legal Theory; First Amendment: Sedition; Governmental Liability; Mexican Law; Japanese Law; National Security Law and Policy; Oil and Gas; Science, Technology, and Law; Taxation of Natural Resources

---

Commentary. Students had various favorable things to say about their education. Some said that many of their professors were very good teachers. Others mentioned the law school's very strong clinical program. And still others noted the great variety of student-run scholarly journals. Students did not, however, claim that these characteristics were not shared by other top law schools and so did not think education at UT unique. One student perhaps described the curriculum best by calling it "mostly legal mainstream." Indeed, that description seems to be entirely consistent with the law school's academic philosophy (above): Texas is a national law school that intends to provide its students both with the tools for practicing law and with a sense of the responsibility that the legal profession and each of its individual members must have for the public welfare. Perhaps what makes the education at Texas unique, and this was a point remarked on by several students, is its cost: a top law school education for just a little over $4,400 per year for residents and about $8,600 per year for nonresidents.

Students reported that during the first year, professors tend to rely on the Socratic method to a greater or lesser extent. One student reported being a member of a first-year section in which all professors used the question-and-answer format, calling students "at random and without warning." Another, however, reported having only one such professor and other professors who either "wove their way through the class in a predictable manner" or who "divided the class into thirds" for the purpose of assigning primary responsibility for class participation on a given day. One student theorized that the administration might be trying to give each first-year student a mix of teaching styles but could not be certain that the pattern was the result of a conscious policy decision. After the first year, the Socratic method is replaced by a "pot-pourri" of teaching styles.

When asked about faculty-student interaction, most students immediately declared that the faculty "are accessible," but subsequent conversation usually indicated that the accessibility is the accessibility of a large school. Students said that faculty are available informally at the end of class and that they post office hours. Even students who said they did not feel uncomfortable dropping in on a professor without an appointment said that one runs the risk of the professor already being occupied and that it might be necessary to return at a more convenient time or even to make an appointment. Students also said that professors and students mix socially on a few occasions, as when an organization invites its faculty advisor to some social gathering. Again, the description of the student-faculty interaction both at the law school and outside of it suggests that it is of the sort characteristic of a large institution—though no one expressed dissatisfaction over that fact.

ADMISSIONS | According to Director of Admissions Rita Bohr, the University of Texas Law School receives applications from many more qualified candidates than the law school's facilities and educational program can accommodate. In a typical year, about 4,400 applications may be filed for only 500 seats in the next entering class.

Approximately 55 percent of the available admissions are granted after summary review to candidates whose Admissions Indices reflect both an outstanding undergraduate grade point average and an outstanding LSAT score. The rest of the offers are made after a more thorough examination of all applicants' files. Because so many applicants present undergraduate records and LSAT scores that demonstrate a strong potential for success in law school, Ms. Bohr explains that the admissions committee takes into account a number of additional factors, including exceptional personal talents, unique work or service experience, rigorousness of the undergraduate course of study as reflected by the applicant's college transcript, graduate study, leadership potential, a history of overcoming disadvantage, ability to communicate, ethnic background, race, cultural disadvantage, maturity, physical handicap, geography, and other factors.

The Personal Statement.   The application form provides space for candidates to comment on their undergraduate academic performance, their employment experience, and their extracurricular activities.

Recommendations.   Letters of recommendation are not required, but Ms. Bohr says that they will be accepted and are considered, provided that they are received by the February 1 deadline.

ADMISSIONS DATA

	Class of 1993	Class of 1994
Applied	3,919	4,364
Median LSAT	N/A	83 percentile
Median GPA	N/A	3.29
Accepted	958	927
Median LSAT	N/A	N/A
Median GPA	N/A	N/A
Enrolled	551	508
Median LSAT	89.7 percentile	92.3 percentile
Median GPA	3.50	3.55

Interviews. Ms. Bohr states that because of the volume of applications that the law school receives each year, personal interviews are not a part of the admission process.

Residence. The Texas legislature has limited non-resident enrollment to 15 percent of the student body.

Application Tips. Ms. Bohr explains that letters of recommendation are not useful unless they provide insights and information about the candidate that are not otherwise reflected in the application. The most useful letters, she continues, are from employers and professors with whom the candidate has had a close working relationship.

Regarding residency, Ms. Bohr also notes that while one out of every four resident applicants is usually offered admission, only one out of every eight non-resident applicants is typically offered a seat.

PLACEMENT The Law School's Career Services Office provides a multitude of programs designed to unite legal employers with law clerks and associates. Prior to the fall interviewing season, the office invites employers who have recruited the previous year, employers who have interviewed in prior years, and employers who have not interviewed in the past. Each year, The University of Texas School of Law attracts over 400 interviewing law firms, corporate legal departments, governmental agencies, and public interest organizations from across the country.

The Career Service Office publishes a handbook designed to assist students with interviewing strategies, resume preparation, and job searching techniques. The office schedules individual counseling sessions for first-year law students to revise resumes and remains available for student counseling throughout the year. Additionally, mock interviews for first-year law students are conducted by Austin attorneys through the Career Services Office.

A variety of programs are sponsored by the Career Services Office each year, including Corporate Counsel Day, Public Service Career Day, a Student Pro Bono Placement Program, and a Solo Practice Series. The office also holds workshops on summer clerkships and professional dress and etiquette.

PLACEMENT DATA

	Class of 1991	Class of 1990
Placed at Graduation	77%	73%
Placed within 90 Days	83%	85%
U.S. Supreme Court Clerks	0	0
U.S. Appellate Court Clerks	4	11
U.S. District Court Clerks	13	14
State Appellate Court Clerks	14	17
Other Judicial Clerks	2	2
Median Starting Salary	$53,000	$52,000

Commentary. Reports suggest that the main activity of the placement office at the law school has traditionally been the operation of its on-campus recruitment program—a program that is primarily geared to finding students jobs with large firms both inside Texas and out. Students interested in such career paths allowed that the placement office does a good job on this score. Students interested in other career paths felt, however, that they were left to "fend for themselves." In defense of the placement office, students pointed out that they are making efforts in other directions. For example, the office has brought in speakers to discuss the position of corporate counsel and recently ran a 10-week series on operating a solo practice. It was not suggested that these initial steps will answer every complaint, but as one student said optimistically, "The placement office has a 'very big ear.'"

A STUDENT SAMPLER The law school has a total enrollment of over 1,500 students, making it one of the largest law schools in the country. While the students are predominantly Texas residents, over one-third of them graduate from a college or university outside of Texas. More than 200 undergraduate colleges and universities are represented in the student body.

Each year, eight entering first-year students are awarded a Rice Scholarship, a grant of full tuition and fees for all three years of law school at the University of Texas School of Law. These scholarships are awarded solely on the basis of past scholastic achievement, performance on the LSAT, and other indicators of academic potential. Financial need is not a factor in the awards. In fact, a recent recipient of a Rice Scholarship had also won the $100,000 grand championship of the television quiz show "Jeopardy."

NOTEWORTHY GRADUATES

James A. Baker III, former Secretary of State; Lloyd M. Bentsen, Jr., Secretary of the Treasury; Tom Clark, former Justice, U.S. Supreme Court (deceased); John Connally, former Governor of Texas and former Secretary of the Treasury; Sam Hurt, cartoonist; Michael Levy, founder and publisher of *Texas Monthly*; Myra McDaniel, first African-American woman to serve in a statewide office in Texas; Frederico Peña, Secretary of Transportation; Robert Strauss, former Ambassador to Russia

---

VANDERBILT UNIVERSITY

SCHOOL OF LAW
NASHVILLE, TN 37240
(615) 322-6452

ADMISSIONS

Applied: 2,400

Accepted: 508

Enrolled: 183

Median LSAT: 89.7 percentile

Median GPA: 3.60

STUDENT BODY

Total: 540

Women: 39%

Minorities: 18%

Average Age: N/A

ACADEMIC RESOURCES

Library Volumes: 208,000

Computer Services: LEXIS, WEST-
LAW, word processors

Student/Faculty Ratio: 20:1

FINANCES (ACADEMIC YEAR)

Tuition:	$15,800
Housing:	$ 4,500
Books:	$ 500
Miscellaneous:	$ 5,050
Total:	$25,850

ENVIRONMENT Nashville, a city of 521,000 and the state capital, offers unique professional, cultural, and recreational opportunities. Within a few minutes of the campus are the state legislature, federal and state courts, government agencies, and modern corporate skyscrapers. Cultural life is greatly enhanced by the Tennessee Performing Arts Center, with auditorium facilities for the Nashville Opera Association, the Nashville Ballet, and a variety of theatrical and musical presentations. The Nashville Sounds (AAA affiliate of the Cincinnati Reds) play ball April through September, and Vanderbilt's Southeastern Conference teams generate sports excitement throughout the year. The city's many restaurants cater to dining preferences ranging from barbecue and turnip greens to Peking duck, and entertainment choices are likewise wide-ranging, from hole-in-the-wall bluegrass joints to swank, showcase supper clubs. Sports and recreation thrive in the rolling green hills of Middle Tennessee. The city's parks host everything from steeplechase to horseshoes, and the area surrounding Nashville is a natural for hiking, camping, and caving. Thus, the city provides the benefits of cosmopolitanism, while avoiding the disadvantages of the megalopolis or the small town.

Vanderbilt's 333-acre campus is located 1½ miles from the Nashville downtown business district, combining the advantages of an urban location with a tranquil parklike setting of broad lawns, shaded paths, and quiet plazas. The law school's supportive environment is reinforced by its host university and city. With 10 schools, 1,400 faculty members, and 9,000 students, Vanderbilt University is large enough to offer the excellence and diversity characteristic of a premier teaching institution, yet small enough to insure a university-wide scale proportioned to that of the law school itself.

Commentary. Students generally observed that one's assessment of Nashville is likely to depend in an important way on prior experience with cities. Those who came to Nashville from small towns in the South remarked that they and their classmates from similar backgrounds view Nashville as a large city filled with new and exciting experiences. Those who came from cities larger than Nashville noted that the city lacks some of the variety of diversions available in the very largest cities. Still, even those from larger cities made it clear that there is more to Nashville than Opryland (a musical theme park) and country music. On balance, all groups seem to be fairly well-satisfied by the law school's host city. It was described as "very livable," "cosmetically pretty," and "definitely a Southern city." One student who claimed to live in "one of the worst areas likely to be inhabited by law students" said that nonetheless she felt "perfectly safe," and a student from a large city marveled at the fact that it is possible to leave one's door unlocked while running a 15-minute errand without fear of being burglarized.

Students, of course, mentioned the strong presence of the country and western music industry, typified by "Twitty City" (devoted to the life and work of singer Conway Twitty), the Country Music Hall of Fame, and the "tacky Elvis shops" on Music Row—not as sites high on the list of law student interests but as institutions that help to define the character of the city—even as they pointed out that the city is generally an important center of the recording industry. Consequently, students reported, the city has a lot of clubs featuring bands hoping to break into the industry.

Since Nashville is an important city in Tennessee and Vanderbilt a major campus, both are included on the schedule of touring artists. Students mentioned a recent concert by Bob Dylan and performances by touring companies of "The Will Rogers Follies" and "Phantom of the Opera." Students noted also that the city has a variety of restaurants, particularly the area around the Vanderbilt campus which includes Thai, Chinese, and Italian establishments. Students also pointed out that the law school is associated with a major university and that its sports teams have the support of many of the law school's students. A few other students mentioned the variety of outdoor activities available within a short drive.

In the final analysis, as a city Nashville may be less important to Vanderbilt law students than the host cities of other law schools are to their student bodies. As one student put it, "Here we make our own fun." Another put questions about entertainment and cultural activities into perspective by noting, "It doesn't really matter anyway because Vanderbilt Law School has all of our money."

Just as the location of the law school does not occasion any strong reaction among students, so too its physical plant doesn't inspire intense opinions. The building was described as "modern but not new," "not very interesting," and "a little outdated." To be sure, some students voiced particular criticisms such as the need to upgrade the computer facilities in the building's subbasement; but on the other hand, students also mentioned the central courtyard, Blackacre, where it is possible to sit on pleasant days and socialize or read. Students also noted that the administration, in response to letters printed in the law school newspaper complaining of the lounge area, installed new carpeting and tables and improved cleaning services.

Given the lack of concern about the physical plant, it might seem curious, then, that one student referred to the physical plant as the single biggest source of dissatisfaction about the law school. The seeming paradox disappears, however, when one asks Vanderbilt law students about their classmates. Several students mentioned that they chose Vanderbilt over other top law schools because of its reputation for having an environment of cooperation and support rather than of competition. Thus, it was not surprising to hear students report that people share notes and outlines and are generally cooperative. But from this background of civility, there stands forth a genuine enthusiasm for one's classmates. Quite remarkable was the frequency of comments such as "I made friends very quickly," "I have made lifelong friends," and "Everyone makes new friends." Students said also that because of the small class size it is possible to know, at least by sight if not by name, all of one's classmates, and they mentioned frequently the Friday afternoon "Blackacre," an informal party with refreshments held every other week. In the final analysis, then, it seems that the environment at Vanderbilt Law School is defined in the main not by the city of Nashville, nor by the university's campus, nor by the law school's physical plant, but by the people who make up the student body.

ACADEMICS According to Dean of the Law School John J. Costonis, the curriculum at Vanderbilt Law School manifests a dual focus on traditional core courses and the relevance of legal doctrine to the complex modern world of legal process. The dean explains that a solid understanding of basic subjects is a necessary foundation upon which students can then fashion an educational experience tailored to their individual interests; but excepting a course in professional responsibility and an advanced writing requirement, the first-year courses are the only ones that students must take. Indeed, a student's course work in the upperclass years may include classes in other schools of the university. In this way, the dean says, the law school helps to provide students with an understanding of the relationship of law to other disciplines.

As for teaching methods, Dean Costonis says that faculty members vary in technique and substantive emphasis, producing an overall balance in perspective. The dean also states that the student-faculty ratio at the law school encourages close rapport between students and faculty and that the law school has an "open door" tradition, under which students are welcome to visit freely with faculty. Furthermore, the first-year writing program at Vanderbilt is taught by the faculty in small groups, providing student-faculty contact from the very first day. According to Dean Costonis, these characteristics, which facilitate the exchange of ideas and encourage the growth of personal relationships, help make the law school a unique institution.

CURRICULUM

First-Year Courses: Appellate Advocacy (spring only), Civil Procedure I and II, Constitutional Law I and II, Contracts I and II, Criminal Law (spring only), Legal Writing (fall only), Property I and II, Torts I and II

Interesting Electives: Advanced Intellectual Property Seminar, Bioethics and the Law Seminar, Children and the Law, The Common Market, Employment Discrimination Law, Environmental Law, First Amendment Constitutional Law, Foreign Relations Law of the United States, Health Law and Policy, International Commercial Transactions, Law of Developing Countries, Legal Problems of the Music Industry, Media Law and Competition Seminar, Social Legislation, Superfund

Commentary. A review of the law school's "Bulletin" suggests, and student reports confirmed, that the academic philosophy at Vanderbilt is fairly traditional. Indeed, the list of second- and third-year courses for the academic year 1991–1992 contains no course names that even hint at "ideological diversity," and it is perhaps the case that most students think the curriculum as presently constituted is well-balanced. Indeed, the recent addition of a single course on gender and the law seems to have occasioned some controversy among students. While the course was fairly well subscribed, a minority of students in what was characterized as a generally conservative student body thought that the new course "just wasn't needed."

While the academic philosophy of the law school is not a subject of heated debate, one criticism of the curriculum is that the first year is too demanding. As the list of first-year courses above shows, students take five academic courses in the fall (plus Legal Writing) and six academic courses in the spring (plus Appellate Advocacy). Some students theorized that first-years simply get spread too thin and that the overly demanding course of study may actually interfere with the learning process. Those who support the present balance are reluctant to decrease the workload for fear of injuring the law school's reputation for academic rigor. Students reported that a faculty committee was appointed to review the first-year requirements, but it is not yet clear what action, if any, will be taken.

On the whole, students seem to be pleased with their faculty but noted that teaching styles vary from professor to professor. Student comments suggest that the use of the Socratic method during the first year at Vanderbilt is perhaps a bit more rigorous than that at some other law schools. A typical description was, "You get called on and are expected to be prepared." Still, students were adamant that the use of the Socratic method, even when rigorous, was neither harsh nor demeaning and that younger professors tended to be less demanding.

Students reported that faculty are accessible and have an "open door policy." They said that it is common practice to go to the faculty suite area and to drop in on professors without making an appointment. Students qualified this view by noting that it might be necessary to return at another time if the professor were already engaged and further, that some professors prefer not to be disturbed just before class while they complete their final preparations. A few students also reported socializing with professors outside of the law school and mentioned sports activities such as basketball and golf. In general, students thought professors to be genuinely interested in teaching and pointed out that the law school assigns those who teach the substantive first-year courses, such as Contracts, to teach the first-year writing program rather than adjuncts hired just for that one task.

ADMISSIONS | According to Anne M. Brandt, Assistant Dean for Admissions and Student Affairs, Vanderbilt Law School has an Admissions Committee composed of the Assistant Dean for Admissions and five faculty members. Vanderbilt does not use a rolling admissions process. Instead, the admissions committee begins its evaluation of files on the application deadline, February 1; decision letters are sent to applicants beginning in the third week of February. Dean Brandt notes that all applicants who have filed timely applications (prior to the application deadline) will receive an admissions decision prior to April 1.

Dean Brandt states that Vanderbilt's admissions process does not rely on any thresholds—either for the LSAT or the GPA. Rather, the admissions committee carefully evaluates several factors in every application: academic performance, LSAT score, letters of recommendation, personal statement, extracurricular

ADMISSIONS DATA

	Class of 1993	Class of 1994
Applied	2,400	2,500
Median SLAT	N/A	N/A
Median GPA	N/A	N/A
Accepted	508	540
Median LSAT	N/A	N/A
Median GPA	N/A	N/A
Enrolled	183	184
Median LSAT	89.7 percentile	92.3 percentile
Median GPA	3.60	3.61

activities, work experience, and any other factor an applicant presents. Dean Brandt notes that because Vanderbilt values nonacademic qualities, a low LSAT or GPA will not automatically eliminate a candidate from serious consideration; each year the law school admits applicants who have a history of poor standardized test scores or who may have had modest accomplishments in college but have been successful in subsequent endeavors.

The Personal Statement. Dean Brandt explains that Vanderbilt does not offer evaluative interviews. Consequently, the admissions process relies heavily on the personal statement to provide in-depth information about applicants. The application asks two questions that encourage open-ended answers. One asks the applicant to provide reasons for the decision to study law. The second is an invitation to submit an autobiographical statement of no specified length. The admissions committee reads carefully each personal statement and gives it "significant weight" in their evaluations.

Recommendations. Vanderbilt requires two letters of recommendation from every applicant, and Dean Brandt states that the admissions committee prefers that these letters come from professors or others who are in a position to give detailed information about the applicant's academic strengths and potential for the study of law.

Interviews.   Vanderbilt does not offer interviews to applicants. Dean Brandt says, however, that the law school does welcome visits by applicants who wish to spend time with faculty and students and to learn more about the law school.

Minority Applications.   According to Dean Brandt, minority status is one of the factors that Vanderbilt considers in making admissions decisions. Not only does the law school give special consideration to members of certain racial and ethnic groups, it also pays special attention to individuals who are socioeconomically disadvantaged, learning-disabled, or who have had similar experiences.

Application Tips.   When asked to give content to the idea of "significant other accomplishments," Dean Brandt responds that this is a broad term used by the admissions committee to describe experiences that "add depth and breadth to an applicant and, therefore, to the student body." With regard to college extracurricular activities, for example, the admissions committee would prefer that an applicant have selected an activity and have committed to it for an extended period of time. Leadership positions are useful in demonstrating both commitment and the ability to persuade others. Dean Brandt emphasizes that whether a student chose to spend time as an editor of the college newspaper or as a volunteer in service to a community organization is not as important as the fact that the student gave time and energy outside of the classroom. Less impressive, notes the dean, is the application that contains a dazzling array of the names of organizations to which the applicant belongs with an unspecified contribution to each. Additionally, the dean notes that the admissions committee looks carefully at the applications of candidates who worked either part-time or full-time during their college years, because they understand that hours required to help pay for college expenses are hours that cannot be devoted to study or to extracurricular activities. The dean continues the analysis of "significant other accomplishments" by explaining that a significant scholarly accomplishment might be published material or participation with a faculty member on a research project. For someone out of school for a period of time, it might mean starting a business.

Given the comments set forth in the preceding paragraph, it is not surprising that Dean Brandt urges applicants to Vanderbilt to use the personal statement to flesh out the information contained in the other parts of the application and to share with the admissions committee those special qualities or experiences which might help them to understand the unique contribution that an applicant could make to the law school.

As for letters of recommendation, Dean Brandt states that the "ideal recommendation" should come from a recommender who is able to describe for the admissions committee specific strengths and weaknesses of an applicant. The "ideal recommendation" will also describe the relationship between the writer and the applicant and the circumstances under which the writer knows the applicant. Finally, the "ideal recommendation" is one that is detailed and thorough and responds specifically to the questions asked on the letter-of-recommendation form provided by the applicant to the recommender.

PLACEMENT | According to Pam S. Malone, Assistant Dean for Placement, about 400 recruiters visit the law school campus each year. Dean Malone explains that the Vanderbilt Law School is able to attract recruiters because it enjoys a national reputation, because Vanderbilt graduates perform well as professionals, and because the law school has a strong alumni network. As part of its efforts to help students find jobs, the placement office mails announcements of on-campus recruiting programs to prospective employers prior to each recruiting season. Employers not able to visit the campus are encouraged to send non-visiting notices of employment opportunities. To students, the placement office offers individual counseling sessions with staff as well as seminars and handouts covering all aspects of the employment process.

PLACEMENT DATA

	Class of 1991	Class of 1990
Placed at Graduation	89.6%	90.6%
Placed within 90 Days	90.0%	91.3%
U.S. Supreme Court Clerks	0	0
U.S. Appellate Court Clerks	6	8
U.S. District Court Clerks	14	11
State Appellate Court Clerks	3	8
Median Starting Salary	$57,399	$55,000

Commentary. Student evaluations of the placement office seemed to vary with expectations about just what a placement office ought to do. Students agreed that the placement office does a pretty good job of attracting recruiters from medium to large firms, particularly from the South, and that the staff tries to keep students informed by placing notes in student folders. There was some small disagreement about certain policies governing the interviewing process, such as the practice of not allowing firms to prescreen students on the basis of grades or the rule preventing students from speculating on their class ranking, but these differences of opinion seemed to be more about style rather than substance.

The sharpest differences of opinion about the placement office were not about interviewing rules but about efforts to find students jobs in other areas. Although one student noted that the placement office is making an effort to cultivate contacts with regional employers, most said that students often found it necessary to take the initiative. One student pointed out, for example, that it was student initiative that created a separate center for information about public interest work. Two others, who noted that relatively fewer firms from the Northeast come to Vanderbilt, mentioned finding jobs in New York by writing letters themselves. Another mentioned that ties to a particular community are often important in landing a job with a smaller firm. Perhaps the fairest assessment would be that the placement office is pretty good at what it knows best how to do, which is attract firms from its own region, that it is only somewhat effective in finding alternative employment, and that it operates within certain inherent limitations, such as the ability of the law school to attract employers from more remote areas or smaller employers with less need to do recruiting.

A STUDENT SAMPLER In recent years, the typical Vanderbilt student body has numbered about 540 students from over 40 states and from over 205 undergraduate institutions. The most represented undergraduate institutions are Vanderbilt (40), Duke (25), Tennessee (16), Pennsylvania (13), Dartmouth (10), Tulane (10), Harvard (9), North Carolina (9), Northwestern (9), and Texas at Austin (9). Many students come from the Southeast—Alabama (30), Florida (30), Georgia (16), Kentucky (26), Louisiana (12), Mississippi (18), North Carolina (7), and Tennessee (111)—but many others come from other areas of the country—California (20), Massachusetts (10), Michigan (10), and New York (42). Recently, the student body has included physicians, a playwright, engineers, a nuclear weapons specialist from the military, a submariner, ministers, musicians, dancers, actors, Peace Corps and VISTA veterans, legislative aides, political operatives, bankers, journalists, scientists, accountants, athletes, missionaries, and artists.

NOTEWORTHY GRADUATES

Hon. Robert E. Cooper, Chief Justice, Supreme Court of Tennessee; Fred Graham, chief anchor and managing editor of the Courtroom Television Network; Ken Masterson, senior vice president and general counsel, Federal Express Corporation; Jim Neal, Chief Trial Counsel on the Watergate Special Prosecution Force, recently listed by *Fortune Magazine* as one of the U.S.'s five top trial lawyers; Bradford Reynolds, Assistant Attorney General of the United States in charge of civil rights

UNIVERSITY OF VIRGINIA

▼

SCHOOL OF LAW
NORTH GROUNDS
CHARLOTTESVILLE, VIRGINIA 22901
(804) 924-7351

ADMISSIONS

Applied: 5,887

Accepted: 953

Enrolled: 381

Median LSAT: 94.5 percentile

Median GPA: 3.59

STUDENT BODY

Total: 1,143

Women: 40%

Minorities: 14%

Average Age: 24

ACADEMIC RESOURCES

Library Volumes: 600,000

Computer Services: LEXIS, WEST-LAW, word processing

Student/Faculty Ratio: 23:1

FINANCES (ACADEMIC YEAR)

Tuition and Fees:
Resident:	$ 4,858
Nonresident:	$11,538

Housing and Food:
Resident:	$ 8,225
Nonresident:	$ 8,225

Books:
Resident:	$ 700
Nonresident:	$ 700

Total:
Resident:	$13,783
Nonresident:	$20,463

ENVIRONMENT Charlottesville is situated about 120 miles from Washington, D.C. and 70 miles from Richmond. A downtown pedestrian mall offers shopping, a variety of restaurants, and entertainment establishments that feature local talent; and in the Court Square area, lawyers

218

and business people occupy offices in buildings dating back to the 1700s. The university was founded by Thomas Jefferson, who also designed the original "academical village" that is still the spiritual and intellectual heart of the university. The special grace and character of Jefferson's design are widely recognized, and that part of the university has been called the single most beautiful and effective architectural group of its kind in the history of American building. The law school itself is housed in a single building of more modern design located on the North Grounds.

According to Assistant Dean Jerome Stokes, Virginia is as free of destructive tension as any high-caliber law school can be because the wealth of placement opportunities and lack of class ranking place the emphasis upon pursuing inquiry for its own sake rather than on scrambling over other students. Moreover, the semi-urban setting focuses attention on the law school, so that the school becomes the social center as well as the study center. For this reason, too, there is considerable socializing between faculty and students.

Commentary.   When a university's literature defines its geographical location by reference to cities other than the one in which it is located, it is almost certain that the host city is not a major metropolitan area, and this is true of Charlottesville. When they responded to questions about the amenities to be found in Charlottesville, many students added by way of a footnote comments such as "Oh, and Washington is only about two hours away." This is not to say, however, that students expressed dissatisfaction with the law school's setting. In fact, most seemed to be quite pleased with their surroundings and mentioned the availability of a variety of medium-priced eating establishments and places for an evening's diversion in the downtown area or in a strip of stores closer to the law school referred to as the Corner. After thinking about the issue for a while, one student opined that while "a real New Yorker might feel somewhat stifled, 90 percent of the students seem to be happy with the location." And, of course, a safety valve—D.C.—is only a couple of hours away.

As for the physical plant, while Jefferson's "academical village" (with the Rotunda that figures prominently in photographs in the university's literature) was acknowledged by students to be very beautiful, the law school building, located an another part of the campus, was described as "utilitarian" and "a typical college building." Students occasionally commented unfavorably on the somewhat cramped quarters and poor climate control. Even so, no student thought the physical plant to be a serious impediment to learning, and the law school intends to take over the nearby business school building and to join the two structures to create an interesting new facility with approximately 50 percent more space than the existing plant. The proposed expansion, however, is scheduled for 1995 and cannot take place until the business school's new quarters have been constructed. So for the next couple of years, entering students can expect to feel a bit cramped.

Students also agreed with Dean Stokes that the grading system, under which most students receive a grade between 3.2 to 2.7, does reduce the temptation to compete vigorously against classmates, though a few students will "break out" from the pack. Students added that the student body itself also helps to foster the atmosphere of noncompetiton through peer pressure. Many people choose Virginia over one or another top school for its reputation as an institution with a noncompetitive atmosphere; and, as students, they work to ensure that the reputation is justified. One student, for example, said that there is an unwritten rule that outlines are to be shared—not hoarded—and that peer pressure would make it difficult to refuse a request to borrow an outline. Again, students who call attention to themselves by being overly aggressive in class are likely to hear about it from others. Or again, *Law Weekly*, the school newspaper, includes a feature entitled the "Bottom Ten," where students who transgress the unwritten rules regarding competition are censured with notes such as "A not-to-be-named second-year was seen rummaging through mail boxes in search of outlines."

Many students said that instead of competing against their fellow students, they cooperate with them. By way of illustrating this attitude, a student described one method of organizing an outline group: on the first day of class, simply circulate a page with numbers for 14 names (one for each week in the semester). The 14 subscribers, taken pretty much at random, then share outlines at the end of the course. Another student cited with approval the practice of dividing the first-year class into sections of 30 or so students. Students in a section are all assigned to the same classes and have one course in which they are the only students. According to this account, the practice creates a warm feeling of having a "homeroom."

Students also agreed with Dean Stokes's comment about the sociability of Virginia students and mentioned as an example the North Grounds softball league, organized primarily for law students. Indeed, softball seems at times to be almost an obsession with Virginia law students, and some people are members of two or even three teams. As a result, softball is more than just the "sport of choice" at Virginia; it is a symbol of sociability at the law school. So those who for one reason or another decline to participate may feel somewhat excluded from the law school community.

ACADEMICS | According to Thomas H. Jackson, former Dean of the Law School and now University Provost, the Virginia School of Law is the modern expression of one of the original ten faculties visualized for the university by Thomas Jefferson. To be sure, the dean said, it is the mission of the law school to *teach*, in the classical sense of transmitting knowledge to generations of law students to equip them to be functioning and valuable members of the legal profession. For law school is, as the dean noted, the place of entrance to the legal profession; but it is also the function of a university-based law school to provide the kind of academic backing to law and the legal profession that universities are expected to provide to society at large. Thus, law schools are the places that examine, in a scholarly way, the legal foundations of our society and that conduct the research that provides the intellectual underpinnings to the myriad ways legal rules affect society.

The dean emphasized, however, that there is a "symbiotic relationship" between the twin missions of teaching and research. They are not two separate functions "coincidentally placed in the same institution." Instead, the dean sees the two functions as parts of an integrated whole. The research done at the law school is intended to inform the day-to-day inquiry in the classroom—not simply to fill the pages of scholarly journals. Thus, the dean believes that the law school's comparative advantage lies in imparting to students (and hence to new members of the profession) the kinds of ideas, perspectives, and inquiries that will allow them to be valuable members of the profession precisely because they are able to relate law to broader social and economic trends.

CURRICULUM

First-Year Courses: Civil Procedure (fall), Constitutional Law (spring), Contracts (fall), Criminal Law (fall), Legal Writing (year-long), Property (spring), Torts (fall), plus a spring elective

Interesting Electives: AIDS and the Law, Children and the Legal System, Complex Litigation, Employment Law, Feminist Jurisprudence, Frontiers of Legal Thought, Immigration Law, Income Redistribution and Gender, Law and Medicine, Legal Control of Violence, Native American Law, Oceans Law and Policy, Sex Discrimination, Soviet Law and Politics

Commentary. Student responses to questions about the educational philosophy outlined by the dean indicate that the theoretical component of the curriculum at Virginia is fairly orthodox "law and economics" analysis. Those students who argue for greater diversity among the faculty described the faculty as "neoconservative" and pointed to a lack of representatives from schools such as Critical Legal Studies and feminist thought. Dean Jackson has defended the current faculty as being "intellectually diverse" but has also conceded that the law school is "comparatively weaker" in the more "radical" intellectual movements. Although the law school has made efforts to recruit representatives of the other schools of thought, most students seem to think it is likely that "law and economics" will remain the dominant tradition at Virginia; and one student perhaps spoke for the vast majority of students in saying, "And that's just fine!"

As is to be expected, students said that classroom style varies from teacher to teacher: some rely heavily on the Socratic method, others do not. Even in the first year, however, where the method is likely to be used more extensively than in upper-division courses, professors often exercise care to take some of the sting out of the question-and-answer format. Although some professors do "cold calling," others proceed by alphabetical or seating order, so that it is possible to predict with some confidence when one is likely to be called upon. In any event, students at Virginia are not likely to submit passively to abuse of the question-and-answer format. Recently, a first-year professor who persisted in being overly rigorous with the Socratic method was permanently assigned to the "Bottom Ten" list, which was renamed for the remainder of the year the "Bottom Nine."

The student-to-faculty ratio at Virginia is a very high 23:1, a figure the administration would like to adjust either by hiring more faculty or by reducing class size. Since the demand for legal education within the state of Virginia is expected to increase, hiring more faculty seems to be the law school's only option. Indeed, Assistant Dean for Administration Elaine M. Hadden said that some progress has already been made in hiring new faculty but could not readily quantify the change in the student-to-faculty ratio. She did say, however, that in the next couple of years, the law school hopes to have it down to about 20:1.

In spite of the high student-to-faculty ratio, students reported that faculty are reasonably accessible: professors are available informally after class, they have office hours, and their doors are often open. On the other hand, student responses to questions about interaction with faculty suggest that teacher–student contact is as a rule initiated by the student and that faculty reserve the right to ask that an inquiry be postponed, perhaps until a scheduled time. Faculty, then, are accorded a measure of deference, and it is implicitly understood that it is generally not a good idea to drop in for a chat about nothing in particular.

Some policies of the law school are specifically designed to facilitate socializing between faculty and students. The first-year students assigned to a professor's small section may be invited for drinks or dinner at the end of the year. The Student Bar Association funds a program to encourage groups of students to take professors to lunch by reimbursing them the cost of the professors' meals. And some professors also participate in the softball league.

ADMISSIONS | According to Albert Turnbull, Dean of Admissions and Placement, the Law School Admissions Services uses a formula created and tested for validity by the law school to calculate an Admissions Index for each applicant. The index has two functions. One, it is a means of analyzing the applicant pool to get a general sense of the overall qualifications of the candidates in the pool in a given year before making any individual decisions. Two, it is also used for rough sorting of applications before the review process begins, though the index itself is not used to make individual decisions.

In addition to the "naked" GPA, the admissions committee considers the quality of the undergraduate institution, the rigor of courses taken, and the degree of grade inflation. Furthermore, the quantitative factors are subject to interpretation in light of any number of variables, e.g., the maturing effect of some years away from formal education; a rising trend in academic performance versus solid but unexceptional work; financial pressure requiring employment during the undergraduate years; significant personal achievement in extracurricular work at college or in a work or military situation; unusual prior training; background or ethnicity that promises a significant contribution to the law school community.

ADMISSIONS DATA

	Class of 1993	Class of 1994
Applied	5,323	5,887
Median LSAT	86.5 percentile	86.5 percentile
Median GPA	3.38	3.46
Accepted	953	953
Median LSAT	96.1 percentile	96.1 percentile
Median GPA	3.62	3.65
Enrolled	380	381
Median LSAT	94.5 percentile	94.5 percentilc
Median GPA	3.57	3.59

The Personal Statement. The application requests a personal statement of not more than 250 words. According to Dean Turnbull, the purpose of the statement is not only to give the admission committee additional insight into an applicant's background but to give the committee an opportunity to appraise the applicant's writing ability. In many cases, said Dean Turnbull, the personal statement is very important and becomes the "glue that holds the application together."

Recommendations. Candidates must supply two recommendations, at least one of which should be from a professor. If an applicant has been out of school for a number of years and so is not able to obtain a recommendation from a professor, then a letter from an employer or perhaps a professional colleague can be substituted; but an explanation of the inability to secure a letter from a professor should accompany the application.

Interviews. Virginia is one of the few law schools that uses personal interviews as a regular part of the admissions process. An interview can be scheduled between October 1 and January 31, but Dean Turnbull notes that the number of requests usually exceeds the number of available appointments. Consequently, a candidate who anticipates that an interview might be an important part of the application should contact the law school as early as possible.

Minority Applications. According to Dean Turnbull, the primary focus of minority recruitment at Virginia is on black applicants, but members of other minority groups are also given special attention by the admissions committee. As part of its commitment to affirmative action, the law school provides special scholarship aid to assist minority students.

Application Tips. As would be expected, Virginia residents fare considerably better in the admissions process than their nonresident counterparts. A resident applicant with a GPA of 3.6 and an LSAT score in the 96th percentile has a better than two out of three chance of being accepted, while a nonresident applicant with similar numbers has but a one out of three chance of acceptance.

The word limit on the personal statement is very severe when compared with those of other law schools reviewed in this book, and the admissions office acknowledges that each year a significant number of candidates violate the explicit instructions on the application form and run on for several pages. Even those applications are read, however, though apparently not without some grousing by the members of the admissions committee among themselves. It would probably be better, therefore, to submit to Virginia a personal statement that observes as closely as possible the word limitation and to offer a supplemental statement if one is absolutely needed to address some pressing matter that cannot otherwise be covered in the shorter statement.

One way of mitigating the severity of the word limitation on the personal statement would be to request an interview. According to the admissions office, an interview provides a good opportunity for a candidate to explain why a GPA or an LSAT score is not truly reflective of the candidate's ability. Unfortunately, the opportunities for an interview are limited: only about 700 appointments per year. By mid-November, all interview slots are likely to be filled, and so it is essential to request an interview as early in the application season as possible.

What if a candidate requests an interview but no appointment is available? According to the admissions office, it is always possible, though not likely, that a cancellation will free up a slot or that a member of the admissions committee will find time to conduct additional interviews. In any event, Dean Turnbull said that those who are unable to schedule an interview for whatever reason are not thereby necessarily put at a disadvantage. In the first place, interviews are rarely dispositive of an application; rather, the Dean explained, they tend to add weight to factors in the written part of the file that already point in a particular direction. In the second place, most of the issues that are discussed in an interview could as easily and as effectively have been treated in writing.

Dean Turnbull also provided further information about the law school's treatment of minority applications. The dean stressed that the summary statement of the law school's policy on minority recruitment (which states that the "primary focus" is on black candidates) should not be read to imply that applications from nonblack minorities do not receive special attention. Indeed, the statement clearly establishes that all minority applications do receive special attention; but the dean explained that, given the history of *de jure* segregation in the state of Virginia, the admissions committee chose to make the recruitment of black candidates a double priority.

PLACEMENT | In a typical year, 600 to 700 recruiters visit the law school campus. Of the 614 that came to recruit from the class of 1991, 544 were law firms, 12 were corporations, 12 were legal aid and public interest organizations, and 7 were city and state agencies. The placement office coordinates and provides logistical support for the on-campus interviewing process and offers students workshops, panel discussions, handouts, and individual counselling regarding the hiring process.

PLACEMENT DATA

	Class of 1991	*Class of 1990*
Placed at Graduation	92%	94%
Placed within 90 Days	94%	96%
U.S. Supreme Court Clerks	1	2
U.S. Appellate Court Clerks	14	16
U.S. District Court Clerks	35	26
State Appellate Court Clerks	7	11
Other Judicial Clerks	7	4
Median Starting Salary	$64,000	$63,000

Commentary. In general, students at Virginia seem to be fairly well pleased with the efforts of the placement office, but some of that satisfaction students attributed to the job-getting power of the Virginia Law School degree and not to the efforts of the placement office. In better times, some students observed, the task of the placement office consisted primarily of coordinating the interviewing

225

schedules of large firms, and so it was easy for the office to satisfy the demands of its constituency. Even so, students said that the placement office does a "decent job," and they mentioned that a new, full-time Public Interest Coordinator has been hired.

A STUDENT SAMPLER A recent entering class included 209 Virginia residents, while the remaining 171 came from 33 different states, the District of Columbia, the Canal Zone, Puerto Rico, and the Virgin Islands. There were 153 women and 42 black students. The most represented undergraduate institution was the University of Virginia with 64, followed by Harvard-Radcliffe with 16, Yale with 14, Dartmouth with 13, and Duke with 13. In total, over 120 undergraduate institutions were represented. The average age of the class was 24, and many students had completed advanced degree work.

Some interesting personalities in recent entering classes include a member of the corps of the Washington Ballet, a championship body-builder, a trader of foreign currency, a New York City plainclothes narcotics officer, a research administrator in epidemiology, an actuary, and a former Franciscan friar.

In a typical year, about two-thirds of the graduates will take positions in private law firms, with a substantial number also accepting judicial clerkships. Although Virginia is a state school, its graduates disperse across the country: California, 43; Georgia, 32; Illinois, 14; Massachusetts, 14; New York, 64; North Carolina, 24; Ohio, 13; Pennsylvania, 17; Texas, 37; Virginia, 83; and Washington, D.C., 119.

NOTEWORTHY GRADUATES

Evan Bayh III, Governor of Indiana; Lowell P. Weicker, Jr., former U.S. Senator and Governor of Connecticut; R. William Ide III, President of the American Bar Association; Robert F. Kennedy, U.S. Attorney General and U.S. Senator; Edward M. Kennedy, U.S. Senator; Tina A. Ravitz, Vice President and Chief Counsel of *Newsweek*; Linda A. Fairstein, Chief of Sex Crimes Prosecution in the Manhattan District Attorney's Office; Evan J. Kemp, Jr., Chairman, Equal Employment Opportunities Commission; Elaine R. Jones, Deputy Director and Counsel for the NAACP Legal Defense and Education Fund

UNIVERSITY OF WASHINGTON

SCHOOL OF LAW
SEATTLE, WASHINGTON 98195
(206) 543-4078

ADMISSIONS

Applied: 2,400

Accepted: 449

Enrolled: 157

Median LSAT: 92.3 percentile

Median GPA: 3.44

STUDENT BODY

Total: 486

Women: 41%[1]

Minorities: 30%[1]

Average Age: N/A

ACADEMIC RESOURCES

Library Volumes: 435,000

Computer Resources: LEXIS, WEST-LAW, word processors

Student/Faculty Ratio: 15:1

FINANCES (ACADEMIC YEAR)

Tuition and Fees:		
Resident:	$ 3,387	
Nonresident	$ 8,472	
Food and Lodging[2]:	$ 5,274	
Books and Supplies:	$ 738	
Insurance:	$ 487	
Personal Expenses:	$ 1,575	
Transportation:	$ 699	
Total:		
Resident:	$12,160	
Nonresident	$17,245	

[1]The Class of 1992 included 24 persons who classified themselves as members of minority groups, the Class of 1993 had 59, and the Class of 1994 had 57. The Class of 1993 had 64 women, the Class of 1994 had 88. For a discussion of the implications of the increases, see "Commentary" sections, below.

[2]This figure is for one person in a residence hall room shared with another. Rooms for married couples in University housing vary depending on income and priority.

ENVIRONMENT The University of Washington School of Law, located in Seattle, was first organized in 1899 and is fully accredited. The new law building, Condon Hall, was completed and occupied in 1974; it is three blocks west of the main University campus and is mostly self-contained. The building houses classrooms; student lounge and locker areas; the Marian Gould Gallagher Law Library; and offices for faculty, administration, and student organizations. Financial aid, registration, and placement functions are run primarily as in-house operations. The building itself is fully accessible to persons in wheelchairs and is equipped with Braille identifiers. Condon Hall is a designated non-smoking area.

Commentary. Student descriptions of Seattle and the surrounding area were uniformly very favorable. It was described as "really beautiful," "a great place," and "unlike other large cities." When asked to be more specific about the advantages of living in Seattle, students mentioned a variety of recreational and entertainment opportunities. Less than an hour's drive to the east of the city are the mountains, which offer hiking, skiing, and other similar activities; to the west are beaches, which offer surf and sun; and the University offers various programs such as sailing and canoeing. Seattle itself offers a rich variety of restaurants, including Thai, Chinese, Mexican, and other ethnic cuisines as well as more traditional "four-star" type restaurants. Indeed, the "melting pot" metaphor often used to describe American society exhibits a redoubling of meaning when applied to the restaurant trade in Seattle, as cuisines such as Thai mix with European styles to produce a "fusion" cuisine that exhibits elements of both but that cannot strictly speaking be called either Thai or European. The city is also a stop for major entertainment tours, and students mentioned recent performances of *Les Miserables* and *Phantom of the Opera* as well as a concert by Sting. Additionally, students said that there is a wealth of coffee houses, pubs, wineries, breweries, ethnic theaters, cinemas, professional sports, and other attractions. And on top of all of that, the people are "friendly" and the lifestyle is "relaxed." Not even the weather is a source of disappointment, which, students said, is much maligned by those who are not really familiar with Seattle.

Paradoxically, amid the glowing descriptions, it seemed at times possible to detect a certain reluctance on the part of students to say too much about Seattle, as though favorable publicity might attract too many people from other parts of the country, thereby upsetting the delicate balance of population that creates Seattle's attractive life-style. Indeed, one student joked that "too many Californians were moving to the region after they had screwed up their own state," and another quipped that recruiters from the East Coast think that visiting the University of Washington Law School is a waste of time because U of W graduates don't leave the Seattle area. (Of a recent graduating class of 148, at least 70 people remained in the Seattle area, with another 21 staying in areas of Washington state.)

The law school is located three or four blocks from the University of Washington's main campus. The main campus was described as "gorgeous" with "beautiful trees, walkways, and fountains"; Condon Hall was described as "a large concrete slab," "a disaster resulting from budgetary pressures," and "an architectural wart." There must be some truth to these observations, as a columnist for one of the Seattle newspapers included the building in a list of the "10 ugliest" buildings in Seattle. On the other hand, students conceded that the building "serves its function." Although space may not be overly abundant, second- and third-year students generally can get a study carrel; there are two student lounges (one "quiet" lounge and one "talking" lounge); computer facilities are generally adequate (except perhaps during exam time); and there is a cafeteria across the street that is patronized by students and professors (too many professors for the likes of some students who were not always well prepared for class).

Regarding the atmosphere at the law school, students thought that their classmates might be a little more "mellow" and "cooperative" than students at other schools, though they did allow that some "hidden competition" is probably inherent in any law school. There is a "peer mentor" program that pairs first-year students with upperclass students, and numerous organizations make available outlines and other study aids. Moreover, students reported that classmates freely exchange their own outlines and textbooks. Additionally, the grading system, under which most students receive a "pass," is designed to relieve competitive pressures. The law school also operates on the quarter system, and the first sets of exams are usually given relatively little weight.

Reports also indicate that the social life at the law school is variegated. Every other Friday (or so), there is a TGIF "keg party" that attracts 50 or more students, and the ethnic student associations stage a variety of events. (A recently concluded Cinco de Mayo celebration featuring food and various exhibits was mentioned frequently and with enthusiasm.) In addition, there are softball, soccer, and "flag football" leagues, and some measure of the student interest in such activities can be gotten from the number of teams fielded by the students for the softball league: six first-year teams and four upperclass teams.

While the features noted above about the quality of life at the law school help to distinguish the University of Washington from other law schools, they may not make it unique. There is, however, one aspect of the student body that does set Washington apart from other law schools: for the Class of 1994, about 35% of the students are members of various minority groups, and over half are women. The current mix was arrived at in a fairly short period of time. The number of minority students increased from 24 to 59 in a single year, and the number of women students from 64 to 88 in the following year. Most students interviewed felt that this rich diversity truly contributes to the learning environment at the law school, but there are some problems. Some students reported that "majority" students feel a certain frustration regarding some school policies. For example, all entering students receive two days of orientation; minority students receive a third day. And some students seem to be haunted by the "PC" specter. They said that there is sometimes a reluctance to speak forcefully and frankly on some issues for fear of saying something that is "politically incorrect." What should be emphasized, however, is that none of the students interviewed thought the awkwardness to be a terrible disadvantage of the law school.

ACADEMICS | According to Dean of the Law School Wallace D. Loh, the University of Washington School of Law is a small, state-assisted law school committed to excellence in teaching, scholarship, and public service. Dean Loh explains that this excellence begins with a solid foundation in traditional curricular offerings, as well as offerings in new areas such as Alternative Dispute Resolution. The dean notes that the law school has earned a reputation for teaching that makes use of small classes, clinical experiences, and a friendly faculty to assist students in becoming practitioners committed to the ideal of ethics and excellence in the profession. And, the dean adds, the Pacific Northwest is known for its leadership in Pacific Rim trade, environmental awareness, sophisticated health sciences community, and high technology industrial base; so, the law school's location enhances its programs in East Asian Law, Environmental Law, and Law of the Sea—programs that draw upon the resources of the broader University and regional community. Finally, the dean adds, the School of Law is committed to serving students of all ethnic backgrounds.

CURRICULUM

First-Year Courses: Contracts, Civil Procedure, Property, Torts, Criminal Law, Basic Legal Skills, Constitutional Law

Interesting Electives: American Indian Law, Arms Control and Disarmament, Copyright Law, Disabled and the Law, Environmental Law, Feminist Legal Theory, Income Maintenance Legislation, Law in East Asia (several offerings), Mediation of Disputes, Natural Resources, Payment Systems, Transmission of Wealth, Transnational Tax, Water Law

---

Commentary. Students echoed the dean's remarks about the structure of the curriculum of the law school and explained that it is the philosophy of the dean to develop areas of emphasis that seem to be extensions of the needs and advantages of the university and surrounding community. For example, the law school's geographical position does suggest that an emphasis on East Asian and

Comparative Law would be appropriate. Also, the law school is developing a program on Health Law because the University has a particularly good medical school. As one student put it, it would be possible to get a more rounded legal education elsewhere, but Washington offers a lot of classes that are "on the cutting edge."

Another unusual feature of the curriculum is its public service requirement. Before graduation, students must perform 60 hours of public service work; they receive 2 hours of academic credit for the work, and the requirement can be fulfilled by doing an externship with a judge or a government agency such as the prosecutor's office. The requirement is relatively new and was not implemented until a vote was taken among the student body. The result of that vote: 85% or more favored the adoption of the new requirement.

The first-year classroom experience does not seem to have left any profound impressions on those interviewed. The use of the Socratic method was described as "nonconfrontational" and even "mellow." Some professors call upon students at random, while others assign specific students to be prepared on particular dates, and still others try to rely mostly on volunteers. For the most part, it was said, if a student is foundering, the professor will move on to another student or try to coach out a correct response.

Finally, though one student said that whether or not faculty are accessible is a "point of controversy," most agreed that the faculty are accessible, though they added that some are "amazingly busy" and so sometimes difficult to reach. Even the dean, however, is available by appointment and will stop in the corridor to chat for a few moments. There are a few opportunities for students and faculty to socialize. During the first year, students are assigned faculty advisors and usually have lunch with them once a quarter, but teachers may or may not be seen at various student functions. (Several teachers attended the Cinco de Mayo celebration, mentioned above, though the students who were interviewed were not clear whether they did so out of interest in the exhibits or the food that was served.)

ADMISSIONS | According to Kathy Swineheart, Director of Admissions, the objective of the law school's admissions program is to select individuals who have the highest potential for achievement in and contribution to the legal profession, legal scholarship, or law-related work. The law school has determined that this objective is best attained by the selection of individuals who have the greatest capacity for high-quality academic work at the law school and who will contribute to the diversity of the student body and of the legally trained segment of the population.

Ms. Swineheart explains that files are considered only when they are complete. They are then read by the Admissions Office staff or the Assistant Dean. Approximately 90 percent of all decisions are made in the Admissions Office, but the last 200 (very difficult) choices are made by the admissions committee.

From this group come the last admissions, the waiting list, and the last denials. Ms. Swineheart explains that the Admissions Office waits until it has a meaningful applicant pool before it begins its deliberations, a process that usually starts by mid-January and is completed by April 1. There is no minimum LSAT score or GPA below which applicants are not considered, but Ms. Swineheart advises prospective applicants to consult the admissions data for the previous year's entering class (published in the law school's admissions bulletin).

Ms. Swineheart goes on to explain that in cases where numerical indicators do not appear to be an adequate measure of academic potential, the admissions decision incorporates a number of other factors such as: the difficulty or ease of the undergraduate curriculum and the scholastic quality of the school, the nature and attainment of an advanced degree, the applicant's post-college experience as it relates to the applicant's academic potential, any substantial changes in the applicant's health or economic position as they would affect academic performance, the quality and strength of recommendations which address the applicant's academic potential, variations in the level of academic achievement over time, social or economic disadvantage experienced by the applicant that may have affected past academic performance, and any other indicators that may aid in the determination of academic potential.

ADMISSIONS DATA

	Class of 1993	Class of 1994
Applied	2,100	2,400
Median LSAT	N/A	N/A
Median GPA	N/A	N/A
Accepted	443	449
Median LSAT	94.5 percentile	94.5 percentile
Median GPA	3.51	3.53
Enrolled	161	156
Median LSAT	92.3 percentile	92.3 percentile
Median GPA	3.39	3.34

The Personal Statement. Ms. Swineheart says that the personal statement is "very important" when it notes diversity characteristics and other information not included in other parts of the application.

STATISTICS: CLASS OF 1994

LSAT Score (percentiles)	Applied	Accepted	GPA	Applied	Accepted
96–99	315	199	3.75 +	208	109
91–95	301	84	3.50–3.74	484	144
81–90	506	65	3.25–3.49	574	105
71–80	321	25	2.00–3.24	524	54
61–70	268	25	2.75–2.99	320	17
41–60	364	30	2.50–2.74	141	6
0–40	329	17	2.25–2.49	69	6
			Below 2.24	22	0

Recommendations. Ms. Swineheart says that recommendations may be very significant, especially in "borderline" cases or in matters of diversity. The strongest recommendations, notes Ms. Swineheart, are those submitted by a teacher who knows the applicant's work and can give a well-substantiated assessment of the applicant's academic potential. For applicants who have been out of school for some time, professional recommendations are appropriate.

Interviews. Ms. Swineheart says that formal interviews are not part of the admissions process but adds that prospective applicants may visit the law school to meet with the admissions staff for answers to any questions they may have.

Minority Applications. Ms. Swineheart notes that the law school looks for a diverse entering class and that it considers a number of factors, including ethnicity.

Application Tips. The Law School will only accept two recommendations. Additional ones will not be considered. Therefore, Ms. Swineheart advises, applicants should choose their recommenders "judiciously" and in light of their function, as described above, Ms. Swineheart notes also that applicants who have a history of poor test-taking skills are invited to submit appropriate documentation of that fact (e.g., an SAT score report) and to comment briefly on that topic in the personal statement. The following data are taken from the table of admissions statistics mentioned above by Ms. Swineheart:

Of course, candidates whose applications combined both a high LSAT score with a high GPA were more likely to be accepted than the summaries above suggest. For example, all of the 45 applicants with LSAT scores in the 96th percentile or better and GPAs of 3.75 or better were accepted. Conversely, candidates whose applications combined a lower LSAT score with a lower GPA were less likely to be accepted.

P LACEMENT According to its director, Earl Young, the Career Development Office schedules interviews at the law school with firms, government agencies, legal service and public defense organizations, corporations, accounting firms, and other employers. Recently, about 120 recruiters visited the campus. In addition, the Career Development Office maintains a file of current job openings; publishes a regular placement bulletin advertising these listings; produces annually updated material on judicial clerkships, federal hiring, Rule 9 certification, resume and interview preparation, and Washington bar examination registration information; counsels students and graduates on resume writing and job hunting techniques; arranges special group programs; assembles employment and bar exam statistics; and keeps a small lending library of useful books and reports on legal employment.

Commentary. Students reported that the placement office at the law school is in transition, a transition, they hope, that is almost complete. It seems that a

PLACEMENT DATA

	Class of 1991	Class of 1990
Placed at Graduation	87%	84%
Placed within 90 Days	N/A	N/A
U.S. Supreme Court Clerks	0	0
U.S. Appellate Court clerks	1	2
U.S. District Court Clerks	4	5
State Appellate Court Clerks	2	1
Other Judicial Clerks	3	5
Median Starting Salary	$46,000	$47,000

couple of years ago, the placement office lost its permanent director and that it was not particularly effective under its interim director. Recently, however, a new permanent director was hired, and the name of the placement office was changed to Career Development. The change in the name, students said, is significant, for it signals a shift from the traditional activity of "placing" students in positions (primarily firms) to a broader approach that includes counseling on long-term career development and alternative career paths. Of course, Career Development also continues to offer the usual support such as assistance on resume preparation and advice on interviewing skills.

A STUDENT SAMPLER | A recent entering class at the law school included students from over 75 undergraduate institutions including Berkeley, Boston College, Brown, California Institute of Technology, Chicago, Colgate, Columbia, Dartmouth, Duke, Rice, Smith, Stanford, Tufts, Washington, Washington State, and Yale. Many of the students have traveled throughout the world, are fluent in many languages, are athletic superstars, have owned their own businesses, have worked in the private and public sectors (including working with top political figures), and many are engineers, teachers, pharmacists, poets, or musicians. Students hold advanced degrees including the MD, the DDS, and the PhD. Many of the JD students also pursue joint degrees, especially in Business, Public Affairs, and International Studies.

NOTEWORTHY GRADUATES

Jeff Brotman, founder and CEO of COSTCO; Representative Thomas Foley, Speaker of the House of Representatives; Larry Mounger, Chairman and CEO of Pacific Trail Inc.

WASHINGTON AND LEE UNIVERSITY

▼

SCHOOL OF LAW
LEXINGTON, VIRGINIA 24450
(703) 463-8504

ADMISSIONS

Applied: 2,345

Accepted: 367

Enrolled: 120

Median LSAT: 89.7 percentile

Median GPA: 3.29

STUDENT BODY

Total: 384

Women: 40%

Minorities: 14%

Average Age: 26

ACADEMIC RESOURCES

Library Volumes: 270,000

Computer Services: WESTLAW, LEXIS, word processors

Student/Faculty Ratio: 13:1

FINANCES (ACADEMIC YEAR)

Tuition and Fees:	$12,226
Housing:	$ 1,840
Meals:	$ 2,000
Total:	$16,066

E NVIRONMENT Founded in 1749, Washington and Lee was named Liberty Hall in 1776, shortly before the signing of the Declaration of Independence. Not long after that, the Trustees changed the name to Washington College, in honor of the country's first president and the college's first major benefactor. The forerunner of the School of Law was Lexington Law School, organized in 1849 by the Honorable John White Brockenbrough, a U.S. District Court Judge for the Western District of Virginia, who also happened to be a trustee of Washington College. The law school became affiliated with Washington College after Robert E. Lee was named pres-

236

ident of the college in 1865. The name was changed to Washington and Lee University in 1870, when General Lee died. He is buried in the university's chapel, and his famous horse, Traveller, is buried right outside.

The law school has gained its national reputation by growing not bigger but better. In fact, W&L is the smallest national law school—with a typical entering class of no more than 120. Lewis Hall contains no classrooms seating more than 75 students, and each student is assigned a carrel or office space. The school's size has enabled it to compete effectively for faculty members who are as energetic as they are well qualified mainly because the size allows the personal involvement, interaction, and intensity W&L professors consider important to teaching law.

The town of Lexington is another important asset of the law school. It offers a community existence instead of a commuter existence, and that is one of the main reasons that faculty members are so available so much of the time. Additionally, Lexington offers many housing options, ranging from apartment to house rentals, in addition to the law school's apartments adjacent to the academic building. Many students get involved in university activities as well. One third-year student has staged his own plays in the theater, with undergraduate and law school actors. Another coaches lacrosse. The scale of the entire university-town community encourages what can only be called a shared "school spirit."

Commentary. When a law school's literature says virtually nothing about its host community, one would naturally suspect that nothing very noteworthy is happening there; that appears to be the case with Lexington. Students said that the town has a Kroger grocery store, a Wal-Mart, and a K-Mart (but no indoor shopping mall), a handful of restaurants (mostly fast food franchises but one where dinner plus drinks for two runs as high as $80), one movie theater (plus a drive-in), some small Civil War museums (including the Stonewall Jackson house), and three bars with a fourth one expected to open soon (described by a student in a perhaps not-so-tongue-in-cheek tone as a much anticipated event). As one student remarked of Lexington, "Night life is not really one of the town's strong points." The favorite hangout of law students is "The Palms." Finally, students made a point of noting that Lexington sits at the junction of I81 and I64 and that Roanoke is only 45 minutes away, Washington, D.C. only 3.5 hours away, and the Atlantic Ocean only 5 hours away. Lexington does not have an airport.

Obviously, the Lexington life-style will not be to everyone's liking, but for those who prefer small-town living, its "quiet and congenial" atmosphere may be very attractive. And students described the Shenandoah Valley (situated between the Blue Ridge and Allegheny Mountains) in very positive terms, calling it some of the "most beautiful country in the world." What Lexington lacks in terms of "prepackaged diversions," it makes up for, students said, by offering an "unlimited" variety of outdoor activities including kayaking, mountain biking, hunting, fishing, tubing, and white-water rafting.

Because Lexington is so small, the focus of student social life tends to be the law school itself. The Student Bar Association has a substantial "beer budget" and organizes many recreational and social activities such as the spring softball tournament, in which "about three-quarters of the school participates," and a string of parties for various events such as Halloween and Mardi Gras. Plus, individual students host parties at their own homes. The result is a fairly tight-knit law school community in which students know their classmates as people and not just as faces and names.

Students said that the law school's physical plant, which was built in the mid-1970s and designed specifically to house the law school, is not particularly imposing from the outside ("it has no ivy and no pillars"), but they also said that the library and other facilities are very functional and even comfortable (though some thought orange a peculiar color for carpeting and other upholstery). Students noted particularly the availability of videotaping equipment that can be used to tape classes (subject to the professor's approval). It is necessary only to contact the AV staff in the library, who control the equipment from a central location. Tapes are also placed on reserve in the library and can be played on machines there to make up missed classes or to review difficult material.

Students are given 24-hour access to the building and are assigned individual carrels that function as both "desk and locker." Students even feel comfortable taking naps on a couch and walking around in socks. This arrangement tends to encourage students to be at the law school even on weekends and at odd hours and helps to foster the sense of community mentioned above. Students noted further that the sense of a close student community also tends to minimize feelings of competitiveness. As one student explained, "At the beginning, 20 or 25 people were really 'go-getters,' but by October everyone had mellowed out." Or, as was also noted, "You don't want people even to think that you are competitive; it's more than just a 'no-no,' it's not even talked about."

ACADEMICS According to Dean of the Law School Randall P. Bezanson, Washington and Lee is a small, private, and highly selective law school with a total student body of about 350 students and a faculty (excluding adjunct professors) of roughly 35. With one of the best student/faculty ratios in the country, the dean says that Washington and Lee's educational philosophy is to provide the most personalized yet rigorous legal education possible, with a very heavy emphasis on writing as the central discipline of the learning process. All writing at Washington and Lee, the dean explains, is supervised by full-time, tenure-track faculty. The clinical programs, too, are run by tenure-track faculty.

The dean elaborates on the emphasis on writing by noting that research and writing are pervasive through the three years of study. In the first year, writing in various forms takes place in virtually all courses. In one course each semester, the research and writing is conducted in a small class (18 to 20 students) and is fully integrated into the substantive coursework in the class. The objective of the first year is to provide the basic jurisprudential and analytical building blocks and to do so through heavy emphasis on research and writing.

The dean continues by pointing out that the emphasis on writing is also found in the second and third years, where it broadens into a wider array of fields. By the third year, the dean says, students work in very small, often tutorial, arrangements on joint projects with faculty, and that the faculty-student relationship has matured into one of mentor and colleague. In the second and third years, students are required to select from a range of special tutorials, interdisciplinary seminars, law review writing, and clinical programs, and to undertake a sustained and synthetic research-based project with one or more faculty members. These projects often explore the relationship between fields of law or between law and other disciplines (commerce, economics, history, medicine, science, and technology). Through the three years, the dean concludes, the educational philosophy is focused on providing intellectually challenging as well as professionally rigorous training and doing so on a scale permitted by what is perhaps the best student/faculty ratio in the country.

CURRICULUM

First-Year Courses: Contracts, Criminal Law, Property I and II, Torts, American Public Law Process, Civil Procedure, Criminal Procedure, Introduction to the Lawyer's Role

Interesting Electives: Bioethics; Communications Law; Comparative Legal Systems; Consumer Protection; Disrupted Transactions; Intellectual Property; International Law; Land Use Regulation; Local Government; Negotiation and Mediation Seminar; Race, Racism, and American Law; Real Estate Transactions; Securities Regulation; Sports and Entertainment Law; Supreme Court Practice

---

Commentary.   When asked about any features that might make the W&L curriculum distinctive, students responded that the law school is very strong on business-type courses, including Securities Regulation, but that its offerings seem pretty standard. One student, who thought the academic philosophy of the law school to be fairly conventional, said, "The first year they scare you to death; the second year, they work you to death; and the third year, they bore you to death."

The small size of the law school is a slight disadvantage, students said, because the number of offerings is somewhat limited; and the small size of Lexington is a disadvantage because the law school just cannot offer the same variety of clinical programs that one might find at a law school in a larger city. The law school has apparently tried to maximize clinical opportunities and has even established a program in West Virginia at a federal prison for women, but students reported that there are still more students interested in such programs than there are positions available. And, it was said, the method for allocating those scarce slots is "a mystery to students."

On the other hand, students said that the small size of the school helps to make the faculty accessible. In fact, it is a policy of the law school that teachers may not have office hours. Instead, it is expected that while they are at the law school they will be in their offices with doors open and available for student consultations. It was remarked, however, that some teachers seem to have "just stepped out to the restroom" with greater frequency and for a longer duration than seems reasonable. Students also said that while some professors are not particularly outgoing, others are especially interested in students as people and attend various law school functions.

Nor does the first year at W&L seem to be particularly stressful. It is necessary "to be prepared," and one professor reportedly requires students to stand for up to 30 minutes as part of the Socratic inquiry; but even that professor is well-liked by students. And, students added, they had the sense that the work load in the first year is fairly distributed and that professors do not unnecessarily burden students with useless reading.

ADMISSIONS | According to Assistant Dean of the Law School Susan Palmer, the admissions committee at Washington and Lee is composed of three members: the assistant dean and two faculty members. The law school does not use any type of index or formula, and there are no "cut-offs" or points below which applicants are withheld from the committee or automatically rejected. In fact, Dean Palmer notes, the range of accepted students' LSAT scores recently ran from the 25th percentile to the top percentile and that GPAs ran from 2.0 to 4.0. The "numbers," Dean Palmer says, are simply tools used to evaluate a student's potential for law study and participation in the legal profession, and if one or the other would lead to an erroneous conclusion, then it is not used. In general, the committee considers undergraduate GPA and transcript, LSAT scores, recommendations, significant employment or post-graduate educational experience, extracurricular activities, special skills and talents, community involvement, and a personal statement if the applicant chooses to submit one. In order to enhance the diversity of the student body, the committee also considers such factors as age and geographic, economic, educational, and ethnic background.

Dean Palmer also explains that the committee reviews the undergraduate transcript itself rather than relying on the summary provided by LSDAS, which, as the dean notes, presumes that an "A" in Calculus is equivalent to an "A" in Volleyball. The review takes into account trends in grades, the rigor of the curriculum, and the level of competition at the school attended.

Dean Palmer says that committee members read everything asked for, including letters of recommendation, personal statements, and resumes. The committee also tries, says the dean, but cannot promise, to read term papers, watch videotapes, or examine works of art that accompany applications. (Recently, the unusual submission of a sample of Chinese calligraphy was passed on for comment to an undergraduate professor expert in such matters.)

ADMISSIONS DATA

	Class of 1993	Class of 1994
Applied	2,001	2,348
Median LSAT	70.7 percentile	75.2 percentile
Median GPA	3.07	3.15
Accepted	406	367
Median LSAT	86.5 percentile	89.7 percentile
Median GPA	3.45	3.50
Enrolled	147	120
Median LSAT	86.5 percentile	89.7 percentile
Median GPA	3.36	3.29

The Personal Statement.   Applicants are invited to submit a personal statement. Dean Palmer explains that the personal statement allows the admissions committee to evaluate unquantifiable factors such as the unique perspective, experiences, and wisdom a potential student can bring to a law school class.

Recommendations.   Dean Palmer states that letters of recommendation can give the admissions committee valuable information about an applicant's aptitude for the demanding academic work required of a law student. A letter from a college professor providing further detail, the dean says, may address whether a student comes to class regularly and well-prepared; contributes thoughtfully to class discussion; shows an ability to think through a problem in a rational, precise manner; uses fact, theory, policy, and logic to support a conclusion; anticipates and responds to weaknesses in a position; writes clearly; speaks well; cooperates with classmates; and is generally motivated and disciplined. The dean adds that non-traditional applicants may have difficulty finding professors who taught years ago and that they should feel free to use employer references;

241

but, the dean cautions, such applicants should keep in mind the sort of information the committee desires and should solicit letters from those best equipped to address those issues.

Interviews.   Members of the admissions committee do conduct personal interviews with applicants; Dean Palmer says, "Yes, impressions and information gained from the interviews can play a role in the admissions process." The admissions interview helps the committee "to assess face-to-face" unquantifiable indicators.

Minority Applications.   Dean Palmer states that because the review process at W&L treats each student individually and does not sort candidates by a mathematical formula, minority candidates are treated in precisely the same way as non-minority candidates.

Application Tips.   Dean Palmer explains that the admissions committee is also interested in learning about factors other than academic ability that may have affected an applicant's grades: having to work while in school; family problems; illness; or an unwise choice of major, whether promoted by parental pressure, ill-advised guidance, or simply the student's uninformed decision. As Dean Palmer notes, an applicant with a cumulative 2.8 who floundered through two years of a pre-med curriculum but then recognized that her strengths lay elsewhere and who turned in a consistently strong junior- or senior-year performance as an English major may have far better qualities than the GPA suggests. And, Dean palmer notes, some students are historically poor standardized testtakers. A student who scored 950 on the SATs but now has maintained a 3.7 at a competitive institution can make an excellent case for disregarding a 40thpercentile LSAT score.

As for letters of recommendation, Dean Palmer says that certain letters are "not terribly helpful": letters from family or family friends (the dean says, "We are delighted that Joe comes from a good home, is an affable young man, a favored escort for the recommender's daughter, and the pride of the neighborhood, but that tells the committee little about the candidate's academic abilities."); letters from elected officials who have no personal basis for their comments; or letters from employers in situations that have little relevance to the admissions committee's task (head bartender, construction superintendent, and so on). The dean explains that it is not that such observations about the applicant's ability to work with all kinds of people, exercise good judgment, and maintain a clear head under pressure are of no interest, but the primary focus of the admissions committee's decision-making is on whether the applicant has the ability to do tough academic work. Dean Palmer advises applicants who wish to submit such "testimonials to their character" not to substitute them for the two academic recommendations but to submit them in addition to professors' letters.

W&L is unusual in that personal interviews are used as a part of the admissions process. Dean Palmer explains that "the legal profession demands intellect and technical skill from its practitioners, but a good lawyer must also be able to work cooperatively with colleagues and clients, to listen well, to articulate a position with some degree of skill, and be a person of compassion, integrity, poise, and, occasionally, humor."

PLACEMENT According to Director of Placement Sandra Philipps, W&L uses several methods to attract recruiters. In February, the placement office mails recruiting information to all alumni and to a large number of prospective employers. Approximately 200 recruiters visit the campus in a typical year, and many of those who do not schedule on-campus interviews nonetheless request resumes from students. In July, the office sends the law school's placement publication, *The Lawyer*, to all alumni as well as to all employers who have interviewed on campus, requested resumes, or hired a W&L graduate within the most recent three years. At the end of the first semester, there is another mailing targeting small firms. In addition, the placement director attends several conferences each year to stay abreast of current trends in the field as well as to encourage employers to consider W&L students.

Ms. Philipps explains also that preparation for the job interviewing process begins even before students are aware of it. As students work with staff on their

PLACEMENT DATA

	Class of 1991	Class of 1990
Placed at Graduation	75%	75%
Placed within 90 Days	86%	85%
U.S. Supreme Court Clerks	1	0
U.S. Appellate Court Clerks	1	3
U.S. District Court Clerks	10	7
State Appellate Court Clerks	4	3
Other Judicial Clerks	7	3
Median Starting Salary	$51,490	$51,312

resumes, the staff are attentive to speech patterns, gestures, and personal habits that are "ingrained" and might be a problem in an interview. Later, students will participate in mock interviews, but the placement office staff will already have had the opportunity to observe them as they act more spontaneously. The placement office also arranges "information interviews" with law school alumni. By talking with alumni, students become aware of subtle differences in a variety of geographic and practice areas and learn "what works and what doesn't."

Commentary. According to one report, students at W&L have a tendency to "hammer" on the placement office. Their frustration, it seems, is partly attributable to the current state of the job market for law school graduates, a situation compounded by the fact that employers just don't want to drive "to the middle of nowhere" to interview law students. But there is also a sense that the placement office is not particularly effective. Indeed, it reportedly has a staff of only two and is tucked into a tiny little office. It seems to be most effective for those who are at the top of their class. Most other students wind up doing a lot of work on their own, e.g., mailing resumes to firms or other employers. Fortunately, most of them are ultimately successful.

A STUDENT SAMPLER The student body at W&L is typically drawn from about 180 undergraduate institutions and from over 40 states. The undergraduate institutions most represented are the University of Virginia with 32 students, Washington and Lee with 16, William and Mary with 10, and Notre Dame with 8. A recent entering class included four students who had earned MBAs and others who held master's degrees in German, journalism, mathematics, and accounting. One student has a PhD in mathematics. Those with "real-world" experiences include military officers, Capitol Hill staffers, and bank vice-presidents. And some of the more unusual positions were a CEO of a general contracting firm, a cartographer, an Alaskan bush pilot and guide, a professor of aerospace studies, an engineer at a nuclear power plant, two college English instructors, a submarine radar scientist, a CIA analyst, a newspaper reporter, and someone already qualified as a lawyer in Russia.

NOTEWORTHY GRADUATES

Lewis F. Powell, Jr., Justice, U.S. Supreme Court (retired)

COLLEGE OF
WILLIAM AND MARY

MARSHALL–WYTHE SCHOOL OF LAW
WILLIAMSBURG, VIRGINIA 23185
(804) 221-3785

ADMISSIONS

Applied: 3,411

Accepted: 587

Enrolled: 173

Median LSAT: 92 percentile

Median GPA: 3.32

STUDENT BODY

Total: 581

Women: 46%

Minorities: 13%

Average Age: 24

ACADEMIC RESOURCES

Library Volumes: 300,000

Computer Services: WESTLAW, LEXIS, word processors

Student/Faculty Ratio: 21:1

FINANCES (ACADEMIC YEAR)

Tuition & Fees:
Resident:	$ 4,622
Nonresident:	$12,002

Living Allowance:
Resident:	$ 8,900
Nonresident:	$ 8,900

Books:
Resident:	$ 800
Nonresident:	$ 800

Total:
Resident:	$14,322
Nonresident:	$21,702

ENVIRONMENT The Virginia peninsula boasts "The Historic Triangle," three treasures of American heritage: Jamestown, site of the first permanent English settlement in America; Yorktown, where American independence was won; and Williamsburg, the colonial capital of Virginia. After a half-century of restoration and preservation, the historic city of Williamsburg offers an unparalleled view of eighteenth-century life. The educational, cultural, and recreational opportunities afforded to all students by the college, the city, and the Colonial Williamsburg Foundation add to the quality of life and education at William and Mary.

The college of William and Mary, a public university supported by the Commonwealth of Virginia, currently has 7,700 students. The campus is a mixture of the ancient and the modern, reflecting the 300 years of the college's past. The Sir Christopher Wren Building, located at the west end of Duke of Gloucester Street, is the oldest educational building in continuous use in the United States. The Wren Building marks only the eastern tip of a campus that includes 1,200 acres, approximately 40 major buildings, a large lake, extensive woods, and many playing fields and tennis courts. Behind the Wren Building and stretching from the Sunken Gardens to Lake Matoaka is a wooded area known as the Jefferson Prospect. Surrounding Lake Matoaka is College Woods, an expanse of acreage which provides hiking trails and an exceptional natural laboratory for William and Mary students.

The law school moved to its new building, located adjacent to the headquarters of the National Center for State Courts, in 1980. One of the major features of the building is the technologically advanced McGlothlin Moot Courtroom, where innovative approaches to the conduct of judicial proceedings both at the trial and appellate levels occur. William and Mary is a university small enough to provide for relationships that cultivate learning and community and large enough to have the resources to achieve excellence.

Commentary. The fact that the Marshall–Wythe Law School is located in the "restored colonial capital of Virginia" helps to define the quality of life outside of the law school in two important ways. First, Williamsburg, for better or worse, is a small town. For worse, its size means the relative scarcity of the entertainment and arts appreciation opportunities that are more plentiful in cities or even larger towns. The College of William and Mary itself has too few students to support the variety of activities that one might find in a college town that is home to a gigantic state university. And, as for diversity, one student quipped that the permanent residents of Williamsburg think that William and Mary's law students are the ultimate in diversity. For better, Williamsburg's small size means that one gets to know one's neighbors and can more easily become a part of the community. And, as might be expected, William and Mary's students are relatively free of the concerns that plague their counterparts in the large cities—although one student remarked, "One never really feels safe here; every two or three months, something bad happens to someone." One should perhaps not make too much of the dearth of diversions. As one student pointed out, the atmosphere is very conducive to study—an activity that law students are likely to spend a great deal of time on. Several students also added that Richmond and Norfolk, each only an

246

hour's drive from Williamsburg, offer the opportunity to hear a symphony or to attend legitimate theater. And Newport News, with its shopping mall, is only 20 minutes away.

Second, for better or worse, Williamsburg's economy is heavily dependent on tourism. For worse, one student complained that living in Williamsburg is like "living next to Disney World in the middle of pancake houses and cheap motels." By pancake house, the student meant a restaurant that opens early (to serve breakfast to tourists) and closes early (once the tourists have returned to their motel rooms). The difficulty with pancake houses is that their schedules are not convenient for law students. Other students helped to put this remark into context by explaining that while Williamsburg probably is the "world's capital of pancake houses," the tourist trade also supports other restaurants, including some that serve ethnic cuisines such as Vietnamese, Italian, Mexican, and Chinese. Furthermore, the historic area, which is within walking distance of the law school, often has interesting programs such as reenactments of colonial life and is said to be a nice place to take visiting friends and relatives.

Reports indicate that law students are likely to remain mostly in the law school building and that they rarely have occasion to visit the rest of the William and Mary campus. Student evaluations of the physical plant were not extreme and included "fairly modern," "adequate," "no grand facades," and "your generic academic building." Only two complaints of the facility were heard, both dealing with space. One complaint about the building, and it was voiced with some frequency, cited its small size. Apparently, the number of students at the law school has grown more rapidly than expected. One student noted that no law school classroom is now large enough to accommodate all of the students in a class; on those special occasions when a class or the entire student body must assemble, they must do so elsewhere on the university campus. Additionally, the lack of space in the library is particularly noticeable during exam time. Students mentioned that the law school is formulating plans for expansion, and Associate Dean Connie Galloway confirmed that the law school would like to increase the size of the physical plant but noted that plans are still in the "formative stages" and cautioned that such projects can take quite a long time to come to fruition. The other "space" complaint mentioned parking space. It seems that recently completed university construction gobbled up some of the parking near the law school and that there was some debate as to how the remaining prime spaces were to be allocated. The fact that such a minor inconvenience could occasion a great "space debate" suggests that, in the overall scheme of things, the concerns of Marshall–Wythe students about the law school's facilities are relatively minor, a point that is fairly readily conceded by students.

If the small size of the town is a disadvantage, then most students regard the small size of the law school as a distinct advantage. They reported that one quickly learns the names of classmates and that friendships are easily formed. The atmosphere was described as "friendly" and "congenial." Students share materials, passing outlines on to classmates (even those in the same year), and form impromptu study groups while sitting in the lounge. The Lawyering Skills component of the first-year curriculum, in which students are divided into groups of only 12 to 15 and assigned faculty and upperclass advisors, also helps to foster a sense of cooperation among students. As one student put it, "As trite as is sounds, when William and Mary students compete, they compete against themselves."

ACADEMICS When asked about the educational philosophy of the Marshall–Wythe School of Law, Dean Timothy J. Sullivan, now President of the College of William and Mary, begins by cautioning that it would be inaccurate to suggest that a single point of view animates the work and teaching of every member of its faculty. Law professors, the dean observes, are intensely individualistic. Yet, the dean continues, there are certain core values that are shared by the faculty as a whole, shared values that impart a cohesiveness and an intellectual unity to the educational experience at Marshall–Wythe that help to make the law school unique.

First, notes the dean, intellectual distinction is a fundamental attribute of a good lawyer, and the admissions process at Marshall–Wythe is sufficiently stringent to ensure that the students selected for study possess the intellectual potential for success at the bar. Once students have enrolled, the law school makes every effort to ensure that their intellectual capacity is tested rigorously and directed along professionally productive lines. Additionally, early on the curriculum emphasizes the acquisition of essential skills.

Second, while allowing the primacy of intellectual rigor in the training of a lawyer, the dean states that the faculty firmly believes that the education of a complete lawyer must be more than training in the life of the mind. Most lawyers perform many functions in their professional careers, and they are often advocates, counselors, and community leaders. In the discharge of these functions, the dean says, more is required than an able intellect; traditional traits of character are equally important. "Of course," the dean adds, "a law school cannot create character, but it can make it clear to its students that these qualities, in common with intellectual ability, are important in the education of a lawyer who aspires to genuine professional excellence." Consequently, the dean explains, the Marshall–Wythe School of Law tries to emphasize the human side of the practice of law.

Finally, the dean points out that the law is a learned profession and its mastery, if attainable at all, requires a lifetime of diligent study and practice. In the dean's view, no law school, however distinguished, should presume to claim that its students, immediately upon graduation, are competent to contend on an equal basis with lawyers of longstanding and substantial experience. Nonetheless, it is the goal of the Marshall–Wythe School of Law to prepare each of its graduates for a life in the law which, says the dean, if pursued with persistence and integrity, will be marked by significant legal achievement and unfailing adherence to the highest ideals of the profession.

CURRICULUM

First-Year Courses: Civil Procedure I and II, Constitutional Law I and II, Legal Skills I and II, Property I and II, Torts I and II

Interesting Electives: Administration of Social Programs, Agricultural Law, Capital Transactions, Computers and the Law Seminar, Economic Analysis of Family Law, Education Law Seminar, Entertainment Law, Environmental Law, International Business Transactions, Land Use Control, Local Government Law, Military Law Seminar, Modern Land Finance, Unfair Trade Practices, White Collar Crime

Commentary.   Perhaps the most unusual feature of the curriculum at Marshall–Wythe is the Legal Skills component, in which students are organized into "firms," complete with senior partners (the firm's faculty and upperclass advisors). The student-attorneys handle simulated cases in which clients are played by other students. During an exercise, students may be required to interview the client, write a memorandum to the senior partner, draft a brief, argue a case, even try the case, and perhaps take an appeal. Descriptions of the Legal Skills program suggest that the role-playing is fairly realistic. For example, students studying at the college to become court stenographers are used to take notes at simulated trials and to prepare transcripts. In addition, the situations are sufficiently complex that no outcome is predetermined. For example, if a case designed to go to trial is settled by the firm, its student-attorneys are assigned another case. Before the program is finished, students must participate in all the important phases of litigation.

A more detailed example will provide a better idea of the complexity of the simulations. One student reported working on a firm's last assignment, a criminal case in which a client was accused of vehicular homicide, more specifically, accused of running over an ex-lover with a car. In the initial interview, the client denied the allegations, claiming an alibi. Over a period of several weeks, the student-attorney argued the appropriate motions and prepared for trial. Two days before trial, the student-attorney decided, almost as an afterthought, to meet once again with the client. In this meeting, the client casually mentioned a theretofore undisclosed substance abuse problem that threatened the client's credibility as a witness and the alibi defense as a whole. At that point, two days away from the simulated trial, the student-attorney had to rework completely the trial strategy. Later the student learned that the client had been told by the professor controlling the simulation that in the event that the student-lawyer had made the mistake of not meeting with the client once more before trial, the client should, on the witness stand, break down and confess to the crime, thereby creating a tremendous headache for the student-lawyer.

Comments about Legal Skills are generally, though not completely, favorable. One student thought that the program is a particularly effective way to teach legal writing skills because students are involved in drafting a variety of documents. Another mentioned the program's practical dimension; for example, even though just a simulation, one case required students to research real estate records in the county records office. Another reported that the required participation can be a plus with recruiters. On the other hand, some students suggested that the program is perhaps overly long, as it continues through the second year and must compete for student energies with other activities such as Law Review and moot court; eventually its novelty wears off.

Teaching styles during the first year were said to vary from professor to professor; but, as one student put it, only one or two professors in the whole school use the "official" Socratic method, meaning by that phrase an artificially formal use of the question-and-answer format. Others call on students according to some pre-established order, for example, alphabetically by last names. Teachers are reported to be accessible to students, giving out home telephone numbers and posting office hours. Students noted that the practice of posting office hours is not intended to create barriers to accessibility but as a convenience to students who can be certain that, for the most part, teachers will be available to them at a certain time.

ADMISSIONS | According to Associate Dean of Admissions Faye F. Shealy, the law school has an Admissions Committee composed of three faculty members appointed by the dean. The Associate Dean of Admissions reviews all application files and has decision-making responsibility for the majority of them. Applications from minority candidates and applicants with unusual circumstances and requests are reviewed and voted upon by the faculty admissions committee. As an example of a candidate whose file might be referred to the faculty admissions committee, Dean Shealy mentions someone with a poor undergraduate record but a high LSAT score or professional work experience. The associate dean does not use a rolling admissions process. Applications are reviewed as they become complete, and the majority of admissions decisions are finalized after the March 1 application deadline. The associate dean does not use a mathematical formula to sort applications and has no minimum LSAT score or GPA below which applications would not be considered.

The Personal Statement. A personal statement is required. According to Dean Shealy, the personal statement provides an applicant with the opportunity to address personal qualities and characteristics that might not otherwise be disclosed by transcripts, test scores, employment history, etc.

ADMISSIONS DATA

	Class of 1993	Class of 1994
Applied	3,248	3,386
Median LSAT	75.2 percentile	79.6 percentile
Median GPA	3.15	3.21
Accepted	627	636
Median LSAT	92.3 percentile	92.3 percentile
Median GPA	3.43	3.45
Enrolled	185	211
Median LSAT	92.3 percentile	92.3 percentile
Median GPA	3.4	3.4

Recommendations. Letters of recommendation are required, and at least one must come from an academic source.

Interviews. Personal interviews play no role in the decision-making process, but the law school does grant requests by applicants to learn more about the law school. Dean Shealy adds, however, that no record is kept of interviews granted.

Minority Applications. Dean Shealy states that the law school strives to achieve equal opportunity and to increase the diversity of the law school student body. Both the ABA and AALS, the dean explains, require law schools to provide full opportunities to members of racial and ethnic minorities who have been victims of discrimination. Applications for minority candidates and applicants with unusual circumstances and requests are reviewed and voted upon by the faculty admissions committee. The admission process is implemented with attention to the expected yield in terms of class size, ratio of residents to non-residents, and the desire for ethnic and cultural diversity.

Residency. William and Mary is a state-supported school, and Dean Shealy explains that the General Assembly has issued guidelines regarding the mix of resident and non-resident students. Traditionally, the law school has had a 60 percent/40 percent mix of Virginia residents and non-residents, respectively.

Non-residents should not, however, be deterred from applying to Marshall–Wythe. Dean Shealy points out that, for various reasons, the proportion of non-residents who ultimately accept offers to the law school is lower than that for residents. Consequently, even though non-residents account for only 40 percent of the typical entering class, the admissions office usually extends more offers to non-residents than to residents.

Application Tips. Although the law school does not use "cut-offs," Dean Shealy notes that an application with an LSAT score below the seventeenth percentile or a GPA below 2.5 is just not really competitive. In fact, a review of published admissions data shows that in a recent year the law school accepted only two of 184 applicants whose LSAT scores were below the twenty-fifth percentile, and one of those had a GPA above 3.75. And the law school accepted only six of the 221 applications it received with GPAs below 2.5. Conversely, Dean Shealy notes that the law school receives many applications from people with outstanding academic records from high-quality educational institutions who also have very high LSAT scores. A significant number of these also have individual accomplishments such as work experience and extracurricular activities, often with leadership roles. The difference between admission and rejection in such cases is many times the quality of these "other factors." And the dean adds, some applicants are admitted who have atypical qualifications, e.g., a very high GPA but mediocre LSAT score. Those with such records who are accepted are able to demonstrate by some means, such as work experience, graduate study, or some other accomplishment, that the traditional admission criteria should not be used in evaluating their applications.

As for the mechanics of the application, Dean Shealy emphasizes that brief "Why I Want to Be a Lawyer" statements are generally of no help. Letters of recommendation are helpful if the writer discloses in what capacity he/she knows the applicant and if the letter addresses desired characteristics, i.e., intelligence, motivation, good character.

PLACEMENT | According to Assistant Dean of Career Planning and Placement Robert Kaplan, the placement office uses several different approaches to attract employers to the law school, including mailings to a national employer data base, personal contact with hiring attorneys and recruiting professionals, contact with professional associations, and participation in 11 off-campus job fairs. Approximately 200 to 250 recruiters visit the campus in a typical year. All students receive extensive written materials about interviewing, and several programs are held each year covering interview tips. The associate dean conducts mock interviews which, upon a student's request, can be videotaped and later critiqued in detail. Through the "Of Counsel" program, entering students are paired with alumni mentors who, among other functions, may provide assistance with interviewing strategies.

PLACEMENT DATA

	Class of 1991	Class of 1990
Placed at Graduation	82%	78%
Placed within 90 Days	87%	81%
U.S. Supreme Court Clerks	0	0
U.S. Appellate Court Clerks	5	6
U.S. District Court Clerks	10	14
State Supreme Court Clerks	3	4
Other Judicial Clerks	15	10
Median Starting Salary	$49,321	$45,000

Commentary. Students' opinions about the placement office varied considerably, and the differences no doubt reflected to some extent individual fortunes in the job search. The most commonly heard complaint mentioned the small staff of the placement office: Dean Kaplan and an assistant with perhaps the part-time support of one or two clericals. Students noted that the dean has only three or four slots per day for student consultations and that during busy times of the year it is very difficult to get an appointment. This is not to say, however, that students thought the people in the placement office to be less than competent. In fact, students praised the staff for doing as much as possible with limited resources. But the lack of resources (and William and Mary is dependent upon scarce public funds) does prevent the placement office from doing more.

A STUDENT SAMPLER A recent entering class at the law school included students from 28 states, the District of Columbia, Taiwan, and England, representing 90 different colleges and universities. About 56 percent of them came from William and Mary, Amherst, Brown, Colgate, Duke, Georgetown, George Mason, James Madison, Mary Washington, Miami of Ohio, North Carolina at Chapel Hill, Notre Dame, Pennsylvania, Virginia, Virginia Tech, and Yale. Fifteen of them had earned graduate degrees, including a Ph.D. in Soviet studies from Johns Hopkins, a master's in international relationships from the University of Chicago, and a master's in electrical engineering from MIT. Over half had full-time work experience in areas such as consulting, engineering, accounting, architecture, nursing, teaching,

253

research, and journalism. The class included a congressional aide, a pharmacist, legislative correspondents, a political analyst for the CIA, a Rhodes Scholarship finalist, the Associate Director of the Institution for a Drug-Free Workplace, the mother of an Air Force Academy linebacker, musicians, and athletes, including the Most Outstanding Athlete of the Year from Amherst College.

NOTEWORTHY GRADUATES

Hon. Rebecca Beach-Smith, U S. District Court, Eastern District of Virginia; Florian Bartosic, Emeritus Dean, University of California at Davis Law School; R. Harvey Chappell, attorney and past President of the American College of Trial Lawyers; Jane Fahey, attorney, clerk to Supreme Court Justice Sandra Day O'Connor; Hon. H. Robert Mayer, U.S. Court of Appeals, Federal Circuit; James McGlothlin, president of The United Company; Robert H. Scott, Dean, University of Virginia Law School

YALE UNIVERSITY

LAW SCHOOL
P.O. BOX 401A YALE STATION
NEW HAVEN, CONNECTICUT 06520
(203) 432-4995

ADMISSIONS

Applied: 5,381

Accepted: 407

Enrolled: 183

Median LSAT: 98.3 percentile

Median GPA: 3.81

STUDENT BODY

Total: 557

Women: 42%

Minorities: 23%

Average Age: N/A

ACADEMIC RESOURCES

Library Volumes: 800,000

Computer Services: WESTLAW,
LEXIS, word processors

Student/Faculty Ratio: 13:1

FINANCES (ACADEMIC YEAR)

Tuition and Fees:	$18,810
Other Expenses:	$ 9,580
Total:	$28,390

ENVIRONMENT New Haven enjoys outstanding cultural attractions for a city of its size. In addition to a full series of concerts and recitals presented by the Yale School of Music, the New Haven Symphony Orchestra performs regularly and annually presents a "Great Performers at Woolsey Hall" concert series with guest artists. The New Haven Chorale also gives concerts at Woolsey Hall, one block from the law school. The Long Wharf Theatre and the Yale Repertory Theatre are two of the leading repertory theaters in the country. The Shubert Performing Arts Center and the Palace Performing Arts Center bring in touring companies and nationally known performers. Many movie theaters are within either walking distance of, or a short drive from, the law school. A number of first-rate museums are within

New Haven proper, including the Yale Art Gallery, the Yale Center for British Art, and the Peabody Museum. New Haven is ringed by parks, including East Rock and West Rock Parks. The city maintains tennis courts; eight golf courses are within the area; the Veterans Memorial Coliseum is the site of various athletic events in the winter; and there are nearby skating and skiing facilities. Additionally, all of the Yale athletic facilities are available to law students. And New Haven is one hour and 35 minutes by train from New York City and about three hours from Boston.

Commentary.   Some students had very good things to say about New Haven; others said categorically that living in New Haven was the single biggest drawback of studying law at Yale. Moreover, it does not seem possible to reconcile these conflicting points of view. The differences of opinion coalesced around two aspects of life in that city. First, while New Haven may have its fair share of cultural amenities "for a city of its size," some students thought that the city "compares poorly" to other, larger cities in terms of its cultural amenities and entertainment opportunities. As one student put it, those coming to New Haven from a city such as New York are in for an "adjustment." These evaluations must be balanced, however, by other, highly specific and favorable observations in reports that indicate that there are many student-type activities, including clubs, restaurants, theaters, etc., in New Haven generally and on the Yale campus in particular. One student mentioned, for example, "Toad's Place," a spot famous for popular music "where bands play before they become famous." A telephone call to Toad's Place connected to a long recorded message detailing the club's program for the upcoming month, a program that included a different musical group almost every night. Another student noted that "New Haven is famous for pizza" and reeled off a list of favorite pizzerias. Yet another student added that New Haven has a "plethora of Indian restaurants." Students also echoed the administration's comments regarding on-campus entertainment, specifically mentioning the university's orchestra and drama department. The university's athletic facility is only a block or so from the law school and was described as "old but complete" and is equipped with weights, pools, and squash and basketball courts. Finally, students noted that New York city is just 95 minutes away by train, that those with established contacts in the city are likely to make the trip with some frequency, and that even those who "come from Kansas" would find it easy to make a weekend trip to take in the sights.

The other aspect of the city that occasioned disagreement is the quality of life in the area immediately surrounding the university. It was specifically described by some students as "definitely not safe," and members of that school of thought referred to reports of muggings, acts of random violence against students, and other crimes. One interviewee who held an unfavorable opinion about the area reported having been "chased recently by three kids." Another student noted an incident in which a classmate had been the victim of a particularly bad beating in the area. Members of the other school of thought tended to downplay the significance of such incidents as isolated events and defended New Haven as being neither more nor less safe than other urban areas.

Again, it just does not seem possible to reconcile these conflicting viewpoints because they are probably to a great extent idiosyncratic and depend in important ways on one's prior experience with cities, and also on one's experience with New Haven in particular. Two facts, however, did emerge during the course of student interviews. One, Yale University, a monied and otherwise privileged institution, sits in the middle of a city that has a great deal of poverty. Two, the university is very responsive to student concerns about personal security. The school operates a shuttle service between 6 P.M. and 7 A.M. that delivers students to their homes; recently, it installed call boxes equipped with an emergency button all around the campus; and the campus is patrolled by campus police officers.

Descriptions of the law school's physical plant conjure up stereotypical images of the "Ivy League." It was described as "Gothic," "covered with gargoyles," and "absolutely beautiful." Students also remarked positively on an abundance of stained glass windows, some with caricatures of lawyers and others depicting "legal" themes—sometimes satirically. One report described a stained glass panel above the entry to the law school that depicts a law school classroom filled with students—all of them asleep. Other students mentioned the "nice courtyard" (the scene of cocktail hours) with its grass, trees, and picnic tables. Of course, Gothic style is not to everyone's liking, and a few students thought the buildings a bit dark and somewhat oppressive.

Despite having different tastes in architecture, students generally agreed that the facility is in need of some "TLC." Students noted that the building has ventilation problems and that classrooms are not air-conditioned. Criticisms of the physical plant, however, should not be given much weight as the law school is now renovating its facilities.

As for the atmosphere at the law school, one student perhaps put it best by describing classmates as "very serious but not competitive in the usual sense." In the first place, Yale law students tend to be very serious and are likely to be very busy working on individual research projects. As one student noted, a typical exchange between classmates might go:

Question: "How are you doing?"

Answer: "Oh, I am doing this, and this, and this."

The point of the anecdote is that the inquiry about "how" one is doing is treated as an inquiry about "what" one is doing.

On the other hand, students were adamant that the atmosphere is not characterized by a mad scramble for grades and insisted that students are very cooperative and share study resources. This absence of the competitive attitudes can perhaps be attributed to two features of the law school as an institution. First, students pointed out that the grading policy is designed to reduce the incentive to study for the sole purpose of obtaining high marks. There are no grades at all the first semester—only "credit" or "no credit"—and thereafter the grading system uses only four marks: Honors, Pass, Low Pass, and Fail. No class ranking is calculated. Second, the small size of each graduating class and the reputation of the law school work together to generate an enviable placement record. Consequently, employers are competing for Yale graduates rather than vice versa. Thus, at least some of the pressures that seem to work to create a competition for grades at other law schools are simply absent at Yale.

While Yale law students may not be competitive "in the usual sense" of competition for grades, reports indicate that the law school is not therefore free of all competition. In fact, reports suggest that there is serious competition for other kinds of rewards such as working for a professor or having research published in a journal. And while Yale students may not have to worry about landing a job with a large firm, they do engage in serious competition for a different kind of position: the judicial clerkship.

A judicial clerkship is a full-time position, usually lasting one year, as a judge's assistant. Students often accept offers of permanent positions with firms or other employers but then defer the start of that employment in order to take advantage of the special educational value of a clerkship. And the more prestigious the court, the more severe the competition for the clerkship. About half of each class end up accepting a clerkship, so even those who at the time they entered law school had no intention of clerking may be caught up in the competition for clerkships; the pressure on those in the hunt begins building in the second semester of the first year.

There is a second way the competition at Yale may be said to be different from that at other law schools: the motivation to succeed. Entering law students at Yale are told that "the pressure is off," meaning that once accepted by the law school, a student no longer has to prove anything by achieving high marks. Further, as one student noted, faculty and students alike recognize that any grading system is inherently arbitrary. Thus, the theory goes, students are free to pursue studies for their own intrinsic worth—not as way of getting good grades. In fact, Yale students do take their studies seriously, and it is at this point that another kind of pressure begins to operate. When one sees classmates producing interesting and scholarly work of very high quality, it becomes necessary to match the quality of their efforts. As one student described the feeling, the "very 'highpoweredness'" of one's classmates is communicated by a kind of induction, stimulating the need to perform at the same level. Thus, the competition at Yale seems to be more internalized and also more a product of self-motivation than at other law schools.

Ultimately, then, Yale Law School is not an institution free of all competition. Indeed, one student wondered how a law school, an institution that selects for highly competitive individuals, could be expected to be free of competition. The game is played at Yale as well—it's just that the rules are a bit different.

ACADEMICS | According to Dean of the Law School Guido Calabresi, the primary educational purpose of Yale Law School is to train lawyers. Its primary scholarly role is to encourage research in law. Throughout much of the law school's history, the dean notes, its teachers, students, and deans have taken a broad view of the role of law and lawyers in society. The law school has sought to train lawyers for public service and teaching as well as for private practice, to advance inquiry at the boundaries of the law as well as to inculcate knowledge at the core. The professional orientation is enriched by a setting hospitable to a wide variety of intellectual currents and designed to produce lawyers who are creative, sensitive, and open to new ideas.

CURRICULUM

First-Term Curriculum: Constitutional Law, Contracts, Procedure, Torts, plus a small-group legal research and writing course and a series of lectures on the history and organization of the legal profession and on problems of legal ethics

Interesting Electives: Advocacy for People with Disabilities; Capital Punishment: Race, Poverty, and Other Issues; Comparative Environmental Law and Politics: The United States, Germany, and the European Community; Designing Public Institutions: The Case of Health Care Reform; Feminism, Gender, and the Law; Financial Market Regulations Justice; Law Secrets and Lying; Law in the People's Republic of China; Limits of Law as an Instrument of Social Control; Narrative in Law and Literature; Nonprofit Organizations Clinic; Procreation and the Law of Family; Power and the American Lawyer; Public Order of the World Community: A Contemporary International Law; Sports and the Law

---

Commentary.   As a comparison of the entries in this guidebook would suggest, there is in general a fair degree of uniformity in the educational process at law schools. One finds, for example, the same courses required of first-year students at most law schools, and certain electives are also offered at most schools. The curriculum at Yale, however, seems to be unique in two respects. First, there are very few required courses, and most of those are taken during the first semester. Second, the course titles of the electives have a noticeably different character from those at other law schools, as evidenced by the list of "Interesting Electives" above.

As for course requirements, students noted that it is not part of the academic philosophy of Yale that the administration or faculty need "to crack the whip" to encourage students to learn nor to "spoon-feed" them the law. Rather, students are expected to be self-motivated and to pursue topics of their own interest. For example, before graduation, students are required to submit two major papers, but they have considerable discretion in their choice of subjects. Someone with a background in anthropology might, for example, choose to use methods of research from that field to study some problem of law. Or, to illustrate again the flexibility of Yale's curriculum, it is even possible to get an entire semester's credit while pursuing an individual research project on another continent. One student, for example, travelled for several months in Europe researching a question of international and environmental law, while another lived for seven months in India, and yet another worked for the Russian office of a U.S. law firm. All got academic credit for their work. In this respect, as one student put it, Yale Law School is more "like a graduate school than a trade school."

Another student described the atmosphere at the law school as "fairly anarchic," a description that was endorsed by classmates. One third-year student pointed out, for example, that official deadlines for course papers tend to be "officially flexible." So much so, that it is possible to dig a hole for oneself by postponing the completion of too many requirements. With graduation only a few weeks away, that student was faced with the necessity of completing two papers before the final official deadline for completing all course work—papers that were not yet begun. But then, as always, anarchy implies an element of danger.

The second element that distinguishes Yale's curriculum from that of other law schools is the distinctly theoretical color of the courses. Virtually every law school, for example, offers a course on "Trusts and Estates"; but at Yale, the course title for that topic is "Trusts and Estates: Family Wealth Transmission," and the first topic listed in the course description is "the policy bases of inheritance and the changing character of intergenerational wealth transfer." In other words, the course is not simply about trusts and estates *per se*, but about the theoretical underpinnings of the very notion of inheritance as well. Indeed, the "anarchy" mentioned above seems also to infuse the curriculum in yet another way as professors are reportedly fairly unfettered in their discretion as to what they will teach. As one student put it, "I don't know if they are ever told specifically to teach anything." The result is an eclectic mix of courses that tend to be highly theoretical. As one student observed, "Yale is definitely not a practical place."

If there is a drawback to studying law at Yale, it is that the extraordinary emphasis on theory and scholarship comes at the expense of "black letter" courses, that is, courses that teach the "nuts and bolts" or the "mechanics" of law. One student, for example, expressed regret at not being able to take a course in ordinary "Commercial Transactions" because the course had not been offered. Other "black letter" courses are, however, available, but they seem almost to be looked down upon as not truly worthy of a Yale student. One student put the issue into perspective by pointing out that while the Yale Law

School experience may not fully equip someone to pass the bar examination, it is always possible to learn the "black letter" law by enrolling in a bar review course (a six- to eight-week course that reviews the basic law needed to pass the bar exam). On the other hand, the student wondered, after spending three years in law school studying "black letter" law in order to pass the bar exam, where would one go for the Yale Law School experience?

Because the experience of studying at the Yale Law School is shaped by the extraordinary flexibility of the curriculum and by the distinctly theoretical element of the coursework, questions about classroom teaching styles do not have the same significance for Yale students that they do for students at other schools. When asked about their first-year experiences, students noted almost in passing that professors ask and entertain questions, and further, that they do not grill students or otherwise make them feel uncomfortable. The whole idea of the "Socratic method" seems to be a non-issue at the school.

As for faculty accessibility, student remarks suggest that teachers *want* to be available to students. Indeed, one student theorized that professors come to Yale because they want to be around Yale students and to become engaged with them. Consequently, professors are available at the end of class, and post-class discussions can spill over into the hallways. Some professors have posted office hours, but others have an open-door policy. In either case, the small size of the law school means that even those professors who are otherwise engaged are likely to be accessible to students when they are at the law school. Students noted, however, that many of the professors are "luminaries" who are almost always engaged in some project.

ADMISSIONS | According to Director of Admissions Jean Webb, the small size of the Yale Law School—approximately 175 in each entering class—requires an extremely selective admissions process. Overall, the law school seeks the most promising students in terms of their professional and academic distinction.

The deadline for applications is February 1, and Ms. Webb notes that applications postmarked thereafter are reviewed only at the law school's discretion and then only after all other complete applications have been reviewed. Applications are considered roughly in the order in which they are completed, beginning in December. An applicant to whom an offer of admission is to be made will be notified of the offer as soon as the decision is made. An application may be "held" for later consideration if the applicant does not quite meet the standard of those currently being admitted but has qualifications sufficiently strong to suggest a favorable decision later in the admission season.

As for the mechanics of the process, Ms. Webb explains that each application file is read first by the Dean or Director of Admissions. A group of the most highly rated files—in the recent past, 20 to 25 percent of the applicant pool—is then considered by faculty file readers. All faculty members participate in this process, each faculty member reviewing between 80 and 100 files. An applicant may be admitted with as few as two readings or as many as four, and the relative weight to be given to experience versus academic achievement is within the discretion of the file readers, who employ ratings based on individual criteria. After the reading process, some candidates may be placed on a waiting list. The use of the list, Ms. Webb notes, varies from year to year, and a number of waiting-list candidates may be held for consideration through registration day.

ADMISSIONS DATA

	Class of 1993	Class of 1994
Applied	5,670	5,381
Median LSAT	N/A	N/A
Median GPA	N/A	N/A
Accepted	377	407
Median LSAT	N/A	N/A
Median GPA	N/A	N/A
Enrolled	179	183
Median LSAT	97.4 percentile	98.3 percentile
Median GPA	3.79	3.81

The Personal Statement.   A 250-word essay, on a topic of the applicant's choice, is required (and should not exceed that length). Personal statements of any length are welcome.

Recommendations.   Two letters of recommendation are required, but additional letters will be considered.

Interviews.   Ms. Webb states that the law school does not grant evaluative interviews.

Minority Applications.   According to Ms. Webb, there is no special procedure for evaluating minority applications. Ms. Webb adds that in rating applicants, file readers are free to consider race, ethnic background, socioeconomic background, and other factors, and that applicants are encouraged to bring to the law school's attention aspects of their personal background and other special characteristics that they believe to be pertinent.

Application Tips.   The applications deadline is fairly severe, and candidates are encouraged to submit applications as soon after October 1 as possible. Ms. Wcbb notes that candidates who file just before the deadline and whose applications are completed late run the risk that the class will be filled before their applications are reviewed. Regarding the personal statement, Ms. Webb notes that the required short essay is likely to play a more important role in the admission process than the optional personal statement. Finally, Ms. Webb states that "letters of recommendation may 'make or break' an application, particularly in the latter stages of the evaluation process." Ms. Webb goes on to explain that an "ideal letter" comes from a person who has had frequent opportunity for direct interaction with the applicant and a basis for evaluating the candidate's academic work. Ms. Webb adds that the "ideal letter" uses specific example rather than abstract adjectives and explains what makes "this particular applicant different from the many other highly qualified applicants in the pool."

For those who want more information about the quantitative qualifications of those typically accepted by the Yale Law School, Ms. Webb suggests that they consult the "grid" that is published annually by the law school:

APPLICANTS FOR THE 1991–92 ACADEMIC YEAR

	Average LSAT Score Percentile						
GPA	0–60	61–70	71–80	81–90	91–95	96–99	Total
3.75+	68/0	46/0	81/3	233/15	214/25	608/236	1,250/279
3.50-3.74	142/1	63/0	111/3	300/12	313/17	647/65	1,576/98
3.25-3.49	173/0	62/0	109/3	228/4	172/4	343/11	1,087/22
3.00-3.24	131/0	46/0	52/0	123/0	79/2	166/4	597/6
Below 3.00	312/0	48/0	43/0	115/0	65/0	100/0	683/0
No GPA	59/1	8/1	8/0	12/0	6/0	11/0	104/2
Total	885/2	273/1	404/9	1,011/31	849/48	1,875/316	5,297/407

In each box, the figure to the left of the slash is the number of applicants; the figure to the right of the slash is the number of acceptances (e.g., 10/2 means 2 of 10 applicants with that combination of LSAT score and GPA were accepted).

263

PLACEMENT According to Director of the Career Development Office Judith A. Lhamon, about 350 recruiters visit the law school campus in a typical year. Additionally, Ms. Lhamon adds, the law school tries to reach out to smaller firms and government and public interest employers of all kinds in order to provide some balance in the view of the profession presented. The Career Development Office does programs on practice areas and sectors of the job market, and publishes many handouts and manuals for students. The Career Development Office also maintains a Career Resource Library and has a part-time Public Interest Counselor. Ms. Lhamon notes also that "the school is small enough that we can give students individualized attention."

PLACEMENT DATA

	Class of 1991	Class of 1990
Placed at Graduation	98.9%	100%
Placed within 90 Days	100%	100%
U.S. Supreme Court Clerks	5	7
U.S. Appellate Court Clerks	40	33
U.S. District Court Clerks	47	44
State Supreme Court Clerks	4	7
Other Judicial Clerks	1	0
Median Starting Salary	N/A[1]	N/A[2]

[1]Starting salaries ranged from $25,000 to $83,000.
[2]Starting salaries ranged from $23,000 to $80,000.

Commentary. Given that the law school has a near-perfect placement record, one would not expect to hear too many negative comments about its placement office. In fact, students said that for those interested in working for a large firm (and the placement office's activities seem to be geared primarily to finding students that type of position), the placement office "works smoothly," contacting employers, scheduling interviews, and otherwise administering the recruitment program. One report said, for example, that students are permitted to request up to 25 interviews for each week of the on-campus interviewing season and can generally expect to get them all. Other activities conducted by the placement office, however, are not so highly regarded. Students said, for example, that they were aware of the interviewing skills workshops offered by the placement office, but implied that few students take advantage of the service, most being confident in their ability to pull off something so routine as a job interview. Finally, the placement office came under fire for its lack of efforts in the area of public interest law; and though students noted that the office is trying to develop a data base on those types of positions, one observed that it really just "lacks the infrastructure" to be very effective in that area.

A STUDENT SAMPLER Nearly 200 different academic institutions are represented in the law school's student body, with the greatest number coming from Yale (73), Harvard (57), Princeton (32), Cornell (17), Brown (15), Stanford (14), Columbia (13), University of California at Berkeley (12), Georgetown (10), University of Michigan (10), and University of Washington (10). Students also represent 45 states and 28 foreign countries.

NOTEWORTHY GRADUATES

Bill Clinton, President of the United States; Hillary Rodham Clinton, Head of the President's Task Force on National Health Care Reform; John C. Danforth, U.S. Senator; Alan Dershowitz, Professor, Harvard Law School; Bill Drayton, head of Ashoka, former head of EPA; Marian Wright Edelman, head, Children's Defense Fund; Fay Vincent, former Baseball Commissioner; Anita Hill, Law Professor, Oklahoma State University, School of Law; Victor Navasky, Editor, *The Nation*; Clarence Thomas, Justice, U.S. Supreme Court; Nina and Tim Zagat, publishers of Zagat's restaurant guides

---

THE
RUNNERS-UP

Boston College

LAW SCHOOL
885 CENTRE STREET
NEWTON, MA 02159
(617) 552-4350

ADMISSIONS

Applied: 6,257

Accepted: 954

Enrolled: 289

Median LSAT: 90th percentile

Median GPA: 3.41

STUDENT BODY

Total: 850

Women: 50%

Minorities: 20%

Average Age: 24

ACADEMIC RESOURCES

Library Volumes: 300,000

Computer Services: LEXIS, WEST-LAW, word processors

Student/Faculty Ratio: 20:1

FINANCES (ACADEMIC YEAR)

Tuition and Fees:	$14,880
Food, Housing, Personal:	$10,805
Books & Supplies:	$ 800
Total:	$26,485

ENVIRONMENT Boston College Law School is located in Newton, Massachusetts, a suburb of Boston. The city of Newton has several parks and public recreational facilities, including tennis courts, golf courses, ponds, and lakes. Numerous theaters, restaurants, shops, and shopping malls are convenient to the law school campus; downtown Boston, just seven miles away, is accessible by public transportation as well as by automobile. Thus, the law school claims the benefits of a campus community in the midst of rich cultural and historical traditions, just minutes away from the many professional opportunities available in the area. The law school is housed in four

269

interconnected buildings, including Stuart Hall, the five-story colonial edifice that is the law school's main building. The main campus of Boston College is located in Chestnut Hill, and its athletic and cultural facilities are available to law students.

ACADEMICS | According to Dean of the Law School Daniel R. Coquillette, the faculty at Boston College Law School strongly believes in the importance of a general legal education that emphasizes preparation for a wide range of professional opportunities. Thus, the curriculum at the law school is designed to develop broad interests and skills which enable its graduates to adapt to the changing demands of society and law practice.

Dean Coquillette also emphasizes that the law school values and attempts to foster a humane and informal learning environment consistent with the acknowledged rigors of a demanding program. Each student is encouraged to create and to utilize opportunities to enrich the others with whom the law school experience is shared. The law school wants students to feel that they are members of a warm, supportive, and vibrant community dedicated to pursuing legal education at the highest academic level.

The dean believes that the law school strikes a proper balance by being "large enough to offer a rich curriculum, yet small enough to allow for scholastic and personal interaction among students, faculty, and staff."

CURRICULUM

First-Year Courses: Introduction to Lawyering and Professional Responsibility, Property, Legal Research and Writing, Civil Procedure, Constitutional Law, Contracts, Torts

Interesting Electives: Asian Law; Entertainment Law; Environmental Law/Hazardous Waste; High Technology Law; Intellectual Property; Law and Lawyers in Literature; Law, Medicine and Public Policy; Regulation of Professional Athletics

---

ADMISSIONS | According to Director of Admissions Louise Clark, Boston College Law School uses a rolling admissions process with the actual decision-making beginning sometime in December. Ms. Clark states that the GPA and LSAT score are the first factors considered and are in the long run the most important ones. An index created from the applicant's GPA and LSAT score is used to direct files to the primary committee reader, but Ms. Clark emphasizes that all files are considered regardless of index and that each is read thoroughly by at least one member of the admissions committee. Furthermore, Ms. Clark notes that the quantitative factors may be interpreted by the committee in light of other factors, such as trends in grades or a history of poor standardized testing. Multiple LSAT scores are averaged (unless there is a compelling reason to prefer a particular score).

A personal statement, though not required, is "highly recommended," and two letters of recommendation are required. At least one of the recommendations should be from a professor. The other letter may come from an employer, an advisor, or some other person familiar with qualities of the applicant that might manifest themselves in a nonacademic setting. Ms. Clark adds that applicants who are removed from college for a significant number of years and who cannot obtain academic letters of recommendation should solicit evaluations from persons acquainted with their intellectual strengths.

The law school strongly encourages applications from qualified minority, handicapped, or other students who have been socially, economically, or culturally disadvantaged, and a special subcommittee evaluates such applicants in an effort to ensure that all relevant credentials are favorably considered. Evaluative interviews play no role in the admissions process at the law school.

ADMISSIONS DATA

	Class of 1993	*Class of 1994*
Applied	5,958	6,257
Median LSAT	N/A	N/A
Median GPA	N/A	N/A
Accepted	1,052	945
Median LSAT	90th percentile	93rd percentile
Median GPA	3.5	3.5
Enrolled	313	289
Median LSAT	87th percentile	90th percentile
Median GPA	3.45	3.41

Application Tips   Ms. Clark notes that the admissions committee may adjust an applicant's GPA in light of the rigor of the course mix and the demands of the academic institution at which grades were earned. The committee looks for any patterns in the grades reported, such as a poor start followed by a strong performance, or a change of majors followed by a dramatic improvement. Further, Ms. Clark notes that outstanding academic achievement despite a history of poor standardized testing may prompt the committee to discount the LSAT score somewhat. Interesting work experience, research endeavors, or graduate study are also all positive factors. Finally, the admissions committee strongly recommends that candidates submit their applications well before the March 1st deadline and that the LSAT be taken no later than December of the year prior to anticipated matriculation.

P LACEMENT According to Jean French, Director of Career Planning and Placement, in a typical year 400 or more recruiters visit the law school campus, while another 1,000 or so employers solicit the resumes of students and graduates interested in summer or permanent positions. The law school is also a member of the Placement Consortium of Massachusetts. The Office of Career Planning and Placement also offers individual counseling, advice on interviewing, national directories and listings of legal employers, and workshops on various topics.

PLACEMENT DATA

	Class of 1991	Class of 1990
Placed at Graduation	N/A	N/A
Placed within 6 Months	95.7%	97.1%
U.S. Supreme Court Clerks	N/A	N/A
U.S. Appellate Court Clerks	N/A	N/A
U.S. District Court Clerks	N/A	N/A
State Appellate Court Clerks	N/A	N/A
Other Judicial Clerks	N/A	N/A
Mean Starting Salary:	$54,900	$52,400

Ms. French says that the Office of Career Planning and Placement does not have available a breakdown by category of the clerkships reported by the law school's graduates, but the office was able to provide totals:

	Class of 1991	*Class of 1990*
Total Judicial Clerkships	31 (12.6%)	31 (15.2%)

A STUDENT SAMPLER In a typical year, the student body at Boston College Law School will represent over 220 undergraduate institutions. The most represented schools are Boston College (97), Boston University (18), Holy Cross (19), Cornell (23), Dartmouth (28), Harvard (22), Notre Dame (11), University of Pennsylvania (14), and Wellesley (16). Nearly 60 percent of entering students have worked, continued their education, or gained some other type of experience before entering law school. Some idea of the diversity of the law school's student body is provided by the following brief student profiles:

A.M. earned a Ph.D. in biochemistry and was already a registered patent agent before entering law school.

B.P. played four years of hockey at Harvard, was part of the 1989 national championship team, and later played two years of professional hockey in Europe.

E.S. earned a master's degree in Renaissance English and was a senior editor with *Cuisine* magazine and a freelance writer for the *New York Times* and *Esquire*.

NOTEWORTHY GRADUATES

Leonard DeLuca, Vice President of Program Planning, CBS Inc.; Hon. Janet Healy-Weeks, Judge, Territory of Guam; Hon. John F. Kerry, U.S. Senator, Massachusetts; Hon. Thomas P. Salmon, former Governor of Vermont, currently President of the University of Vermont; Hon. Joseph P. Warner, Chief Justice, Massachusetts Court of Appeals; Hon. Diane Wilkerson, Massachusetts State Senator (first African-American woman elected to the Massachusetts State Senate)

Boston University

SCHOOL OF LAW
765 COMMONWEALTH AVENUE
BOSTON, MASSACHUSETTS 02215
(617) 353-3100

ADMISSIONS

Applied: 5,943

Accepted: 1,779

Enrolled: 444

Median LSAT: 89.7 percentile

Median GPA: 3.3

STUDENT BODY

Total: 1,200 (plus 200 graduate students)

Women: 46%

Minorities: 19%

Average Age: N/A (54% out of school
one year or more)

ACADEMIC RESOURCES

Library Volumes: 420,000

Computer Services: WESTLAW,
LEXIS

Student/Faculty Ratio: 27:1

FINANCES (ACADEMIC YEAR)

Tuition and Fees:	$16,160
Housing, Food, Books, and Personal:	$10,850
Total:	$27,010

ENVIRONMENT Boston, the largest city in New England, is rich in early American colonial and revolutionary history. Boston University School of Law is located in the heart of the Boston University campus in view of the downtown skyline, in a modern facility completed in 1964. The university campus stretches along the banks of the Charles River and is only a few minutes from the city's downtown area. Within a short streetcar ride are the elegant shops of Copley Square, the sporting events at the Boston Garden, or the diversions of the restored Faneuil Hall market area. Beaches to the north and south, including those of the famous Cape Cod, are within easy reach by car or bus, and the mountains of New Hampshire and Vermont are but a few hours' drive away.

ACADEMICS According to Dean of the Law School Ronald A. Cass, the educational goal of the Boston University School of Law is to teach students to understand the nature of the law, to provide them with training in legal principles and professional techniques, and to equip them to succeed in a rapidly changing world. Thus, the school emphasizes law's relation to other disciplines and the evolutionary nature of legal rules, reflected in the increasing application of law to international transactions and to new technologies.

CURRICULUM

First-Year Courses: Contracts, Criminal Law, Procedure, Property, Research and Writing, Torts, Elective Course (one from Administrative Law, American Legal History, International Legal Process, Law and Economics, Legal Institutions, or Legislation)

Interesting Electives: Communications Law; Computers and the Law; Dimensions of Difference: Legal Rights of Individuals with Disabilities; Environmental Law; Feminism and Gender Discrimination; International Trade Law; Medical Care and Public Policy Issues: The Role of Legal Institutions; The Minority Underclass: Law, Poverty, and the Failure of Community

ADMISSIONS According to Dr. Marianne Spalding, Director of Admissions, the law school typically receives about 6,000 applications for 410 places. Despite the volume of applications, the admissions staff reads each file carefully at least once, and many files go through a number of readings by both staff and faculty. While the admissions process places the primary emphasis on LSAT score and GPA, Dr. Spalding stresses that various factors are considered. A personal statement is required, and it is the first part of the application to be read because, says Dr. Spalding, "It informs the reader about the rest of the file." Additionally, the law school requires two letters of recommendation. Given the volume of applications, the committee does not grant personal interviews, but applicants are encouraged to visit the law school to sit in on first-year classes and to take advantage of the Friday informational sessions held in the Admissions Office. The law school has an affirmative action program and actively recruits minority students. Applicants are given the opportunity to identify themselves as belonging to a racial or ethnic group, if they wish.

ADMISSIONS DATA

	Class of 1993	Class of 1994
Applied	6,165	5,943
Median LSAT	N/A	71 percentile
Median GPA	N/A	3.17
Accepted	1,979	1,779
Median LSAT	89.7 percentile	89.7 percentile
Median GPA	3.39	3.42
Enrolled	422	444
Median LSAT	86.5 percentile	89.7 percentile
Median GPA	3.3	3.3

Application Tips. According to Dr. Spalding, the personal statement should be more than a narrative of jobs held and courses taken, for that information is already provided in answers to questions on the application form, in a transcript, or in an accompanying resume. The most interesting personal statements are those that have a central theme buttressed by several illustrative examples or anecdotes. The best letters, according to Dr. Spalding, are most often from faculty members who have taught the applicant in at least one but preferably more courses. Applicants who graduated from college a number of years ago should attempt to obtain at least one academic recommendation if possible. It is understood, however, that some applicants will have to rely entirely on work or volunteer work recommendations. Dr. Spalding adds that the admissions committee is concerned more with the quality and content of the recommendation than with the importance of the recommender. A generic recommendation from an important government official is much less useful than is the thoughtful recommendation of an instructor who is very familiar with a student's intellectual attributes.

PLACEMENT According to Michael L. Leshin, Director of Career Planning and Placement, over 500 employers nationwide recruit students from the law school in a typical year for both summer and permanent positions. In addition to inviting employers to interview students on campus, the Career Planning and Placement Office organizes off-campus recruiting in popular cities at times when many employers and students can attend. The law school is also a member of the Massachusetts Law School Consortium and the Boston Area Legal Recruiters Association.

The Career Planning and Placement Office also gives support to students by helping them with their resumes, counseling them on job opportunities (both traditional and nontraditional options), and directly assisting with the interview itself. The office staff regularly conducts interviewing workshops, mock interviews, and videotape interviews with professional critiques.

PLACEMENT DATA

	Class of 1991	Class of 1990
Placed at Graduation	48%	75.1%
Placed within 90 Days	51%	82.1%
U.S. Supreme Court Clerks	0	1
U.S. Appellate Court Clerks	2	1
U.S. District Court Clerks	7	2
State Appellate Court Clerks	6	2
Other Judicial Clerks	7	15
Median Starting Salary:	N/A	$55,413

A STUDENT SAMPLER

The undergraduate institutions most represented at the law school are the University of Pennsylvania (71), Cornell University (64), Boston University (60), University of Michigan (48), Tufts University (37), Brandeis University (36), Brown University (34), SUNY Binghamton (31), Columbia University (26), Harvard University (24), and Wellesley College (23). The student body at the law school includes people with different pre-law-school experiences: legal assistants, paralegals, and police officers; management consultants, financial consultants, and insurance brokers; legislative aides, political budget analysts, an examiner from the Federal Reserve Bank of New York, and a former Assistant for the Minister of Education in Poland; medical researchers and physicians; military personnel (including two who served in Operation Desert Storm); academics (several Ph.Ds in various fields); and a waitress, a hotel desk clerk, a ski-lift operator, a chaplain, a florist, a chef, a painter, a press secretary, a translator, a fitness instructor, a former member of the CIA, and even a former LSAT instructor.

NOTEWORTHY GRADUATES

F. Lee Bailey (Trial Attorney); Hon. Edward W. Brooke (United States Senator, 1967–79, Massachusetts); Richard Donahue (President and CEO, Nike, Inc.); Hon. Barbara Jordan (Former United States Representative, Texas); David Kelly (Executive Producer and Chief Screenwriter, "LA Law"); Hon. Paul J. Liacos (Chief Justice, Supreme Judicial Court, Massachusetts); Beverly Woolf (General Counsel, Metropolitan Museum of Art, New York)

UNIVERSITY OF CALIFORNIA, HASTINGS

HASTINGS COLLEGE OF THE LAW
200 MCALLISTER STREET
SAN FRANCISCO, CALIFORNIA 94102
(415) 565-4623

ADMISSIONS

Applied: 3,568

Accepted: 995

Enrolled: 460

Median LSAT: 92.3 percentile

Median GPA: 3.39

STUDENT BODY

Total: 1,271

Women: 48%

Minorities: 25%

Average Age: 27

ACADEMIC RESOURCES

Library Volumes: 500,000

Computer Services: LEXIS, WEST-LAW, word processors

Student/Faculty Ratio: 25:1

FINANCES (ACADEMIC YEAR)

Tuition and Fees:	
Resident:	$ 2,730
Nonresident:	$10,429
Housing:	$ 6,210
Food:	$ 2,790
Books and Supplies:	$ 770
Transportation:	$ 770
Personal Expenses:	$ 3,060
Total:	
Resident:	$16,330
Nonresident:	$24,029

ENVIRONMENT Hastings College of the Law is located in the heart of San Francisco, one of the most beautiful and cosmopolitan cities in the United States. The city is situated on the tip of a peninsula on the central California coast at the entrance to a spectacular harbor. Known for its mild weather and dramatic vistas, San Francisco offers Hastings students a myriad of cultural and social activities, as well as easy access to some of the nation's most beautiful parks. Among its many amenities, San Francisco boasts an outstanding opera, symphony, and ballet (all of which perform within walking distance of the campus); the San Francisco 49ers; the San Francisco Giants; and an extraordinary array of events that reflect the cosmopolitan nature of the city, such as a firecracking Chinese New Year parade, a Carnaval celebration, and the famous Bay-to-Breakers run. Recreational possibilities abound in every direction outside of the city. To the south are Monterey, Carmel, and Big Sur; to the north, the redwood forests and the wine country; to the east, Yosemite and Lake Tahoe; and to the west, the Pacific Ocean.

Hastings is located in San Francisco's Civil Center. This central location offers Hastings students unparalleled access to observe and participate in the legal community. The California Supreme Court and Court of Appeals are virtually adjacent to the college. Two blocks away is City Hall, housing the civil departments of the superior and municipal courts and the San Francisco Law Library. Within three blocks are the United States District Court and the Court of Appeals for the Ninth Circuit.

The college moved to its present location in 1953 and expanded its classroom facility in 1970. In 1980, the college completed construction of its academic facility, which houses the law library, faculty offices, student services, the dining commons, and the bookstore. In 1982, the college opened McAllister Tower, a student housing facility, located one block from the academic buildings. McAllister Tower, built as a luxury hotel in 1927, is 24 stories tall and includes a melange of student apartments from simple efficiencies to large two-bedroom apartments.

ACADEMICS According to Dean Frank T. Read, the Hastings College of Law seeks to impart not only a theoretical understanding of the law but also the essential skills for entry into the legal profession. Hastings' graduates depart with both a familiarity with current law and the analytical tools necessary to shape the laws of the future. Hastings has evolved over the years, the dean explains, to have a broad purpose and mission both to train lawyers and to contribute to the body of national and international legal scholarship. The faculty, the dean notes, is diverse, containing senior scholars who compose the famous "65 Club," other nationally prominent scholars, and newly

---

CURRICULUM

First-Year Courses: Civil Procedure, Contracts, Criminal Law, Legal Writing and Research, Moot Court, Property, Torts

Interesting Electives: Banking Regulation, Capital Punishment, Employment Rights, Feminist Theory, International Law, Mass Media Law, U.S. and Japanese Corporate Relations, Water Resources

emerging scholars. The school has never, the dean insists, lost sight of the need for its faculty to be caring and effective classroom teachers.

ADMISSIONS | According to Director of Admissions Janice Austin, the admissions committee is composed of faculty members, current students, and the Director of Admissions. The review process begins in the middle of January when the applications are placed in a ranked order based on LSAT index. Candidates at the high and low ends are screened first. Decisions are sent beginning in early February and continue through the middle of May. Ms. Austin says that the college does not use cut-off numbers to establish minimum GPA or LSAT scores and that candidates should be aware that if they fall within the "competitive range" (80th percentile or better and 3.15 or better), then they have a realistic chance of acceptance. Applicants who do not fall within the "competitive range" must possess exceptional additional qualifications in order to be accepted.

ADMISSIONS DATA

	Class of 1993	*Class of 1994*
Applied	5,118	3,568
Median LSAT	79.6 percentile	79.6 percentile
Median GPA	3.22	3.24
Accepted	1,266	995
Median LSAT	92.3 percentile	92.3 percentile
Median GPA	3.47	3.47
Enrolled	422	460
Median LSAT	92.3 percentile	92.3 percentile
Median GPA	3.46	3.39

Ms. Austin explains that Hastings does not grant interviews; therefore, the personal statement should be used to discuss or to describe one's background, skills, and abilities. Letters of recommendation can be useful, especially those from academic institutions and particularly if they come from a recommender who has evaluated other candidates to the law school. The college actively recruits and otherwise encourages minorities to apply. Many do so through the Legal Education Opportunity Program which reflects the college's commitment to admitting students from disadvantaged backgrounds. Many other minority group applicants, however, are admitted apart from the LEOP program, and the LEOP program is not limited to minority group applicants. Candidates who apply for LEOP are reviewed by a faculty and student committee. Admissibility into LEOP is based on a determination that the applicant has a disadvantaged background. Criteria reflecting disadvantage may take many forms, including economic, geographic, social, and physical.

Ms. Austin explains that applications that are typically accepted by the college include good grades with a varied curriculum, extracurricular campus or community activities, and perhaps work experience, along with outstanding letters of recommendation, and show that the candidate has strong writing ability as well as some extra dimension such as an advanced degree, fluency in a language other than English, or travel experience. Applications that are typically not accepted show poor or inconsistent grades, "fluffy courses," little or no work experience or involvement in community or campus activities, evidence a lack of writing skills, and include equivocal letters of recommendation.

PLACEMENT | According to Director of Career Services Kristen Flierl, the placement office sends out informational mailings and invitations to interview on-campus twice a year. In a typical year about 400 recruiters visit the campus. The placement office also works with student groups to "market" the College of Law, provides free job listing services to employers nationwide, and is active in national and local placement organizations.

PLACEMENT DATA

	Class of 1991	Class of 1990
Placed at Graduation	81%	82%
Placed within 90 Days	85%	85%
U.S. Supreme Court Clerks	0	0
U.S. Appellate Court Clerks	4	2
U.S. District Court Clerks	8	7
State Appellate Court Clerks	2	4
Other Judicial Clerks	3	2
Median Starting Salary	$53,500	$62,000

Ms. Flierl explains further that it is part of the philosophy of the Career Services Office that on-campus recruiting represents only one component of the job search process. Beginning the first year, students are also encouraged to develop the skills necessary to conduct a comprehensive and continuing career plan rather than rely solely on on-campus recruiting. Students are provided with individual and group career counseling, mock interviews using practicing attorneys, informational programs featuring practicing attorneys, resume and interview skills workshops, and alumni mentor programs.

A STUDENT SAMPLER | While a substantial number of students in each entering class come from California, in recent years over 20 percent have come from other areas of the United States and from abroad; together they represent nearly 300 different undergraduate colleges and universities. About half graduated from a University of California school. Ten percent have advanced degrees, and one in five holds a degree in political science with a slightly smaller percentage graduating in the humanities and social science. Recently the student body has included a U.S. Olympic Boxing Team qualifier, a doctor active in Physicians for Human Rights, a country-western radio station broadcaster, a public health administrator, immigrant boat refugees, a television producer, and a Habitat for Humanity volunteer.

NOTEWORTHY GRADUATES

Willie L. Brown, Speaker, California State Assembly, named one of the "100 Most Influential Lawyers in America" by the *National Law Journal*; Joseph W. Cotchett, partner, Cotchett, Illston, & Pitre, Burlingame, CA, named one of the "100 Most Influential Lawyers in America" by the *National Law Journal*; Fr. James T. Hammer, SJ and public defender; William W. Hodgman, Deputy District Attorney, Los Angeles County, who successfully prosecuted Charles H. Keating, Jr.; Carl A. Leonard, Chairman, Morrison & Foerster, San Francisco, named one of the "100 Most Influential Lawyers in America" by the *National Law Journal*; Anne Cecile Molgaard, Earl Johnson Fellow, State Bar of California

---

CASE WESTERN RESERVE UNIVERSITY

SCHOOL OF LAW
11075 EAST BOULEVARD
CLEVELAND, OH 44106
(216) 368-3600

ADMISSIONS

Applied: 2,201

Accepted: 637

Enrolled: 224

Median LSAT: 83rd percentile

Median GPA: 3.4

ACADEMIC RESOURCES

Library Volumes: 280,000

Computer Services: LEXIS, WEST-LAW, word processors, access to over 700 electronic services and library catalogs

Student/Faculty Ratio: 20:1

STUDENT BODY

Total: 681

Women: 46%

Minorities: 9%

Average Age: 25

FINANCES (ACADEMIC YEAR)

Tuition:	$15,880
Fees:	$ 640
Meal Plan:	$ 2,050
Graduate Room:	$ 3,100
Living Expenses:	$ 4,090
Total:	$25,760

ENVIRONMENT Case Western Reserve is an independent, comprehensive, research-oriented university with total enrollment of a little over 8,000, about 35 percent of whom are undergraduates, 45 percent graduate students, and 20 percent students in professional graduate schools. The university occupies a single campus of 128 acres at the eastern edge of the city of Cleveland. The law school building is a comfortable space for both students and faculty. The faculty have little reason to retreat to their home studies, and students determined to live the law can spend virtually all their waking hours in and around the building. The result is an intense shared experience and unusual sense of community.

Greater Cleveland is home to more than two million people and many of the country's largest companies and law firms. Ranking "most favored" locations for corporate headquarters, *Forbes* magazine put Cleveland fourth in the country. Seven of the city's law firms have more than 100 attorneys, and five of these are among the 50 largest firms in the country. There are innumerable mid-sized and small firms; and besides the lawyers in private practice, there are lawyers in corporate offices, government agencies, and the courts. For the law student, the professional community is the city's chief asset, but Cleveland offers in addition all the other attractions of a major city, including music of all sorts, night life, films, restaurants, museums, parks, theater, dance, and professional sports. The Cleveland Museum of Art and the Cleveland Museum of Natural History are near neighbors of the law school. Housing costs are lower in Cleveland than in most other cities: a typical two-bedroom apartment rents for about $500 per month, utilities included.

ACADEMICS | According to Dean of the Law School Peter M. Gerhart, the mission of the Case Western Reserve University School of Law is to guide the growth of men and women so that they become leaders of the legal profession in the next century. To fulfill that mission, the dean says, the law school has carefully evaluated the knowledge and capabilities that will distinguish leaders of the profession in the decades ahead and has identified six areas of mastery and skills that are likely to be critical: problem solving and analysis, theories of law, preventive law, communication, information management, and professionalism. Dean Gerhart explains that the educational

---

CURRICULUM

First-Year Courses: Fall Semester: Contracts; Criminal Law; Torts; Spring Semester: Constitutional Law; Civil Procedure; Property; Conflicts Resolution; Research, Analysis, and Writing (both semesters).

Interesting Electives: American Indian Law; Bioethics and Law Seminar; Condominiums, Homeowners' Associations, and Co-operatives; Discrimination in Employment; Intellectual Property; International Human Rights; Medical-Legal Concepts; Natural Resources

program of the law school is designed to weave material concerning these proficencies throughout the curriculum in a coherent and systematic way so that the students develop a platform of knowledge, insight, and skill that will serve them in any arena of the legal profession, and will allow them to integrate new information as they continue lifelong learning and development.

ADMISSIONS | According to Barbara F. Andelman, Assistant Dean for Admissions and Financial Aid, the admissions committee at Case Western Reserve is composed of faculty, administrators, and two current students (who assist only in decisions regarding admission policy). The application deadline is April 1, but the majority of decisions are made on a rolling basis between January 1 and May 15. Each application file is reviewed by members of the admissions committee, and Assistant Dean Andelman says that a candidate should view the application as the opportunity for an "interview" with the committee. She urges candidates to put the appropriate amount of time and care into completing the application.

In reviewing applications, committee members look for nonquantitative factors such as the rigor of the undergraduate major, the selectivity of the undergraduate institution, grade trends, the applicant's writing ability, the applicant's work experience, any disadvantages overcome, and whether or not the applicant's first language was other than English. A personal statement is required and, according to Assistant Dean Andelman, is a "very important part of the

ADMISSIONS DATA

	Class of 1993	Class of 1994
Applied	1,832	2,201
Median LSAT	56 percentile	56 percentile
Median GPA	3.01	3.09
Accepted	645	637
Median LSAT	79.6 percentile	79.6 percentile
Median GPA	3.27	3.37
Enrolled	261	224
Median LSAT	75.2 percentile	83 percentile
Median GPA	3.3	3.4

application." It allows the applicant the opportunity to bring to the committee's attention information that the applicant feels is important to the admissions decision, and it allows the committee to assess the applicant's writing ability. Although letters of recommendation are not required, applicants may submit up to three. Assistant Dean Andelman stresses that they should be written by a faculty member or employer who knows the candidate well and can speak to the candidate's intellectual abilities and academic achievements. The law school does not offer formal interviews, but does encourage applicants and prospective applicants to visit the law school and to sit in on classes and speak with current students. Finally, according to Assistant Dean Andelman, the law school actively seeks applications from students of color and takes care during the admissions process to evaluate carefully not only the quantitative credentials of applicants, but other unquantifiable factors as well.

Application Tips.   Assistant Dean Andelman notes that many applicants, in an attempt to overwhelm the admissions committee, provide a lengthy list of every organization in which they have participated, but the assistant dean cautions that more is not necessarily better. A more effective strategy is for an applicant to focus on the one or two that were of the greatest significance and to explain, if possible, the impact that they had on the applicant.

Regarding the personal statement, Assistant Dean Andelman stresses that applicants should try to distinguish themselves from other applicants with similar academic records. The assistant dean says, "Tell us about your three years spent as a volunteer at a New Mexico rural legal services office, or your background in canon law or fifteenth-century Icelandic sagas, or of your interest in admiralty and the salvage of Spanish shipwrecks off the Florida coast." The assistant dean also advises students to make sure that the personal statement is grammatically correct and otherwise free from error: "A sloppy personal statement reflects poorly on an applicant seeking to join a profession in which attention to detail is necessary for success." Finally, the assistant dean says specifically, "Do not describe yourself as a member of the plant kingdom," meaning that essays that attempt to be clever, while sometimes successful, also carry a very high risk of failure.

P LACEMENT   According to Director of Career Planning Debra S. Fink, the law school uses a variety of means to compile its mailing list of employers, and somewhere between 100 and 130 employers visit the campus each year. The Career Planning Office gives all entering students a comprehensive 150-page manual covering a variety of topics, including job search approaches, resume writing and correspondence, interview tips, and information on the office's collection of career planning information and directories. In addition, the Career Planning Office holds regular seminars on interviewing and job search skills and offers students individualized critiques on resumes, correspondence, and mock interviews.

PLACEMENT DATA

	Class of 1991	Class of 1990
Placed at Graduation	51%	57.3%
Placed within 90 Days	75%	85%
U.S. Supreme Court Clerks	0	0
U.S. Appellate Court Clerks	1	2
U.S. District Court Clerks	6	8
State Supreme Court Clerks	0	0
Other Judicial Clerks	6	9
Median Starting Salary:	$40,325	$40,000

A STUDENT SAMPLER The law school's total enrollment is around 675, nearly all full-time students. About half are "from Ohio"—a disparate group that would include the 22-year-old Cincinnati native who has spent the past four years at the University of California and the 35-year-old New Yorker who moved to Cleveland two years ago and has decided to get a law degree. In every entering class, more than 130 undergraduate institutions are represented, and no one college supplies a noticeable block of students. About half of the entrants come straight from college, but the rest have had a year or more—in some cases, very many more—between college and law school. Recently, the student body included the first Peace Corps volunteer in the Kingdom of Rey Bouba, a research assistant to the House of Commons of the British Parliament, a public health officer with the Zairian Ministry of Health, a National Park Ranger, the president of the Game Manufacturers Association, a thoracic surgeon (among other physicians), two caseworkers from the Department of Human Services, a member of the Cleveland Orchestra Chorus, the author of a bicycle touring series, a former director of secondary marketing for a savings and loan, a supervising senior accountant at a Big Five accounting firm, a member of the French parachuting team, a novelist, a geologist, a pharmacist, a member of the Israeli army, a T.V. news anchor, a critical care registered nurse, an intelligence analyst with the U.S. Air Force, and a 25-year veteran police officer.

NOTEWORTHY GRADUATES

William W. Falsgraff, Baker & Hostetler, Cleveland, OH, and Past President, American Bar Association; Fred D. Gray, civil rights attorney, Tuskegee, AL, and Past President, National Bar Association; Hon. Robert B. Krupansky, U.S. Court of Appeals, 6th Circuit; Major General Robert E. Murray, U.S. Army, Assistant Judge Advocate General; Sherwood M. Weiser, Chairman and CEO, Continental Companies, Miami

UNIVERSITY OF COLORADO, BOULDER

SCHOOL OF LAW
BOULDER, CO 80309
(303) 492-7203

ADMISSIONS

Applied: 2,694

Accepted: 480

Enrolled: 165

Median LSAT: 92.3 percentile

Median GPA: 3.28

STUDENT BODY

Total: 490

Women: 48%

Minorities: 18%

Average Age: 26

ACADEMIC RESOURCES

Library Volumes: 255,000

Computer Services: LEXIS, WEST-LAW, word processors

Student/Faculty Ratio: 18:1

FINANCES (ACADEMIC YEAR)

Tuition:	
Resident:	$ 3,078
Nonresident:	$10,080
Housing and Food:	$ 2,048
Fees:	$ 230[1]
Total:	
Resident:	$ 5,356
Nonresident:	$12,358

ENVIRONMENT The University of Colorado was founded in 1876 at the present Boulder campus, which encompasses 600 acres and has more than 160 buildings. The city of Boulder has a population of about 85,000 and the University's student body of 20,000 includes 3,800 graduate students. The campus lies at the base of the Rocky Mountains, accented by Boulder's noted Flatiron Mountains; and Denver, the state capital, is only a 40-minute drive away. The Fleming Law Building, located on the Southwestern

---

[1]Includes a $15.00 one-time registration fee.

corner of the campus, includes the law library (expanded fifteen years ago along with major additions to the law building), teaching facilities, complete trial and appellate courtroom, suites for professional organizations, offices for various student organizations, faculty and administrative offices, and a student lounge.

ACADEMICS When asked about the educational philosophy of the law school, Dean Gene R. Nichol quotes Karl Llewellyn, who wrote, "Technique without values is wickedness." Thus, says the dean, the goal of the University of Colorado School of Law is to ensure that its students graduate "not only with a sound foundation of professional skill, but also with a strong sense of the legal profession's greatest traditions and an equal dedication to public service."

CURRICULUM

First-Year Courses: Contracts, Property, Civil Procedure, Torts, Criminal Law, Appellate Advocacy, Legal Writing

Interesting Electives: American Indian Law, Church and State Relations, Conservation Philosophy and the Law, Death Penalty in America, Patent and Trademark Law, Toxic and Hazardous Wastes, White Collar Crime, Women and the Law

---

ADMISSIONS According to the Director of Admissions, Carol Nelson-Douglas, the small size of the law school and the large number of applicants make for a selective admissions process. Ms. Nelson-Douglas stated that the importance of the personal statement as an element of this selective process cannot be over-emphasized. In *all* cases, the committee wants to get to know each applicant as an individual; and both the quality of the writing and the topic chosen provide important information. Letters of recommendation too can make a significant difference—provided that the writer can cite specific examples of the qualities ascribed to the applicant. The law school does not, however, use interviews in the evaluative process. Finally, the law school believes that the educational experience of all students is enhanced when the student population is diverse. Ms. Nelson-Douglas notes that as part of the law school's commitment to achieving a diverse student body, an application from a candidate with minority or ethnic status is not rejected until it has been reviewed by the entire admissions committee. In the past several classes, she notes, almost 20% of the students have been black, Hispanic, Native American, or Asian-American.

ADMISSIONS DATA

	Class of 1993	Class of 1994
Applied	2,150	2,694
Median LSAT	70.7 percentile	75.2 percentile
Median GPA	3.10	3.15
Accepted	489	480
Median LSAT	89.7 percentile	92.3 percentile
Median GPA	3.35	3.35
Enrolled	177	165
Median LSAT	89.7 percentile	92.3 percentile
Median GPA	3.30	3.30

Application Tips. According to Ms. Nelson-Douglas, the admissions committee does not have formal cut-offs for the LSAT score or the GPA. On the other hand, in recent history, few applications with LSAT scores below the 90th percentile or GPAs below 3.0 have been admitted. Moreover, applicants with LSAT scores below the 50th percentile are almost never admitted. But, Ms. Nelson-Douglas adds, there are exceptions! Ms. Nelson-Douglas advises people trying to assess realistically their chances of acceptance to check the median scores for the most recent entering class.

Candidates should keep in mind, however, that numbers are not the whole story. According to Ms. Nelson-Douglas, "The whole person is who we're looking for *and* what we're looking at." When asked to describe some of the diverse accomplishments of Colorado law students (see "Student Sample" below), Dean Nichol said the attitude of the admissions committee is reflective of a general feeling among Coloradans: "We figure that there are hundreds of ways that a person can prepare for law school."

PLACEMENT

According to Irene Honey, Director of the Office of Career Services, the law school uses two mass mailings each year—one in the fall and one in the spring—to invite recruiters to participate in the On-Campus Interviewing Program. Approximately 100 recruiters visit the campus each year. The Office of Career Services also conducts workshops on interviewing skills and job search strategies and holds mock interviews, and it offers help on creating resumes and on developing interviewing skills.

EMPLOYMENT DATA

	Class of 1991	Class of 1990
Placed at Graduation	N/A	N/A
Placed within 90 Days	86%	92.6%
U.S. Supreme Court Clerks	0	0
U.S. Appellate Court Clerks	1	0
U.S. District Court Clerks	4	3
State Apellate Court Clerks	3	6
Other Judicial Clerks	14	9
Median Starting Salary:	$35,000	$30,000

A STUDENT SAMPLER The median age of the typical entering class at Colorado is about 26, but ages range from 20 to the middle 40s—and occasionally as high as the middle 50s. Most recently, the entering class included journalists, engineers, an astrodynamic programmer for NORAD, a professional basketball player, several artists (working in various mediums from wood to music), and outdoors people "galore" such as a trail ranger from Appalachia and agroforesters from Chad and the Philippines.

NOTEWORTHY GRADUATES

Senator Hank Brown (Colorado); Hon. Allen P. Compton, Justice, Alaska Supreme Court; Hon. Linda Newman, Justice, Iowa Supreme Court; Governor Roy Romer (Colorado); Hon. Luis Rovira, Chief Justice, Supreme Court of Colorado

EMORY UNIVERSITY

SCHOOL OF LAW
GAMBRELL HALL
ATLANTA, GEORGIA 30322
(404) 727-6802

ADMISSIONS

Applied: 3,576

Accepted: 889

Enrolled: 219

Median LSAT: 89.7 percentile

Median GPA: 3.4

STUDENT BODY

Total: 700

Women: 45%

Minorities: 10%

Average Age: N/A

ACADEMIC RESOURCES

Library Volumes: 250,000

Computer Services: LEXIS, WEST-LAW, word processors

Student/Faculty Ratio: 23:1

FINANCES (ACADEMIC YEAR)

Tuition and Fees:	$ 7,330
Living Expenses:	$ 7,500
Total:	$14,830

ENVIRONMENT With a population of 2.8 million, Atlanta is the ninth largest city in the country and one of the fastest growing. Over 400 of the nation's Fortune 500 companies have principal or major offices in Atlanta, and the city is the headquarters for the U.S. Court of Appeals for the Eleventh Circuit as well as the capital of Georgia. The city is home to the Braves baseball team, the Hawks basketball team, and the Falcons football team; the Woodruff Arts Center comprises the High Museum of Art, the Alliance Theater, and the Atlanta Symphony and Chorus. The International Olympic Committee has named Atlanta as the host city for the 1996 Olympic Games.

The Emory University campus is located just six miles from the city center in a residential area called Druid Hills, the setting for the film *Driving Miss*

Daisy. Despite its proximity to the heart of a big city, the campus provides Emory's 9,000 undergraduate and graduate students with an environment as secluded and quiet as that of any rural college. Peavine Creek, a free-running waterway with footbridges, meanders through the verdant lawns, shaded areas, and masses of azaleas and other flowering shrubs that characterize the Emory campus.

The law school is housed in a large, modern building on the southern edge of the campus. In addition to the usual classrooms, offices, interview rooms, and student lounge areas, Gambrell Hall includes a 450-seat auditorium and a state-of-the-art courtroom equipped with studio-quality video equipment. The law library occupies a portion of all three floors on the south side of the building. Most faculty offices are clustered around several classrooms on the third floor, and the doors to these offices are usually open.

ACADEMICS According to Dean of the Law School Howard O. Hunter, the Emory University School of Law strives to develop mature, sensitive judgment in persons who will be among the country's decision makers. Sensitive leadership, the dean explains, requires more than a knowledge of rules of law and an ability to analyze problems. Sensitive leadership requires also an understanding of the role of law in the process of society's orderly change and development. Thus, the dean concludes, the study of law at Emory is more than a process of learning law; it is a process of continuing intellectual development.

CURRICULUM

First-Year Courses: Business Associations, Civil Procedure (I and II), Constitutional Law, Criminal Law, Contracts, Legal Writing and Advocacy, Property, Torts

Interesting Electives: Asset-Based Lending, Communications Law, Constitutional Law: Church and State, Entertainment Law, Juvenile Law, Prisoners' Rights Workshop, Trademark Law

ADMISSIONS According to Director of Admissions Betsy Orr, choosing 225 students from an application pool of more than 3,000 is a difficult process, and many factors are taken into consideration. Ms. Orr notes, however, that an applicant's undergraduate GPA and LSAT score are particularly important. Further, Ms. Orr explains, because the faculty of the law school want to maintain a diverse, well-rounded student body, the admissions committee also considers such factors as extracurricular activities, work experience, level of quality and difficulty of undergraduate courses, performance in graduate school, letters of recommendation, and other nonacademic factors, The application invites candidates to submit an optional one-page personal statement. Two letters of recommendation are required; according to Ms. Orr, these should come from persons who are not relatives of the applicant, who know the applicant personally, who have recent knowlege of the applicant's academic performance and activities, and who can speak of the applicant in personal terms. Finally, Ms. Orr states that the law school recognizes that certain minority groups are underrepresented in the legal profession and that applications from members of those groups are given special consideration in the decision-making process. Personal interviews are not usually granted (though the admissions committee may require some applicants to come to the law school for an interview), but applicants are invited and encouraged to visit the law school to sit in on classes and talk with law school personnel and students.

ADMISSIONS DATA

	Class of 1993	Class of 1994
Applied	3,353	3,576
Median LSAT	N/A	N/A
Median GPA	N/A	N/A
Accepted	930	889
Median LSAT	N/A	N/A
Median GPA	N/A	N/A
Enrolled	267	219
Median LSAT	86.5 percentile	89.7 percentile
Median GPA	3.3	3.4

Application Tips.   The instructions for the optional personal statement specify a limit of one page but do not provide any specific direction regarding content. This lack of direction, explains Ms. Orr, is intentional. The admissions committee wants applicants to distinguish themselves as individuals. Consequently, the choice of subject matter may be just as informative as the treatment given to the theme. The most effective recommendations, according to Ms. Orr, are academic letters, so applicants should solicit them from professors with whom they have actually studied. If someone has been out of school for some time, then a recommendation prepared by an employer who knows the applicant's qualifications may be substituted. Finally, Ms. Orr notes that applicants with both a GPA of 2.8 or below and an LSAT score below the forty-fifth percentile are not usually accepted.

PLACEMENT According to its director, Martha Fagan, the Emory Law Career Services Office invites about 10,000 prospective employers to visit the campus each year. The Career Services Office also schedules off-campus recruitment programs in cities other than Atlanta for the convenience of recruiters. In a typical year, over 225 recruiters will participate in the on- and off-campus interviewing programs. Additionally, Ms. Fagan says that the Career Services Office contacts Emory Law School graduates in the targeted cities to alert them to the fact that Emory students will be interviewing in the area.

The Career Services Office also uses a variety of techniques to prepare students for the job search, including videotaped practice interviews with critiques, an "interviewing dress rehearsal" during which graduates of the law school return to campus to play the roles of prospective employers, and a networking program in which students are matched up with Emory law graduates who talk

PLACEMENT DATA

	Class of 1991	Class of 1990
Placed at Graduation	65%	75%
Placed within 90 Days	N/A[1]	N/A[1]
U.S. Supreme Court Clerks	0	0
U.S. Appellate and District Court Clerks	24	13
State Supreme and Appellate Clerks	10	14
Average Starting Salary	$43,554	$48,103

[1]Placed within six months:
Class of 1991: 92%
Class of 1990: 95%

with them about the realities of the practice of law. Ms. Fagan notes that Emory students have the advantage of a placement office with four full-time staff members who serve a fairly small student body. Consequently, students don't have to wait for attention.

A STUDENT SAMPLER Nearly half of the students at the Emory University School of Law come from the Southeast, but they represent about 200 colleges and universities. About 30 percent of them worked at least one year between college and law school. The schools that are most consistently the largest sources of Emory students are Emory, Cornell, Duke, the University of Virginia, the University of Pennsylvania, and the University of Michigan. Some idea of the diversity of the law school's students can be obtained from the following biographical sketches.

E.R. was captain of Emory's first NCAA Division III varsity basketball team and began to think about law as a career during an internship sponsored by the Georgia Governor's Office working with "adjudicated youths" and their families.

C.K. graduated from Princeton and worked first in Australia on a statistical analysis of teachers' behavior toward male and female students in the classroom and later as a legislative aide to the National Organization of Women.

J.M. earned an M.A. from Columbia in Russian history and particiated in a year-long exchange program at the Moscow State University, attending regular university classes taught in Russian and researching police and judicial archives for a master's thesis.

NOTEWORTHY GRADUATES

Hon. Richard Bell, Justice, Georgia Supreme Court; Hon. Stanley F. Birch, Judge, U.S. Court of Appeals for the Eleventh Judicial Circuit; Robert S. Harkey, Senior Vice President and General Counsel, Delta Air Lines; Hon. Willis Hunt, Justice, Georgia Supreme Court

UNIVERSITY OF FLORIDA

COLLEGE OF LAW
GAINESVILLE, FLORIDA 31611
(904) 392-0421

ADMISSIONS[1]

Applied: 2,150

Accepted: 457

Enrolled: 187

Median LSAT: 86.5 percentile

Median GPA: 3.43

STUDENT BODY

Total: 1,059

Women: 42%

Minorities: 12%

Average Age: 24

ACADEMIC RESOURCES

Library Volumes: 500,000

Computer Services: WESTLAW,
LEXIS, personal computing lab

Student/Faculty Ratio: 19:1

FINANCES (ACADEMIC YEAR)

Tuition:		
Resident:	$ 2,744	
Nonresident:	$ 8,876	
Food and Housing:	$ 4,490	
Books and Supplies:	$ 550	
Clothing and Maintenance:	$ 370	
Personal and Health:	$ 660	
Transportation:	$ 480	
Total:		
Resident:	$ 9,294	
Nonresident:	$15,426	

ENVIRONMENT The University of Florida, with a student enrollment of approximately 24,000, is the largest university in the Southeast and the tenth largest in the nation. It is a residential campus with rich resources because of its size. In addition to opportunities to interact with a

---

[1]Class that entered Fall 1991. The University of Florida College of Law also admits an entering class in the spring of each year.

distinguished faculty, students have ample opportunity to attend concerts, lectures, theater productions, art shows, seminars, athletic contests, and a myriad of other events featuring nationally and internationally known leaders and talents. UF offers students one of the nation's most diverse educational experiences, plus the opportunity to enjoy Florida's year-round outdoor activities.

The College of Law is housed primarily in two adjacent buildings on the west side of the University campus. Spessard L. Holland Hall, named in honor of the former Florida governor and U.S. Senator, Class of 1916, houses classrooms, an auditorium, administrative and faculty offices, and the law library. Bruton-Geer Hall, dedicated in 1984 and funded largely through alumni contributions, is named in memory of the parents of retired Circuit Judge James D. Bruton, Jr., Class of 1931, and of his late wife, Quintilla Geer Bruton. Bruton-Geer Hall houses a modern courtroom, a sophisticated media services department, the Civil and Criminal Clinics, the Center for Governmental Responsibility, the Legal Research and Writing Program, the Career Planning and Placement Office, a student lounge, and a dining facility.

ACADEMICS | According to Dean of the Law School Jeffrey E. Lewis, the University of Florida College of Law is one of the nation's most dynamic and progressive major law schools. The dean describes the study of law at the University of Florida as a "challenging and enriching academic experience." Specifically, the dean says, it prepares students for a life of creative problem solving, dispute resolution, planning, and counseling. The curriculum includes an extensive offering of skills courses and a variety of courses with an international perspective, as well as courses and seminars dealing with fundamental subject matters and issues of current significance in the law. Skills courses are supported by a modern courtroom and state-of-the-art audio-visual resources. Student and faculty research is supported by one of the nation's leading law libraries.

One of the greatest strengths of the college, the dean explains, is its faculty. Known nationally and internationally, faculty members have produced a number of leading textbooks, and they annually contribute dozens of scholarly articles. The dean notes that two members of the faculty are past presidents of the Association of American Law Schools, the preeminent position for a legal educator, and that the college offers a student-teacher ratio of 18-to-1. Another strength of the college, the dean adds, is the student body, which meets the highest national standards as a result of the tremendous demand for admission to the school.

Finally, the dean goes on to explain that the College of Law combines traditional and innovative approaches to the study of law to provide a dynamic professional program. The three-year Juris Doctor curriculum is designed to develop students' analytical ability, practical knowledge, ethical consideration, and communication skills to produce proficient members of the legal profession.

The dean notes also that a variety of teaching methods are employed. In the first year, the "case" and "Socratic" methods provide for stimulating and challenging classroom interaction. Courses that focus on problem solving and seminars that allow for close interaction and individualized research are part of the second- and third-year curriculum.

CURRICULUM

First-Year Courses: Contracts I and II, Civil Procedure I and II, Constitutional Law I and II, Torts I and II, Property I and II, Criminal Law, Jurisprudence, Legal Research and Writing, Appellate Advocacy

Interesting Electives: Agricultural Law; Art Law Seminar; Environmental Law: Control of Toxics, Hazardous Waste, and Governmental Action; Human Rights, Law, and Policy Seminar; Patent, Trademark, and Copyright Law; Products Liability Law; Workers' Compensation and Other Employment Rights

---

ADMISSIONS | According to J. Michael Patrick, Assistant Dean for Admissions and Financial Aid, approximately 50 percent of each entering class at the law school is chosen solely by reference to a combination of LSAT scores and undergraduate grade point averages (ones leading to the first baccalaureate degree). In the absence of disciplinary problems, the dean notes, applicants with "superior" records will be automatically admitted. Approximately 40 percent of each class is selected from a "hold" or "continuing review" category. In addition to the LSAT score and GPA, the admissions committee takes into consideration the flow of effort (ascending or descending) reflected in undergraduate or other academic performance; the colleges or universities where, and the disciplines in which, the applicant's degree was earned; academic accomplishment subsequent to the earning of the first baccalaureate degree; leadership and other relevant activities; evaluations by persons in a position to form an objective judgment as to the potential of the applicant (e.g., undergraduate professors or employers where the type of work is likely to indicate potential for the study and practice of law); maturing experience (employment, military service, and the like); and the applicant's racial, ethnic, and economic background and geographical origin.

Dean Patrick explains further that the personal statement is regarded as an "interview on paper." When an applicant provides a statement that meets that description, the dean says, it can be a "significant factor" in the admissions decision. Similarly, letters of recommendation that are evaluative, providing first-hand, objective information bearing upon an applicant's qualifications for the study of law can be helpful to an applicant's chance of gaining admission to the College of Law. The college does not make available individual interviews.

Regarding minority applications, the dean explains that in accordance with the Florida Board of Regents' policy and the University's Affirmative Action Program, approximately 10 percent of each entering class may be admitted through the Minority Admissions Program. This program, the dean explains, is limited to African-American applicants and further to applicants qualifying under the pre-law study program of the Council on Legal Education Opportunity.

Finally, the dean notes that the Board of Regents also has ruled that the state university system of Florida will accept non-Florida residents in numbers not to exceed 10 percent of the total systemwide enrollment. Consequently, admissions standards for non-residents are significantly higher than those for residents.

ADMISSIONS DATA

	Class of 1993		Class of 1994	
	Spring	Fall	Spring	Fall
Applied	949	2,005	1.058	2,150
Median LSAT	N/A	N/A	N/A	N/A
Median GPA	N/A	N/A	N/A	N/A
Accepted	284	496	329	457
Median LSAT	75.2 percentile	89.7 percentile	79.6 percentile	89.7 percentile
Median GPA	3.25	3.43	3.26	3.50
Enrolled	202	196	210	187
Median LSAT	75.2 percentile	86.5 percentile	79.6 percentile	86.5 percentile
Median GPA	3.24	3.40	3.22	3.43

PLACEMENT | According to Ann L. Skalaski, Director of Career Planning and Placement, the full-time staff of the Career Planning and Placement Office coordinates recruitment activities between students and employers and provides individual counseling workshops, seminars, and an extensive career resource library for law students and alumni. The office participates in regional and national job fairs and receives news of job openings from publications and individual employers. For UF law alumni, the office publishes a monthly alumni placement bulletin and provides a job-listing telephone service. Approximately 250 employers visit the campus in a typical year.

PLACEMENT DATA

	Class of 1991	Class of 1990
Placed at Graduation	55%	58%
Placed within 90 Days	N/A	N/A[1]
U.S. Supreme Court Clerks	N/A	N/A
U.S. Appellate Court Clerks	N/A	N/A
U.S. District Court Clerks	N/A	N/A
State Appellate Court Clerks	N/A	N/A
Median Starting Salary	N/A[2]	N/A[2]

[1]Placed at six months after graduation: 65%.
[2]For graduates of the December 1989, May 1990, and July 1990 classes, average starting salaries were:

Law Firms:	$44,811
Federal Government:	$29,800
Military:	$29,400
Public Defender:	$23,400
State Attorney:	$23,358

A STUDENT SAMPLER   The majority of UF law students enter law school soon after receipt of the baccalaureate degree; a substantial portion of the student body, however, is made up of second-career students and others in that age group and includes former military personnel, teachers, social workers, journalists, businesspersons, and professional athletes.

NOTEWORTHY GRADUATES

Marshall M. Criser, President, University of Florida 1984–89; Stephen O'Connell, Justice, Florida Supreme Court 1955–67; Talbot D'Alemberte, President, American Bar Association 1991–92; Carol M. Browner, Director, Environmental Protection Agency.

GEORGE WASHINGTON UNIVERSITY

NATIONAL LAW CENTER
WASHINGTON, D.C. 20052
(202) 994-7230

ADMISSIONS

Applied: 8,232

Accepted: 1,734

Enrolled: 465

Median LSAT: 89.7 percentile

Median GPA: 3.42

STUDENT BODY

Total: 1,100 (full-time day)
      300 (part-time evening)

Women: 42%

Minorities: 16%

Average Age: 24 (full-time day)
           28 (part-time evening)

ACADEMIC RESOURCES

Library Volumes: 400,000

Computer Services: LEXIS, WEST-
    LAW, word processors

Student/Faculty Ratio: 25:1

FINANCES (ACADEMIC YEAR)

Tuition:	$17,650
All Other:	$12,190
Total:	$29,840

ENVIRONMENT Of special significance is the location of the National Law Center in a central area of the nation's capital, the focal point of the law in action, both American and international. The work of the law center goes on in this environment, presenting a unique opportunity for observation and study of federal agencies—judicial, legislative, and administrative. Readily accessible are the Supreme Court of the United States, the federal trial and appellate courts of the District of Columbia, and federal courts of special jurisdiction, such as the United States Court of Appeals for the Federal

Circuit, the United States Tax Court, and the Court of Military Appeals. Current federal legislation can be studied as it is considered on the floor of the House of Representatives and the Senate.

The National Law Center has a total enrollment of about 1,600 students. Approximately 1,100 students are in the full-time day division for the J.D. degree, and 300 are enrolled in the part-time evening division. More than 200 students, many from abroad, are enrolled in the post-J.D. degree programs. The law center comprises three adjoining buildings: Theodore N. Lerner Hall, Stockton Hall, and the Jacob Burns Law Library. Lerner Hall is a modern and innovative teaching facility. Its five levels contain classrooms, the dean's suite, and the Moot Court Room. Four of its eight classrooms are constructed in amphitheater style and are equipped with advanced sound systems and full video and viewing capabilities. Stockton Hall contains administrative offices, the Community Legal Clinics, classrooms, faculty offices, a reading room, a media center, and a student lounge. The Jacob Burns Law Library houses faculty and student organization offices and a computer room as well as its extensive collection.

ACADEMICS According to Dean of the National Law Center Jack Friedenthal, the National Law Center wants to instill into each of its students a sense of the law: its history and development, the various philosophies that have affected it, its use in the establishment and enforcement of economic and social policies, and its role in the future of our nation and the other nations of the world. Thus, the dean explains, the faculty at the National Law Center seek to establish an understanding of how the law operates within a number of basic contexts in order that students, once they graduate, will be able to serve clients and to give sound advice. The dean cautions that the faculty do not pretend to prepare students for practice at the most sophisticated levels, as that often takes years of training in the field, but they do strive to give graduates

---

CURRICULUM

First-Year Courses: Constitutional Law I, Contracts I and II, Civil Procedure I and II, Criminal Law, Introduction to Advocacy, Legal Research and Writing, Property, Torts

Interesting Electives: Chemical and Biotech Patent Practice, Government Procurement Law, Employment Discrimination Law, International Arbitration, Mass Communications Law—Electronic Media, Refugee and Asylum Law, Sports Law, Toxic Tort Seminar

all the tools necessary to absorb the practical lessons in the shortest possible time and to remain flexible in order to incorporate into their calculations the inevitable alterations of the law that constantly occur. The dean adds that the National Law Center is not just concerned to teach basic lawyering. It also hopes to inspire a commitment in its students to the highest ethical standards befitting a profession that touches the lives of so many citizens. Thus, Dean Friedenthal emphasizes, it is also a goal of the National Law Center to ensure that every student understands the need of each individual in the community for able and fair representation whenever it is required and whatever the individual's status.

ADMISSIONS According to Assistant Dean for Admissions and Financial Aid Bob Stanek, the entering class of the National Law Center is selected from an applicant pool of over 8,000 candidates. Dean Stanek explains that admissions decisions are made by a Faculty Committee on Admissions, composed of full-time faculty members, and the Assistant Dean for Admissions. A majority vote of the committee is required for admission of a candidate. The admissions committee begins to review completed files in December, though, Dean Stanek notes, the majority of decisions are made in February and March. All material submitted by the applicant is considered, and there are no levels of grades or LSAT scores which have been designated as automatic "admits" or "denies." The personal statement, says Dean

ADMISSIONS DATA

	Class of 1993	Class of 1994
Applied	7,340	8,232
Median LSAT	79.6 percentile	79.6 percentile
Median GPA	3.19	3.22
Accepted	1,721	1,734
Median LSAT	89.7 percentile	92.3 percentile
Median GPA	3.46	3.50
Enrolled	480	465
Median LSAT	86.5 percentile	89.7 percentile
Median GPA	3.40	3.42

Stanek, is "taken very seriously" by the admissions committee. Interviews are not part of the admissions process; they are granted only for the benefit of applicants. Finally, Dean Stanek says that the National Law Center does not have any special procedure for handling minority applications but notes that minority status is a factor taken into account by the Faculty Committee on Admissions when an applicant's file is reviewed, and he adds that the committee "feels strongly" that minority representation in the classroom and the profession should be assured.

Application Tips.   Although the National Law Center does not use "cut-offs" either to accept or to reject applications, the data supplied by the Admissions Office on a recent entering class makes it clear that "numbers" are nonetheless important determinants of an application's chance for favorable action:

LSAT Score Percentile		GPA	Applied	Accepted
91–99	and	3.75–4.0	84	82
81–90	and	3.50–3.74	268	220
71–80	and	3.25–3.49	304	83
61–70	and	3.00–3.24	236	12

Dean Stanek notes also that the personal statement is read for writing ability as well as for content. Finally, of recommendations, Dean Stanek notes that the "ideal letter" paints a portrait of the applicant as a student first and then as a person and that the role of recommendations varies with the quality of the letter itself.

P LACEMENT | According to Nancy Saltsman, Director of Career Development, each year the Career Development Office sends a brochure to approximately 16,000 legal employers, including private firms of all sizes, government agencies, public interest organizations, corporations, legal services offices, public defender services, and National Law Center alumni. The brochure advertises all interviewing programs, both on and off campus, the resume collection service for employers not able to make a recruiting visit to Washington, D.C., the "direct writes" option for employers who wish to have students contact them individually, and the regular job posting which lists summer and full-time positions. In a typical year, approximately 575 recruiters visit the campus. To assist students with the interviewing process, the Career Development Office organizes workshops on "Legal Employment Interviews" and invites speakers from legal organizations to come to the National Law Center to speak on how to conduct a legal interview and to offer tips from the employer's side. Additionally, the Career Development Office offers a mock interview program using either staff or graduates of the National Law Center to play employers. These mock interviews can be videotaped for student review. Students are also given a handout on legal employment interviews, which discusses what students should expect in an interview and provides a list of typically asked questions.

PLACEMENT DATA

	Class of 1991	Class of 1990
Placed at Graduation	75%	80%
Placed within 90 Days	78%	85%
U.S. Supreme Court Clerks	N/A	N/A[1]
U.S. Appellate Court Clerks	N/A	N/A
U.S. District Court Clerks	N/A	N/A
State Court Clerks	N/A	N/A
Other Judicial Clerks	N/A	N/A
Median Starting Salary	N/A	$61,000

[1]The total number of graduates of the Class of 1990 who accepted a judicial clerkship was 38.

A STUDENT SAMPLER The 10 undergraduate institutions with the highest number of graduates at the National Law Center in a recent entering class were the University of Michigan, the University of Pennsylvania, Cornell University, the University of Maryland, the University of Virginia, George Washington University, Duke University, SUNY Binghamton, Princeton University, and the University of Illinois. The student body includes several former Peace Corps volunteers, a former Navy "Top Gun," and a number of other students starting second careers after military service. Many of the evening (part-time) students continue to work full-time, and that division includes an airline pilot, a nurse, a State Department official, and a small business owner (computers). The entering class also usually includes several students with Ph.D. degrees in engineering or the sciences (who often have a special interest in intellectual property or environmental law).

NOTEWORTHY GRADUATES

William P. Barr, former U.S. Attorney General; Hank Brown, U.S. Senator, Colorado; Hon. Harry L. Carrico, Chief Justice, Supreme Court of the Commonwealth of Virginia; Robert P. Casey, Governor, Commonwealth of Pennsylvania; Frankie Sue Del Papa, Attorney General, State of Nevada; Earle H. Harbison, President and CEO, Monsanto Co.; Daniel K. Inouye, U.S. Senator, Hawaii; Marvin L. Warner, co-owner, Tampa Bay Buccaneers

HOFSTRA UNIVERSITY

SCHOOL OF LAW
HEMPSTEAD, NEW YORK 11550
(516) 463-5916

ADMISSIONS

Applied: 3,384

Accepted: 943

Enrolled: 295

Median LSAT: 83.0 percentile

Median GPA: 3.2

STUDENT BODY

Total: 823

Women: 40%

Minorities: 15%

Average Age: 24

ACADEMIC RESOURCES

Library Volumes: 375,000

Computer Services: LEXIS, WEST-
LAW, word processors

Student/Faculty Ratio: 22:1

FINANCES (ACADEMIC YEAR)

Tuition:	$13,696
Housing:	$ 3,260
Board:	$ 2,200
Total:	$19,156

ENVIRONMENT Hofstra University is an independent, nonsectarian, coeducational institution in Hempstead, New York, on suburban Long Island, 25 miles east of Manhattan. Hofstra offers an extensive intercollegiate and intramural sports program as well as recreational facilities in the Physical Fitness Center. The campus has been designated a registered arboretum accredited by the American Association of Botanical Gardens and Arboreta. An Olympic-sized swimming pool is available for student use. The Student Center's cinema screens many feature films during the academic year, and there are other film events presented by various departments during the year. Hofstra is outstanding in the area of fine and performing arts, with performances far above usual college standards. Each year a formal pro-

310

gram of plays, operas, operettas, and concerts is held, reaching a climax each spring with the nationally known Shakespeare Festival, and later the Festival of the Arts. Law students with musical interests are welcome to audition for the University's Concert Band, Orchestra, Collegium Musicum, Mixed Chorus, Opera Theater, and Music Repertory Company Jazz Ensemble. The Emily Lowe Gallery mounts some eight exhibitions a year and, while not large, has an international reputation. The Student Center houses three self-service restaurants, a bookstore, a game room, an arts and crafts workshop, a Rathskeller, and an ice cream parlor, as well as meeting rooms, a theater, and a multipurpose room for special events.

The law school is located in an air-conditioned, three-level building, designed to be in harmony with the brick neoclassic buildings on the South Campus. In the law school's Moot Courtroom, designed to simulate actual courtroom conditions, students view and criticize their own moot court practice through the use of advanced audio-visual equipment, including remote-control, closed-circuit television cameras and recording devices.

ACADEMICS | According to Dean of the Law School Stuart Rabinowitz, Hofstra prides itself on providing its students a high-quality and rigorous legal education in a diverse and nurturing atmosphere. Dean Rabinowitz notes that though the law school is only a little over twenty years old, it has already achieved a national reputation for academic excellence. As a relatively young institution, however, the law school continues to question, to grow, and to develop. The law school has always emphasized teaching as well as research and publication. The faculty are persons of academic distinction, and many of them are recognized as national authorities in their fields. They are also committed, the dean stresses, to excellence in teaching. The faculty cares deeply about legal education in general and about their students in particular. They make it a point to be accessible to students outside of the traditional classroom setting.

The dean goes on to explain that the curriculum at Hofstra is designed to provide a broad-based legal education that will equip students to practice law in every state and federal court in the nation. The emphasis is primarily on the teaching of legal analysis, lawyering skills, and professional responsibility. The first-year curriculum includes a course on "Lawmaking Institutions in Context" which explores the process of lawmaking through an examination of recent legislation. The law school takes special care to provide the rigorous first-year legal training in as personal an atmosphere as possible. For example, each first-year student has one class in a section of fewer than 30 students; this experience enables a closer relationship between students and faculty in a seminar-like environment. In the second and third years, the law school provides the opportunity for interested students to develop expertise in a number of particular areas of the law, e.g., extensive offerings in litigation and trail practice consisting of a

311

mix of classroom, simulation, and skills and strategy. Other areas of possible concentration include corporate, constitutional, criminal, family, health, labor, and tax law as well as alternative dispute resolution.

Finally, Dean Rabinowitz notes that learning takes place not only in the classroom and clinical settings, but also at frequent special lectures when prominent judges, scholars, and practitioners address students and faculty, and during more informal exchanges among faculty and students in faculty offices and student lounges. This intentionally challenging, yet nurturing, atmosphere makes Hofstra a "very special place" at which to obtain a legal education.

CURRICULUM

First-Year Courses: Civil Procedure I and II, Contracts I and II, Criminal Law, Lawmaking Institutions in Context, Legal Writing and Research, Property I and II, Torts I and II

Interesting Electives: Alternatives to Litigation, Collective Bargaining, Environmental Law, Land Use Regulation, Law and Literature, Law and Psychiatry, Lawyer Malpractice, Sex-Based Discrimination

---

ADMISSIONS | According to Director of Admissions Amy Engle, the structure of the admissions process at the Hofstra University School of Law is designed to ensure that applications are given a "personalized review." While acknowledging that the admissions process does place "significant weight" on the LSAT score and GPA, Ms. Engle emphasizes that it does not use any numerical threshholds for accepting or rejecting applications. Rather, Ms. Engle stresses that the median test scores and GPAs found in the table below are just that, medians, and that an equal number of entering students had credentials both above and below the particular median. This range of "numbers," Ms. Engle says, is evidence of the important value that the dean and faculty admissions committee attach to other aspects of an application, such as undergraduate school, grade trend, major, personal statement, letters of recommendation, geographic origin, minority group status, work experience, extracurricular activities, and other factors.

Ms. Engle says that the personal statement provides applicants with the opportunity to communicate important information to the faculty admissions committee. It serves, Ms. Engle explains, in many respects, as a substitute for a personal interview. Applicants are advised to consider their key strengths and to highlight these points in the personal statement. Conversely, if a glaring weakness exists, the personal statement is a suitable forum in which to address that point. In sum, Ms. Engle says, "Personal statements can and do sometimes make a difference." Beyond that, Ms. Engle notes that letters of recommendation can provide an important additional dimension to an application. For example, letters of recommendation from former professors often contain insights about an applicant's analytical skills, intellectual sophistication, and academic potential. Sometimes they provide reasons why an applicant experienced difficulty adjusting to college or had a particularly poor semester. Letters of recommendation from employers frequently set forth information about the amount of time applicants worked during college, and they can also describe an applicant's personal traits such as discipline, ability to work with others, or career interests. As noted above, personal interviews are not ordinarily a part of the admissions process and are granted only "under exceptional circumstances." Finally, Ms. Engle notes that the faculty admissions committee exercises great care in evaluating all facets of applications and that it devotes substantial attention and resources to processing minority applications. As in the review of other applications, this effort may include particular emphasis on factors in addition to the GPA and the LSAT score. The law school, Ms. Engle points out, has a longstanding commitment to attracting a diverse student body, has attracted an increasingly large pool of highly qualified students of color, and expects to continue to do so in the future.

ADMISSIONS DATA

	Class of 1993	Class of 1994
Applied	3,159	3,384
Median LSAT	N/A	N/A
Median GPA	N/A	N/A
Accepted	779	943
Median LSAT	N/A	N/A
Median GPA	N/A	N/A
Enrolled	291	295
Median LSAT	75.2 percentile	83 percentile
Median GPA	3.2	3.2

PLACEMENT According to Senior Assistant Dean for Career Services Gail Cutter, Career Services pursues potential employers on behalf of its students in a variety of ways. It invites all employer members of the National Association for Law Placement to recruit on campus or, alternatively, to participate in its resume referral program; it sends similar invitations to non-NALP member private sector employers in major cities throughout the United States; it sends invitations to local, state, and Federal government agencies; it does a comprehensive mailing to public interest employers; it cultivates alumi/ae recruitment contacts; and the Dean of Career Services serves as a member of City and County Bar Association Committees in order to expand lawyer networks and personal contacts for recruitment and referral of the law school's students. Each year between 75 and 90 recruiters visit the campus.

PLACEMENT DATA

	Class of 1991	Class of 1990
Placed at Graduation:	N/A	N/A
Placed within 6 months:	87%	N/A[1]
U.S. Supreme Court Clerks:	0	0
U.S. Appellate Court Clerks:	2	1
U.S. District Court Clerks:	6	2
State Appellate Court Clerks:	2	3
Other Judicial Clerks:	3	0
Median Starting Salary:	$51,082	$43,000

[1]Placed within 6 months: 90%.

In order to prepare students for the job search, Career Services offers to students a number of programs. University faculty members in Communications provide individual, one-hour videotaped mock interview training sessions. Two professional Career Services staff members provide individual counseling for students, including preparation for hiring interviews and post-interview reviews. The Career Services Resource Center develops employer information files on on-campus recruiters, including NALP forms, employer resume and reports, news articles, and student feedback forms, all designed to assist students in researching jobs and preparing for interviews. Instruction in the use of computerized databases to research firms is also provided. Finally, Career Services also distributes an information packet that includes sample question guidelines, articles, and a resource bibliography to promote skills development. Frequent panel discussions and workshops on a variety of career choices are also offered.

A STUDENT SAMPLER A recent entering class at the law school was drawn from nearly 110 undergraduate colleges and universities. Several of its members held master's degrees and doctorates. The class included CPAs, the owner of a pool construction company, the owner of a trucking company, a sports referee, a clothing designer, musicians, a disc jockey, athletic coaches, a writer of children's books, a ferry captain, computer experts, a tax examiner, a jewelry designer, a cantor, armed services personnel, the manager of a retail store, an international dancer, a Shakespearean actor, an investment manager, an official of the ASPCA, a hotel detective, a chemist, a physical fitness instructor, and a ski instructor. Members of the class had participated in a variety of activities such as the United Way, a volunteer ambulance corps, a volunteer fire department, the Audubon Society, the Special Olympics, the Red Cross, the Salvation Army, the ACLU, Project Literacy, and various religious organizations. Finally, their extracurricular activities and hobbies include wine tasting, cheerleading, photography, body building, martial arts, every imaginable sport (including water polo and frisbee), chess, astronomy, photography, and music (including composing and performing).

NOTEWORTHY GRADUATES

Hon. Maryanne Trump Barry, U.S. District Judge, U.S. District Court for the State of New Jersey; Gordon J. Crane, President, Apple & Eve Juice Company; Jonathan Gradess, Executive Director, New York State Defenders Association; Hon. David A. Levy, Congressman, United States House of Representatives; David Paterson, New York State Senator; Barbara Patton, Commissioner, New York State Workers' Compensation Board; Kenneth Randall, Thomas E. McMillan Professor of Law and Vice Dean, University of Alabama Law School; Robert Rosenthal, President and CEO, First Long Island Investors, Inc., and Co-Chairman of the New York Islanders

---

UNIVERSITY OF ILLINOIS, URBANA-CHAMPAIGN

COLLEGE OF LAW
504 EAST PENNSYLVANIA AVENUE
CHAMPAIGN, IL 61820
(217) 244-6415

ADMISSIONS

Applied: 2,265

Accepted: 554

Enrolled: 222

Median LSAT: 89.7 percentile

Median GPA: 3.44

STUDENT BODY

Total: 622

Women: 35%

Minorities: 16%

Average Age: 24

ACADEMIC RESOURCES

Library Volumes: 480,000

Computer Services: LEXIS, WEST-LAW, word processors

Student/Faculty Ratio: 19:1

FINANCES (ACADEMIC YEAR)

Tuition:	
Resident:	$ 4,166
Nonresident:	$11,778
Food & Lodging:	$ 4,666
Fees:	$ 862
Books:	$ 660
Transportation:	$ 400
Other:	$ 1,570
Total:	
Resident:	$12,324
Nonresident:	$19,936

ENVIRONMENT The University of Illinois at Urbana-Champaign has a student body of 35,000 and is located in East Central Illinois, about 130 miles from Chicago, 120 miles from Indianapolis, and 170 miles from St. Louis. Major airlines offer air-travel connections throughout the United States, and Amtrak's City of New Orleans and Illinois trains stop in town, making it easy to get back and forth to Chicago.

The University's academic resources are complemented by a rich collection of cultural opportunities. A number of nationally and internationally renowned artists perform each year in the Krannert Center for the Performing Arts, one of the finest and most active performance complexes in the country. Its four major theaters present student and faculty performances as well as appearances by major symphonies, jazz and chamber groups, dance troupes, and soloists from throughout the United States and abroad. Recent performers include Isaac Stern and Kiri te Kanawa. Also on campus, the Assembly Hall hosts entertainment shows, rock concerts, and major sporting events. Recent performers include Aretha Franklin, INXS, Bonnie Raitt, and Hammer. The Krannert Art Museum and Kinkead Pavilion, second only to the Art Institute of Chicago among Illinois public art museums, is directly adjacent to the College of Law.

Sports and other forms of recreation are popular, and many law students participate in the individual and team recreational opportunities sponsored through the University's Division of Campus Recreation. Directly across the street from the law building is the Intramural Physical Education Building—one of the largest facilities of its kind nationwide, with indoor and outdoor swimming pools, tennis courts, four gyms, weight and exercise equipment, and ball courts of all kinds.

The cities of Champaign and Urbana boast two of the nation's outstanding park systems, with 67 parks totaling more than 908 acres. Picnic shelters, play equipment, and outdoor performances make the parks a vibrant part of community life. Nearby there are golf courses and natural areas equipped for boating, fishing, and camping. With miles of bike paths and an excellent local bus service (free to students), many students live in Champaign-Urbana without a car. Graduate housing offered through the University Residence Hall system includes two halls with single and double rooms and two apartment housing areas for students with families. Apartments in the community come in all sizes and locations and typically are quite affordable.

The College of Law, established nearly 100 years ago, recently completed a major addition to and renovation of its physical plant. The construction added 70,000 square feet of new space and includes more study and shelf space in the library, four new classrooms, new offices for student organizations, and a new student lounge and dining area.

ACADEMICS | According to Dean of the College of Law Richard Schmalbeck, for almost a century the University of Illinois College of Law has provided a strong combination of practical and theoretical training in the law. Although the principal objective of the College of Law is to prepare students for the practice of law, the dean notes that its total mission is much broader. In the first place, the dean explains, it is the College of Law's purpose to expose students to the legal issues of the society, to develop their analytical and communications skills, to instill in them an awareness of the interrelationship of law and society, and to prepare them to use law as an implement of societal development. Thus, the dean notes, students at the College of Law are equipped to serve their communities not only as advocates and counselors but as policy makers and active, responsible citizens as well.

In addition to its primary objective, Dean Schmalbeck continues, the coordinated program of the College of Law has three other objectives: to contribute significantly to the body of legal scholarship; to render appropriate service to the University, the judiciary, practicing members of the bar, and the public; and to provide educational opportunities for those who wish to gain an understanding of the legal system but do not intend to practice law.

Consistent with the purposes of the College of Law, the dean notes, the methods of instruction vary with the subject matter and objectives of individual courses. Most classes, the dean explains, are conducted primarily through discussion rather than by lecture. The Socratic method of probing interchanges between student and professor is used in many classes, particularly in the first year. Judicial opinions and statutes are studied and the principles extracted are used in arguments about hypothetical situations. Other methods of instruction include research and writing, drafting of legal documents, seminars, and practical experience both in clinical programs involving actual clients and simulations.

CURRICULUM

First-Year Courses: Contracts & Sales I and II, Property I and II, Criminal Law, Criminal Procedure, Civil Litigation I and II, Legal Writing & Research, Torts, Moot Court

Interesting Electives: American Indian Law, Commodities and Futures Law, Employment Discrimination, Feminism and the Law, International Trade Policy, Natural Resources, Russian Law, Sports Law

ADMISSIONS | According to Pamela Coleman, an admissions officer at the College of Law, though the deadline for applying for admission is March 15, the College of Law uses a rolling admissions process that begins in October. Ms. Coleman notes that candidates who apply before January 15 may enjoy some competitive advantage and so advises all candidates to apply as early as possible in the application season. Ms. Coleman explains that applications are read by a committee consisting of faculty members and the Assistant Dean for Student Affairs. The committee attempts to identify applicants whose LSAT scores or grades appear to underpredict their performance in law school as well as applicants whose admission would contribute diversity to the College of Law. In evaluating applications, the committee places great weight on the undergraduate grade point average and LSAT score. The committee also considers graduate work in other fields, employment experience, and demonstrated leadership ability. Ms. Coleman stresses that applicants are *not* judged on the basis of Illinois residency.

A personal statement is requested as part of the application and is, says Ms. Coleman, an opportunity for applicants to introduce themselves to members of the admissions committee. The statement is a "significant part" of the application, and applicants should feel free to discuss any of the following: education, background, community involvement, strengths and weaknesses in certain courses or activities, personal and professional goals, significant achievements, and any other information that might be relevant to the admission decision. Letters of recommendation, according to Ms. Coleman, should provide the admissions committee with an appraisal of an applicant's character, maturity, motivation, and scholarly ability. The most useful letters come from individuals who can offer sound judgments about the candidate's qualifications for the study of law; for example, former or current instructors. Ms. Coleman notes that applicants who have been away from college for some time may need to substitute recommendations from employers, but Ms. Coleman also points out that recommendations from judges or other public figures who have only a passing knowledge of a candidate are likely to be of "little value." The College of Law does not conduct evaluative interviews of applicants, though prospective students are encouraged to visit and to take

ADMISSIONS DATA

	Class of 1993	Class of 1994
Applied	2,150	2,266
Median LSAT	75.2 percentile	75.2 percentile
Median GPA	3.23	3.22
Accepted	496	554
Median LSAT	89.7 percentile	92.3 percentile
Median GPA	3.55	3.50
Enrolled	206	222
Median LSAT	86.5 percentile	89.7 percentile
Median GPA	3.48	3.44

a tour, sit in on a class, and talk with an admissions officer who can answer questions. Finally, Ms. Coleman says that the admissions committee favorably considers applicants whose admission would contribute diversity to the College of Law.

PLACEMENT According to Joyce Elliott, Director of Career Services, each spring the Office of Career Services invites legal employers nationwide to participate in the College of Law's on-campus interviewing programs and/or student resume solicitation. These employers include law firms; corporations; banks; accounting firms; public interest organizations; and local, state, and Federal government agencies. Additional contacts are made with prospective legal employers at legal association functions, i.e., alumni events, bar association meetings, and law school association conferences. In a typical year, 200 employers will visit the College of Law's campus.

Ms. Elliott goes on to explain that interview skills workshops are held each semester for all students. The workshop speakers are practicing attorneys who are involved in the interviewing and hiring process. Mock interviews with an attorney are also available to students who wish to sharpen their interviewing skills. The Director of the Office of Career Services and the Assistant Dean for Student Affairs are also available for individual consultations with students. In addition, written materials and articles on preparing for an interview are available to each student.

PLACEMENT DATA

	Class of 1991	Class of 1990
Placed at Graduation	73.0%	75.7%
Placed within 90 Days	86.1%	85.7%
U.S. Supreme Court Clerks	0	0
U.S. Appellate Court Clerks	4	1
U.S. District Court Clerks	6	1
State Appellate Court Clerks	4	5
Other Judicial Clerks	2	2
Median Starting Salary	$50,000	$49,100

A STUDENT SAMPLER Students at the College of Law come from 29 states and 159 undergraduate institutions. Some have enrolled immediately after graduating from college; others have pursued careers in fields as diverse as theater, accounting, farming, and biochemistry. Recently, the student body included a West Point graduate who had a brief career as a professional football player, someone born in Hong Kong who went to college in the Netherlands, a chemical engineer, a member of a Big Ten college football team, and a former Marine.

NOTEWORTHY GRADUATES

John B. Anderson, former U.S. Congressman and Presidential candidate; Edward W. Cleary, former Professor of Law at the University of Illinois and Reporter to the Advisory Committee on the Federal Rules of Evidence; John E. Cribbet, former Dean of the College of Law and Chancellor of the University of Illinois; Grover G. Hankins, former Chief Legal Counsel, NAACP and Principal Deputy Counsel, U.S. Department of Health and Human Services; Albert Jenner, Jr., litigator at Jenner & Block and Chief Counsel to the Warren Commission; Peer Pedersen, Partner, Pedersen & Houpt, Chicago, Illinois; Hon. Harlington Wood, U.S. Court of Appeals for the Seventh Circuit

---

INDIANA UNIVERSITY,
BLOOMINGTON

SCHOOL OF LAW
BLOOMINGTON, INDIANA 47405
(812) 855-2704/855-4765

ADMISSIONS

Applied: 2,171

Accepted: 530

Enrolled: 207

Median LSAT: 85 percentile

Median GPA: 3.44

STUDENT BODY

Total: 600

Women: 34%

Minorities: 11%

Average Age: 25

ACADEMIC RESOURCES

Library Volumes: 475,000

Computer Services: LEXIS, WEST-LAW, computer room

Student/Faculty Ratio: 19:1

FINANCES (ACADEMIC YEAR)

Tuition:	
Resident:	$ 4,011
Nonresident:	$11,036
Books and Supplies:	$ 900
Food & Lodging:	$ 4,440
Personal Expenses:	$ 3,645
Total:	
Resident:	$12,960
Nonresident:	$20,021

ENVIRONMENT Founded in 1842, the Indiana University School of Law—Bloomington is one of the oldest law schools in the nation. Located on the beautifully wooded campus of one of the nation's largest teaching and research universities, the school is a charter member of the Association of American Law Schools and is approved by the American Bar Association. The presence of the university, including its world-famous School of Music, offers students cultural opportunities available in few urban areas, while retaining the advantages of a small town. In 1985, the law building was completely remodeled to provide comfortable, attractive classrooms, including trial and appellate courtrooms. A student lounge, canteen, and offices for student groups were part of the remodeling. The remodeling included state-of-the-art electronics and video equipment. An addition to the law building was also completed in 1985 to house the Law Library's extensive collection. The library is fully carpeted with an atrium extending through all six floors, and it faces several acres of woodland on the southwest corner of the campus.

ACADEMICS According to Dean of the Law School Alfred Aman, the educational program of the University of Indiana at Bloomington School of Law is designed to prepare its graduates for the many roles that lawyers play both in the United States and abroad. The dean notes that in addition to engaging in the private practice of law for clients at all income levels, lawyers serve in legal or executive posts for a variety of government agencies, business organizations, and educational institutions. As a member of the legal profession, the dean emphasizes, an attorney is called upon and expected to provide civic and political leadership and to devote a portion of his or her time to the public interest. For example, the community often entrusts the lawyer with elective and appointive offices in local, state, and national government.

Further, Dean Aman continues, global and economic political changes are placing new demands on the profession and providing new opportunities for its members. With the increasing awareness that political, legal, and economic issues transcend national boundaries, the School of Law is committed to preparing students for a global age. A world characterized by a truly interdependent global economy, global communications networks, and global environmental issues places new demands on the legal profession and provides new opportunities for its members. International solutions and international law are more important now, and lawyers of the future will need to be aware of how international economic trends and political events affect legal transactions even within our national boundaries. The interdependent global economy and the worldwide markets and firms that now exist mean it is highly likely that the law student of today will be representing clients who do business in other parts of the world. While acknowledging that not all of the law school's graduates will be directly involved in international law, Dean Aman stresses that international issues will increasingly affect their clients. With this in mind, the law school has designed a curriculum to prepare students for the international dimensions of legal problems. More important, the dean adds, the faculty work to equip law students with the broad perspective they will need to understand law and its place in the new global age in which we live.

To meet the diverse challenges its graduates will encounter, the law school stresses the development and discipline of reasoning ability, verbal and writing skills, and the interpersonal skills of communication and negotiation. The student is expected to become familiar with the basic institutions, rules, and doctrines of the legal order, to appreciate their development in social context and historical perspective, and to understand the processes by which the legal order is adapted to meet social needs.

The dean notes that the law school has recently implemented an innovative program to assure that its graduates have the necessary writing skills to meet the demands of practice now and in the future. In the first year, students work in small groups under the supervision of a lecturer and the director of legal research and writing to become familiar with the conventions and requirements of legal writing. In the second, they select a regular substantive course in which they further exercise and sharpen their writing skills in a small-group setting. During the second or third year, students must also complete a substantial research and writing project.

In addition, the law school offers several clinics for academic credit, such as the Community Legal Clinic, the Student Legal Services Clinic, and the Federal Courts Clinic. A course entitled Independent Clinical Project enables students to create their own clinical educational experiences. Also, many students earn academic credit by doing independent research under faculty supervision in areas of special interest. Joint degree programs are also available in business administration, public affairs, environmental science, and library science.

Finally, the dean says that the relatively small size of the first-year class affords students and faculty a chance to get to know one another informally. Seminars and independent study projects provide many opportunities for students to work one-on-one with faculty members. Upperclass elective courses are often small (fewer than 20 students). Besides the regular classroom contact, faculty and students join together in activities throughout the year. Among these activities are a "gong show" sponsored by the Black Law Students Association and a Women's Caucus auction sponsored by the Women's Caucus. There is an annual faculty-student softball game and a spring picnic at a park not too far from the law school. Each fall, there is a welcome party at a local winery owned by a member of the law school faculty. What is achieved, the dean hopes, is a small, intimate learning community that has a sense of a shared academic and collegial responsibility to one another as professionals.

CURRICULUM

First-Year Courses: Contracts I and II, Criminal Law, Constitutional Law I, Property, Torts, Civil Procedure I and II, Legal Research and Writing

Interesting Electives: Communications Law, European Legal History, Fact Investigation and Analysis, Land-Use Controls, Law and Medicine, Law and Sports, Negotiations, Social Science Applied to Problems in Law

ADMISSIONS | According to Assistant Dean for Admissions Frank Motley, in recent years the number of applicants for admission to the law school has exceeded the number of available spaces by as much as 10 to 1, so admission is selective. Decisions are made by a six-person admissions committee, composed of faculty and students. Dean Motley explains that the admissions committee looks first at the LSAT score and the GPA and uses a mathematical index that ranks applicants. Those with the highest LSAT scores and GPAs are the most likely candidates for admission. The dean adds, however, that there are no LSAT or GPA cutoffs.

Dean Motley says that the admissions committee considers the quality of a candidate's undergraduate institution, the level and rigor of courses taken, graduate work (if any), employment during and after college, extracurricular activities, potential for service to the profession, educational diversity, and residency. Applicants are encouraged to explain matters that may have adversely affected their undergraduate performance, for example, necessary employment that took time from studies or initial selection of a course of study for which the applicant was not suited, as well as factors indicating potential for law study that might not be elicited by questions on the application form.

Dean Motley explains further that the admissions committee finds it useful to have a personal statement regarding an applicant's experiences, backgrounds, talents, or any other matters that indicate why the application should receive favorable action. Letters of recommendation, while not required, are also helpful to the committee in assessing the qualifications of many applicants, particularly if they are from faculty members who are familiar with the candidate's academic

ADMISSIONS DATA

	Class of 1993	Class of 1994
Applied	2,106	2,171
Median LSAT	N/A	N/A
Median GPA	N/A	N/A
Accepted	548	530
Median LSAT	N/A	N/A
Median GPA	N/A	N/A
Enrolled	212	207
Median LSAT	85th percentile	85th percentile
Median GPA	3.38	3.44

strengths. Interviews, however, are not a part of the admissions process. Finally, the dean notes that applicants who feel that they have been disadvantaged because of economic, educational, racial, or cultural factors are urged to bring such information to the attention of the committee.

PLACEMENT | According to the Assistant Dean for Career Services, Kelly Toole, the law school does an annual mailing to approximately 2,000 employers. Approximately 160 to 200 visit the campus in a typical year, and the Career Services Office posts information about another 650 to 800 job openings. The Career Services Office provides students with hand-outs describing effective interviewing techniques and holds meetings on the interviewing process. Students are also invited to meet individually with the staff of the Career Services Office for mock interviews that are videotaped and then critiqued.

PLACEMENT DATA

	Class of 1991	Class of 1990
Placed at Graduation	70%[1]	70%[1]
Placed within 90 Days	N/A[2]	N/A[2]
U.S. Supreme Court Clerks	0	0
U.S. Appellate Court Clerks	2	5
U.S. District Court Clerks	6	6
State Appellate Court Clerks	5	9
Other Judicial Clerks	3	3
Median Starting Salary	N/A	$40,000

[1]Estimated.
[2]At six months, 93% for Class of '90.

A STUDENT SAMPLER | The majority of students at the Law School—over 80 percent—come from Indiana and other midwestern states. About 50 percent of the students have under-graduate majors from the social sciences, 20 percent from the humanities, and 20 percent from business/commerce. The median age of the student body is 25, with ages ranging from 20 to 48; and about one-fifth of the students are married.

NOTEWORTHY GRADUATES

Senator Birch Bayh; Representative Lee H. Hamilton, U.S. Congress, 9th Indiana District; Michael Kanne, Judge, 7th Circuit Court of Appeals; Edward King, Judge, Supreme Court of Micronesia; Sherman Minton, former Associate Justice of the U.S. Supreme Court; Milton Thompson, founding partner of Sports Venture, a sports and entertainment company responsible for hosting the annual Pan Am Games; Michael Uslan, executive producer of *Batman* and *Batman II*

THE OHIO STATE UNIVERSITY

COLLEGE OF LAW
THIRD FLOOR LINCOLN TOWER
55 WEST 12TH AVENUE
COLUMBUS, OHIO 43210
(614) 292-8810

ADMISSIONS

Applied: 2,099

Accepted: 498

Enrolled: 230

Median LSAT: 86.5 percentile

Median GPA: 3.56

STUDENT BODY

Total: 640

Women: 45%

Minorities: 18%

Average Age: 24

ACADEMIC RESOURCES

Library Volumes: 550,000

Computer Services: LEXIS, WEST-LAW, word processors

Student/Faculty Ratio: 19:1

FINANCES (ACADEMIC YEAR)

Tuition and Fees:	
Residents:	$ 4,204
Nonresidents:	$10,798
Food & Housing:	$ 3,921
Books and Supplies:	$ 500
Miscellaneous:	$ 800
Total:	
Residents:	$ 9,245
Nonresidents:	$16,039

ENVIRONMENT Since its founding in 1812 on the banks of the Scioto River, Columbus has been a dynamic, expanding city, achieving early recognition as an important government and transportation center. Presently, Columbus is undergoing dramatic aesthetic and cultural development. Downtown, the Ohio Center houses a convention center, hotel, shopping mall, and restaurants. Columbus City Center Mall, a three-level, million-square-foot enclosed mall of more than 140 specialty shops and department stores, opened in 1989. Several restorations have been completed, and the renovated community of German Village—200 blocks of 19th-century shops, restaurants, and homes—lies a few blocks south of downtown. Opportunities for entertainment are many and diverse. The historic Ohio Theatre and Palace Theatre host Broadway shows. The Columbus Symphony Orchestra, Ballet Met, Opera Columbus, and Dancecentral, as well as university and private community theatre groups, present plays, musicals, and concerts. Sports fans attend the Columbus Horizon (basketball), Columbus Clippers (baseball), and Columbus Chill (hockey) games, Jack Nicklaus' Memorial Golf tournament, the Nationwide/ Bank One Marathon, and Big Ten football and basketball at Ohio State. Outdoor recreation sites include 11,500 acres of public parks, the Scioto and Olentangy rivers for water sports, and miles of bicycle paths. Housing is diverse and plentiful, and a 15-minute drive in any direction from downtown puts one in a country setting.

The beautifully landscaped campus of the University stretches across 3,200 acres and encompasses 380 buildings, ranging from lecture halls to high-rise brick and glass laboratories, from hospitals to computer centers. Ohio State has two superb golf courses and houses one of the largest collegiate recreational complexes under one roof. The College of Law moved into its modern, air-conditioned building on the southeast corner of the campus in 1959. The building, which was even then one of the finest in the country, still provides study, research, and classroom facilities for all law students. The College of Law completed a nineteen million dollar addition and renovation of the building in 1993 that doubled the size of the facility and provided additional space for library acquisitions, student activities, evolving technology, programmatic development, and offices for faculty and staff.

ACADEMICS According to its dean, Francis X. Beytagh, the College of Law, founded in 1891, has grown and prospered in its first century through innovative program development, commitment to teaching excellence, support for outstanding research facilities, and attraction of highly qualified students. The dean notes that the college is an integral part of a major land-grant university and shares the basic educational goals of quality education and program accessibility. The general educational philosophy of the College of Law is to provide an environment conducive to the learning process and to assure that students acquire a solid foundation of knowledge about the law and the legal system, together with the analytical and lawyering skills that will best serve their professional careers in a changing, increasingly complex, global environment. This philosophy, says the dean, is focused upon the centrality of the student in the College of Law's educational endeavors. Integral to the fulfillment of these goals is the willingness of the faculty to reassess and to reevaluate periodically what the College of Law seeks to accomplish, including the institutional commitment to public service and professionalism.

The dean goes on to explain that despite increasing pressure on tuition, the cost of an Ohio State legal education remains attractive and competitive given the national stature of the College of Law. Successful recruitment, financial aid, and affirmative action programs produce a talented and diverse student body. The college also aggressively recruits talented teachers and scholars to supplement the faculty's ranks. The dean notes that recent appointments include two former clerks to U.S. Supreme Court justices and two experienced practitioners with special interests in bankruptcy and environmental litigation.

Dean Beytagh goes on to note that a modest-sized student body and favorable faculty-to-student ratio create a learning environment for individual student attention. This philosophy, the dean explains, is reflected in a "small section" enrollment for every first-year student in at least one of the required courses and in enrollment limitations on upper-level seminars and clinical courses. Students engage in analytical and problem-solving skills in traditional classroom and seminar settings and have unique opportunities for in-depth study in special core areas of curricular concentration. As a pioneer in clinical education, the College of Law offers students varied and interesting opportunities for practical application of lawyering skills. The dean also notes that the college's extensive involvement in alternative methods of dispute resolution, including publication of the *Journal on Dispute Resolution*, puts the school at the forefront of this important trend. Additionally, international perspectives are integrated into course development through extensive programmatic contacts with Oxford University in England, with the University of Genoa in Italy, and (in conjunction with the University's East Asian Studies program) with China. Furthermore, as part of an outstanding University graduate center, the College of Law gives students additional opportunities to enrich their legal education through enrollment in diverse graduate-level courses, and students may pursue dual degrees in many established or individualized master's programs. Finally, the dean notes that the college's location within a dynamic city, an active center of government, business, state and federal courts, and the legal profession, offers further learning opportunities through various internships.

CURRICULUM

First-Year Courses: Contracts, Torts, Property, Civil Procedure, Constitutional Law, Appellate Practice, Legal Research and Writing

Interesting Electives: Comparative Legal History, Criminal Procedure: Police Evidence Gathering Practices, Environmental Law, Gratuitous Transfers, Regulated Industries, Right of Privacy, Sex-Based Discrimination and the Law, Social and Environmental Litigation

ADMISSIONS | According to Associate Dean to Student Affairs Karen Cutright, applications to the College of Law are read and evaluated by members of an admissions staff and faculty members of an admissions committee. There is no minimum LSAT score or GPA below which an applicant is not given full consideration, though candidates should keep in mind that the median LSAT score for recent entering classes has been between the 85th and 90th percentile and the median GPA between 3.40 and 3.60. Dean Cutright explains that those applicants who present strong academic credentials, recommendations, and other information consistent with their academic performance can usually be admitted after an initial review of the completed admission file. At the other end of the continuum, applicants with weak academic credentials may be denied after one review. For the many candidates who fall into neither of those extreme categories, the committee members evaluate their applications in light of the coursework taken, the caliber of the undergraduate institution, any trends in grades, graduate work (if any), and information found in letters of recommendation and the required resume. The College of Law uses a rolling admission process, so the earlier an application is complete, the earlier the candidate will have a final decision.

ADMISSIONS DATA

	Class of 1993	Class of 1994
Applied	1,903	2,099
Median LSAT	N/A	N/A
Median GPA	N/A	N/A
Accepted	513	498
Median LSAT	86.5 percentile	86.5 percentile
Median GPA	3.58	3.59
Enrolled	215	230
Median LSAT	83.0 percentile	86.5 percentile
Median GPA	3.54	3.56

Ohio State does not require but does encourage applicants to submit a personal statement. They are "occasionally helpful," especially if the applicant explains an unusual occurrence that may have affected academic performance. Two faculty recommendations are required, though candidates who have been out of college for more than 12 months and cannot secure faculty evaluations can substitute recommendations from an employer or an attorney. Recommendations can be helpful, Dean Cutright says, especially if they comment on the candidate's analytical skills, critical thinking ability, reasoning ability, and ability to communicate. Interviews are granted to applicants who request them for informational purposes; the college may occasionally ask an applicant to come to the campus for an interview. Finally, Dean Cutright says that Ohio State encourages applications from underrepresented minority applicants. Those candidates must submit the same information as all other candidates, and their applications are evaluated in light of any cultural, economic, or educational disadvantage they may have experienced.

PLACEMENT | According to its director, Pamela Lombardi, the placement office at the College of Law maintains contacts with a wide range of employers through a variety of formal and informal programs, including membership in the National Association for Law Placement, the Ohio Law Placement Consortium, the Columbus Bar Association, and the National Association for Public Interest Law. The placement office contacts approximately 1,000 potential employers each year by mail. About 100 to 150 recruiters visit the campus in a typical year.

In addition, Ms. Lombardi explains that the college provides programming, informational packets, and individual assistance to students. These programs include a practice interview program (co-sponsored by the Columbus Bar Asso-

PLACEMENT DATA

	Class of 1991	Class of 1990
Placed at Graduation	66%	68%
Placed within 90 Days	76%	80%
U.S. Supreme Court Clerks	0	1
U.S. Appellate Court Clerks	4	3
U.S. District Court Clerks	7	6
State Appellate Court Clerks	6	6
Other Judicial Clerks	3	0
Average Starting Salary	$41,346	$41,300

ciation) in which students are matched with practicing attorneys for an interview and given a critique, a day-long Interviewing Skills Workshop (also co-sponsored by the Columbus Bar Association), and a variety of alumni presentations including "Introduction to Law Firms" and "Judicial Clerkships," as well as a library containing written publications, electronic databases for job-prospecting, and audio and video tapes on various aspects of the job search.

A STUDENT SAMPLER The student body at the College of Law typically has representatives from 30 or more states and several foreign countries. Recently, it included two Fulbright scholars in addition to numerous National Merit Scholars and Phi Beta Kappas. One recent entering class included a medical doctor, two students who were called up for active duty during Desert Storm, several varsity football or basketball players, and a professional golfer, as well as stockbrokers, business executives, engineers, published authors, and musicians.

NOTEWORTHY GRADUATES

Edwin Cooperman, former CEO of American Express, now CEO of PrimeAmerica; William Isaacs, former Chairman of the Federal Deposit Insurance Corporation; Senator Howard M. Metzenbaum, member of the U.S. Senate since 1976; Aaron Moriarty, lead reporter and news commentator for CBS News in New York; Chief Justice Thomas J. Moyer, Supreme Court of Ohio; Governor George V. Voinovich, former mayor of Cleveland, elected governor of Ohio in 1990

U NIVERSITY OF U TAH

▼

COLLEGE OF LAW
SALT LAKE CITY, UT 84112
(801) 581-7479

ADMISSIONS

Applied: 1,105

Accepted: 280

Enrolled: 129

Median LSAT: 88.9 percentile

Median GPA: 3.52

STUDENT BODY

Total: 382

Women: 42%

Minorities: 12%

Average Age: 26

ACADEMIC RESOURCES

Library Volumes: 260,000

Computer Services: LEXIS, WEST-LAW, word processors

Student/Faculty Ratio: 15:1

FINANCES (ACADEMIC YEAR)

Tuition:		
Residents:	$ 2,495	
Nonresidents:	$ 6,128	
Other Expenses:	$ 7,000	
Total:		
Residents:	$ 9,495	
Nonresidents:	$13,128	

E NVIRONMENT Salt Lake City, framed by 11,000-foot snow-capped peaks, offers many urban bonuses. It is a city on the move that blends subtle sophistication with the comfortable pace and friendliness characteristic of the West. Culture flourishes on the scale of much larger cities, with the Utah Symphony, Ballet West, Repertory Dance Theatre, Ririe-Woodbury Dance Company, Utah Opera Company, and Pioneer Theatre Company being major attractions. Sports enthusiasts will find NBA basketball, professional hockey, and baseball, plus spirited college rivalries. Sun and low humidity combine for pleasantly warm, dry summers and moderate winters. Law students can enjoy world-famous skiing at seven resorts within 45 minutes of the campus or take advantage of a dozen national parks less than a day's drive away. Vast outdoor areas near the city invite a variety of activities, including hiking, mountaineering, camping, bicycling, fishing, hunting, wind-surfing, boating, and photography.

The 1,500-acre University of Utah campus, located on the northeastern edge of Salt Lake City, reaches to the foothills of the majestic Wasatch Mountains. Academic and research activities coalesce in more than 200 buildings linked by walks, fountains, grassy hills, and trees that lend an open, parklike quality to the campus.

The law building and law library serve as educational and informational resources for students, faculty, lawyers, and others from the local community. The library, adjoining the law building, contains more than 260,000 volumes of law and law-related materials. The College of Law recognizes the critical need that law students have for private on-site study space and provides individually assigned carrels to *all* students.

ACADEMICS According to Dean of the Law School Lee E. Teitelbaum, legal professional training must coherently address three fundamental aspects of what it means to be a lawyer: knowledge of doctrine; skills in applying doctrine to new problems and in assessing the impact of doctrine on problems and institutions; and an understanding of the relationship between law and the social and ethical values it reflects and reproduces. Dean Teitelbaum explains that in order to accomplish these goals better, a few years ago the law school adopted a major curriculum reform called "Cornerstone-Capstone," a program designed to provide each year of legal education with a distinctive purpose and character, a logical progression of knowledge and skills, and diverse teaching and evaluation methods. Elaborating on the function of the various courses, the dean notes that while the first-year curriculum focuses on typical foundation courses, Cornerstone courses, taken in the second year, offer students a wide choice of broad, doctrinal courses in subjects considered essential to a well-rounded, contemporary legal education. In the third year, the dean continues, Capstone courses—numerous clinical and skills courses, advanced specialty courses, and directed research opportunities—offer students a rigorous, innovative, and exciting advanced educational experience incorporating extensive research, writing, and "live" practice opportunities. The dean concludes by

---

CURRICULUM

First-Year Courses: Civil Procedure, Constitutional Law, Contracts, Criminal Law, Property, Torts, Legal Writing and Research

Interesting Electives: Art and the Law, Employment Regulation, Federal Indian Law, Health Law, Military Law, Teaching Law in High Schools, Writing for the Courts

---

adding that the law school believes that frequent and close association between faculty and students contributes to the quality of the educational experience as well as to the development of professional values. A favorable student-to-faculty ratio, active faculty advisor and mentor programs, and small classes foster a friendly, intimate, and personal atmosphere at the law school.

ADMISSIONS | According to Reyes Aguilar, Director of Admissions at the College of Law, the admission committee is made up of faculty members and the Director of Admission. The law school typically begins to accept applications on November 15 for admission the following year. The admission office uses a rolling admission process with decisions being made as early as mid-January. In order to receive "priority" consideration, files should be complete by January 15. The regular application deadline is February 1, and the file completion deadline is March 1.

Mr. Aguilar explains that the College of Law has no "minimum" requirements for admission. All files, no matter how low or high the GPA or LSAT score, are given full consideration by the admission committee. Mr. Aguilar explains further that the College of Law does not grant personal interviews, so the personal statement allows the applicant to let the admission committee know more about himself/herself. The admission committee also uses the personal statement to evaluate a candidate's writing ability. The College of Law requires one letter of recommendation, and Mr. Aguilar notes that it should come from

ADMISSIONS DATA

	Class of 1993	Class of 1994
Applied	968	1,105
Median LSAT	61.2 percentile	70.4 percentile
Median GPA	3.19	3.27
Accepted	277	280
Median LSAT	86.5 percentile	88.9 percentile
Median GPA	3.51	3.61
Enrolled	130	129
Median LSAT	84 percentile	86.5 percentile
Median GPA	3.47	3.52

someone who knows the applicant well and adds that no more than three letters are desired by the admission committee. Finally, Mr. Aguilar states that the College of Law does not have any special procedure for handling minority applications but adds that members of ethnic and racial minorities are affirmatively recruited to apply to and to attend the College of Law. The College of Law reaches out to members of these groups through such services as the Candidate Referral Service and the Western Interstate Name Exchange. Furthermore, members of the admission committee do make recommendations for candidates to be considered for participation in the Academic Support Program. The College of Law also utilizes the services of the Minority Law Caucus and members of the Utah Minority Bar Association in its recruitment and retention efforts.

PLACEMENT | According to Francine Curran, its director, Legal Career Services (LCS) has a database of over 5,000 potential employers and contacts those employers two or more times a year. In a typical year, Ms. Curran says, about 100 recruiters visit the campus. Ms. Curran goes on to explain that LCS also fosters an Alumni Career Information Exchange network for career guidance. Additionally, LCS sends focused mailings to

PLACEMENT DATA

	Class of 1991	Class of 1990
Placed at Graduation	N/A[1]	N/A[1]
Placed within 90 Days:	N/A[2]	N/A[2]
U.S. Supreme Court Clerks:	0	0
U.S. Appellate Court Clerks:	N/A[3]	N/A[3]
U.S. District Court Clerks:	N/A[3]	N/A[3]
State Appellate Court Clerks:	N/A[3]	N/A[3]
Median Starting Salary:	$32,538	$37,803

[1]Placed four months before graduation: 53% and 57% for Class of 1991 and Class of 1990, respectively.
[2]Placed between six and nine months after graduation: 83% and 88% for Class of 1991 and Class of 1990, respectively.
[3]For Class of 1991 and Class of 1990, a total of 20 judicial clerks in each year.

employers with specific requirements, lists employer job announcements in a monthly mailer, and sponsors an Outreach Interview Program for students to travel at their own expense to interview at employers' offices.

To assist students in the job search, the office offers seminars and workshops several times each year on resume and letter writing, on using the computer for direct mailings, and on interviewing skills. And, Ms. Curran adds, mock interviews with videotaped practice sessions are conducted by volunteer attorneys, and personal counseling is provided to improve interviewing skills.

A STUDENT SAMPLER | The typical entering class at the University of Utah College of Law will include people with practical work experience as well as experience in community and public services. For example, a recent class included a doctor, a ballet dancer, a firefighter, paralegals and legal secretaries, a reporter, a singer, a former farm worker, a gymnastics coach and stunt team member, and military officers, one of whom served in the Persian Gulf. The class also included people who had participated in varsity sports such as football, wrestling, skiing, and track and others who are competitive runners and marathoners, and still others who are rock climbers and hikers. The class included students from the former Soviet Union, the Philippines, Jamaica, Taiwan, Iran, Korea, New Zealand, Japan, and 29 different states.

NOTEWORTHY GRADUATES

Roberta Achtenberg, Assistant Secretary for Fair Housing and Equal Opportunity, Department of Housing and Urban Development; Hon. Stephen Anderson, U.S. Court of Appeals, 10th Circuit; Hon. Judith Billings, Presiding Judge, Utah Court of Appeals, President, National Association of Women Judges; Larry Echohawk, Attorney General for the State of Idaho; Jan Graham, Attorney General for the State of Utah; Hon. Gordon Hall, Chief Justice, Utah Supreme Court; Hon. Bruce Jenkins, Chief Judge, Federal District Court, Utah

UNIVERSITY OF WISCONSIN, MADISON

LAW SCHOOL
975 BASCOM MALL
MADISON, WI 53706
(608) 262-5914

ADMISSIONS

Applied: 2,653

Accepted: 690

Enrolled: 285

Median LSAT: 86.5 percentile

Median GPA: 3.36

STUDENT BODY

Total: 843

Women: 47%

Minorities: 14%

Average Age: 25

ACADEMIC RESOURCES

Library Volumes: 400,000

Computer Services: LEXIS, WEST-LAW, NEXIS, DIALOG, word processors

Student/Faculty Ratio: 17:1

FINANCES (ACADEMIC YEAR)

Tuition & Fees:
Resident:	$ 3,875
Nonresident:	$10,311

Other Expenses:	$ 7,000

Total:
Resident:	$10,875
Nonresident:	$17,311

ENVIRONMENT The University of Wisconsin–Madison is a public, land-grant institution, founded in 1849. The law school is a part of the larger University community, which numbers 43,000 students and over 7,000 faculty and staff. The law school building, completed in 1964, is located halfway up Bascom Hill, close to the classroom buildings and administrative offices of the University, the Memorial Union, the Memorial Library, and the College Library. Classrooms; offices for faculty, administrative staff, and student groups; the extensive law library; and faculty and student lounges are located within this air-conditioned building. The library wing provides study space in its several reading rooms. There are locked carrels available to some graduate students in law and special research workers.

ACADEMICS According to Dean of the Law School Daniel O. Bernstine, Wisconsin Law School has historically been noted for its "law in action" approach to legal education. The dean explains that the "law in action" philosophy recognizes that law does not exist in a vacuum. Rather, students are taught to consider law not simply as a set of rules and cases but as a behavioral system and to understand how the various parts of that system interact. Although Dean Bernstine acknowledges that the "law in action" approach to the study of law is no longer unique to the law school, Wisconsin was a pioneer in this area and has used the principle more consistently than any other school. The dean goes on to explain that the "law in action" approach has led the faculty to develop many programs that have influenced not only legal scholarship but the behavior of institutions and lawyers throughout the world. The dean gives as examples the seminal work of Professor J. Willard Hurst in legal history that unfolds the mutual interplay of legal and social forces over time; the view of criminal justice as an administrative system that was developed by Professor Frank Remington; the vision of Professor Stewart Mccaulay of "law and society" as a distinct field of knowledge, with its use of the social sciences to illustrate the dynamic nature of the legal process; and the empirical studies by Professor Marc Galanter of the so-called litigation explosion that call into question the accepted wisdom that such a phenomenon exists. The dean notes that examples could be multiplied but indicates that these illustrate the basic, continuing philosophy of the University of Wisconsin Law School.

Dean Bernstine also says that the law school is noted as a leader in clinical education and mentions several of the law school's programs, including Legal Assistance to Institutionalized Persons (assistance to those incarcerated in prisons and mental institutions), the Legal Defense Project (public defender work), the Center for Public Representation (emphasis on administrative advocacy in providing assistance to underrepresented and unrepresented groups), the Public Intervenor Program (placement in the office of the state that represents the environment), judicial internships with federal and state judges, placements with the NAACP's Legal Defense Fund in the summertime, and an unusual course in general practice, which provides simulation of the actual practice of law in a variety of areas, divided into units taught each week by a different team of practicing attorneys under the supervision of the law school's director of the General Practice Program.

Finally, the dean says, in the tradition of public service as part of "law in action," the faculty at Wisconsin Law School had major responsibility for drafting corporation, family, and criminal laws. In recent years, the dean notes, law school faculty have served on the Wisconsin Supreme Court, as United States Attorney for the Western District of Wisconsin, and as head of Wisconsin's

Division of Corrections. On the national level, faculty have served as members of or advisers to the Federal Trade Commission's Bureau of Consumer Protection, the U.S. State Department, the Watergate Special Prosecutor Force, the National Collegiate Athletic Association, and the Wisconsin Project on Nuclear Arms Control (located in Washington, D.C., it detects violations of the Nuclear Arms Proliferation Treaty).

CURRICULUM

First-Year Courses: (Fall) Contracts I, Introduction to Substantive Criminal Law, Civil Procedure I, Torts Legal Research and Writing: (Spring) Property, Introduction to Criminal Procedure, Legal Research and Writing, plus one from Constitutional Law I, Contracts II, Civil Procedure II, or Legal Process

Interesting Electives: African Law, Environmental Law and Institutions, Equal Employment Law, Health Law and Administration Seminar, Modern American Legal History, Product Safety Liability, Trademarks, Water Rights Law

ADMISSIONS | According to Professor Gordon Baldwin, Director of Admission, when an application file is completed, it is reviewed by a member of the law school's admissions committee and receives one of three dispositions. If the applicant is outstandingly qualified on academic factors, an acceptance is sent promptly and without further screening. If the applicant represents an unacceptably high academic risk because of low academic credentials not counterbalanced by other factors, then a denial is sent. A substantial group of strongly qualified applicants will be selected by the initial reviewer for the "Hold" category. Applicants placed in "Hold" are so notified. "Hold" files are reviewed again by the entire admissions committee when substantially all files have received initial review. At that time, the "Hold" files are accepted, denied, or placed on a waiting list.

Professor Baldwin explains that the first step in the evaluation of the academic factors in an application is the calculation of "prediction index" that combines GPA and LSAT score using a mathematical formula. The admissions committee also considers a number of unquantifiable factors as well, including trend of college grades, course selection, the quality of the undergraduate institution, part-time student employment, graduate study (if any), and the interval between graduation and application (if applicable). The committee also takes into account non-academic factors such as minority status, unusual cultural background, and diversity of experience or background. The law school has a Legal Education Opportunities Program that was founded to recruit students from minority groups that have been historically disadvantaged and underrepresented in the legal profession, including but not limited to black Americans, American Indians, Puerto Ricans, and Chicanos. Finally, Professor Baldwin adds that the faculty has determined that non-residents should make up no more than 20 to 30 percent of an entering class. This limitation works to impose somewhat higher standards on nonresident applicants.

The application gives candidates the opportunity to submit a personal statement; and Professor Baldwin says that among candidates with similar GPAs and LSAT scores, this statement "may be critical." The personal statement is examined for writing skills as well as for content, and Professor Baldwin cautions that poor grammar and spelling errors will "almost invariably lead to rejection." Letters of recommendation, while not required, are "strongly encouraged." A "careful, thoughtful letter from a teacher or employer" may tell the committee enough about the intellect, imagination, or diligence of an applicant that the committee will judge the applicant's prospects for academic success to be better than mere numerical factors might suggest. Professor Baldwin says that personal interviews are not part of the decision-making process.

ADMISSIONS DATA

	Class of 1993	Class of 1994
Applied	2,675	2,653
Median LSAT	75.2 percentile	75.2 percentile
Median GPA	3.30	3.23
Accepted	656	690
Median LSAT	89.7 percentile	89.7 percentile
Median GPA	3.49	3.50
Enrolled	287	285
Median LSAT	86.5 percentile	86.5 percentile
Median GPA	3.40	3.36

PLACEMENT According to Assistant Dean Edward J. Reisner, who is responsible for operation of the law school's Career Services Offices, Career Services regularly invites up to 750 employers to conduct on-campus interviews. Somewhere between 150 and 200 generally accept. Dean Reisner adds that many who cannot visit the campus will nevertheless solicit resumes from the law school's students. In addition, Career Services periodically targets employers by practice area or geographic areas, in response to expressed needs of students. For example, several years ago the Career Services expanded its database for the Twin Cities in order to attract more employers from that area because surveys had shown high student interest in the area. Also, the staff has recently begun to personally visit employers in areas where the law school has a concentration of alumni in order to inform employers about the school and its programs and to promote the interests of students who may be applying for positions.

Dean Reisner goes on to explain that Career Service offers a wide variety of career planning programming efforts on a variety of topics, including resume preparation; electronic job hunt techniques; and panel discussions on various career tracks, specific careers, and clerkships. Dean Reisner also notes that the placement office has established a close working relationship with the Wisconsin Bar and has created a mentor program that matches students with experienced lawyers. This program allows students to learn about the profession and to help create their own job hunting network. The Bar also offers a one-day "Tag Along Program" in which students follow an attorney around during a typical day's activities. Finally, the Career Services Office also provides career planning videotapes on topics such as large firm practice, small firm practice, criminal law, women in the law, and government practice.

PLACEMENT DATA

	Class of 1991	Class of 1990
Placed at Graduation	80%	85%
Placed within 90 Days	90%	92%
U.S. Supreme Court Clerks	0	0
U.S. Appellate Court Clerks	3	3
U.S. District Court Clerks	7	2
State Appellate Court Clerks	4	4
Other Judicial clerks	5	6
Median Starting Salary	$38,500	$39,300

A STUDENT SAMPLER The entering class at Wisconsin Law School usually includes a high percentage of Wisconsin residents; for example, of 286 students who recently began their three years of study at Madison, 212 were Wisconsin residents. Yet the class also had representatives from over 100 undergraduate institutions and from 24 home states. The class included a former staffer for *Ms. Magazine*, the recipient of the Oklahoma University President's Leadership Award (among others), an ice cream and frozen foods route sales representative (who went to law school to get away from lifting heavy, frozen objects), and the coordinator of test marketing and regional sales manager for L'Eggs Hosiery.

NOTEWORTHY GRADUATES

Hon. Shirley S. Abrahamson, Justice, Supreme Court of Wisconsin; Clark Byse, Professor of Law, Emeritus, Harvard Law School, and suggested by some to be the inspiration of the Professor Kingsfield character in the movie "The Paper Chase"; Judith Lichtman, President of the Women's Legal Defense Fund; Charles F. Luce, former CEO of Consolidated Edison; Gaylord Nelson, former United States Senator; Tommy Thompson, Governor of Wisconsin; Arnold Weiss, former General Counsel at the American Development Bank

YESHIVA UNIVERSITY

▼

BENJAMIN N. CARDOZO SCHOOL OF LAW
BROOKDALE CENTER
55 FIFTH AVENUE
NEW YORK, NEW YORK 10003
(212) 790-0274

ADMISSIONS[1]

Applied: 2,230

Accepted: 802

Enrolled: 263

Median LSAT: 83 percentile

Median GPA: 3.18

STUDENT BODY

Total: 960

Women: 43%

Minorities: 10%

Average Age: 23

ACADEMIC RESOURCES

Library Volumes: 310,000

Computer Services: LEXIS, WEST-LAW, word processors

Student/Faculty Ratio: 23:1

FINANCES (ACADEMIC YEAR)

Tuition:	$15,400
Food:	$ 8,600
Housing:	$ 3,790
Books:	$ 860
Fees:	$ 220
Travel:	$ 860
Miscellaneous:	$ 1,370
Total:	$31,100

ENVIRONMENT | Benjamin N. Cardozo School of Law is located virtually midway between the Washington Square Arch (the symbol of the charming and historic neighborhood of Greenwich Village) and the Empire State Building. Cardozo is convenient to public transportation connecting all parts of Manhattan and the other boroughs. In a few minutes by bus or subway, students can get to major courts and law offices; to the business,

---

[1]Figures are for class that entered in September and will graduate in June 1994. Cardozo also enrolled 43 students in January and 47 in May.

financial and theatre districts; and to the great museums and libraries of New York. Attractive housing is available in Cardozo's immediate vicinity, as well as in neighborhoods easily accessible by public transportation. Although Cardozo does not offer housing facilities, the law school provides a student housing exchange newsletter and bulletin board.

ACADEMICS According to Dean of the Law School Frank J. Macchiarola, the study of law is the pursuit of a delicate balance: an academic exploration of the philosophy of social structure balanced with training in the processes which form and sustain that structure. Benjamin N. Cardozo School of Law's reputation, the dean explains, is built upon an understanding of this balance. Building a bridge between the academic and professional worlds, Cardozo meets the challenge of legal education with a commitment to excellence in traditional classical legal training coupled with a dedication to clinical education and professional development.

The dean goes on to explain that many of Cardozo's faculty and even many of its students hold advanced degrees in areas other than law. Economics, history, literature, philosophy, and other disciplines mix with law in the analysis of current issues. The dean adds that much of the faculty's research is seminal, that is, they break new ground. Widely published in fields as diverse as law and literature, corporate governance, international law and human rights, entertainment law, and legal history, the law school's faculty is, according to the dean, an important source of Cardozo's distinction. Finally, Dean Macchiarola also notes that the faculty teach as "passionately and creatively" as they pursue scholarship and adds that Cardozo is "nationally renowned for its hospitality to ideas, for the persistence of its faculty in exploring those ideas, and as a forum for their discussion."

CURRICULUM

First-Year Courses: Contracts, Criminal Law, Elements of the Law, Civil Procedure, Property, Torts, Legal Research, Writing, and Appellate Advocacy

Interesting Electives: Advanced Criminal Law: Conspiracy and Racketeering; Contract Drafting in Entertainment Law; Education Law; Law and Literature; Main Institutions of Jewish Law; Mental Disability Seminar; Terrorism and the Law; War Crimes, Reparations, and Human Rights

---

ADMISSIONS | According to Anita T. Walton, Director of Admissions, the admissions committee at the law school consists of the Director of Admissions, the faculty chairman of the committee, two additional faculty members, and the Dean of the Law School. Ms. Walton explains that the admissions process is "collaborative," with the chairman, director, and dean working closely together. Decisions are made on a rolling basis, and candidates are notified of dispositions on a "timely basis" once applications are complete.

The application consists of three parts: the LSAT score and GPA; a personal statement and other "subjective" materials; and letters of recommendation (plus dean's certification). Ms. Walton explains that the committee will consider the surmounting of economic, social, physical, educational, or other obstacles as evidence of an applicant's ability to achieve. Applicants who wish such achievements to be considered are encouraged to elaborate on them in their personal statements.

Ms. Walton notes that the personal statement is "one of the most important parts of the application" because it is "the one chance the applicant has to 'face the committee'" and to "advocate" the case for admission. In light of the function of the personal statement, applicants are advised to "consider the things that would distinguish their files from all the rest." In addition, Ms. Walton notes that personal statements should be well-written, provide insight into the applicant's

ADMISSIONS DATA

| | Class of 1993 | | | Class of 1994 | | |
	January	*May*	*September*	*January*	*May*	*September*
Applied	227	115	2,187	209	109	2,230
Median LSAT	N/A	N/A	N/A	N/A	N/A	N/A
Median GPA	N/A	N/A	N/A	N/A	N/A	N/A
Accepted	58	70	857	47	70	802
Median LSAT	N/A	N/A	N/A	N/A	N/A	N/A
Median GPA	N/A	N/A	N/A	N/A	N/A	N/A
Enrolled	47	55	256	43	47	263
Median LSAT	79.6 %	75.2 %	83 %	83 %	75.2 %	83 %
Median GPA	3.06	3.07	3.10	3.13	3.11	3.18

character and desire to study law, and elaborate on personal accomplishments that might be of interest to the committee. Statements should be moderate in length, typed, double-spaced, and "with no misspellings." It is not necessary to limit one's statement to a single page, but Ms. Walton advises applicants "to be mindful of the person reading the essay." Applicants are also invited to enclose a resume but are cautioned against including large writing projects, though "a sample of short articles" might be appropriate.

Ms. Walton says that recommendations are "important" in all files and "especially important" in borderline cases—they can "make the difference between acceptance and denial." Interviews are not a part of the regular admissions process. Applicants may request an interview in writing, but the committee reserves the right to grant interviews only when it deems them "appropriate." Consequently, it is important to "put one's best foot forward" in the written application.

Finally, Ms. Walton notes that the law school is committed to providing opportunities for legal education to diverse populations. It has a special Legal Experience Program that was developed to provide opportunities for minority students to work as paralegal/legal assistants while completing their first year of law school in two consecutive summers.

PLACEMENT According to Associate Dean Ellen R. Cherrick, the services offered by the law school's Center for Professional Development are designed to help both students and graduates to find permanent, summer, and part-time employment. Each year, the Center does an extensive nationwide invitational mailing for its on-campus interviewing program. Later, it does telephone follow-ups to maintain contacts with hiring partners, recruitment coordinators, and graduates at major firms and government agencies. The center's staff (which includes two professionals whose sole responsibilities are job development and recruiter contact), deans, administrators, and faculty also make personal visits to hiring personnel and to the law school's graduates at major firms and government agencies. About 120 recruiters visit the law school in a typical year. In addition, the center sends invitations for seminars and other programs held at the law school and distributes a quarterly newsletter to firms, agencies, and members of the judiciary.

Dean Cherrick explains further that the center distributes to all first-year students a "Student Manual" and begins its intensive personal counseling during that first year as well. The staff also operates a mock interview program, and it puts on panels and other presentations with graduates, search firm members, and other experts in interviewing techniques. The center also distributes a broad selection of handouts and makes available to students books and other materials in the center's resource library.

PLACEMENT DATA

	Class of 1991	Class of 1990
Placed at Graduation	N/A	N/A
Placed within 90 Days	N/A	N/A[1]
U.S. Supreme Court Clerks	0	0
U.S. Appellate Court Clerks	1	1
U.S. District Court Clerks	3	8
State Appellate Court Clerks	3	N/A[2]
Other Judicial Clerks	8	3
Median Starting Salary	N/A	N/A

[1]88% of those reporting were employed as of seven months after graduation.
[2]One state supreme court clerkship reported but no information about other state appellate courts.

A STUDENT SAMPLER   A recent entering class at the law school included students from over 100 undergraduate colleges and universities, including representatives from Amherst, Barnard, Brandeis, Bryn Mawr, Bucknell, Colgate, Columbia, Cornell, Dartmouth, Duke, Emory, Harvard, MIT, Mt. Holyoke, Skidmore, Swathmore, Trinity, Vassar, and Yale. Some idea of the variety of pre-law school accomplishments of members of the student body can be gotten from the following brief descriptions:

G.A. holds a Red Belt in Tae Kwon Do and worked as an electron microscopy technician.

R.A. was a computer science major who earned an MBA in finance and was later a senior systems analyst for New York City Health and Hospital Corporation.

S.L. was a domestic reports analyst at the Federal Reserve Bank of New York.

L.L. worked as a confidential investigator for the New York City Department of Investigations while in college.

T.Y. was captain of her women's basketball team and worked at a battered women's shelter during college.

M.A. worked as a bank teller, a life guard, and a sales consultant during college.

NOTEWORTHY GRADUATES

Dean Cherrick points out that Cardozo is a relatively young school—it was founded in 1976—and that its graduates are only now moving into prominent positions. For example, in New York State one must have practiced law for at least ten years before becoming eligible to run for a judgeship

Appendix—Methodology

▼

The law schools included in this directory were pre-screened using admissions data published in *The Official Guide to U.S. Law Schools, 1990–91*. A mathematical formula was devised to generate an artificial but ready-at-hand index for each school using the median GPA and median LSAT score of its most recent entering class, giving approximately equal weight to those two measures. In those cases where information was nonstandard or incomplete, interpolation, approximation, or *ad hoc* adjustment was required. A list of 45 target schools was created using the highest indexes. Two other schools were included in the list because anomalies in the admissions data suggested that the schools might be more competitive than indicated by median LSAT score and GPA; two schools that did not publish admissions data were added to the list because their names regularly appear on other lists of top schools; and two schools subsequently asked to be added to the list. In all, survey questionnaires were mailed to 51 schools, a number that represents about one-fourth of the total number of law schools accredited by the American Bar Association. After initial responses were received, reminders were mailed to schools that had not yet responded. Ultimately, a total of 40 complete or nearly complete responses were received and they are the foundation of this directory.[1]

The survey questionnaire solicited from each law school admissions and placement data for two years, descriptive information, and published reports about the law school. With the more detailed numerical information provided by the schools, a second ranking system was created using three measures: selectivity, reputation, and placement record. "Selectivity" was defined to be a function of median LSAT score and GPA of student body and the ratio of acceptances to applications; "reputation" was defined as the percent of graduates accepting a

---

[1]Three law schools that have appeared in other "top twenty-five" rankings presented particular problems. Boston College and George Washington were unable to supply detailed clerkship data; and since "reputation" is solely a function of a school's success in placing students into selected clerkships, it did not seem reasonable to estimate a figure (as opposed, for example, to estimating an LSAT score—one of three components of "selectivity"). The University of California at Los Angeles did not file a response. (The University's Public Relations office apparently let three copies of the survey questionnaire "fall between the cracks"; and a final, good-faith effort to provide the information, unfortunately, was made too late.)

351

clerkship with the U.S. Supreme Court, a U.S. Court of Appeals, a U.S. District Court, or the high court of a state; and "placement record" was defined as a function of percent of class placed upon graduation and the median starting salary. Data for the two years covered were averaged. Where data were missing, estimates were arrived at in a variety of ways, e.g., by projecting data from schools comparable on other measures. (In the following tables, estimates are indicated by asterisks.)[1]

For each subcomponent, law schools were assigned a numerical ranking corresponding to their positions in the hierarchy. In cases of ties, the sum of the tied rankings was divided among the tied schools and each received the same ranking. "Selectivity" is the average of the three subcomponent rankings and "placement" is the average of the two subcomponent rankings; and for each of those two measures law schools were assigned a numerical ranking corresponding to their positions in the hierarchy. The average of those three numbers determined final rankings.

The ranking system can perhaps be more easily visualized than described:

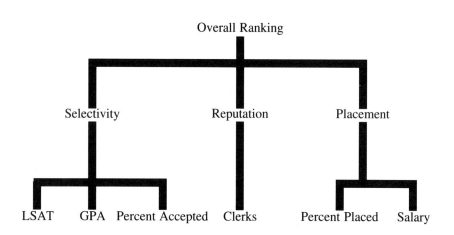

Based on the overall ranking, the list of responding law schools was divided. The schools with the top twenty-five overall rankings were targeted for a second inquiry, to wit, student interviews; for the remainder, shorter entries were prepared using just the information provided by law schools. And a final ranking of the top twenty-five was prepared as a reference guide.

ADMISSIONS DATA

	CLASS OF '93				
	TOTAL APPLIED	TOTAL ACCEPTED	MEDIAN LSAT	MEDIAN GPA	PERCENT ACCEPTED
Cal. at Berkeley	5936	807	94.5	3.65	13.6
Cal. at Davis	3242	661	92.3	3.44	20.4
Chicago	3600	307	97.8*	3.73*	8.5
Columbia	6208	997	97.4	3.6	16.1
Cornell	4650	818	94.5	3.51	17.6
Duke	4254	601	96.1	3.51	14.1
Fordham	4395	916	89.7	3.3	20.8
Georgetown	9500	2065	94.5	3.5	21.7
Harvard	8516	834	96.1*	3.7*	9.8
Michigan	6645	1083	96.1	3.57	16.3
Minnesota	2245	702	89.7	3.54	31.3
New York University	7105	1176	97.4*	3.65*	16.6
North Carolina	3419	549	89.7	3.39	16.1
Northwestern	4934	686	95.3*	3.55*	13.9
Notre Dame	3147	637	89.7	3.4	20.2
Pennsylvania	4879	1013	94.5	3.6	20.8
Southern California	3184	673	94.5	3.4	21.1
Stanford	5719	456	96.1	3.75	8
Texas	3919	958	89.7	3.5	24.4
Vanderbilt	2400	508	89.7	3.6	21.2
Virginia	5323	953	94.5	3.57	17.9
Washington	2100	443	92.3	3.39	21.1
Washington & Lee	2001	406	86.5	3.36	20.3
William & Mary	3248	627	92.3	3.4	19.3
Yale	5670	377	97.4	3.79	6.6

*Estimated

353

ADMISSIONS DATA

	TOTAL APPLIED	TOTAL ACCEPTED	MEDIAN LSAT	MEDIAN GPA	PERCENT ACCEPTED
			CLASS OF '94		
Cal. at Berkeley	6527	741	96.1	3.7	11.4
Cal. at Davis	4006	675	92.3	3.41	16.8
Chicago	3500	296	97.8*	3.75*	8.5
Columbia	5395	930	97.4	3.6	17.2
Cornell	4426	779	94.5	3.55	17.6
Duke	4345	810	96.1	3.65	18.6
Fordham	4176	846	89.7	3.3	20.3
Georgetown	9400	2030	94.5	3.51	21.6
Harvard	7415	837	96.1*	3.7*	11.3
Michigan	6666	945	96.1	3.63	14.2
Minnesota	2423	657	89.7	3.56	27.1
New York University	7241	1172	97.4*	3.64*	16.2
North Carolina	3290	570	89.7	3.51	17.3
Northwestern	4654	728	95.3*	3.55*	15.6
Notre Dame	3600	729	89.7	3.4	20.3
Pennsylvania	4492	934	94.5	3.62	20.8
Southern California	4010	754	94.5	3.4	18.8
Stanford	6006	471	96.1	3.64	7.8
Texas	4364	927	92.3	3.55	21.2
Vanderbilt	2500	540	92.3	3.61	21.6
Virginia	5887	953	94.5	3.59	16.2
Washington	2400	449	92.3	3.44	18.7
Washington & Lee	2348	367	89.7	3.29	15.6
William & Mary	3386	636	92.3	3.4	18.8
Yale	5381	407	98.3	3.81	7.6

*Estimated

CLERKSHIP DATA

	CLASS OF '90				CLASS OF '91			
	U.S. SUP.CT.	U.S. APP. CTS.	U.S. DIS. CTS.	STATE HIGH CTS.	U.S. SUP. CT.	U.S. APP. CTS.	U.S. DIS. CTS.	STATE HIGH CTS.
Cal. at Berkeley	1	15	18	3	1	15	18	3
Cal. at Davis	0	3	12	8	0	1	5	5
Chicago	4	32	6	3	5	28	9	6
Columbia	1	12	30	3	1	14	22	4
Cornell	0	8	6	0	0	6	12	1
Duke	0	13	7	0	0	16	8	4
Fordham	0	8	12	1	0	8	12	1
Georgetown	0	14	12	11	2	6	14	4
Harvard	10	45	63	17	12	61	66	15
Michigan	2	11	33	6	1	26	25	6
Minnesota	0	6	9	9	1	7	4	5
New York University	0	14	43	3	1	6	32	4
North Carolina	0	0	4	6	0	2	6	5
Northwestern	1	16	11	1	0	7	12	4
Notre Dame	0	2	6	0	0	5	2	1
Pennsylvania	0	8	21	1	0	3	21	2
Southern California	0	0	11	0	0	0	13	2
Stanford	2	18	18	6	2	19	10	3
Texas	0	7	14	6	0	3	13	2
Vanderbilt	0	8	11	4	0	6	14	3
Virginia	2	16	26	5	1	14	35	6
Washington	0	2	5	2	0	1	4	0
Washington & Lee	0	3	7	3	1	1	10	2
William & Mary	0	0	10	1	0	5	10	3
Yale	7	33	44	7	5	40	47	4

Table shows the number of graduates who accepted clerkships with various courts.

355

PLACEMENT DATA

	CLASS OF '91		CLASS OF '91	
	JOBS	SALARY	JOBS	SALARY
Cal. at Berkeley	94.3	$65,000	96.6	$65,000
Cal. at Davis	72	$47,497	75	$43,804
Chicago	98	$70,000	98	$70,000
Columbia	97.76	$78,325	95.85	$74,030
Cornell	78	$61,000*	84	$62,000*
Duke	92	$60,172	91	$58,753
Fordham	72	$64,402	89	$64,880
Georgetown	90	$62,000	86	$62,705
Harvard	98	$67,815	98	$66,601
Michigan	92	$65,000	93	$60,000
Minnesota	72	$45,598	70	$40,862
New York University	96	$77,287	97	$76,677
North Carolina	70	$45,000	75	$42,000
Northwestern	90	$67,000	98	$59,918*
Notre Dame	82	$50,671	81	$53,177
Pennsylvania	97.4	$65,000	97.4	$64,600
Southern California	82	$65,750	90	$66,934
Stanford	100	$65,000	100	$58,000
Texas	76	$53,280	74	$55,994
Vanderbilt	8936	$57,399	90.6	$55,000
Virginia	92	$64,000	94	$63,000
Washington	87	$46,000	84	$47,000
Washington & Lee	75	$51,312	75	$51,490
William & Mary	82	$49,321	76	$47,700
Yale	98.9	$71,825*	100	$72,825*

*Estimates
Table shows percent of class that had jobs at graduation and median starting salaries.

TABLE OF RANKINGS

	SELECTIVITY				REPUTATION	PLACEMENT			OVERALL RANK	
	LSAT	GPA	ACC	RANK	RANK	JOBS	SALARY	RANK	AVG	FINAL
Cal. at Berkeley	9.5	5	5	6	13	8	7	7	8.7	8
Cal. at Davis	17	19	15	15.5	14	23	24	23.5	17.7	17
Chicago	2	2	3	2	3	3.5	4	2	2.3	2
Columbia	3.5	9.5	10.5	8	8	6	2	3.5	6.5	6
Cornell	13	15	13	12.5	16	18	14.5	17	15.2	14
Duke	6.5	11.5	8.5	9	12	12	16	14.5	11.8	12
Fordham	22.2	25	20	25	19	19	9	14.5	19.5	18
Georgetown	13	17	23	17.5	21.5	14	13	13	17.3	16
Harvard	6.5	3	4	4	2	3.5	5	5	3.7	3
Michigan	6.5	9.5	7	7	5	11	12	12	8	7
Minnesota	22.5	11.5	25	22	17	25	22	23.5	20.8	23
New York University	3.5	6	8.5	5	8	7	1	3.5	5.5	5
North Carolina	22.5	18	10.5	15.5	21.5	24	25	25	20.7	22
Northwestern	9.5	13.5	6	10	8	9	11	9.5	9.2	10
Notre Dame	22.5	22	19	24	24.5	17	19	18	22.2	25
Pennsylvania	13	7	21	12.5	11	5	8	6	9.9	11
Southern California	13	22	18	17.5	20	15	6	11	16.2	15
Stanford	6.5	4	2	3	4	1	14.5	8	5	4
Texas	19.5	16	24	21	24.5	21.5	18	20	21.8	24
Vanderbilt	19.5	8	22	14	10	13	17	16	13.3	13
Virginia	13	11.5	12	11	6	10	10	9	8.8	9
Washington	17	20	17	19	23	16	23	19	20.3	21
Washington & Lee	25	24	14	23	15	21.5	20	22	20	20
William & Mary	17	22	16	20	18	20	21	21	19.7	19
Yale	1	1	1	1	1	2	1	1	1	1

The table shows the rankings for various measures used to identify the "top twenty-five law schools" for this directory. A "1" is the highest possible ranking, while "25" is the lowest possible ranking. In the case of ties, points were divided among the schools tied, e.g., if two schools were tied for tenth place on a certain criterion, they were treated as occupying positions 10 and 11 and were each awarded 10.5 points. Data for the two years were averaged. The "Selectivity" rank is the average of ranks for LSAT (median LSAT score of entering students), GPA (median GPA of entering students), and ACC (percent of applicants accepted); "Reputation" ranks schools according to the percent of graduates accepting clerkships with the U.S. Supreme Court, U.S. Courts of Appeal, U.S. District Courts, or highest state courts; and the "Placement" rank is the average of "Jobs" (percent of students placed at graduation) and "Salary" (median starting salary). The "Overall Rank" is computed by taking the average of ranks for "Selectivity," "Reputation," and "Placement" and ordering those results.

BOOKS FOR JOB HUNTERS

CAREERS / STUDY GUIDES

Airline Pilot
Allied Health Professions
Automobile Technician Certification Tests
Federal Jobs for College Graduates
Federal Jobs in Law Enforcement
Getting Started in Film
How to Pass Clerical Employment Tests
How You Really Get Hired
Law Enforcement Exams Handbook
Make Your Job Interview a Success
Mechanical Aptitude and Spatial Relations Tests
Mid-Career Job Hunting
100 Best Careers for the Year 2000
Passport to Overseas Employment
Postal Exams Handbook
Real Estate License Examinations
Refrigeration License Examinations
Travel Agent

RESUME GUIDES

The Complete Resume Guide
Resumes for Better Jobs
Resumes That Get Jobs
Your Resume: Key to a Better Job

AVAILABLE AT BOOKSTORES EVERYWHERE

PRENTICE HALL